Buffalo Soldiers
and Officers
of the Ninth Cavalry
1867–1898

Buffalo Soldiers
and Officers
of the Ninth Cavalry
1867–1898

Black & White Together

CHARLES L. KENNER

UNIVERSITY OF OKLAHOMA PRESS : NORMAN

ALSO BY CHARLES L. KENNER

The Comanchero Frontier: A History of New Mexican–Plains Indian Relations (Norman, 1969, 1995)

Library of Congress Cataloging-in-Publication Data

Kenner, Charles L.
   Buffalo soldiers and officers of the Ninth Cavalry, 1867–1898 :
black and white together / Charles L. Kenner.
      p.   cm.
   Includes bibliographical references (p.   ) and index.
   ISBN 978-0-8061-4466-5 (paper)
   1. Afro-American soldiers—West (U.S.)—History—19th century.
2. United States. Army. Cavalry, 9th—History.   3. United States.
Army—Afro-American troops—History—19th century.   4. United
States. Army—Officers—History—19th century.   5. Indians of North
America—Wars—1866–1895.   6. West (U.S.)—History—1860–1890.
   7. Frontier and pioneer life—West (U.S.)   I. Title.
   E185.925.K394   1999
   355'.008996073—dc21   99-33394
                                                                              CIP

The paper in this book meets the guidelines for permanence and durability of the Committee on Production Guidelines for Book Longevity of the Council on Library Resources, Inc. ∞

Copyright © 1999 by the University of Oklahoma Press, Norman, Publishing Division of the University. Paperback published 2014. Manufactured in the U.S.A.

Contents

Illustrations

Acknowledgments

Any researcher who devotes a decade of his life to a topic is obviously indebted to numerous institutions and individuals. Since the majority of my research has been conducted in the National Archives, its staff has been my greatest benefactor. Among the many archivists there who patiently provided me the benefit of their expertise, William Lind and Mike Meier have been called on most often. I am also indebted to the librarians and archivists at the Library of Congress; the United States Military Academy; the United States Military History Institute in Carlisle, Pennsylvania; the Barker American History Center in Austin, Texas; the Arizona Historical Society in Tucson; the Colorado Historical Society in Denver; the New Mexico Historical Society in Santa Fe; the Oklahoma Historical Society in Oklahoma City; the Kansas Historical Society in Topeka; the Nebraska Historical Society in Lincoln; and the Denver Public Library. I owe a special debt to Margaret Daniels and her aides in the interlibrary loan department of Arkansas State University for their assistance in securing research materials.

While I am very much a lone wolf in regards to research and writing, I benefited from discussing the buffalo soldiers with such scholars as Bruce Dingis of the Arizona Historical Society; John P. Wilson and Karl Laumbach at Las Cruces, New Mexico; and my colleague at Arkansas State University, Larry Ball. Karl, a historical archeologist, graciously took the time to guide me over the site of the Hembrillo Canyon battle between Victorio's Apaches and Captain Henry Carroll's buffalo troopers, giving me a perception of the realities of Apache warfare that no amount of reading in the sources could provide. I am also deeply indebted to William Leckie and Thomas R. Buecker for critiquing the manuscript and making valuable suggestions as well as correcting some of its most egregious errors. My book is the better for their efforts. I and every other historian who takes up the subject of the buffalo soldiers will be indebted to Frank N. Schubert for his meticulous collation of biographical items in *On the Trail of the Buffalo Soldier.* Although most of my research was completed before it was published, it proved of great benefit, especially for the post-1890 period.

Most of all, I would express my appreciation to Mildred, my wife for the past forty-four years, for the interest and help she has always shown in my endeavors. She tolerated my insistence that the perfect "vacation" could be built around visits to West Point, Carlisle, or the National Archives and often worked side-by-side with me. My daughter, LaQuita Saunders, painstakingly tutored me in the basics of word processing and cheerfully cleaned up my copy. In closing, I wish to dedicate this book to the memory of my parents, Marshall and Hazel Kenner. Circumstances limited them to eighth-grade educations in one-room schools in western Oklahoma and to a hard life raising cotton on a small farm, but they gave me an abundance of love and support and a set of genes that made me an inveterate habitant of libraries and archives. I would have had it no other way.

Life among the
Buffalo Soldiers

Introduction

Among the unique features of the post–Civil War army were the four regiments consisting of black enlisted men and white officers that were stationed at minuscule posts scattered across the west from border to border. Like it or not, the men and their officers were partners, for the success of each group depended on the ability of the other. Although skin color, prejudice, and cultural background worked against harmonious relations, the soldiers shared a common bond: a thirst for honor. For African American soldiers, "honor" primarily meant respect and recognition of their entitlement to the privileges of citizenship; for the officers, the term implied recognition from their peers and the approval of their superiors.

Obviously, both officers and rank and file included every possible type. Heroes and charlatans, the ingenious and the unbalanced, racists and idealists—all were found among the officers. Some enlisted men might have been as ignorant and irresponsible as the stereotypes depicted in the press, but others were as scholarly, conscientious, and considerate as anyone in the military. Regardless of their characteristics, however, they have shared a common fate. Their lives and deeds have largely been overlooked.

I first encountered the Ninth Cavalry in the files of Southwestern newspapers while researching the range cattle industry. Curious because I was reading about matters of which I knew nothing, I discovered that the topic, with the notable exception of William Leckie's *The Buffalo Soldiers*, had largely been overlooked. Soon my psychological affinity for underdogs launched me on a ten-year quest to unearth as much as possible about life in the Ninth Cavalry.

When I started my research I had not even heard of most of the individuals whose lives I have delineated. As I assembled data on such men as Colonel Edward Hatch, Major Guy Henry, Lieutenants Charles Parker and Charles Young, Sergeants Brent Woods and Emanuel Stance, and Private James Miller, I determined to record their remarkable stories. It is my hope that the drama of their lives will confront stale stereotypes with fresh facts.

I confined my efforts to the Ninth Cavalry in order to permit a more in-depth exploration of the records. I suspect that another reason is that much more had been written about the Tenth Cavalry. William and Shirley Leckie have, of course, published extensively on Colonel and Mrs. Benjamin Grierson. Lieutenant Colonel John W. Davidson has also been the subject of a biography. In addition, several officers in the Tenth, including Captain George Armes and Lieutenants Henry Flipper, John Bigelow, and Richard H. Pratt, have penned memoirs or campaign accounts. Except for Major Guy Henry, the officers of the Ninth, on the other hand, could not have been more mute concerning their lives if they had taken vows of secrecy.

With the obvious exception of Colonel Edward Hatch, every officer whose career I have included was chosen because of his unique relation-ship—good or bad—with the men under his command. Several were among the most heroic and admirable figures in the history of the regiment; others, the most racist. In each case I have tried to understand why they acted as they did as well as to relate what they did. In addition, I think it essential that they be judged by the standards of their times.

Although all nineteenth-century officers would be considered racists by modern criteria, the best, such as Major Henry, Captain Francis Moore, and Lieutenants Matthias Day and Charles Taylor, also appreciated the intrinsic worth of the black soldiers and relied upon such talented sergeants as George Mason, George Jordan, and Moses Williams to mold their com-mands into some of the best units in the military. In contrast, such racist tyrants as Captains Ambrose Hooker and J. Lee Humfreville literally tortured the men under their command. By the same token, some sergeants such as Emanuel Stance and Melvin Wilkins, given too much leeway by their superiors, could be equally brutal.

With a few exceptions, each essay attempts to deal both with specific individuals and with the company in which they served. As a result, the same battle or campaign may be referred to in more than one chapter. I had neither the space nor the desire to describe in any detail the wars with the Apaches. For that, excellent works by William Leckie, Monroe Billington, Dan Thrapp, and Stephen Lekson are listed in my bibliography. The engagements that I do describe, moreover, are viewed from the perspective of particular individuals. I have unearthed a few sources unused by previous writers.

Three of the first four African American officers in the regular army were assigned to the Ninth. In contrast to the numerous studies devoted to Lieutenant Henry Flipper of the Tenth Cavalry, the lives of Chaplain Henry Plummer and Lieutenants John H. Alexander and Charles Young of the Ninth have received little attention. Although each of them had excellent rapport with the men they commanded, their acceptance by white officers was another matter. Charles Young, in particular, merits a full-length biography.

The enlisted men singled out represent all degrees of competence. Their lives and careers, though matched in valor and significance by many others, chanced to generate sufficient data to provide a greater insight into their personalities. It is an unfortunate reality that among the richest sources for the personal lives of buffalo soldiers are the proceedings of courts-martial. The recorded testimony and written depositions therein, self-serving though they may have been, allow them to speak for themselves, often voicing their aspirations and fears with remarkable eloquence. These voices are frequently more convincing than the writings of their commanders.

It is ironic that such men as Brent Woods, Emanuel Stance, and George Lyman can be portrayed in more depth than others not so much because of their considerable merits as because of their inability to stay out of trouble. Meanwhile, men such as First Sergeants George Mason and Madison Ingoman performed their tasks so smoothly that the primary attestation to their worth is found in the record compiled by their troops. One marvels at the perfection that marked everything that a George Mason did, but there is little information concerning his thoughts and aspirations. In contrast, the tragic life and execution of one of the most unimpressive privates in Mason's troop, James Miller, provides a moving portrait of a trooper's psyche and martyrdom. Because of this anomaly, it is likely that life in the Ninth Cavalry was not as turbulent as the following pages may indicate.

Although the spirit of racial harmony so painfully achieved in the regiment would be subverted by the upsurge of intolerance at the turn of the century, all had not been in vain. Some remarkable men of both races created an elite regiment whose history provides unique examples of both the best and worst aspects of human nature. May this work be considered a tribute to some of the most fascinating figures I have ever encountered.

PART ONE

⚔

The Regiment
and Its
Commander

1

All That Soldiers Should Be

On 23 July 1866, Congress established the framework for the post-Civil War army. In recognition of the other contributions made by almost two hundred thousand black soldiers to the Union's victory, it mandated that two of the ten cavalry regiments and four of the forty-five infantry companies (reduced to two out of twenty-five in 1869) were to consist of African American enlisted men. Although the race of the officers was not specified, it was assumed they would be white. All men initially commissioned as lieutenants and at least two-thirds of those at higher ranks were to have served with Civil War volunteer regiments and to have passed rigorous exams. Although regular officers who transferred to the black regiments received a one-grade promotion, Lieutenant Colonel Wesley Merritt (Second Cavalry) and Major James Wade (Sixth Cavalry) were the only regulars of note to switch to the Ninth Cavalry.[1] As late as 1870, Merritt was the only West Point graduate in the regiment.

Although both Merritt and Wade reached the rank of major general, and five other original appointees attained brigadierships before retirement,[2] many of the original appointees were lacking in competence, character, or physical fitness. Of the first thirty officers commissioned, five, including three captains, were cashiered, while others escaped disgrace only by resigning. Several resigned because of poor health, and another six died during the regiment's first six years.[3]

Because the Ninth Cavalry was organized in Louisiana, it has been assumed that most of its early recruits were ignorant field hands. The basis for this misconception was a historical sketch written in 1896 by

Lieutenant Grote Hutcheson, a West Point graduate who had never been on a single campaign with the buffalo soldiers. Ordered to prepare the manuscript because he was the regimental adjutant, he described the early recruits as "woefully ignorant, entirely helpless" blacks who "knew nothing, . . . had no independence, no self-reliance, not a thought except for the present, and were filled with superstition." Some were so hapless that they had to be taught "how to care for themselves."[4]

Providing no evidence for these assertions, Hutcheson lauded the officers for remaining "enthusiastic" even though they had to "assume nearly all the duties" of the noncommissioned officers, who "for years . . . were such only in name." It was "related" that only one man could write well enough to serve as sergeant major.[5]

In contrast to Hutcheson's unfortunate sketch, the companion essay on the Tenth Cavalry drafted by Lieutenant John Bigelow, who was noted both as a soldier and as a historian,[6] emphasized that its officers recruited "colored men sufficiently educated to fill the positions of non-commissioned officers, clerks and mechanics" and other "*superior* men" who

K Troop, Ninth Cavalry, 1889. Courtesy of the Nebraska State Historical Society, Lincoln.

would be a "credit to the regiment."[7] Although historians have accepted both essays as reliable, statistics suggest that recruiters for the Ninth were as selective as those in the Tenth. During the first year, 818 men were enlisted in the Ninth compared to 1,147 in the Tenth.[8]

A study of Ninth Cavalry death statements for its first three years indicates that almost 40 percent of its recruits had prior military service. Although laborers and farmers constituted most of the remainder, more than 10 percent were artisans or domestic servants. Louisiana recruits predominated during 1866, but afterwards most were from Kentucky, Virginia, and the rest of the upper South.[9]

Most of the difficulties in the training camps were primarily a result of the scarcity of officers. With political maneuvering slowing the selection process, only fifteen officers were on duty with their companies at the end of 1867. It was human nature for them, overwhelmed by their workload, to blame their troubles on their men. At least one officer later rated

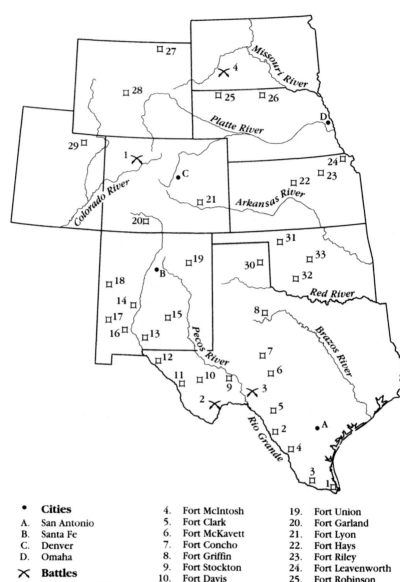

- **Cities**

A. San Antonio
B. Santa Fe
C. Denver
D. Omaha

✕ **Battles**

1. Milk River, 1879
2. Horsehead Hills, 1868
3. Howard's Well, 1872
4. Drexel Mission, 1890

□ **Posts**

1. Fort Brown
2. Fort Duncan
3. Fort Ringgold

4. Fort McIntosh
5. Fort Clark
6. Fort McKavett
7. Fort Concho
8. Fort Griffin
9. Fort Stockton
10. Fort Davis
11. Fort Quitman
12. Fort Bliss
13. Fort Selden
14. Fort Craig
15. Fort Stanton
16. Fort Cummings
17. Fort Bayard
18. Fort Wingate

19. Fort Union
20. Fort Garland
21. Fort Lyon
22. Fort Hays
23. Fort Riley
24. Fort Leavenworth
25. Fort Robinson
26. Fort Niobrara
27. Fort McKinney
28. Fort Washakie
29. Fort Duchesne
30. Fort Elliott
31. Camp Supply
32. Fort Sill
33. Fort Reno

Stations of the Ninth Cavalry, 1867–98

the original recruits as superior to later ones. Asked to evaluate the black recruits of the mid-1870s, Captain Lewis Johnson replied that they were the equals of "a good many" whites, but they were "not as good as *they were immediately after the war closed.*" At that time, he explained, "many colored soldiers from the volunteer service joined the Army."[10]

In striking contrast to the veterans was the youthfulness of many recruits. An analysis of regimental death certificates indicates that 15 percent had been teenagers at the time of their enlistment—some as young as sixteen. Fifty-five percent were aged twenty-one or below, and 87 percent, twenty-five or below. Less than 3 percent were above the age of thirty.[11]

A tabulation of more than three hundred enlistments in the Ninth between 1868 and 1877 indicates that the emphasis on the upper South as a recruiting ground increased. By then, only one in six recruits was from the deep South (from Louisiana eastward through South Carolina). Approximately 40 percent hailed from Kentucky, while another 33 percent were from the balance of the upper South. Eight percent, predominately from Pennsylvania, came from nonslave states. Most surprising, five were born in Canada or the West Indies, while only four were from the southwestern states of Texas and Arkansas.[12]

In accordance with regulations, recruiters carefully noted such items as complexion and color of eyes and hair. Almost two-thirds of the recruits were classified as "black," while the remaining third was segmented into such categories as "brown," "yellow," "mulatto," and "copper." Since many of those described as brown were also referred to as mulattos, the nonblack descriptions usually denoted mixed ancestry. Place of origin had more to do with success than did ancestry. Black and mulatto recruits of the 1870s had virtually identical failure rates.

While 15 to 20 percent of the recruits in each category either deserted or received dishonorable discharges during the initial five-year term of enlistment, southerners, especially those from the upper South, made the transition from civilian to military life much more successfully than their northern counterparts. A survey of L Company recruits shows that twenty-eight of the thirty-six Kentuckians who joined the company between 1871 and 1877 completed their initial enlistments in good standing, while only two deserted or received dishonorable discharges. Of the fourteen recruits from states north of the Mason-Dixon line, on the other hand, six completed their tours successfully while another six either deserted or received dishonorable discharges. (The remaining two received medical discharges.)[13] Free-state African Americans found it more difficult to accept the harsh discipline and discrimination that pervaded army life and probably had more attractive prospects in civilian life than did those from the South. The Kentuckians, most of whom had enlisted at Lexington in the heart of the Blue Grass region, may also have found cavalry life especially attractive.

The troopers were far from imposing in stature. Less than 10 percent were five feet ten inches or more in height, while about the same percentage was below five feet four inches. The median height was five feet six inches. While weights were not listed, recruits were required to weigh less than 155 pounds to avoid placing undue burdens on their horses. Thus, all save the shortest were likely to have been of relatively slender build.[14]

The rate of illiteracy varied widely from company to company. According to the 1870 census rolls, only five members of L Troop were literate; in contrast, in E Troop, twenty-seven of sixty-one claimed the ability to read and write.[15] Whatever the rate, it usually increased whenever an opportunity for learning presented itself. At Fort Concho in 1869 an officer observed that a "limited number" of black troopers were "industriously and successfully studying," even though most, not surprisingly, were passing "their leisure in social amusements."[16]

Opportunities for study were severely curtailed. Although the chaplains of black regiments were charged with instructing illiterate soldiers, they were few and far between. The Ninth Cavalry in 1869, for example, was dispersed in seven forts scattered from the mouth of the Rio Grande almost to El Paso. Its first two chaplains, John C. Jacobi and Manuel Gonzales, moreover, were in such bad health (or so uninterested) that they spent two-thirds of their time on sick leave.[17] As a consequence, troopers rarely saw a chaplain, much less attended classes under one.

At a post with a dedicated padre, however, results could be striking. At Fort Davis, Texas, in 1876, Chaplain George Mullins, assigned to the Twenty-fifth Infantry, reported that some eighty black soldiers, none of whom had known the alphabet a year earlier, had learned to read and write.[18] These included both infantry and cavalrymen. Many soldiers, such as E Troop's William Howard and Benjamin Hockins and K Troop's

George Jordan, gradually progressed from almost total illiteracy to becoming quite proficient in grammatical skills.[19]

Chaplain Mullins was one of the few who sensed the characteristic that more than any other singled the blacks out from their fellow troops—an intense pride in wearing the uniform and a hunger for respect. In Mullins's words, they ardently desired to "be *all that soldiers should be*" because they were convinced that "the colored people of the whole country" were affected by their conduct in the army. He was especially "touched" by their "manly anxiety" for respect both from superiors and "throughout the States." As a result, he asserted, they gambled relatively little, seldom stole from one another, and were "not at all given to quarreling and fighting among themselves." Of 395 black infantry and cavalrymen at Fort Davis, he reported in 1875, only three were under arrest.[20]

Although isolated in frontier outposts, the buffalo soldiers maintained a keen interest in events affecting their race. On 11 March 1874, Senator Charles Sumner of Massachusetts, one of the foremost champions of black freedom, died. On learning of this, the men of L Troop, stationed at Ringgold Barracks on the Rio Grande, adopted a resolution deploring the demise of the "advocator of our equal rights with all men." With his death the country had lost "one of its most faithful servants" and "the colored people of the United States . . . a true friend." Expressing sympathy for the family and friends of Sumner, they voted to send copies of their resolution to the *New York Times* and the *Army and Navy Journal.*[21]

Charles Chinn, a Kentucky veteran of the Civil War with a reputation as a "most excellent soldier," wrote the tribute to Senator Sumner. More than two decades later he again made the pages of the *Army and Navy Journal.* A fifty-six-year-old ordnance sergeant in 1897, he was ordered to Fort McPherson, Georgia. Army regulations stated that noncommissioned officers serving as staff officers were entitled to sleeping car accommodations. As Georgia had recently enacted a Jim Crow law concerning railroad travel, Chinn was told that he could ride in a sleeper only if he "leased all the berths in the car." Upon reaching Atlanta, he engaged an attorney to sue both the state and the company.[22] Although nothing could come of a suit in the wake of the *Plessey* v. *Ferguson* decision upholding segregation, the desire for equality that motivated him would show itself repeatedly among the black troopers.

Sumner was not the only champion of black freedom honored by Ninth Cavalrymen. In 1890, Sergeant Joseph Moore of F Troop spearheaded an effort to raise money to buy the site of John Brown's "fort" at Harper's Ferry, West Virginia, hoping to create a monument to commemorate Brown's effort to liberate the slaves. Although the project was obviously beyond the troopers' modest means, Moore's idealism was not quenched. In 1895 he raised $150 from his troop to assist African American flood victims.[23]

All, of course, was not seriousness among the troopers. Although few suffered from alcoholism, the bane of white regiments, they indulged in their share of vices. An unusually candid description of the aftermath of a paymaster's visit was penned by one signing himself "Africus." For two nights following payday, games of monte raged as "frantic 'buckers'" made the "night hideous with yells of 'turn down,' 'pay de jack,' 'two bits on that ace,' varied by a . . . stampede and 'dousing of glims,'" when the officer of the day made an appearance."[24]

Unfortunately, the "glims" were not doused quickly enough; the following morning, several men were "toting logs" as they paced "to and fro." The punishment reportedly resulted in a "vigorous alacrity" by the "remainder in the performance of duty."

It is likely that the rampant gambling usually went undetected. By chance, Africus's confession appeared in the *Army and Navy Journal* adjacent to a comment by the Ninth's most verbose booster, Major Guy Henry, that at his post (Fort Sill) "the arrival of the paymaster, with its glad welcome for the men," had been followed by "no drunks or confinements."[25] Major Henry may have induced sobriety among his troops, but not even he asserted that they were averse to risking part of their pay at the monte table.

While black soldiers likely had little edge on whites in their proclivity for gambling, they excelled in at least one respect. In the eyes of whites, their most pronounced trait was their affinity for music. At Fort Concho, Post Surgeon William Notson observed that at "every permissible hour," music from a wide variety of instruments could be heard. Many had a "most extraordinary talent," and some could play with either hand. In sounding the bugle calls, they were "disposed to improvise, and vary even upon the orthodox calls."[26]

Notson was not alone in commenting on the troopers' musical talents. Visitors at Fort Bayard, New Mexico, in 1876 noted that "the evening was whiled away listening to a squad of . . . colored troopers who are well up in plantation melodies as well as *au fait* in the jig and other dances." A report from Fort Riley, Kansas, six years later was much the same: "A fine minstrel troupe organized by Company M (Ninth) performed at the post dance hall to the applause of a delighted audience of officers, soldiers, and civilians."[27]

At Fort Stockton, Texas, in 1872, the soldiers treated Emily and Maud Andrews, the visiting wife and daughter of Colonel George Andrews, to an extraordinary performance. Exhibiting only the most genteel over-tones of racism, Mrs. Andrews described the "very funny entertainment" in which the "singing and dancing were something wonderful. . . . Being genuine darkies they entered into it with great zest. We sat in front, while behind us was row after row of the men who really made the room so dark with their bronze faces, that the lights seemed to have no effect."[28]

On the same trip Mrs. Andrews enjoyed the impromptu singing that broke out after the day's march ended. The men seemed never "too tired to dance and sing about their camp fires." Their voices were so "rich and full of melody that I am very glad if I can hear them as I go to sleep."[29]

The penchant for singing contributed to an ability to maintain high spirits in the face of miserable conditions. After the suppression of Sioux resistance following the massacre at Wounded Knee in 1891, four troops of the Ninth remained behind to stand guard over the Pine Ridge Agency. Forced to sleep on the ground with nothing but Sibley tents, each holding fifteen men and heated by a single stove, for shelter from blizzards that piled up snow drifts twenty feet high, many contracted colds or pneu-monia. Through it all they astounded their commanders by their ability each evening, after a Spartan repast of "bread and coffee, and sometimes a little bacon," to settle down in their tents to "have a good time. . . . Song and story, with an occasional jig or a selection on the mouth-organ or the banjo . . . occupied the night hours till 'taps' sounded for bed; and the reveille . . . seemed to find these jolly fellows still laughing."[30]

An even more striking example of the ability to handle adversity was noted by Lieutenant Walter Finley during a desert pursuit of Victorio's Apaches in October 1879. In his first year of service with the regiment, the young West Pointer still regarded the troopers as curiosities: "Darkeys are better on these long marches than white men. They ride along singing and even when they lose their horses they walk beside the column laughing and cracking jokes as if a 40 mile walk was a mere bagatelle."[31] While black troopers undoubtedly loved music, it is also likely that observers were predisposed to exaggerate. After thirty years' service in the Tenth Cavalry, Captain William H. Beck wrote that blacks might "sing more than white troops, but . . . I have not found the difference so very noticeable."[32]

Confined largely to garrison service after the mid-1880s, the buffalo soldiers found the time to stage elegant balls that delighted all fortunate enough to be invited. The troopers were gratified by the attendance of officers and their wives. Grace Paulding, wife of an infantry officer, recalled that the commanding officer and his wife had the first dance, after which she danced once with the post's senior enlisted man. After that, the whites sat on the sidelines "as the soldiers continued the festivities late into the night."[33]

The patronization by officers of their galas presented an illusion of brotherhood. A correspondent to the *Cleveland Gazette* in 1886 applauded the "harmony that exists between the two races when once they don the blue; ladies and gentlemen, regardless of color, waltzing and dancing together. I could not tell from the caste of the floor when in full blast whose dance it was."[34]

A different type of racial intermingling was provided by athletics. Although baseball had become a popular pastime among infantrymen in the 1870s, another decade passed before the buffalo soldiers had time for it. Since they often shared posts with white infantry units, games between the two were hotly contested and occasions for vigorous wagering. The son of Major Anson Burt recalled the "championship game" at Fort Robinson between the Ninth Cavalry and Seventh Infantry. With two outs in the last half of the ninth inning, a "burly" cavalryman cleared the bases with "a tremendous home run to win the game." As the exultant troopers "poured on the field," the umpire, an infantry lieutenant, ruled that the batter was out because he had "stepped clear across the plate" to strike the ball and proclaimed the infantry nine to be the winner. A "near riot" ensued before calmer heads worked out a compromise whereby the game was declared a tie that resulted in the opposing teams' shaking hands and—most important—no money changing hands.[35]

At Fort Duchesne, Utah, the team representing B Troop, coached by Lieutenant James Cavanaugh, who doubled as its pitcher, regularly trounced all competition on the post. The opportunity to demonstrate their prowess against outsiders, however, was limited because of Duchesne's isolation. In May 1897, after making a practice march to Fort Douglas on the outskirts of Salt Lake City, they promptly challenged the nine representing the Twenty-fourth Infantry units at Douglas. Perhaps because of their fatigue, they were soundly trounced. In August they challenged a nine from Vernal, Utah. This time, Lieutenant Cavanaugh's pitches were hammered unmercifully. Eventually he surrendered the mound duties to Private Pettis Jackson, who proceeded to throw "the ball by the man at bat as though it was shot from a cannon." Despite Cavanaugh's ineptness, the troopers were undoubtedly pleased by his participation.[36]

Rivaling baseball in popularity were track and field contests, a regular feature of holiday celebrations. The most hotly contested events matched athletes from different regiments. In these the buffalo soldiers demonstrated that they were as adept on foot as in the saddle. In May 1890 the officers at Fort Leavenworth organized a "hare and hound" race over a nine-mile course across the rolling countryside. Although L Troop of the Ninth was the only black unit involved, along with a dozen white ones, its representatives dominated the race. Private George Wilson, described as "a famous long-distance runner," and a white lieutenant served as the "hares," pursued by twenty-two "hounds." The hares received a fifteen-minute head start but were confined to the course, while the hounds could take shortcuts whenever in sight of a hare. With Private Wilson in the lead, the hares completed the course nine minutes ahead of the closest hound. Two of the three hounds who shared the money awarded the top finishers were also from L Troop. All contestants, black and white, then "devoured" the picnic lunch awaiting them.[37]

Members of the Ninth also excelled at a more ambitious meet at Denver in October 1896. Forty-eight athletes, one from each company stationed in the Department of the Colorado, assembled for the two-day affair. Since Fort Duchesne was the only post manned by the Ninth within the department, it was represented by only two contestants, in contrast to ten from the Seventh Cavalry and eight from each of four infantry regiments. The two, however, dominated the meet.

Running on a track laid out before a grandstand seating an audience that included Denver's most "fashionable belles" and numerous officers, Private William Morris of B Troop easily won the 100- and 220-yard dashes. The following day he trounced several "champion professional" racers in a special sprint.[38]

Morris's exploits were eclipsed by those of Blacksmith Patrick Ross in a variety of contests combining horsemanship, marksmanship, and swordsmanship. Of eight contests designed for cavalrymen, Ross won three and placed second twice. His first victory, entitled "tent pegging," allowed a trooper eight seconds to ride fifty yards to a peg, knock it down with his saber, and return with it balanced on his blade. His second win, a manikin race, required the contestants to mount, race the length of the track, jumping a hurdle en route, snatch up a manikin weighing twenty pounds, place it under an arm, and return. Ross edged out the runner-up in a "pretty and exciting scene."

Ross's wins were all the more remarkable because they occurred on the heels of the broadsword competition. Helmeted and wearing a "plastron" (padded tunic), two troopers battled with broadswords until time expired and the judges declared a victor. Winners advanced to fight in the next round until a champion was determined. The victor had only one tough match, his semifinal battle with Ross. The two fought "two bouts to a draw," evoking "the greatest enthusiasm from the crowd," before the buffalo soldier succumbed. How he emerged from such a slugfest to win the next two events is remarkable.

On the second day, Ross won the "novelty race," in which contestants rode the length of the course while "standing with crossed stirrups," remounted "faced to the rear," and returned to the starting line. Although this was his last victory, he finished second in two of the remaining four events. His first runner-up performance involved "firing, cuts, and thrusts" with revolver and saber while racing over a course that contained twelve obstacles, including hurdles and a water jump. This evoked bursts of "applause that were hearty and well deserved" from the spectators. Ross also placed second in a "potato race" in which contestants raced back and forth to transport a number of potatoes to a basket. When the last potato was securely in place, the trooper remounted and fired a pistol to signal completion.

Perhaps exhausted, Ross failed to place in two especially grueling contests. One was "mounted gymnastics: five minutes at command; five minutes at will," while the other involved "wrestling bareback . . . in blue shirts and leggings."

After the last event, Miss Octavia Wheaton, daughter of the departmental commander, attached medals to the tunics of winners and runners-up before pinning the "general's medal"—going to the outstanding contestant—on Patrick Ross. It must have been heartening to the buffalo soldier to be congratulated by General Frank Wheaton while spectators applauded loudly.[39]

Important as games, music, and other diversions were, the buffalo soldiers did not ignore the serious aspects of life. This was especially true whenever a death occurred. When that happened, they insisted upon due respect for the deceased. While on a scout in New Mexico's Black Mountains in October 1877, Corporal James Betters, an eleven-year veteran of C Troop, was accidentally shot. Before dying, he was promised that he would be returned to Fort Bayard for burial. The manner in which this was carried out was disgraceful.

Betters's body was returned to the fort while the troopers continued their scout. At the fort, with no pretense of following regulations, the body, without even an "arrangement of clothing," was deposited in a coffin and hauled away in a garbage cart. Two military convicts, most likely white infantrymen, rode atop the coffin as they drove to the cemetery and deposited it. There was no flag over the coffin, no military escort, not a "single mourner or friend to follow the poor fellow's remains to their last resting place." To complete the travesty, there was "not even a prayer said above his grave."

Obviously incensed upon returning to the post, Captain Charles Beyer demanded an investigation. Stressing the negative impact on morale, he stated that the insensitive burial had evoked "an intense feeling of indignation" among the buffalo soldiers and their officers.

A hasty investigation by Major Wade consisted primarily of questioning the infantry officers who had handled the burial. Wade accepted their explanation that the body was so decomposed when it arrived at the fort (only thirty-six hours after death and in a mountainous region where October nights were frigid) that it seemed unwise to handle it any other way. Lame as this excuse was, Wade failed to find anyone negligible.[40]

Such disrespect became rare as officers recognized the importance of proper funerals for morale. A burial while a detachment under Colonel Edward Hatch was in Colorado in October 1882 was more likely the norm. James H. White had enlisted in 1878 and had transferred to the regimental band the following year. Popular among his comrades because of his "generosity and affable, pleasant manner," he was also "valued by his commander as an efficient and faithful soldier." Unfortunately, he became ill and, "in spite of every care and attention," died. He was accorded full military honors as the battalion, officers included, escorted the coffin to the camp's limit, from where it was taken to a cemetery for burial.

Africus, who had earlier described the troopers' payday gambling, sent an account of the service to the *Army and Navy Journal* together with a stanza lifted from Sir Walter Scott's *Lady of the Lake:*

> Soldier rest! thy warfare o'er
> Sleep the sleep that knows not breaking:
> Dream of tented fields no more,
> Days of danger, nights of waking.[41]

Descriptions abound of equally impressive funerals. In July 1882, Sergeant Bushrod Johnson and Private Washington Grimke were murdered by a horse thief they were escorting near Fort Sill in what is now western Oklahoma. Two days later they were accorded a "most impressive" funeral: "Each body was followed by his horse, trimmed in the usual manner. The sun had set as we left the post and when the last volley was fired and taps sounded, the full, clear moon rose upon the scene."[42]

Funerals also indicate the bonds that developed between officers and men. At Fort Robinson in the mid-1890s, Robert Emmett, recently retired, was visiting Colonel and Mrs. Biddle when "the funeral call sounded." After the colonel left to attend the services, Emmett learned the identity of the deceased soldier. A "serious look came over [his] face," and he hurried to attend, "as the man to be buried was in the troop he had commanded."[43]

While death was always near at hand, the mortality rate was an area in which African American troopers made considerable progress. During the year ending 1 October 1868, fifty-one of every one thousand black soldiers died, compared to twenty-six per thousand white soldiers. The difference was attributed to their being stationed in areas where cholera and yellow fever were prevalent, but—after subtracting the deaths from these diseases—there was still a discrepancy of twenty-six to thirteen. Since *fewer* blacks than whites were admitted to hospitals or granted disability discharges, it seems likely that army surgeons paid less attention to their ailments.[44]

In succeeding years the gap between black and white mortality rates narrowed dramatically. By 1873 the white rate had dropped to seventeen per thousand, and the black, to twenty-one. Despite this improvement a black soldier admitted to a hospital was almost twice as likely to die as a white one and was much less likely to receive a disability discharge.[45]

By 1879 the respective figures per thousand for black and white soldiers had dropped to fourteen and twelve, respectively. The gap in deaths because of disease, eight (blacks) and seven (whites) per thousand, had virtually disappeared. In addition, the death rate for hospital admission had evened out as fewer than one per thousand of both blacks and whites failed to survive his stay.[46] Although much of the gain resulted from improvements in the quality of drinking water, the disposal of human and animal wastes, housing, and personal hygiene, black soldiers also undoubtedly demanded and received more conscientious treatment.

Desertion rates were another area in which black soldiers excelled. Even during its turbulent organization and move to the Texas frontier, the Ninth's desertion rate was much lower than that of comparable white regiments. During its first twelve months, 118 men from the Ninth deserted; the comparable figures for the Fourth and Seventh Cavalries were 299 and 512, respectively. The Fourth, unlike the newly organized Ninth, had been in existence since the early 1850s.[47]

Never again was the number of desertions in the Ninth half as great as during its first year. Falling to 48 the following year, the rate declined steadily until 1877, when only 6 men deserted in the entire regiment. That same year, the Fourth Cavalry had 184 desertions and the Fifth, 224. After a modest increase during the Victorio War (37 during the twelve months ending 30 June 1880), the levels again became negligible, falling to 13 by 1888.[48]

The low desertion and alcoholism rates did not lead to a corresponding reduction in courts-martial. Fewer problems resulting from desertion and drunken misbehavior were offset by numerous insubordination and negligence cases. An analysis of general courts-martial involving Ninth Cavalrymen from 1882 through 1884, as shown in Table 1-1, indicates the frequency of various types of misbehavior.

TABLE 1-1.

General Courts-martial in the Ninth Cavalry, 1882–84.

Type of Offense	No. of Offenses	% of Total
Insubordination	26	24.3
Negligence	20	18.7
Absence without Leave	18	16.8
Theft	17	15.9
Assault	10	9.3
Desertion	9	8.4
Intoxication	6	5.6
Sexual Deviance	1	0.9

Source: Based on General Court-Martial Orders (GCMO), Dept. of the Missouri, Records of the U.S. Army Continental Commands, RG 393, NA.

Note: Although offenses often involved more than one of these categories (for example, assault on a noncommissioned officer may also have involved insubordination or alcohol abuse), I have tabulated them only according to the most serious and/or obvious offense.

Since 95 percent of all court-martial cases ended in convictions, the most practical purpose of a trial was to determine the punishment. In this the defendant's prior record was as important as the facts of the case. An excellent soldier might get away with murder; a sorry one might be imprisoned and dismissed for a relatively minor offense. The major exceptions involved desertion and theft, which almost always resulted in a dishonorable discharge plus imprisonment.

The thefts punished by dishonorable discharges were of two plugs of tobacco in one case, a spur worth twenty-five cents in another, and a ramrod in a third. Stealing the stakes in a poker game evoked a discharge and a three-year prison term. At Fort Elliott, Texas, in November 1883, Private Fred Freeman of A Troop committed the heinous crime of giving two saddle blankets to a woman so that she could "keep her children warm." He received three months' imprisonment plus the inevitable discharge.[49]

Reviewing authorities often disallowed or mitigated sentences. Ironically, it was their efforts to discourage leniency that tended to benefit prisoners the most. In the spring of 1881, Private Edward McBain of G Troop was convicted of stealing a sack of potatoes and sentenced to three months' imprisonment and a fine of thirty dollars. The verdict was condemned on the contradictory grounds that there was "no legal evidence" to support a conviction and that the sentence was too light for the crime: "Any conviction for a felony should carry a dishonorable discharge." McBain was ordered to be returned to duty. In a more serious case, Private Albert Dennis of I Troop was convicted of stealing a gold watch from a citizen. His sentence—a dishonorable discharge plus two years in prison—was overturned because the court-martial failed to record his plea.[50]

There was less uniformity in the punishment of insubordination than any other offense. While nine out of twenty-six such trials resulted in dishonorable discharges, most of the accused received only token punishments. In May 1881, Private Fred Evans of A Troop attacked his first sergeant with intent to inflict bodily harm and did not stop until another sergeant "broke a carbine over his head." Although Evans was convicted, he escaped with a fine of twenty dollars.[51]

Because of their low desertion rate, black units often developed a high esprit de corps. This helped to win the respect of most of their officers and to endure the most racist. Although officer-enlisted relations had improved greatly by the 1880s, racism was always a factor. A remarkably frank letter to the *Army and Navy Journal* by an unidentified officer illustrates the contradictory feelings held by the best of officers. After stressing that he was "no admirer of the African, believing he will *ultimately destroy the white race*," the writer admitted he would have been as prejudiced as his peers in white regiments had he never served with blacks. His tenure with buffalo soldiers, however, had led him to "think the world of the men of my company. When I look at them I do not see their black faces, I see only something beyond. . . . They are far ahead of white troops. They are more like a lot of devoted servants and retainers, *faithful and trustworthy in every respect, and brave and gallant.*"[52]

While the quality of the officers is easier to evaluate, the noncommissioned officers, especially the first sergeants, primarily determined the worth of a troop. Nothing was more valid than Guy Henry's declaration to a congressional committee that good noncommissioned officers were more important than a good captain. Henry argued that since the first sergeants actually "ran the companies," their pay should be raised from twenty-three dollars to fifty dollars per month. If necessary, he offered to accept a reduction in his own pay to compensate them.[53]

To help improve quality among noncommissioned officers, Henry prepared a booklet entitled an *Army Catechism for Non-Commissioned Officers and Soldiers* that contained 375 questions and answers on topics as simple as how to deal with sore feet or rattlesnake bites to ones as complex as, "If on the march and attacked by the Indians, what formation should be made?" Most important, he admonished NCOs to respect the dignity of men under their command. Discipline should be enforced without "swearing or roughness." If a man had to be confined, "direct two of the privates, or more if necessary, to carry out the order, keeping one's temper, and hands off a man as long as possible. Such conduct will be more effective than brute force, and command more respect and obedience."[54]

A comparison of the desertions and dishonorable discharges among troops in the Ninth from 1885 to 1887 (Table 1-2) demonstrates the validity of Henry's axiom and the wide range of discipline within the regiment. First sergeants such as Emanuel Stance of F Troop who frequently lost their temper and resorted to violence were repaid with more defiance. Others, such as George Mason, first sergeant of L Troop for two decades, seemed to maintain discipline almost effortlessly.

Captains Francis Moore (Troop L), Edward Rucker (M), and J. S. Loud (D), whose troops had the fewest offenders, were low-keyed individuals who shared an ability to support the first sergeants, who were mainly responsible for the records of their units. Ironically, the qualities that made Sergeants Mason, Madison Ingoman (D), and George Washington (M) successful ensured that their actions generated few records.

The variations were also related to the post at which troops served. Nowhere was this so obvious as at Fort Robinson, Nebraska, the regi-

TABLE 1-2.
Desertions and Dishonorable Discharges, Ninth Cavalry, 1885–87

Troop	A	B	C	D	E	F	G	H	I	K	L	M
Desertions	15	6	11	3	10	10	13	4	4	10	3	2
Dishonorable Discharges	9	7	9	2	4	5	7	3	4	5	1	3
Total	24	13	20	5	14	15	20	7	8	15	4	5

SOURCE: Derived from the Regimental Returns, Ninth Cavalry, for the 1885–87 period, M 744, NA.

mental headquarters from 1887 to 1898. Black soldiers there were court-martialed three times as often as those at smaller posts such as Forts Duchesne and McKinney. With a garrison comprised of approximately six troops of black cavalry and two companies of white infantry, Fort Robinson provided an excellent breeding ground for racist resentments that affected the treatment of soldiers. Things got so bad that in May 1887, Lieutenant Colonel J. L. Brisbin, during a brief tenure as the post commander, challenged the necessity of many of the courts-martial. Alarmed that black soldiers were being court-martialed at a rate more than twice that of whites, he warned that good soldiers could be "spoiled by the contamination" of guardhouses, where they came "into contact with the most worthless and vicious characters." In addition, too many courts-martial could "bring the method into contempt and remove the odium that a true soldier should feel, if court-martialed."[55]

Systematic discrimination was also seen in the preference given whites in the allotment of duty assignments. Eventually a buffalo soldier complained to the *Cleveland Gazette* that even though black soldiers at Fort Robinson outnumbered whites by almost four to one, virtually all clerical positions went to the infantrymen. Three white clerks were on duty in the commissary department and two each in the post bakery, adjutant's office, and officers' club. In addition, the post librarian, the two men who worked in the post pump house, and the five employed in the quartermaster department were all white.[56]

In contrast to racism imposed from above, individual black and white soldiers often got along well. After a visit to Fort Duchesne, a "Deputy Marshall Brooks" stated that black and white troopers "fraternize without any fine discrimination as to color." Perhaps with some exaggeration he asserted that they "associate, eat and for all he knows sleep and fight the festive bedbug together."[57] Also indicative of the tolerant climate at Duchesne, its first band included both blacks and whites, as did the choir.[58]

Although the buffalo soldiers were usually stationed in areas with few black inhabitants, they had excellent relations with those they encountered. In October 1880, Lieutenant Matthias Day was ordered to search for black deserters rumored to be in the vicinity of Las Vegas, New Mexico. He was unsuccessful because the "whole colored population here seems to be in league with them and spy around to find out everything I do. They . . . lead me on a wild goose chase all over town."[59]

A more common type of soldier-civilian relationships was noted by a racist editor at Hays, Kansas. The "colored folks" at nearby Fort Ellis had enjoyed a "big time" at a party for which the string band from the Ninth Cavalry had furnished the music. Lest anyone doubt his prejudices, the editor mockingly speculated that "de boys had a high ol time you bet your sweet life, Yah, yah!"[60]

Taunting and snide remarks were mild compared to many of the indignities inflicted on the buffalo soldiers by the civilians they were assigned to protect. Soldiers were also harassed by so-called law officials. While Texas was worst, conditions improved little in New Mexico. In 1878, Troop E was en route to Colorado in response to a rumored Ute uprising. As it passed through Santa Fe, two troopers were arrested for the possession of arms (in a society where "nearly all citizens go armed"). Hauled before a judge, they were fined the amount of money found on their persons and released—minus their weapons, which had been confiscated. Colonel Hatch bitterly protested that the arrest "had no other purpose than to commit robbery under the color of law."[61]

In addition to such harassments, it has often been assumed that black regiments received inferior arms, food, and horses. The best documented example of this occurred at Fort Sill in 1873, when an inspector stated that the Tenth Cavalry was forced to use "mounts [that] were castoffs from the more favored Seventh Cavalry," many as old as fifteen years.[62] This was either an exception to the norm or else the inspector was taken in by the grousing of Lieutenant Colonel John Davidson, the post commander. The most authoritative study on the matter, by Thomas Phillips, indicates that black and white units usually received the "same arms and equipment" and the same "quality of horses."[63]

There is little evidence that the Ninth Cavalry was issued horses, arms, or food that differed from those of white regiments in the same areas. They obviously received poor-quality food at times and occasionally ran low on ammunition, but this was largely a result of being located hundreds of miles from the nearest railroad. This isolation made it especially difficult to procure the grain necessary to keep eastern-bred horses from breaking down. When the Ninth arrived in Texas in 1867, for example, a local editor noted that the troopers were mounted "on superb horses, all of which were in remarkably good condition."[64] Within months so many had broken down because of alkali water and lack of grain that many observers thought the army should purchase local range horses. These, however, were considered too small to carry a trooper laden with rifle, ammunition, canteen, and sleeping gear.

Only once did Colonel Hatch complain of the quality of the horses sent to his regiment. In the fall of 1879 he sharply criticized the latest arrivals. It was not that they were old or broken down, but that they were "entirely too small," because some were "but four years old."[65] Obviously, an officer's idea of the optimum age for a horse differed widely from that of a modern race trainer.

Each theme heretofore discussed will be revisited during the biographical sketches that constitute the bulk of this study. While I would never be so bold as to assert, as did Ralph Waldo Emerson, that there "is properly no history; only biography," I do believe that generalizations are more meaningful when related to the lives of particular individuals. It is only by knowing as much as possible about their lives and aspirations that stereotypes can be corrected.

2

The Colonel of the Buffaloes

It seems almost logical that the Ninth Cavalry should be commanded by one of the army's most underrated and ignored officers, Edward Hatch. Paul A. Hutton's *Phil Sheridan and His Army*, for example, mentions Benjamin Grierson of the Tenth Cavalry on twenty-four pages and Ranald S. Mackenzie, of the Fourth, on forty. Hatch receives not a single word.[1]

Obscurity has led to belittlement. Richard Wormser, author of a respected history of the U.S. cavalry, asserted that Hatch was only the "nominal" head of the Ninth, whose "real commander" was Lieutenant Colonel Merritt.[2] Nothing could be further from the truth.

Little is known of Hatch's youth. He was born in Bangor, Maine, on 22 April 1831, and his father, Nathaniel, was an attorney prosperous enough to send him to the Norwich Military Academy in Vermont. Three years of "unceasing study" there would stand him in good stead later, but his "roving disposition" led him to leave school for a fling as a sailor. After collecting "numerous adventures" on his first voyage, he sedately went to work for his father, who had become a lumber merchant in Pennsylvania. While his stay in the Keystone State was brief, it was probably then that he met Evelyn Barrington, the teenaged daughter of a Philadelphia naval surgeon.[3]

Seeking to carve out a niche in the business world that would allow him to support a family, Hatch invested in a "manufacturing establishment" in Norfolk, Virginia—a holding later confiscated by the Confederates. In 1854 his search for greener pastures took him to the West, where

Edward Hatch, colonel of the Ninth Cavalry, 1866–89. Courtesy of the Massachusetts Commandery, Military Order of the Loyal Legion, and the U.S. Military History Institute, Carlisle, Pa.

he "met with numerous adventures" during a visit with some Plains Indians. A winter in a logging camp in Wisconsin inspired him to change occupations. The following spring, he moved to Muscatine, Iowa, on the banks of the Mississippi. Floating logs downstream from Wisconsin and sawing them into lumber to sell was so lucrative that he was soon able to return east and wed Evelyn. By 1861 he was feeling "comparatively rich."[4]

Visiting in Washington when the bombardment of Fort Sumter occurred, Hatch foolhardily attempted to salvage his Virginia investment. Carrying a fake "pass as a British subject," he traveled to Norfolk to collect "certain claims." Unfortunately, he was recognized, accused of spying, and confined. While his fate was being decided, he escaped "and by means of an oyster boat" reached a Union warship anchored outside the harbor. In late May he returned to Muscatine and set to work helping to organize a volunteer cavalry regiment.[5]

By late July 1861 he had enlisted a company for the nascent Second Iowa Cavalry, had been "elected" its captain, and had conducted it to Camp McClellan in nearby Davenport. Placed in command of the camp because of the absence of the regimental field officers, he so impressed officers and enlisted men alike that they became his most ardent backers.

When a major resigned in August, a "petition . . . signed by every commissioned officer in camp" nominated Hatch for the vacancy. When the lieutenant colonel resigned three weeks later, Hatch was again promoted at the request of the regimental officers. Although he was in charge of the regiment by December, his formal promotion to colonel did not occur until June 1862.

After taking part in the campaign against Island No. 10, he was shifted to western Tennessee, where he spent the next two years protecting rail and telegraph lines from raiders and destroying Confederate installations and foodstuffs.[6] In one hard-fought battle after another he built a solid reputation with men and superiors alike. A no-nonsense taskmaster, he soon led the best-drilled and -disciplined regiment in the Army of the Tennessee. Richard Surby, a proud member of the Seventh Illinois Cavalry, observed that the Second Iowa was "the best drilled regiment" in the cavalry and that, under Hatch's "intrepid" leadership, it was "invincible."[7]

Surby's view from the ranks was echoed from above. General S. A. Hurlbut, commanding Union forces in western Tennessee, described Hatch as the "best cavalry officer in the field and in the camp I have ever met with." Major James H. Wilson, on an inspection tour for General Grant in 1863, reported that the Second Iowa was "by far the best cavalry regiment in the Department of the Tennessee; and what is more, Hatch is the best officer." He commented gratuitously that "I always thought Hatch Grierson's superior, and today I became thoroughly convinced my judgment was properly founded."[8]

Attached to Hatch's staff during the Battle of Nashville, Surby penned the most detailed description of him. He was about five feet ten, "well proportioned," with "dark hair lightly tinged with grey," a "Roman nose, thin lips, and a heavy black mustache." Surby was especially struck by his "blue eyes, beaming with intelligence," that in battle "shine like meteors," and his "cool, collected mind, that sees things at a glance." A "splendid horseman," he was "the last man to sleep when on the march and the first up in the morning." Although a "strict disciplinarian," he required "no more of his . . . men than he performs himself."[9]

Wilson, under whom Hatch served during the last year of the war, was never slow to criticize fellow officers, including Grierson and Hurlbut. He declared that Hatch, possessed of a "splendid constitution and striking figure," had "only to be told what he was to do and then attended to the rest himself." His only fault was that "he always declared himself ready without reference to feed, forage, or ammunition." Brave to a fault, he feared "nothing but that he and his command might not do their full share of the work, or get their full share of the glory." In summation, Wilson stated that it had been an "express pleasure to command" both him and his troops.[10]

Surby and Lyman Pierce of the Second Iowa, the historians of their respective units, stood in equal awe of Hatch. Surby's description of him as "a rare military genius" was echoed by Pierce's statement that he was "by nature" a "military genius of the first magnitude" who became "the idol of the regiment."[11] Hatch never disappointed their confidence that he knew "how to get into a fight and how to get out again." He seemed instinctively to know when to attack vigorously and when to extricate his troops from an untenable situation. As a result, his command suffered relatively few casualties. Skirmishing almost daily and participating in several major battles, the regiment lost only one officer and fifty-nine enlisted men killed. Even the number of deaths from disease (209), was smaller than in most regiments.[12]

Hatch's personal bravery also inspired his men. A member of the Second Iowa described an encounter at Jackson, Tennessee, in which "the rebs got behind the bridge and logs in a manner that defied us to dislodge them." To break the standoff, Hatch "took a rifle and called for four men to follow him." He ran towards the Confederates and had gotten "within fifty yards of them when they raised and fired." He "threw himself on the ground and the balls passed harmlessly over his head." He then fired, "giving a long macilent [sic] Lieut, a *chance to officiate at his own funeral.*" As the Confederates began to fall back, he called out, "draw sabers, forward," and led the charge. The correspondent closed by avowing that men would "rather die than shrink from following one so brave."[13]

Placed in command of a brigade in the autumn of 1862, Hatch only once was disparaged by a superior. General William T. Sherman, irked that Hatch had failed to prevent a Confederate attack on the train on which Sherman was riding, complained that the colonel always "seems to hover around when he should dash in with the saber and pistol."[14] Although stung by the criticism, Hatch said nothing and continued in almost constant action until December 1863. In a fiercely contested battle at Moscow, Tennessee, a bullet passed through his right lung. According to Pierce, he "refused to give up the command or leave the field though the ball had passed entirely through his body. Ordering an ambulance to the spot, he was placed therein and driven from point to point on the field, while he directed the movements of the men. In this way he fought and won the battle."[15]

Converted into one of Hatch's strongest supporters, Sherman declared it was a "travesty" that he had not been promoted to brigadier general even though he had participated in more battles than any other officer from Iowa and had been endorsed for promotion by every general he had served under, including Grant. Promotions, however, depended as much on patronage as on merit. Hatch, in Sherman's opinion, suffered because he had "but few acquaintances among the more prominent men of his state." This offset the fact that he was "universally considered one of the best cavalry officers in the volunteer army."[16]

Sherman undoubtedly appreciated that Hatch, like himself, believed that "war is hell" and did not hesitate to devastate Confederate foodstuffs and railway lines. As early as July 1863, Rebel officers charged that the depredations committed by Hatch's men were "by his orders" and that he had "threatened our people to treat them worse in every succeeding raid."[17]

There is no doubt that Hatch tolerated considerable looting and ransacking. After capturing Jackson, he reported that some of his men had found a cache of whiskey, which caused "as much trouble to save the town from fire . . . as it did to whip the enemy." Although he kept Jackson from burning and protected private dwellings from looters, he was unable to keep "negroes and stragglers" from plundering businesses. A Tennessee officer in his command, however, stated that Hatch's troops openly engaged in plunder. Some "took . . . buggies and wagons and loaded them with goods and boots, etc," and "nearly every man had something that had been taken out of the place."[18]

Jackson's fate was mild compared to that of Oxford, Mississippi, in August 1864. In 1867 a writer blamed Oxford's incineration and plundering upon the "brutality and rapacity of . . . General Edward Hatch." When his troops had completed their work, of "what was an attractive little city on the morning of August 22nd, . . . there only remained at night skeletons of houses and smoldering ruins."[19]

Hatch allegedly established his headquarters in the "ornate mansion" of Jacob Thompson, a former cabinet officer under James Buchanan. Setting up temporary headquarters in the house, he ignored the plundering of its contents. When Mrs. Thompson asked him to stop the looting, he leaned back "in a comfortable arm-chair" and "superciliously answered that his men could take anything they might wish, except the chair in which he was seated." Before leaving the scene, he "caused his ambulance to be filled with pictures, china, . . . and such other articles . . . as had attracted his fancy."[20]

This was followed by the torching of the emptied mansion. A Union soldier, writing to the *Dubuque Times*, confirmed that the troops "made free with Oxford; burning all the fine brick blocks fronting on the public square, also the Court House . . . [and] the houses of some prominent rebel officials." He specifically stated that "the splendid mansion of Jacob Thompson . . . went up in crackling flames" as a "burnt-offering to the Moloch of Treason."[21]

Although Hatch's actions must have been crude indeed to be recalled so vividly, he may not have been as villainous as described. Since he left the war much poorer than he entered it, it seems doubtful that he loaded his ambulance with valuables. As to the charge that he ordered the burning of Oxford, the most contemporary Confederate account stated that it was General Andrew Smith, Hatch's superior, who "superintended" the arson and refused to allow the owners to "remove anything of value from their burning dwellings." The report described the actions of Smith and his command as "brutal in the extreme." Oddly enough, the same work that vilified Hatch contained a second version of Oxford's burning omitting Hatch's name entirely and stating that General Smith "sent an officer of his staff with a detachment to burn" the house. This time, Mrs. Thompson was given fifteen minutes in which to remove any articles she wished to save.[22]

Fortunately, Nashville, not Oxford, determined Hatch's place in the annals of Civil War leaders. In October 1864, Confederate General John Bell Hood, smarting from the loss of Atlanta to Sherman, began an invasion of Tennessee. Sherman chose to continue his march on Savannah while General George Thomas confronted the Confederates. While Thomas was assembling his scattered units into a coherent army, he needed someone to monitor and delay the Confederate advance.

Fortunately, Hatch was in the process of leading a division of cavalry from Memphis to report to Sherman at Atlanta. Since his detachment was the only sizable cavalry force in southern Tennessee, he was transferred to Thomas's command. Although James Wilson assumed command of Thomas's cavalry on 24 October, he was too busy procuring troops, horses, and supplies to leave Nashville until 20 November. In his absence, Hatch, in command of nine regiments and one battery of light artillery designated as the Fifth Cavalry Division, confronted Hood's army.

Deploying his troops along the Tennessee River, he maintained constant reconnaissances that monitored and contested each Confederate move. Frequent counterattacks forced the Rebels to deploy for battle, thus slowing their advance. At the same time, he evaded every effort by Nathan Forrest, Hood's wily cavalry commander, to envelop his command. Wilson lauded his "vigilance" in discovering "every movement" of the enemy and the "coolness and steadiness" with which he handled his troops.[23]

Thomas's corps commanders in southern Tennessee, Generals D. H. Stanley and John Schofield, were also impressed. Stanley stated that he

"dispersed his forces so judiciously that not a movement of any consequence could be made by the enemy in any direction that we were not
immediately appraised of it . . . ; for nearly one month he maintained a
line of pickets and outposts fifty miles in extent . . . without any serious
loss to his command." Schofield wrote that "no cavalry ever performed"
reconnaissance service "more efficiently."[24]

At the Battle of Franklin on 30 November, Rebel cavalry sought to
outflank the Union forces, but Hatch's troops, in Wilson's words, "made
a beautiful fight" and drove them back "with great gallantry." Although
the infantry at Franklin played the major role in defeating Hood's army,
the cavalry's success kept Forrest away from the vital supply trains.
Wilson exulted that in Hatch he had a subordinate "of rare ability and
experience" who was the equal, if not the superior, of the "vaunted"
Confederate cavalry commanders.[25]

The Battle of Nashville provided Hatch his supreme challenge. As
Thomas began his attack on 15 December, Hatch's division and A. J.
Smith's infantry corps were ordered to envelop Hood's left wing. Delayed
first by a dense fog and then by an infantry division's marching in front
of his lines, Hatch was not able to move against Hood's line until almost
noon. After driving the skirmishers from his front, he was faced with five
fortified hilltop redoubts that secured Hood's left flank.

Elsewhere along the battle line, Hood's forces held, but Hatch's dismounted cavalry, supported by a detachment of General John MacArthur's
infantry, broke the stalemate. After routing the units in front of him, Hatch
found his command under artillery fire from the redoubt nearest at hand.
Rather than endure the shelling, he "threw forward" his Second Brigade
in a charge that broke through the opposing infantry and captured the
redoubt with its cannon intact.

Sergeants Surby and Pierce, in the midst of the fighting, penned the
most colorful accounts of the successes that followed. After taking the
first redoubt, Hatch and his command were exposed to the fire of
another, located five hundred yards away and "far above." To capture it
seemed impossible, but "Hatch was with us, and failure is nowhere in
his vocabulary." Having already charged more than a mile laden with
ammunition and gear, and unaccustomed to fighting on foot, the troopers
were exhausted. Nevertheless, in the teeth of "brisk cannonading" and
heavy musketry fire, they struggled up the steep slope toward the

redoubt. "Many . . . crawled on their hands and knees" to its base. Hatch, astride a charger that made him a special target, spotted a trooper too spent to continue. He "told him to get hold of his horse's tail, and hold on, and he would help him up the hill, which was done."[26] Under his urging, the brigade stormed over the redoubt's embankments and captured another six cannon and 175 Confederates.

While the men exulted and caught their breath, Hatch galloped away to send his First Brigade against another redoubt. He continued the assault on the reeling Confederates until darkness forced his troops to bivouac on the field. Astride his horse, always in the thick of the action, he left his men amazed that he "came out untouched."[27] His cavalry had pushed Hood's left flank back four miles.

During the night Hood shifted an entire corps to shore up the exposed flank and laid out a new defense line along the crest of the Brentwood Hills. The next day, Schofield, whose XXIII Corps was now on Hatch's immediate left, considered the Rebel defenses so formidable that he refused to attack until after Hatch's cavalry had decided the outcome of the battle. Even Wilson complained to Thomas that the terrain facing his troops was "too difficult for cavalry operations" and asked permission to move his cavalry to Hood's right flank. His request was granted, but by the time he returned to the front line, Hatch's troops, in the face of fierce resistance, were already fighting their way up the densely wooded Brentwood heights that lay to the left and rear of the main Confederate defenses.

Gaining the crest sometime before 3 P.M., Hatch hauled "with great labor" an artillery battery to the top and opened fire on the main Confederate lines exposed below. Then he launched an attack on the rear of the Confederate positions at the same time that MacArthur's infantry made a frontal assault.

Assailed from front and rear, and with Hatch's battery pelting them from above, the Rebel lines abruptly collapsed as men attempted to escape before they were encircled. Proud of the cavalry's decisive role in routing Hood, Wilson stated that Hatch's troopers "had closed in upon the enemy's entrenchments and entered them from the rear before the infantry reached them in front. They had captured fifteen more field guns, thus bringing their score up to twenty-seven for the two days, and had picked up several hundred prisoners."[28]

As darkness fell on the battlefield on 16 December, Wilson exulted to a subordinate that "the day is glorious! Hatch and Knipe have done splendidly." Years later, he still maintained that Hatch, "*more than anyone else, should have credit for the active and aggressive advance of the cavalry against Hood's left in front of Nashville.*" Hatch was largely responsible for "*the principal successes of both the first and second days*" of the battle. This praise was all the more remarkable because it was written almost twenty years after Hatch's death. In summation, Wilson said it was "impossible to give any adequate account" of Hatch's "gallant deeds."[29]

Confirming Wilson's evaluation, he and Hatch, recently promoted to brigadier general of volunteers, were the only officers recommended by Thomas for promotion to major general after the battle. Hatch's selection was because of the "good management and bravery, . . . skill, [and] untiring energy with which he commanded his division."[30] Not surprisingly, Wilson, senior in rank and with more advocates in high places, was the only one to gain the second star.

Nashville offers a glimpse of chivalrous behavior by Hatch that is in sharp contrast to his reported actions at Oxford. As Hood's forces retreated on the evening of 16 December, Colonel E. W. Rucker covered the withdrawal with a rear-guard stand. Hood escaped, but Rucker, his left arm shattered by a bullet, was captured and escorted by Hatch to a house serving as Wilson's headquarters. Later that evening, Rucker recalled, Hatch "came to me and . . . offered me his bed. I thanked him and he made a courteous reply. . . . Hatch laid down on the floor by my side, and (God bless him) got up frequently during the night and gave me water, and the next morning, when we left for Nashville, he provided me with a small flask of good whiskey."[31] This is a far cry from his alleged behavior as the ogre of Oxford.

For two weeks Hatch's command pursued the Confederates, clashing repeatedly with Forrest's cavalry. After the close of action on the seventeenth, Wilson wrote that "Hatch's division . . . made several beautiful charges, breaking the rebel infantry in all directions. . . . Hatch is a brick!" Confederate General Stephen Lee, describing the "bold and vigorous" pursuit, wrote that a "more persistent effort was never made to rout the rear guard of a retiring column." But with streams out of their banks from torrential rains and with horses rapidly breaking down, the pursuers were unable to prevent the remnants of Hood's army from escaping across the

Tennessee River. On Christmas Day, unable to bridge the flood-swollen stream, the Federal troops gave up the chase. Hatch's division then went into camp at Eastport, on the Alabama-Mississippi border.[32]

For all intents and purposes, Hatch's Civil War service had ended. Like his troops, he needed rest. Still recovering from the wound received at Moscow when he began the campaign, he had been in the field for more than one hundred days, part of the time subsisting on parched corn. Two weeks of nonstop fighting and marching, while pelted by winter rains, had left him so sick "from exposure and over-exertion" that Wilson ordered him to take a twenty-day leave of absence. He did not return to duty until 20 February 1865.

As a result of his illness, he was unable to draft a report of his division's actions during the campaign. In his absence, an adjutant submitted a brief outline of the division's activities. Meanwhile, Colonel Datus Coon, in command of Hatch's Second Brigade, filed a detailed, seventeen-page report emphasizing his own role in the campaign. The richness of his account, in contrast to the blandness of Hatch's, has led historians to overlook the latter. An example of this is Stephen Starr's three-volume *The Union Cavalry in the Civil War*. So overlooked are the crucial initiatives taken by Hatch at Nashville that one has no idea why he was recommended for promotion (a detail casually inserted in a footnote attached to a summation of Wilson's leadership). Much worse is Stanley F. Horn's *The Decisive Battle of Nashville*, in which Hatch receives almost no mention.[33]

In Hatch's absence, Wilson, planning a new offensive against Selma, Alabama, found himself so short of horses that he decided to mount his other divisions by taking Hatch's horses. Wilson later explained that the taking of the Iowan's horses was intended as a reward so that "his division should be remounted, re-armed and re-equipped in the best possible manner." Unfortunately, the Cavalry Bureau "would not or could not" furnish replacements in time for Hatch to join the campaign. Wilson admitted that "I have always felt that I made a serious mistake" in leaving this "splendid division" behind.[34] Instead of complaining, Hatch voluntarily helped to outfit the raiders by lending them the prized Spencer repeating rifles that had played a major role in his men's successes.

Finishing the war as the commander of all forces in northeastern Mississippi, Hatch had the satisfaction of relaying the surrender terms to

Forrest's command. During the summer of 1865, he relieved the misery of impoverished former rebels by distributing confiscated grain. His own terse summation of his Civil War service was incredibly modest: "Though I cannot show my career to have been a brilliant one, I have never met with disgrace, have never lost a gun or any portion of my command and think my experiences of the past four years have made me of some value."[35]

Peace left Hatch unemployed. In September 1865, with little left of his prewar assets other than his "homestead," he asked General Grant for a recommendation for any position "you think me worthy of." Grant gave him a sterling endorsement: "Hatch has been one of the most active and efficient Cavalry Officers in service. I most heartily recommend him for a Field Officer of Cavalry on the reorganization of the Army."[36]

On 2 August 1866, soon after the passage of the Army Reorganization Act, Hatch and Benjamin Grierson were selected by Grant to command the two new "colored" cavalry regiments. Fortunately, the flamboyant George A. Custer, offered the lieutenant colonelcy of the Ninth, declined in favor of the Seventh. Wesley Merritt, with a record equal to Custer's and a much stabler disposition, then accepted the position.[37]

The personality of the man who commanded the Ninth Cavalry for twenty-three years is illusive. Wilson related an example of Hatch's tendency to indulge in "harmless gasconade." After describing his visit with Sheridan's army in Virginia in early 1865, Hatch exclaimed fervently that he'd "be willing to die" to "just have command of Sheridan's cavalry one day." A staff officer retorted, "Wouldn't you like to live just one day more to brag about it?" Hatch "cheerfully" joined in the laughter and admitted, "Yes, I would." To prevent a negative connotation being given to his anecdote, Wilson added that Hatch "was a cheerful and magnanimous soul who had the love of every officer and man in his command."[38]

The most detailed description of Hatch's garrulity was by M. L. Meriwether, the teen-age son of a Memphis journalist making an excursion through the Indian Territory in 1883. Allowed to share an ambulance with Hatch between Fort Sill and Fort Reno, he described the "splendid looking soldier" as a "fluent talker" who "poured forth a stream of amusing personal reminiscences, stories of war, the Indians, and a thousand hair breadth escapes by land and sea."[39] One can only wish there had been a James Boswell on Hatch's staff.

Relatively little is known about his family life. His wife bore him two children, a daughter named Bessie and a son named Barrington. According to one account, Evelyn Hatch was domineering and prudish. William Paulding, who served under Hatch in the early 1870s, later recalled that Hatch was a "fine old soldier" but that his wife was "a terror" who "wanted to command the post and . . . must have made the general's life a burden." Once, while Paulding was visiting the Hatches, Mrs. Hatch began to complain "about the amount of gambling . . . going on in the post, and that he should stop it." Eventually the "old man [Hatch would have been in his mid-forties] . . . turned to her and said, 'My God, Hattie, I wish you would mind your own business and let me run the post.'" Paulding, a dedicated gossip-monger, added that he had heard that Mrs. Hatch was the inspiration for the domineering and snobbish colonel's wife described in Captain Charles King's popular novel, *The Colonel's Daughter*.[40]

Other than Paulding's remarks, there is little indication that Hatch's marriage was unhappy. In September 1881, Mrs. Hatch took their son Barrington east to enroll in college. While visiting her sister in Washington, D.C., she fell ill and died.[41]

Hatch's daughter, Bessie, a "young girl still attending school" when her mother died, by the mid-1880s had become her father's idol and the center of social life at Fort Robinson, Nebraska. It was most likely she who produced a remarkable mellowing in Hatch. As depicted in the diary of Captain A. W. Corliss, also stationed at Fort Robinson, the fierce disciplinarian had become a relaxed, at-ease-with-the-world soul who enjoyed twelve-day hunting excursions and frequent balls and picnics with his daughter and her friends. On 22 March 1888, for example, Bessie hosted a "grand ball" for a newly wed lieutenant and his bride to which a special train brought a large number of guests from Fort Niobrara. The ladies all stayed at Colonel Hatch's house.[42]

Hatch delighted in driving ladies, almost always in groups, at high speeds around the post grounds. Innocent as this was, it provided grist for gossip. After the wife of Major Frederick Benteen returned from a ride in his buggy, Benteen was told by Captain J. A. Olmsted that "many officers of the 9th Cavalry . . . considered [it] compromising to the character of a woman to be seen driving with General Hatch." Benteen gave little credence to the remark because the Olmsteds were "continually" inviting Hatch to dine with them.[43]

Hatch's tolerance and receptiveness to innovations alarmed more traditional officers. In May 1888, Captain Corliss complained that Hatch had established a "canteen or post beer-house which I predict will be a damned nuisance." More likely, the canteen represented an effort to provide soldiers cheaper and more wholesome entertainment than that found in the grog houses of nearby Crawford. Hatch's relaxed demeanor during field exercises inspired Corliss to complain of widespread drunkenness and poor discipline among the troops: "If Gen. Hatch showed as much interest in guard duty, drill, etc. as he does in the welfare of the sutler's store," he wrote, "there would be a different state of affairs."[44]

Hatch was as dashing in the saddle as while driving a spirited team. In March 1883, Meriwether participated in a moonlight "wildcat" hunt with Hatch and Major Guy Henry near Fort Sill. The youth was thrilled by the "exhilarating . . . mad scamper across the plains that silvery night" as the "blue capes of the officers . . . formed streamers in the rushing wind." The "erect Colonel Henry and dignified General Hatch entered the chase with as keen a zest as the commonest private soldier."[45] Hatch was also a crack shot who took regular turns at the rifle range. In 1885, for example, he was one of only eleven men in the Ninth Cavalry to qualify as a sharpshooter.[46]

Hatch especially enjoyed card games with his fellow officers. This resulted in a charge by his waspish lieutenant colonel, Nathan Dudley, that he used his office for gambling. Hatch admitted that the "room adjoining" his office had been used for "such social purposes" as card parties for years, but he denied there had been frequent gambling. On one occasion he had invited a group of officers, including Dudley, to play whist. At the "earnest solicitations" of Dudley, and over his own objections, the group decided to play poker. Hatch stipulated that it "be made a game purely of amusement, and, as usual in these cases, limited to one dollar with five cents ante. . . . That any officer present actually fancied for a moment he was gambling is absurd."[47]

As a commander, Hatch carried out his assignments efficiently, never questioning a superior's judgment or complaining of a lack of resources. Since he made few demands of his superiors, it was easier to ignore his needs than those of more strident officers. Colonel Grierson, in contrast, was a notorious complainer. He may have been held in less esteem by superiors, but his demands were not ignored. Stationed in Texas, where most of the Indian troubles had subsided, the Tenth Cavalry in 1877 had 927 men; the Ninth, in contrast, although confronted by more responsibilities, had scarcely half as many. Three of its troops had fewer than 30 men each, but recruits continued to go to the Tenth.[48]

By the time Hatch protested in early 1878, the Ninth had only 274 men available for duty and another 34 on detached assignment. Five of its depleted companies were en route to the Ute frontier in Colorado, four were maintaining a truce between Anglos and Hispanics at El Paso, two were watching the Warm Springs Apaches, and one was monitoring the bloodbath in Lincoln County. Complaining that his manpower was "entirely inadequate," Hatch asked General Pope to "represent to the War Department" the need for more recruits.[49] It was only luck that all-out war with the Apaches did not break out until 1879, by which time the Lincoln County and El Paso crises had cooled and the Ninth's strength had greatly increased.

The worst error Hatch made while commanding the Ninth Cavalry occurred in 1879. In September, Victorio initiated the bloodiest Apache uprising in New Mexico's history, and the Utes at the White River Agency in Colorado killed agent Nathan Meeker and decimated a relief detachment under Major Thomas Thornburgh. Instead of concentrating his forces against the Apaches and leaving the Utes for others to combat, Hatch took part of the Ninth into Colorado, leaving Major Albert Morrow to contend with Victorio.

After Ute resistance collapsed, Hatch compounded his error by agreeing to head a commission to negotiate the cession of the Ute lands in northern Colorado and the surrender of Meeker's killers. Allowed to make no concessions to the Utes, who were determined not to allow tribesmen to be tried by a Colorado jury, Hatch and the other commissioners risked their lives daily as the Indians became more desperate. Only when he was finally allowed to assure the Indians that the trials would be by a military commission, perhaps in Washington, did the crisis end.

Speaking of the ordeal, Colonel Mackenzie, also sent into Colorado, observed that Hatch was "a very brave man, . . . in a difficult place, doing the best he can." Mackenzie exclaimed that General Sherman "should have allowed no officer to be placed" in such a position.[50]

Confident that Morrow could handle the Apaches, Hatch refrained from requesting reinforcements or recommending the formation of a volunteer militia force. Although it is doubtful his superiors would have agreed to either measure, since they refused a request for more Indian scouts, his seeming indifference while Morrow's undermanned forces were being bloodied during late 1879 made him the prime target for the resentments of settlers.

In the eyes of his critics, no evil was beyond him. He had deliberately deprived Morrow of sufficient troops to defeat the Apaches, had denied that "serious trouble" existed in New Mexico, had convinced Governor Lew Wallace not to ask permission to call out the militia, and had gone to Colorado to enhance his chances of obtaining a promotion to brigadier general.[51]

Some editors charged that Hatch was deliberately prolonging the war to provide contracts for his cronies in the notorious Santa Fe Ring. Concurring in this charge, one paper all but advocated his assassination: "A terrible retribution is awaiting Hatch. . . . Some scalps other than Indians [the newspaper had been demanding a scalp bounty] may be taken without the offer of reward other than to satisfy deep and burning hate."[52]

Hatch expected his subordinates to provide him the same degree of cooperation he gave superiors. Always gracious and genial with those who were loyal, he could be ruthless with anyone who was not. Like many commanders, he was greatly influenced by his staff. Chief among these were Lieutenants John S. Loud and Louis Rucker. Loud, a New Yorker who served as the regimental adjutant for sixteen years, enjoyed Hatch's trust to the extent that he was left in charge whenever the colonel was absent. In 1879, Lieutenant Colonel Peter Swaine of the Fifteenth Infantry, the second ranking officer in New Mexico, complained that Hatch, while absent in the East, had left the administration of affairs to Loud without even informing Swaine.[53] Rucker, a brother-in-law of General Sheridan, served as regimental quartermaster. Captains hesitated to cross either lieutenant, whose own promotion date would be advanced by each superior's termination.

Following the conclusion of its epic struggle with Victorio's Apaches in 1881, the Ninth traded stations with the Fourth Cavalry. The transfer presented the regiment with a novel task. Instead of guarding settlers from Indians, it now protected Indian lands from intruders.

With his regimental headquarters at Fort Riley, Kansas, Hatch depended upon subordinates to handle the intrusions until December 1884, when

W. C. Couch and several hundred Boomers, entrenched near present-day Stillwater, Oklahoma, and defied all requests to submit.[54] Authorized to meet strength with strength, Hatch assembled some four hundred buffalo soldiers and laid siege. Enfilading the Boomers' positions so that they would be exposed to his troopers' fire, he "rode forward and advised a surrender." His position hopeless, Couch capitulated. Hatch was applauded for the "coolness, good judgment and knowledge of handling men" that allowed him to settle the matter without bloodshed.[55]

The confrontation with the Boomers was Hatch's last campaign. Transferred to the Department of the Platte, he spent his last years at Forts McKinney (Wyoming) and Robinson (Nebraska). Routine administrative duties allowed time for frequent parties and balls presided over by his daughter. The monotony was broken by occasional hunting trips and rumors of his promotion whenever one of the five brigadier generals in the regular army retired or was promoted.

Hatch's seniority, plus his adroit handling of the Ute, Apache, and Boomer crises, ensured that his name would be bandied about for each vacancy. This began in 1882, when he was considered a prime candidate for the star that went to Mackenzie. In 1885 the *Kansas City Times* reported it was "official" that the next brigadier would be Hatch or Colonel John Gibbon of the Seventh Infantry.[56] Needless to say, it was not Hatch. The losses to Mackenzie and Gibbon were the first of many as vacancies were filled by men who had more political support.

It must have been galling when officers such as Joseph Potter and Orlando Willcox, who had seen little or no combat duty since the Civil War, received brigadierships. In 1887, Hatch was leapfrogged by Wesley Merritt, his former lieutenant colonel. By then, Hatch and Grierson were the senior colonels in the army. Because the latter had been bloodied by frequent bouts with General Sheridan, he was seldom mentioned as a prospect. With the promotion of George Crook to the rank of major general impending in early 1888, speculation was once more rife. Colonel H. A. Morrow of the Twenty-first Infantry asserted that Hatch "was almost certain" of the promotion because he was "the senior colonel of the Army," had a "brilliant record," and was "surpassed by none other as a cavalry leader."[57]

It may have been long overdue for the brigadier's star to "descend" upon Hatch's shoulders below "hair silver white with exposure and frontier work," but it was not to be. President Cleveland, undoubtedly reacting to political clout, skipped over him and the other logical contenders to choose Colonel John Brooke of the Third Infantry. The new brigadier was labeled the "officer least thought of" by the shocked military columnist of the *Kansas City Times*, who knew only that Brooke was serving "at some remote post in Montana."[58] Since Brooke had little to commend himself save routine garrison service, and had less than nine years' experience as a colonel, his choice was most disheartening.

On 27 November 1888, Hatch gave his daughter in marriage to Edgar Hubert, an infantry officer stationed at Fort Robinson.[59] Since his son Barrington was employed by the railroad line that ran past the fort, he had the satisfaction of close contact with both children.

As was his habit, he remained on the job at Fort Robinson throughout the frigid winter of 1888–89 in an office whose "chilliness and general dilapidated condition" were styled a "disgrace to the race of administration buildings."[60] When 15 March turned out to be "fine and warm," he hitched four "spirited" horses to his buckboard and, accompanied by three officers' wives, set out for nearby Crawford. About half a mile from the post, a single-tree broke and clipped the heels of a horse, which bolted and spooked the others. Hatch was fighting to keep them under control when a wheel hit a hole, capsizing the drag. The women, thrown clear, escaped with "slight bruises," but Hatch, caught under the buggy and dragged a considerable distance, suffered a broken right thighbone, a sprained left leg, cuts on his head, and a badly bruised body. Help was delayed because no one knew of the accident until the team reached the fort.[61]

After being taken to the post hospital in critical condition, Hatch seemed to be recovering. On 10 April, twenty-six days after the accident, Lieutenant Colonel Brisbin reported that he was "cheerful and happy" and looking forward to sitting in a wheelchair within two weeks. At five o'clock the next morning, he told his nurse he had slept well and requested some breakfast. A short time later, just as the "gun fired for reveille," he clasped his head and called out. Within minutes he was dead as a result of a massive brain clot.[62]

For reasons unexplained, his children neither united him in death with their mother nor had him interred at Arlington. Instead, they chose the national cemetery at Fort Leavenworth, Kansas, a post at which he had never served. Escorting the body to its resting place was a delegation of

The eight sergeants who served as the honor guard when the body of Colonel Edward Hatch was transported from Fort Robinson, Nebraska, to Fort Leavenworth, Kansas, for burial in 1889. They are, *seated, left to right*: Sergeant Zekiel Sykes of B Troop, Sergeant Robert Burley of D Troop, Sergeant Edward McKenzie of I Troop, and Chief Trumpeter Stephen Taylor. Sykes enlisted in E Troop in 1866 and endured both the brutality of Lieutenant E. M. Heyl at San Pedro Springs (chapter 4) and the mistreatment

of Captain Ambrose Hooker at Ojo Caliente (chapter 7). *Back row, left to right:* First Sergeant Nathan Fletcher of F Troop, Sergeant Thomas Shaw of K Troop, First Sergeant David Badie of B Troop, and Sergeant James Wilson of I Troop. In December 1890, Shaw would be awarded a medal of honr for his bravery at Carrizo Canyon in August 1881. Fletcher replaced Emanuel Stance as first sergeant of F Troop after the latter's murder in 1887. Courtesy of Special Collections, U.S. Military Academy Library, West Point.

officers and enlisted men headed by Major Henry. Two members of the escort, Lieutenant Matthias Day and Sergeant Thomas Shaw, were Medal of Honor awardees; all had years of service under their fallen chief. Although an impressive array of officers headed by Generals Merritt and Brooke were listed as the official pallbearers, it was "eight stalwart sergeants" who placed his body upon a caisson drawn by four "jet black steeds" and followed by a riderless horse "equipped with the General's saddle, boots, sword and spurs." At the cemetery the post band played "Nearer My God to Thee" as the body was lowered into the grave; three salvos from artillery aligned along the east side of the cemetery gave a final salute. Stephen Taylor, a twenty-year veteran and chief trumpeter of the Ninth Cavalry, blew "in notes strong and long the soldier's last call, 'taps,' and all was over."[63]

Major Henry penned an eloquent eulogy in which he closed by proclaiming that he could "only recall loving and thoughtful acts" on Hatch's part. "That he was perfect no one claims, but if all can obey the reveille summons of their Maker with as clean a record as a soldier, officer and gentleman as General Edward Hatch, the future ought not to be dreaded."

Hatch's memory faded slowly. At a Fort McKinney reception the following winter, several toasts were drunk "with gusto." The only sad one was simply to "the memory of our late chief, General Hatch, a soldier." It was drunk "in silence and with much feeling."[64] The final tribute from his command occurred on Memorial Day 1890, when a "cold, gray granite" monument was placed over his grave. Three sides were inscribed with a comprehensive list of his Civil War battles. On the fourth was a statement that it had been erected "by the officers and enlisted men of the 9th Cavalry in Token of Their Admiration and Esteem for the one who was Their Friend and Commander for Twenty-Three Years."[65]

There is little doubt that Hatch thought highly of his men and was esteemed by them. For more than two crucial decades he had provided stability and understanding. Perhaps the most convincing testimony to his worth as a commander was provided by the high regard in which he was held by such outstanding officers as James Wilson, George Crook, Guy Henry, and Ranald Mackenzie. In contrast, malcontents such as N. A. M. Dudley and Frederick Benteen disliked him intensely. He may not have been a perfect commander, but the regiment fared much better under him than the aging and biased mediocrities who followed.

PART TWO

Years of Crisis

3

Victory, Slander, and Doubt

The Image of the Ninth Cavalry
1866–81

The buffalo soldiers' first fourteen years were marked by a series of ups and downs. Every success was followed by a defeat; every honor, by charges of unreliability. At times the bond between officers and men seemed near collapse. For every officer who valued his men there was a racist goading them to defiance. Every incident, however trivial, fed prejudices that permeated the military command structure. At times the very survival of the black regiments was in question.

Although several regiment's engagements occurred in late 1867, the first spectacular success occurred nine months later in the Horsehead Hills of the remote Big Bend region. On 8 September 1868, Mexican teamsters at Fort Davis reported that forty miles to the south they had seen about two hundred Lipan Apaches headed eastward. Ireland-born Lieutenant Patrick Cusack, an enlisted man until he was commissioned during the Civil War, set out with sixty troopers to follow their trail. Marching at night to avoid detection, he tracked them southeastward. Shortly after sunrise on 12 September his troopers struck the Apache camp.

Although the Lipans fought desperately, superior firepower routed them. After a five-mile pursuit, the buffalo soldiers turned back to collect their spoils. They had killed twenty-five Apaches, most of them left on the battlefield; liberated two Mexican boys; and recaptured hundreds of mules, horses, and cattle. Although Cusack declared that all of his men were entitled to citations for gallantry, he especially lauded three privates from C Troop, Ross Alsie, John Harrison and Lewis White, each of whom had been released from confinement to accompany the scout. Recommending that all charges be dropped against them, he virtually nominated White for a Medal of Honor. During the initial charge, White received a severe arrow wound in his side and had his horse shot from under him. Though told to fall back, he remained in the foremost of the fight.[1]

Cusack gave his men free rein in collecting souvenirs, including scalps. He rewarded the Mexican guides with some of the horses, burned the camp and its equipage, and led his jubilant men back to Fort Davis. An observer noted that some were "rigged out" in "full Indian costume," with the "most fantastic head-dresses" and their "faces painted in a comical style." There was nothing comical, however, with the scalps suspended from "long poles," along with numerous robes, shields, and arrows, which were peddled to those who had remained at the fort. A correspondent of the *San Antonio Herald* gave them a rare compliment: "All honor to . . . the brave soldiers who so thoroughly did their duty."[2]

Cusack's victory was the first of several successes during the next eighteen months. In 1869, Colonel Mackenzie, with authority over the six troops of the Ninth stationed in the Sub-District of the Pecos, launched four successive expeditions that struck Apache and Comanche camps from the mouth of the Pecos to the headwaters of the Brazos. In October, for example, he combined detachments from each of the forts under his command—Concho, McKavett, Clark, and Duncan—to create a 150-man strike force under Captain John M. Bacon, a youthful Kentuckian commanding G Troop. Mackenzie augmented the buffalo soldiers with twenty-six Fourth Cavalry troopers from Fort Griffin and twenty-six Tonkawa Indian scouts. On 28 October the multiracial force routed five hundred hostiles on the upper Brazos, killing fifty and administering the "most important blow to the Indians since [Earl] Van Dorn whipped them nine years ago."[3]

All accounts of the battles of 1869 stressed that the buffalo soldiers fought with great valor. Captain Henry Carroll, who led ninety-eight troopers in a successful encounter with the Comanches on 16 September, lauded his men, most of whom "had never seen an Indian before," for bravery and "excellent behavior."[4] Unfortunately, he did not cite a single soldier by name.

Carroll's engagement, for example, began about 6:30 A.M. when eleven Indians charged his supply train in an effort to stampede the horses. The

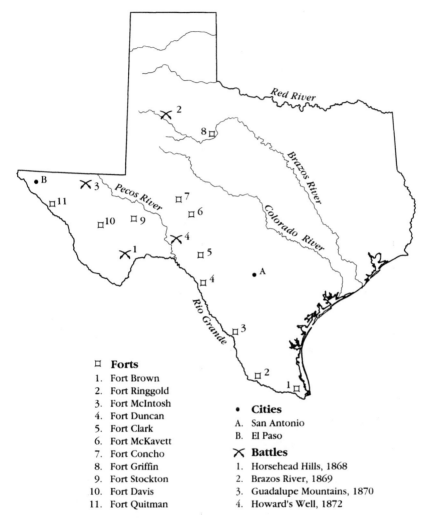

□ **Forts**
1. Fort Brown
2. Fort Ringgold
3. Fort McIntosh
4. Fort Duncan
5. Fort Clark
6. Fort McKavett
7. Fort Concho
8. Fort Griffin
9. Fort Stockton
10. Fort Davis
11. Fort Quitman

• **Cities**
A. San Antonio
B. El Paso

✕ **Battles**
1. Horsehead Hills, 1868
2. Brazos River, 1869
3. Guadalupe Mountains, 1870
4. Howard's Well, 1872

Ninth Cavalry in Texas, 1867–75

attempt failed because Lieutenant George Albee and two troopers, the only men with the train whose mounts were saddled, met and in a sharp skirmish repulsed the attackers. Although Albee was later awarded a Medal of Honor, the names of the two men who fought by his side were unrecorded.[5]

In the Trans-Pecos in April 1870, Colonel Hatch combined detachments from Forts Stockton, Davis, and Quitman under the command of Major Albert Morrow. For fifty-three days the buffalo soldiers, often

marching afoot to rest their horses, scoured the canyons of the Guadalupe Mountains in southern New Mexico, locating several Mescalero
camps. Although the Indians escaped, the troopers destroyed "immense
amounts" of food, robes, and other booty and captured forty horses and
mules.

Morrow lavished praise on the troopers, who had marched until their
boots had to be replaced with makeshift moccasins. Throughout the
campaign they remained "cheerful" despite enduring "short rations" and
extended periods with little water. He concluded that black troops were
"peculiarly adapted" to Indian campaigning because of their bravery and
endurance.[6]

The buffalo soldiers' successes evoked appreciation from the readers
of the anti-Reconstruction *San Antonio Herald.* A letter from Menardsville,
a few miles east of Fort McKavett, enthused that "for bravery in battle, for
endurance of fatigue and hardship, for *elan* in a charge, [and] for obedience and discipline," the "colored soldiers . . . compare favorably with
any soldiers in the world." Although the letter writer had been "raised in
the South" and had "imbibed most of the local prejudices towards the
Negro race, I deem it just to say that no officer who was ever in battle
with them can say that they ever showed the least tendency to
cowardice."[7]

After 1870 the troopers, dispersed in small garrisons and confined to
escort and patrol duty, had no chance to repeat these successes. Inevitably, the Texas press resumed its taunting. When a battalion of recruits
passed through San Antonio, the *Herald* jeered that they were "as common looking niggers as we have seen" and predicted that frontiersmen
would not "receive much protection from their sort." It regularly spiced
its pages with such jibes as, "The Indians are terribly disgusted with the
Negro troops on the frontier—they are difficult to scalp."[8]

All memory of the earlier successes was obliterated by the tragedy of
Howard's Well. In April 1872, Lieutenant Colonel Merritt, with Troops A
and H, the regimental band, and a wagon train carrying the dependents
and "paraphanalia [sic] of a moving garrison," was en route from Fort
Stockton to Fort Clark. Not anticipating an engagement, he had lightened
the horses' load by restricting the troopers to half the normal amount of
ammunition. In addition, so few old soldiers had reenlisted that most of
the men were raw recruits.

The caravan crossed the Pecos at Fort Lancaster on 20 April and headed eastward. As it neared Howard's Well, the next watering station, smoke was seen curling into the sky. Soon the troopers reached the remains of a Mexican wagon train, whose eight teamsters had been scalped, tied to wagon wheels, doused with kerosene, and set afire. Miraculously, two were still alive.

Captain Michael Cooney, commanding A Troop, and Lieutenant Fred Vincent, in charge of H, immediately started in pursuit down the deepening course of Howard's Creek. Suddenly, Indians opened fire from the heights above, dropping nine horses in their tracks. Cooney's mount stumbled, throwing Cooney from the saddle with a foot caught in a stirrup. When the horse righted itself and started dragging the officer towards the Indians, Privates William Nelson and Isaac Harrison risked their lives to free the badly shaken officer. His mishap had caused such a commotion that the fighting was over before the men could regroup.

Lieutenant Vincent, meanwhile, had ordered his troop to attack the Indians on foot. As they pushed up the steep slope, he was shot through the thigh, and an artery was severed. Despite the loss of blood, he spurred his men on until he finally collapsed. Surgeon Peter Cleary tended him, but he became the first officer of the Ninth Cavalry to die on the battlefield. With both officers hors de combat and themselves almost out of ammunition, the troopers had no recourse but to rejoin Merritt and the train at Howard's Well. The raiders, a band of Kiowas, exuberantly returned to their reservation north of the Red River to boast of their victory.[9]

Although the buffalo soldiers had done as well as possible under the circumstances, rumors immediately spread that they had betrayed their officers. The *San Antonio Herald,* increasingly hostile to their presence in Texas, was the most vituperative. Relying solely upon innuendos, it claimed the Kiowas had been joined in their attack by eight black deserters and that the soldiers, although outnumbering the raiders, had "behaved badly." According to one scurrilous libel in circulation four years later, the officers had to draw their pistols and shoot some of their men to force the remainder "to make a stand."[10]

Although it is unlikely that the Ninth's officers doubted their men's courage, many harbored fears concerning the men's licentiousness. Simply speaking, they feared the men might assault white women.[11] As a result, any offense committed in the presence of a woman was punished severely. In August 1869, for example, Corporal Reese Winn, after a long march across the arid plains west of Fort Concho, took undue exception to an order to stand guard. Exclaiming, "I won't do guard duty when I have mules to take care of," he muttered that there had "been some God damned officers killed by our men and there can be more killed" within the officer's earshot. Worse, an officer's wife being escorted to Fort Stockton was also present. A court-martial presided over by Colonel Mackenzie sentenced Winn to be shot. Fortunately, the judge advocate general mitigated the sentence to five years' imprisonment at hard labor.[12]

At Fort Davis, Texas, in November 1872 the latent sexual fears erupted with virtually no warning. Martin Pedee, a member of the Twenty-fifth Infantry, was accused of attempting to rape Annie Williams, the white wife of a member of his regiment.[13] Pedee was in his second enlistment and had an excellent record. The evidence [against] him was far from conclusive, being only Annie's statement that she had identified him in the dark by "feeling of his head." Annie had emitted a single cry of "murder!" well after the intruder had left. Although no other evidence indicated that he had been anywhere that night save asleep in his quarters, the court-martial, consisting of Fort Davis officers, sentenced him to be discharged and confined at hard labor for seven years. After reviewing the case, the judge advocate's office observed that there was not sufficient evidence either to prove there had been "an attempt at rape" or to establish the identity of the intruder. Pedee's discharge was disallowed, and he was required to spend only twelve months at hard labor.[14]

Before the Pedee case had been resolved, a more serious transgression traumatized the officers at Fort Davis. In the predawn hours of 21 November, the wife of Lieutenant Fred Kendall, who was absent on detached duty, awoke to see a man forcing his way through her window. She screamed, but he continued his efforts. Mrs. Kendall picked up a pistol kept beside her bed and fired at point-blank range, shattering the intruder's skull.

The dead man was identified as Corporal Daniel Talliaferro of the Ninth Cavalry. Although there were other possible explanations for the entry,[15] the officers at Fort Davis had no doubt that it was an intended rape. In reporting the incident, Colonel George Andrews of the Twenty-fifth Infantry was almost hysterical. In the seventeen months since he had "commenced service with Colored Troops," similar attempts had been made "upon the officers quarters at Forts Duncan, Stockton, and Davis, and I think McKavett and Concho. While stationed at Fort Clark, five such attempts were reported to me."[16]

Andrews stated that fears of rape were so inflamed that officers were afraid to leave their families after dark and that to order one to perform any duty away from the post was an act of "positive cruelty." Since post and departmental records do not substantiate any of his assertions, they obviously reflected racial fears more than actual facts. In response, General C. C. Augur expressed regret that such a "state of affairs exists" and his pleasure that "retribution was vested" upon Talliaferro."[17]

To the Texas press, the incident at Fort Davis was a godsend. The *Galveston Daily News* declared it proved that the black soldiers' "brutal instincts" would lead "to the commission of every description of outrage" and applauded the "lady at Fort Davis who sent the black scoundrel to his last account."[18]

Although Corporal Taliaferro's ill-fated foray marked the nadir of officer–enlisted man relations among the buffalo soldiers, fears subsided slowly. The excessively harsh reaction to the "near-mutiny" at Fort Stockton the following summer (see pp. 85–91) was undoubtedly a result of the lingering fears.

Nothing that the black troops did helped their image. They escorted thousands of cattle across the plains, captured rustlers too powerful for local authorities,[19] and patrolled the Rio Grande border incessantly. Instead of receiving credit, they were harassed by the very people they were protecting.

Small detachments and camps were especially vulnerable. One night in December 1873, for example, a detachment camped near Fort Concho was peppered by gunshots. It was assumed to be an Indian attack, but Merritt, after investigating the matter, concluded that it was the work of Texas cowboys. He explained that during one of his earlier visits a "lot of drunken Texans about twelve at night rode along the valley below the camp at full speed, yelling and firing their arms. It is a way they have, when under the influence of liquor, of amusing themselves."[20]

One of the few positive evaluations of the buffalo soldiers was made by an "exceptionally qualified" observer in a letter to the *Nation* in late 1873. After observing both black and white troops in the Southwest, the correspondent stated that the "colored troops (called by the Comanches the 'buffalo soldiers,' because, like the buffalo, they are woolly)" were "in excellent drill and condition." The Indians at first held them in "utter contempt," but after "a taste of their fighting capabilities, they began to respect them." Describing the buffalo soldiers as "active, intelligent, and resolute men," he concluded that they were superior to the average white soldier.[21] He explained that this was because "the best colored young men" could be recruited, while "only indifferent or inferior whites" would enlist.

When these remarks were reprinted in the *Army and Navy Journal,* there was a barrage of protests. Taken aback, the editors recanted for having, "unfortunately for us," printed the comparisons. Although it received numerous white protests, they decided they had "better use for our space than to print them."

During the Red River War in 1874–75, units of the Ninth did their full share of the fighting. In October 1874, four troops led by Major Morrow spearheaded the expedition commanded by Lieutenant Colonel George P. Buell. The troopers captured two hostile camps, destroyed more than six hundred lodges, and pursued their occupants all the way to the Canadian River. Although unequipped for cold weather, they campaigned in the teeth of fierce blizzards until January. Their only reward was a compliment for "manly endurance without complaint."[22] All attention was focused on the expeditions of Colonels Nelson Miles and Ranald Mackenzie. Except for William Leckie, recent historians of the Red River War continue to overlook them.[23]

While part of the Ninth pursued Comanches across the Llano Estacado, the remainder continued the risky patrols along the Rio Grande. In early 1875, a five-man detachment from Troop G, led by Sergeant Edward Troutman, was fired upon as it approached a ranch about sixteen miles from Fort Ringgold. As the troopers withdrew toward the fort, they were again ambushed. Privates Moses Turner and Jeremiah Owsley were killed in the opening salvo, but the survivors returned the fire, killing one and wounding two assailants before resuming their retreat. Upon reaching Ringgold, they reported to Colonel Hatch, who had recently moved his headquarters to the post.

The following morning, Hatch led sixty troopers to the ambush site. Finding the troopers' bodies "horribly mutilated," he proceeded to the ranch where the trouble had originated, searched it, and arrested "every suspicious character" he could find. Even as he incarcerated them, he gloomily foresaw that "not a jury in the state will convict them."[24]

Feigning indignation that Hatch had cast aspersions upon the integrity of Texas juries, the *San Antonio Herald* branded him a "political trickster . . . reeking from the stench of Radicalism." His statement demonstrated that he was "an incendiary" capable of "inciting his negro soldiery to do what they are now doing, robbing and murdering."[25]

Hatch's prediction proved accurate. Although nine suspects were indicted, only one was tried, and he was promptly acquitted. Adding injury to insult, the three troopers who had survived the ambush, called as witnesses for the trial, were then arrested and charged with murder—for having killed an attacker in defending themselves. Hatch and Lieutenant J. H. French were indicted for burglary; they had broken into an outbuilding to recover the blood-stained uniforms of the slain soldiers. Although after considerable expense all were ultimately released, the animosity had made the Ninth's situation untenable.[26]

Never had the black regiments been so beset. Some of their officers, resentful at having been "exiled for eleven years . . . at the most disagreeable and unhealthy posts" in the nation, were seeking ways to avoid their "perpetual banishment from the advantages of civilization." Unable to secure more attractive posts for their troops, they had become "the persons principally engaged" in seeking to discontinue segregated units.[27]

The officers stressed that their actions were not because of the quality of black soldiers, who made "as good soldiers as white men, and are more easily disciplined than the human driftwood that finds a haven in the Army." They had "no objection to commanding negro [sic] companies if they can be assigned to duty as the officers of other regiments are."[28]

Unlike the officers serving with them, many officers still branded black soldiers as inferior. Foremost was Brigadier General E. O. C. Ord, who assumed command of the Department of Texas in early 1875. Reared on a Maryland plantation and quick to demean African Americans, he was incensed that all four of the black regiments were stationed in his department. Within weeks of assuming command, he proposed that white troops replace them because the "colored" troops could not be trusted on scouts without officers, "who are not always available." In asserting this, he was ignoring the fact that dozens, if not hundreds, of scouts had been capably led by black noncommissioned officers. In his anxiety to purge blacks from the ranks, Ord even proposed that Mexicans "be considered as Negroes" and used in African American regiments.[29]

In early 1876, Ord told a reporter for the *New York Herald* that black soldiers were untrustworthy and could not be controlled by their officers. Providing not a shred of evidence for this charge, he next appeared before a congressional committee dominated by Southern Democrats. According to a reporter for the *New York Times*, the committee, although hesitant "to take the responsibility of reporting for their abolition," believed that black troops "are worthless and unreliable; that on the Mexican border, where they are stationed, they fraternize with Mexicans and assist in their depredations, and that they cannot be used to fight the Indians." They were searching for "some plan by which . . . [black troops] can be gradually obliterated from the service."[30]

As the committee's star witness, Ord spewed forth a series of false-hoods and exaggerations. He argued that black recruits represented "only the lowest class of colored men," such as "'drifters' and fugitives from the law . . . driven to enlist by the police authorities in order to get rid of them." With "no idea . . . of the management of things for themselves" and with "confused ideas of property," such misfits would require twice as many white officers per company to be molded into efficient soldiers. Supplying not one iota of evidence to support his concoctions, he recommended that all recruits be dispersed throughout the service.[31]

Although Ord's attacks were echoed by several other officers, all were from white regiments. Colonel H. B. Clitz, the nondescript commander of the Tenth Infantry, was uniquely inventive. Black units were so ineffi-cient that they cost at least one-third more than white ones; black caval-rymen broke down their horses at an appalling rate, used up or lost more equipment, and wore out their clothing more rapidly than whites. They were incapable of serving as clerks or mechanics, requiring the hiring of civilians for tasks handled by enlisted men in white companies. Again, not one example was provided.[32]

Clitz's criticisms were echoed by Major Thomas Anderson, also of the Tenth Infantry. Anderson endorsed all of Clitz's assertions and added that whites, unlike blacks, "can build . . . their own posts." Since black soldiers had built or repaired virtually every post in Texas, this was brazen indeed. Lest anyone doubt his racism, he baldly declared that blacks lacked "habits of thrift, economy, or . . . responsibility, and they are, with few exceptions, thieves and liars."[33]

Racism also characterized the testimony of Lieutenant Colonel John S. Mason, Ord's inspector general. Mason admitted that the black soldiers had never displayed any lack of courage and that he had heard nothing but praise from their officers. Despite this, he thought, based upon "conversations with others," that they were "of little or no use on the frontier." In support, he offered an ingenious bit of racist logic: "The class of Mexicans along that frontier are generally of the lowest order, part Indians, and they fraternize with the negro [*sic*] more readily than with the white people; and the consequence is that there is great demoralization among the black troops, and it has extended to the officers."[34]

The blatant distortions evoked few rebuttals. Major Henry C. Corbin of the Twenty-fourth Infantry appeared before the committee and defended the reliability of black soldiers. The *San Antonio Herald*, hoping to create a rift, asserted that Corbin insinuated that "Gen. Ord did not know what he was talking about. The colored troops were not only 'perfectly orderly,' but 'really better behaved than the white soldiers'; which makes a very plain and pretty issue between Ord and Corbin."[35]

The *Army and Navy Journal* received at least two letters upholding the black troops. One, a twenty-year veteran signing himself simply "White Soldier," stated that he had "seen them in Indian campaigns in Kansas standing all night at their horses' heads during a heavy storm, . . . seen them in the hot months of July and August marching thirty miles a day on the 'Staked Plains' without a murmur, [and] . . . put up with ill-treatment and injustice without complaint." Based on this, he labeled "all the tales . . . told against them to be false." Anyone who had served with them, he continued, could attest that "they are sober, obedient and trustworthy, and will fight as long as their officers will stand."[36]

A second writer, signing himself "Nine Years," simply stated that he had always found black soldiers to be "willing and faithful, evincing a pride of being soldiers." He had never heard "of an instance of their being uncontrollable or unreliable" and that the records would "show that they have been good soldiers."[37]

These tributes led to a spate of vituperative retorts. To its regret, the *Army and Navy Journal* printed a letter from Fort Richardson, Texas, signed "11th Infantry," whose mixture of half-truths and fabrications were the most slanderous denigration of black soldiers that ever appeared in its pages. Alluding to the San Pedro Springs mutiny of 1867 (see pp. 000–000), the writer charged that there had been similar uprisings at Fort Stockton, including one in 1869, "when the officers sent their families out of the post for safety, again in '74 and many more instances that I could mention." With these fabrications out of the way, he charged them with cowardice, spewing out a torrent of distortions.

Many of the alleged incidents were so vague that it is impossible to know to what, if anything, they referred. At Eagle Springs, Texas, a "brave officer was killed by their cowardice when their strength was 3 to 1 Indian" (perhaps referring to the death of Lieutenant Vincent at Howard's Well), and at Johnston Station they "hid in the bush until the Indians ran off 32 of their best horses."

Other allegations were obvious lies. At the Wichita Agency in 1874, it was claimed, "four full companies turned their backs on a few miserably armed Indians, until two companies of the 11th came up from Sill." No other description, official or otherwise, of the fight at the Wichita Agency supports this assertion.

Indicating sexual origins for his tirade, "11th Infantry" speculated that the men who called "the colored troops good" were likely living "with a *dusky companion* smarter than you are, and expressing her opinions. You are like a good many renegades, . . . *no matter what the color as long as it is a woman.*"[38]

Although soldiers from each of the black units answered the slurs, the *Army and Navy Journal* refused to print their replies. Instead, it published an ill-chosen letter signed, "An officer of colored troops for thirteen years." Although stating that the black troops needed no defense against the "manifest injustice of 11th Infantry's" attack, the officer agreed that General Ord's remarks referring to black troops were just and explained "why we get . . . only the lowest class of colored men."[39]

Black soldiers knew that the termination of separate regiments would eliminate them from military service. In December 1876, E. K. Davies, a black veteran residing at Brownsville, Texas, complained of this to Congressman Benjamin Butler. Butler assumed the letter was from E. J. Davis,[40] a former Reconstruction governor of Texas, and forwarded it as such to Secretary of War J. D. Cameron. Davies charged that most recruiting officers were so prejudiced that they required "all kinds of credentials," including the ability to read and write, of blacks that were not required of whites. Then they "raise the cry that the colored regiments can't get recruits." Other "haters of the Negro" compiled "bogus returns" showing that black regiments were more costly. As soon as the separate regiments were eliminated, Davies predicted, "they will refuse to enlist any more colored men, and . . . they would soon be a thing of the past" except for a few assigned duties as "cooks, officers' servants, and teamsters."[41]

Calling Davies's remarks "a lible [sic] on the army," Cameron asserted that blacks made poor soldiers because they "are a quiet, kindly, peaceful race of men. Naturally not addicted to war; better suited to the arts of peace." The attempt to convert them into soldiers had been "partially successful," but the army would save money if it relied solely on white regiments.[42]

Cameron was simply echoing the sentiments of General Sherman. Sherman had admitted in 1874 that the black soldiers "stood up to their work as well as white troops would, and I am pleased to hear testimony to their courage and their fidelity." The Ninth Cavalry, he noted, had "fulfilled the best expectations entertained by the friends of the negro [sic] people." They made "first-rate sentinels," were "faithful to their tasks," and were "as brave as the occasion calls for." Although they had done "everything expected of them," he still "preferred" white troops. By 1877 he had decided that blacks were too "docile" to make good soldiers. Indicating that they lacked the "muscle, endurance, will, and courage . . . to combat the enemies of civilization," he argued that black soldiers should be used only in malaria-ridden areas too dangerous for whites.[43]

In October 1877, Senator Ambrose Burnside introduced a bill opening all regiments to white recruits. It passed the House of Representatives and then went before the Senate. Fortunately, Texas senator Samuel B. Maxey, a former Confederate general, boasted too soon that its passage would "convert" the black regiments into "good white" ones. As a result, Republican senators mustered just enough Reconstruction fervor to kill the bill.[44]

The officers and men of the Ninth Cavalry, transferred to New Mexico in 1875, were only marginally involved in the debate concerning black regiments. The Ninth was, however, dangerously depleted by a directive that recruiters were to take only a "superior class of men." Nationwide in 1876, fewer than 20 percent of applicants were accepted. Although the percentage for blacks was not specified, it was much lower. In the cavalry, for example, 93 percent of the new recruits were white.[45] With new enlistments curtailed and the second wave of five-year terms expiring, the Ninth rapidly contracted. By mid-1877 it had only 276 men "present for duty."[46]

Although Colonel Hatch never questioned his troops' valor, he shared the belief that they were uniquely adapted to subtropical service. He argued, therefore, that all units—infantry, cavalry, and artillery—stationed in torrid or swampy regions should be composed of blacks. "Prejudice to color" should have nothing to do with assigning them. Since "the colored recruits make a superior artillerist and excellent garrison soldier," they should be enlisted for all service in the deep South.[47]

Stationed in New Mexico until 1881, the Ninth carried out one demanding assignment after another. But no success had any impact in refurbishing the tarnished image of black troopers. Reporters for eastern papers accompanied many expeditions of white troops;[48] not one went near a camp of the Ninth. By the time Hatch's terse reports reached the press, they had lost all relevance. As long as the black troops campaigned in isolation in the remote New Mexican mountains, their engagements, no matter how hotly contested, were instinctively downgraded. The real wars were fought on the plains against the Sioux, Cheyenne, and Nez Percé. Only if their valor was displayed in direct comparison to that of white troops could they gain credibility.

The opportunity came with dramatic suddenness in October 1879. Ever since arriving in New Mexico, the Ninth had monitored relations between the Utes and settlers in Colorado. Although the troopers carried out their duties so fairly that neither side was displeased, it was a never-ending chore. In 1879, Troop D under Captain Francis Dodge had the assignment.

All summer long, the White River Utes of northwestern Colorado had been harassed by both settlers and their narrow-minded agent, Nathan Meeker. Seeking to force the Utes to plow up the pastures on which their ponies grazed, he evoked such resistance that he called upon the military for protection. Although the nearest troops were Dodge's command, investigating spurious complaints that the Utes were setting fires on Colorado ranches, the military dispatched Major Thomas Thornburgh of the Fifth Cavalry from Wyoming. Thornburgh, who in four years had

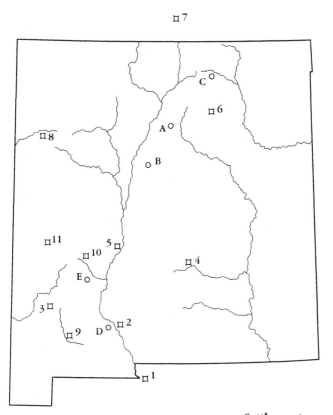

Forts		Settlements
1. Fort Bliss	6. Fort Union	A. Santa Fe
2. Fort Selden	7. Fort Garland	B. Albuquerque
3. Fort Bayard	8. Fort Wingate	C. Cimarron
4. Fort Stanton	9. Fort Cummings	D. Las Cruces
5. Fort Craig	10. Ojo Calinente	E. Cañada Alamosa
	11. Fort Tularosa	

Ninth Cavalry in New Mexico, 1975–81

been promoted from lieutenant to major as a result of political machinations, had neither tact nor caution.[49] On 29 September, after he failed to honor a promise to halt his advance, the Utes confronted him in the valley of the Milk River, some fifteen miles east of the agency. A shot rang out, both sides opened fire, and within minutes the troopers had fallen back to their train as bullets poured down from nearby heights. Thornburgh and ten of his men lay dead; another twenty-three were wounded, including the new commander, Captain J. Scott Payne. Payne ordered his demoralized men to dig rifle pits and dispatched couriers for help. As soon as the Indians at the agency heard of the battle, they slaughtered Meeker and nine of his employees. It would be a week before a relief expedition under Colonel Merritt could reach Payne's beleaguered command—if he held out that long. Luckily, help was closer at hand.[50]

Dodge, some seventy miles away, learned of the disaster from a freighter at midafternoon on 1 October. Although Dodge's force numbered only thirty-five, he immediately ordered a march towards the agency, but he stopped to set up camp a few hours later. Waiting until dark to foil possible Ute spies, he issued 125 rounds of ammunition and three days' rations to each soldier and set out, leaving his supply train behind. Although following a hunting trail instead of the wagon road to reduce the chances of an ambush, Dodge's command made amazingly swift time. By 4:30 the next morning they had reached the besieged troopers. Not a man was harmed as they rode down the valley, at every step exposed to the Ute rifles, and paused in front of Payne's entrenchments. Holding seniority over Payne, Dodge assumed command of the united force. After considering an assault on the Ute positions, he discarded the idea because of the steepness of the bluffs on which they were posted. Blacks and whites then dug in together to await reinforcements.[51]

For the white troopers, the buffalo soldiers' arrival was a godsend. The bizarre mixture of prejudice and admiration in their remarks portray both admiration and racism:

> We were getting pretty d____d tired. . . . It was the third morning after we were corralled, and . . . we didn't know whether any of our messengers . . . had struck help or not . . . when Captain Dodge came up at a canter, leading the rest of his men. . . . We forgot all about the danger of exposing ourselves and leaped up out of the pits to shake hands all around. Why, . . . we took those darkies in right along with us in the pits. We let 'em sleep with us, and they took their knives and cut off slips of bacon from the same sides as we did.[52]

Another cavalryman recalled that one afternoon a "*moke* got terribly thirsty; . . . and says he, 'Well, boss, I be powerfully dry, and somebody's got to git water fo' me, or Ise got to git water fo' somebody,' so what does that *moke* do but take two pails in broad daylight, and go down and bring 'em back both full of water, and the Injuns never lifted a hair on him."[53]

The grit displayed by the buffalo soldiers won over the most diehard racist. John Gordon, their guide during the march to Payne's camp, was dumbfounded: "I was a captain in the rebel army and very much prejudiced against 'nigger' soldiers but if the Lord will forgive me for what I have said about them, I will never repeat it after what they did today."[54]

A statement by Captain Joseph Lawson of the Fifth Cavalry, ostensibly intended as a compliment, exceeded any remark from the ranks in offensiveness: "The boys of the Fifth Cavalry have forgotten about the smell of niggers. . . . The men of the Ninth Cavalry are the whitest black men I ever saw."[55]

In his official report, Dodge failed to cite any of his men by name. Collectively, however, he was generous. By enduring a "forced march of seventy miles," the loss of sleep, lack of food, and "other deprivations attendant upon their situation" without a murmur, they had proven themselves to be "good soldiers and reliable men."[56]

Although no buffalo soldier was cited for gallantry at the time, Sergeant Henry Johnson eleven years afterwards applied for and received a Medal of Honor. He has been credited with leaving his rifle pit after dark to carry instructions to the troopers and with having "shot his way to the river," also after dark, to procure water.[57] In his application, he stated he was on "guard outside the main entrenchment on the night of October 3rd and on the skirmish line to the creek for water for the wounded." Lieutenant Martin Hughes recalled only that Johnson had gone after water and had helped remove dead and decaying horses from the rifle pits. He added that a noncommissioned officer whose name he had forgotten had led a charge that dislodged some Indians from a position "in dangerous proximity" to the besieged troopers. Captain Charles Parker, Johnson's troop commander at the time of his application, stated that he said he was "one of" the noncommissioned officers Hughes referred to.[58]

Since contemporary accounts indicate that the Indians did relatively little firing after dark and that many soldiers went for water each night, there must have been considerable activity in the entrenchments. Indeed, piling dirt on the bodies of the slain horses aligned in front of the rifle pits to protect against Ute snipers and reduce the stench kept many troopers busy during the nocturnal hours. As there is no reason to doubt the word of Hughes in supporting Johnson's application, he most likely deserved it. But it may not have been because he "shot his way to the river" for water.

After the arrival of Merritt's column ended the siege, it became obvious that Dodge's troopers were needed more in New Mexico than in Colorado. Since the Santa Fe Railway had recently been extended into northern New Mexico, the quickest return route was to march to the Union Pacific station at Rawlins, Wyoming, and travel by rail. For the buffalo troopers, it turned out to be a trip of triumph.

Upon reaching Fort Fred Steele at Rawlins on 19 October, they received a greeting such as never before accorded a black unit. On horses loaned them to replace the ones slain by the Utes, they rode into the post between two lines of soldiers awaiting "the Brunettes." Dodge, "his face worn with fatigue," dismounted and crisply saluted post commander Albert Brackett. Halting beside him were his troopers, whose "honest, beaming darky visages" seemed to belie the "dashing bravery which signalized the rescue on Milk River." Colonel Brackett lifted his hat and started a round of applause from all present that "caused the whites of some forty . . . eyes to gleam like the risen moon." Erect in their saddles, the buffalo soldiers brought their hands to their temples in salute and then "nearly every one of them bowed with real grace in acknowl-edgment of the greeting."[59]

A more rousing reception awaited them two days later at Denver. When word of their pending arrival reached the city, Governor Frederick Pitkin and Denver's "colored citizens" joined forces to give them a "grand recep-tion." They secured the YMCA hall, had "plenty of eatables" brought in, and engaged Denver's "only colored band" to await them at the depot. When the men stepped from the train, the "air was rent with cheers and everything assumed the aspect of a grand jollification." Soon the troopers were marching in a procession headed by the band "playing national airs."

At the YMCA hall a large crowd, including most of Denver's black community, was waiting. After the band stopped playing, Sergeant Johnson mounted the platform to a chorus of "tremendous cheers" and told how his comrades had "made the most wonderful march upon record, making forty-five miles in seven hours, to relieve Payne's command" and how "all their horses were shot . . . but not a man scared."

Speaking next, Sergeant John Olney recounted their exploits "in a very enthusiastic manner." Soon all the men were besieged with well-wishers seeking to hear of their heroics. In the words of a local reporter, "a number of wild assertions, concerning what the command had done, were made, which, owing to the excitement and enthusiasm, can not be credited as strictly true, and hence can not be given publicity." After the speeches ended, the soldiers were provided with "an elegant repast."[60] It would be years before buffalo soldiers again received such a reception.

Compared to Morrow's desperate battles with Victorio's Apaches, the actions of Dodge's command at Milk River were almost trivial. Without incurring a single casualty, perhaps without killing an Indian, they had buoyed up the spirits of a demoralized white command and, above all, had their deeds recorded and even exaggerated by the nation's press. It is ironic that saving white troops was the only way they could establish credibility.

The acclaim accorded Dodge's command, combined with a belated recognition of the Ninth's epic struggle with Victorio, did much to establish the right of the black regiments to exist. It would soon become an impossibility for the most ardent racist to make headway toward abolishing their right to remain an integral part of the army.

4

E. M. Heyl, the Genteel Racist of San Pedro Springs

Under leaden winter skies on 6 January 1895 a train rolled into Union Station in Washington, D.C. On it rode the body of fifty-year-old E. M. Heyl, assistant inspector general of the U.S. Army; his widow; and two minor children. Waiting to escort the body to its final resting place were four troops of cavalry, Secretary of War Daniel Lamont, Major General Nelson Miles, Adjutant General J. C. Breckinridge, and many other officers. The cortege wound its way down the mall and was ferried across the Potomac to Arlington National Cemetery. It proceeded up the slope, passed the Custis-Lee mansion, continued on another hundred yards, and halted.

General Breckinridge solemnly recited the highlights of the departed officer's career. Heyl had rallied a broken regiment at Antietam, had led a charge at Willis Church, and had killed a Comanche warrior in hand-to-hand combat, among many other feats. More important, he had been a "kindly gentleman" with a "fine sense of honor."[1] Only his premature death had prevented him from ascending to the command of the inspector general's department.

Omitted from the eulogy were two controversial actions that had stained Heyl's early career. Lieutenant Robert G. Carter, for example, never forgot that at Blanco Canyon, Texas, in October 1871, Heyl without warning had taken flight with a dozen troopers, leaving Carter and two enlisted men to face a host of onrushing Comanches. Carter was awarded a Medal of Honor for his desperate stand, but he also incurred a leg wound that forced him into a premature retirement.[2]

Despite Carter's belief that Heyl's action was cowardly, Colonel Mackenzie chose to ignore the matter in his report on the engagement. In addition, Heyl remained popular with most of his fellow officers. James Parker, a West Pointer assigned to Heyl's troop, described him as a "fine looking man" who believed in "having everything in the best condition" and was "always ahead of the other officers in looking out for the interests of his company."[3]

This may have been true where white troops were concerned, but the buffalo soldiers of the Ninth remembered Heyl as an alcoholic racist guilty of the most sadistic actions in the regiment's history. Unlike Parker, they understood why he named his "well-bred, powerful . . . black horse" Nigger.[4]

Edward M. Heyl was born on Valentine's Day, 1844, to a Philadelphia bureaucrat and a "devoted" mother whose many "good acts" during the Civil War would keep "her memory bright as a friend of the soldier."[5] After attending the Plainfield Military Academy at Carlisle, Pennsylvania, he had entered the University of Pennsylvania when he joined the Third Pennsylvania Cavalry in 1861. Rising to the rank of captain by August 1862, he participated in every major battle of the Army of the Potomac. For the most part, his duties were relatively nonlethal: "escorting . . . Generals, driving up stragglers to their regiments, . . . taking [prisoners] . . . from the front line of battle to places of security in the rear, filling gaps on the picket line until larger bodies should come up to occupy them."[6]

Although the regimental history was not compiled until several years after Heyl's death, he was remembered with affection. Time having healed the war's scars, the writers emphasized interludes between battles during which gentlemen exchanged courtesies and demonstrated prowess. On one such occasion some officers were discussing the distance to the Confederate troops. When one "made a bet that they were out of carbine range," Heyl accepted it and borrowed a carbine that he "knew to be a good one . . . [and] aimed it carefully . . . at the man on the right of the skirmish line, fired, and the man tumbled off his horse. That settled the question."[7]

Even his capture had a romantic air. In November 1862 he was with a detachment on picket duty at Hartwood Church, twenty miles west of Fredericksburg, Virginia. The officer in command, instead of tending to his duties, "amused himself" painting murals of "gallant cavalry encounters" on its inside walls. While he was so engaged, Confederate troops under General Wade Hampton surprised and captured the entire company.

After the enlisted men were started afoot toward Richmond, the officers, having exchanged respects with Hampton, set out horseback under a token guard. When Heyl's horse broke down, a courier remained to escort him while the others went ahead. A short time later, the guard secured a promise that Heyl, "as a gentleman," would make no attempt to escape and hurried on to overtake the others. By the time Heyl reached the station, the last train had departed. With night falling, he trudged up to a "fine old Virginia mansion" a few hundred yards away and knocked on the door.

A "handsome young chap" of eighteen and wearing a new uniform sent by his mother, he soon won the confidence of the mistress of the house, a "stately . . . iron-grey-haired Virginia matron, and her two "lovely" daughters. Seeing "no evidences in his smiling face of a disposition to commit immediate murder," they invited him in, where his "personality" won them over. The husband and father was "a colonel in Lee's army." The next morning, "with true Virginia hospitality," they asked him to stay longer, but he "pointed out that he was a 'Yankee'" and had promised to rejoin the other captives. Although reassured that "he was not a Yankee . . . but like one of their own Southern gentlemen," he reluctantly departed. On reporting to Libby Prison, he "seemed a little distraught and like a man dreaming dreams."[8]

This account, embellished as it surely was, indicates the high regard Heyl's comrades had for him. That so personable a comrade could harbor such intense contempt and hatred of African Americans seems almost inexplicable. The black soldiers of the Ninth Cavalry would have no reason to suspect what a "true gentleman" their torturer had once been.

Mustered out of service in 1865, Heyl applied for a commission in the postwar army shortly after the army act of July 1866 was passed. Armed with recommendations from Generals Grant and George Meade, he was slated for a lieutenancy in the Ninth Cavalry. Although a person of his background and education should have found the exam required of appointees easy, he failed miserably. His answers on the geography and history sections, in particular, displayed colossal ignorance.

Q. "Where is the Amazon River?" A. "Don't know."

Q. "Where is Hudson's Bay?" A. "At the mouth of the Hudson River."

Q. "Into what body of water does the Nile River flow?"

After first writing "Pacific Ocean," Heyl scratched through his answer and substituted "Don't know."

Asked to name the principal rivers of Europe, he took a desperate look at the preceding question and wrote "The Nile."

Asked to identify the English king during the Revolutionary War, he replied, "I think George II but I don't remember."

His prize answer, however, was on a Civics question:

Q. "How is the President of the United States selected according to the Constitution?" A. "He is chosen from the Senate."[9]

Needless to say, the examining board refused to certify an apparent moron for a commission. When General Grant ordered a new examination, the board dutifully found that he had passed. On 25 February 1867, eleven days after his twenty-third birthday, Heyl reported for duty, the first officer assigned to Company E, Ninth Cavalry. For two ghastly months he remained the only one.

Heyl, whose only experience had been with the Third Pennsylvania, may have been overwhelmed by the sea of blacks around him. With only eleven officers, each struggling with a backlog of paperwork and responsibilities, on duty in the entire regiment, there was no one to guide him or to curb excesses. Frustration fueled by prejudice and alcohol did the rest. Just when harsh discipline evolved into sadistic abuse cannot be determined, but by the time the regiment reached Texas in early April, the transition had occurred.

Although there are no known cases of abuse during Heyl's first month on duty, Private James Williams, soon to become the troop's first sergeant, testified that he had seen Heyl striking men with a saber at Greenville, Louisiana.[10] Matters grew worse during the sea and land trip to Texas. Leaving New Orleans on 27 March, the first units, including E Troop, arrived at San Antonio on the evening of 4 April. During the march inland a flare-up in Lieutenant Frederick Smith's K Troop was "suppressed with great difficulty." This may have increased Heyl's contempt for his charges. The day before the command reached San Antonio, Private Williams testified, he knocked a man down with a "stick of wood."[11]

Despite their troubles, the troopers displayed a proud face as they marched through San Antonio en route to San Pedro Springs, north of the city. An anti-Reconstruction paper was impressed by their "tidy and soldier-like appearance" and stated that the precision of their marching "gave every indication of strict discipline."[12]

On 8 April, Heyl's mistreatment of his troopers worsened. That evening, for unknown reasons, he exploded at Private Robert Winthrop, slashing the private's shoulder with the blade of his saber and following that with blows with the flat of the blade as blood streamed from the wound.

The following morning, already under the influence of alcohol, he lost all control of himself. As Private Lewis Brown stated, "I never saw him go on as he did that morning, before in my life." He first became enraged when three men failed to remove the nose-bags after feeding their horses. He ordered them to be trussed and suspended from their wrists, their feet dangling about six inches above the ground. Riding to a nearby saloon, he consumed more liquor. His actions thereafter were those of a maniac.

Returning to camp, "he came running [his horse] . . . over the soldiers of the company . . . striking them with his whip and calling them sons-of-bitches." As he reeled towards his tent, he noticed that one of the three suspended soldiers, John Hill, was resting his weight on a tree stump. Infuriated, he drew his revolver and fired several shots towards the help-less troopers. When Hill still sought to ease his suffering on the stump, Heyl stormed up, saber flailing. Most of the blows were with the flat of the blade, but at least one cut deep into Hill's side. His fury dissipated, Heyl allowed them to be cut down, and he retired to his tent.[13]

The brutalities were too much for First Sergeant Harrison Bradford. A twenty-four-year-old mulatto from Kentucky, he had served in the 104th U.S. Colored Infantry during the Civil War. His only apparent recourse was to go to Lieutenant Colonel Merritt. Wanting his troop to appear as impressive as possible, he assembled them in formation, each dressed formally with his saber strapped to his belt, and marched them towards Merritt's tent.

All hope of a peaceful presentation of grievances vanished when Heyl emerged from his tent and ordered them to halt. Bradford complied, his troopers standing in rank. When Heyl called him forward, he again obeyed. According to Heyl, he asked Bradford where the men were going, and Bradford replied, "To see General Merritt." Bradford added that "he did not like the way I treated the men," Heyl claimed. Then the sergeant pulled his saber and lunged at the officer. Backing up while firing his pistol and fending off the saber blows with his hand, Heyl received two slashes on his palm and wrist before he collapsed. Revealing the sad state of his relations with his troop, he admitted that, save for Bradford, he was unable to recognize or name a single soldier.[14]

The soldiers' testimony differed dramatically. When asked why he was going to see Merritt, Bradford had replied, "The way these men are treated."

"The way who treated them?"

"The way you treated them . . . last night you cut one man to pieces, . . . this morning you tried to run your horse over one; and then . . . you tied up three men clear from the ground, and then stood off and shot at them and that would not do; and you . . . cut at them with your saber as if they had been hogs, . . . and that's what I'm going to report."

For a few seconds the two confronted each other. Three times Heyl blustered, "I do them so, hey?" and three times the sergeant responded firmly, "You do them so!" It was Heyl, the men said, who broke the standoff by fumbling for his revolver and firing. Bradford's first saber thrust was directed at Heyl's hand, as though to knock the revolver aside. After a second shot ripped into his mouth, he could only fight desperately to survive.

Hearing the shooting, Lieutenants Seth Griffin and Frederick Smith, both veterans of wartime service with black regiments, rushed from their tent. As Smith turned back to procure his pistol, Griffin opened fire on Bradford. The sergeant swung wildly at this new assailant, his sword cleaving Griffin's skull. As an unidentified soldier yelled, "Rally, Company E," several men sprang to Bradford's aid. At least one also slashed at Griffin as he slumped to the ground.

By this time Smith, gun in hand, reemerged and fired two more bullets at Bradford, killing him instantly. As the sergeant fell, four or five troopers sprang at Smith, slashing with their sabers. Private Irving Charles, identified as one of the attackers, asserted that he had "got frightened and stepped out of ranks" when Lieutenant Smith fired at him because "he saw my saber out of the scabbard." Terrified, he "ran toward Lt. Smith, he shot at me again—I ran towards my quarters, threw off my saber in my tent and I kept right on . . . toward Lt. Smith . . . because I was frightened and did not know which way to run."[15]

When Merritt and Captain George Purrington arrived on the scene, the men around the officers fled, panic-stricken at what had occurred. Amazingly, the great majority of the troop, although stunned by the confrontation and endangered by the wild firing by the officers, had remained in their ranks. As Merritt and Purrington arrived, they suddenly bolted for their quarters. The "mutiny" was over.[16]

Never regaining consciousness, Lieutenant Griffin died two days later. The fleeing "mutineers" set out as best they could towards the Louisiana border. Despite an extensive search, it was 25 April before the last of them, "hungry and emaciated" and with their clothes shredded by the chaparral, were in custody.

During the manhunt, Private Washington Wyatt, a twenty-year-old Louisianan, became separated from his comrades. A week later, searchers found his decomposed body, a bullet through the head. Although his saber was still in its scabbard, his carbine and other valuables had been taken. It was assumed that he had been killed by local thieves.[17]

After a hasty investigation, Merritt excoriated Heyl for the "cruel . . . brutal treatment of his men" and recommended a "thorough examination into his conduct." Nevertheless, only the enlisted men were court-martialed. Before a panel that did not include anyone from the Ninth Cavalry, eight troopers were tried in early June, found guilty, and sentenced to be executed. General Philip Sheridan, commanding all forces in Louisiana and Texas, quickly concurred, but Judge Advocate General Joseph Holt was less accommodating.

Holt, a Kentucky Democrat, had won acclaim (or notoriety) for securing death sentences for such controversial defendants as Henry Wirz, superintendent of the Andersonville military prison, and Mary Surratt, the mother of one of John Wilkes Booth's accomplices, by ignoring due process of law. After reviewing the trials of the mutineers, however, he blamed the tragedy on Heyl's "flagrantly cruel and illegal" actions. He was especially impressed by the "quiet attitude and demeanor" of the great majority of the men during the altercation. Although the convicted men had obviously engaged in an unpremeditated act of mutiny, it had been because of extreme provocation. They had already suffered so much from "anxiety and imprisonment" that any additional punishment should be "extremely light."

Agreeing with Holt, Secretary of War Stanton recommended that, in view of Heyl's "outrageous" actions and the suffering the prisoners had already endured, their sentences should be reduced. Two, including

Private Irving Charles, were restored to duty; the other six were to serve from one to two years at hard labor at Ship Island, Mississippi. Six months afterwards, all were released.[18]

The leniency granted the mutineers was dwarfed by that afforded Heyl. Few have been condemned so harshly and dealt with so lightly. Although Holt had demanded a court-martial, and Colonel Hatch, "for the good of the service," had drawn up charges, Sheridan refused to order one. Undoubtedly he and General Grant feared a trial would encourage more defiance of authority and undercut the morale of the officers in black regiments. Arguing that the mutiny was largely a result of the shortage of officers in the Ninth Cavalry, they demanded that all vacant positions be filled immediately. In response, Stanton in July 1867 directed that the existing vacancies were to be filled by promoting the senior officers of the next lower grade. As an obscene result, Heyl, the senior lieutenant in the regiment, was promoted to the captaincy of M Troop.[19]

Heyl's promotion was a godsend for all concerned. Since M Troop was stationed at Fort Brown near the mouth of the Rio Grande, its members had not witnessed the tragedy at San Pedro Springs. Heyl was also removed from the immediate supervision of Hatch and Merritt, both of whom had condemned him. Repairing the shattered morale of their command would be hard enough without his presence making it more so.

At Fort Brown, Ranald Mackenzie, head of the black Forty-first Infantry, became Heyl's commander. Although Mackenzie was not one to tolerate the abuse of soldiers, he seems not to have prejudged the newcomer. Heyl, for his part, also learned from the tragedy. Never again was there even a hint of excessive drinking on his part. He even kept his racism under sufficient control to win accolades in the Indian campaigns of 1869. Transferring to the Fourth Cavalry in 1870, he served with it for fourteen years before his brother-in-law, Senator William T. Sewell of New Jersey, secured him a highly coveted slot in the inspector general's department. It is an all too revealing commentary on the racist mores of the late nineteenth century that misbehavior as heinous as Heyl's actions at San Pedro Springs would have so little impact on his subsequent career.

Others involved in the San Pedro Springs affair did not fare as well. Lieutenant Smith, the slayer of Sergeant Bradford, showed considerable promise as an officer. Stationed at Fort McKavett, he led frequent scouts and was building a solid reputation with his superiors. It all ended three days before Christmas, 1869. His wife received a letter from home, contents undisclosed, and began packing to leave him. He sought to dissuade her, to no avail. An hour before sunset, he gave up. Taking a revolver, his wife still in the room, he fired a bullet into his brain.[20]

The men of E Troop fared little better than Smith. None of the mutineers and only three of the others made the army a career. Mutineer Ephrain Bailey's fate in a way was symbolic. Released from Ship Island in March 1868, he rejoined the troop at Fort Stockton. Less than a month afterwards, he died in the post hospital.[21]

Heyl's ability to emerge from the San Pedro Springs affair unscathed (and, in effect, rewarded) seems all the more atrocious when compared to the fates of officers charged with fraternization with enlisted men. At least three officers in the Ninth Cavalry were dismissed for fraternization. While this may have been practiced throughout the army in order to maintain discipline, racial considerations undoubtedly added a sense of urgency to the policy of maintaining the distance between officers and the rank and file.[22]

The first casualty of the no-fraternization policy was Captain William Frohock of K Troop, a veteran of the Forty-fifth Illinois Infantry who was wounded at both Shiloh and Vicksburg. After recovering, he was breveted a brigadier general and placed in command of the Sixty-sixth U.S. Colored Infantry.[23] After joining the Ninth, he distinguished himself by winning the first major battle between the buffalo soldiers and the Comanches at Fort Lancaster, Texas, in October 1867 (see p. 141). Despite his excellent record, on 11 January 1870 he was tried by a court-martial, presided over by Colonel Hatch, for conduct unbecoming an officer and gentleman. In February 1868 he had engaged in a game of poker with a stagecoach driver, lost heavily, and tried to renege on paying the loss. The driver pulled a pistol and gave him "half a minute to return that money." He was found guilty and sentenced to be dismissed from the military."[24]

The sentence's harshness prompted a quick reversal and the restoration of Frohock to duty. He immediately tendered his resignation, odd behavior for one who had ample opportunity to resign before enduring the court-martial. His reasons for doing so remained a secret until Colonel Hatch revealed during the court-martial of Frohock's successor that he had also gambled "*with the men and employees of his company.*" After resigning, he "raffled off his effects among the men of the company [and] gambled in their presence with these employees."[25]

A similar transgression ended the service of Lieutenant Francis Davidson, a beneficiary of political patronage. Although a native of Massachusetts, he secured the slot allocated to Kansas at West Point in 1861 and remained in the academy for four years, always on the verge of dismissal for poor scholarship and conduct. Finally dismissed in July 1865, he served three months as a lieutenant in a Massachusetts cavalry regiment awaiting deactivation. Despite his mediocre record, political backing produced a lieutenant's commission in the Ninth in July 1867.[26]

Although Davidson showed that he was capable of excellent service during his eight years with the Ninth Cavalry, he refused to conform with military discipline. After surviving four confinements and two courts-martial with little more than token punishments, he committed a calamitous infraction on 31 July 1875.

While stationed at El Sanz, Texas, a temporary camp set up on the lower Rio Grande to patrol for cattle rustlers, he was charged with disobeying orders. Although confined to his quarters by First Lieutenant E. D. Dimmick, he went to a nearby cantina that evening and "did gamble with, winning money from, and exchanging and dividing money with certain enlisted men" from his company until four in the morning. Confronted by Dimmick after he returned, he exploded: "I am no G____ d____ boy; go away from here you G____ d____ sneaks [Lt. J. H. French was with Dimmick]; I suppose those G____ d____ idiots at Fort Brown sent you here to spy on me."

After refusing requests to resign to "avoid the disgrace" of a court-martial, he was tried at Fort Brown. Although exonerated on the charges that had led to his initial arrest, his gambling escapade proved decisive. Convicted of insubordination and misconduct, he was dismissed from military service as of 15 November 1875.[27]

Socialization with enlisted men occasioned the demise of at least one other lieutenant. In 1873, Polish émigré Lieutenant Gustave Radetski of Ambrose Hooker's E Troop was accused of visiting a "public bar-room" for a round of drinks with "an enlisted man" of his company. When the proprietor notified Radetski's superiors, charges were promptly filed. Within four months' time the hapless officer had been dismissed from service by a court-martial.[28] Radetski would have had a better chance of escaping punishment had he maimed or killed the enlisted man instead of taking a drink with him.

With the possible exception of Captain Frohock, none of these officers were particularly talented. But there is no reason to think that they might not have enjoyed lengthy and successful careers in the army had they not fraternized with black enlisted men.

5

"Hoodoos" and Kangaroo Courts

The "Near Mutiny" at Fort Stockton

No officer in the Ninth Cavalry received more recognition than Francis Dodge, for thirteen years the leader of D Troop. A native of Massachusetts who had risen from the ranks during the Civil War, he was obviously one of the regiment's most efficient officers. His moment of glory came in October 1879, when he led his troopers on a dramatic march to relieve the survivors of the Thornburgh "massacre" at Milk Creek, Colorado. For that he received a Medal of Honor and, as "a Christmas gift from the President," a transfer to the Pay Department with the rank of major. When he retired twenty-six years later he was head of the pay branch and held the rank of brigadier general.[1]

Dodge first demonstrated his capacity for leadership during a campaign against the Mescalero Apaches in January 1870. Ostensibly confined to a reservation near Fort Stanton, New Mexico, the Mescaleros found the emigrant trails that skirted their lands all too tempting. Swooping down from the Guadalupe and Sacramento Mountains, they wreaked havoc upon wagon trains, stagecoaches, and cattle herds.

For the first two years that the Ninth was in Texas, the Mescaleros had things their own way, because officers were too busy rebuilding Forts Stockton, Davis, and Quitman to make more than token pursuits of raiders. By 1870, Hatch was able to spare the manpower for an expedition into the heart of the Mescalero country. Combining men from the garrisons at Forts Davis and Stockton, Hatch assembled almost two hundred men under the command of Captain Dodge. With his own D Troop in the van, Dodge on 12 January marched northwestward from

Fort Davis. Even though the midwinter nights in the Trans-Pecos were bitterly cold, he forbade campfires in order to reduce the chances of discovery. Five days out, he struck an Indian trail along Delaware Creek just below the New Mexico line. Following the Delaware to its head near towering Guadalupe Peak, he discovered the Mescalero camp.

Despite his efforts to avoid detection, the Mescaleros had time to retreat to a nearby mesa, from which they peppered the buffalo soldiers with gunfire. Ordered to advance, the troopers moved "spiritedly to the attack." The Apaches fought fiercely, "disputing every step of the ascent," but the soldiers, most in their first battle, did not flinch. Shortly before sundown they reached the top, putting the Mescaleros to rout. Rarely did Apaches leave their dead behind, but so rapid was the last surge up the mesa that the bodies of ten of them were found. Dodge estimated the Indians might have lost as many as fifty warriors in the battle. After a brief pursuit the following day, the victors turned back to burn the lodges and destroy the captured buffalo robes and food supplies.[2]

Dodge's campaign had been a spectacular success, showing the mettle of men and officers alike. Such a shared venture often forged a lasting bond between an officer and his men, but this was not the case with Troop D. While the reason for this is not clear, it was at least partially a result of Dodge's austere and unforgiving nature. The regimental returns for the early 1870s indicate that he was unusually quick to place men under arrest. Men in his troop were confined at a rate more than twice that of the regimental average. Since the numerous arrests were not accompanied by increased numbers of desertions or dishonorable discharges, most incarcerations were likely for minor offenses.[3]

Demonstrating the sad state of morale in D Troop was its dismal reenlistment record. Its members simply did not reenlist. Ten of the survivors of the San Pedro Springs mutiny in E Troop, including most of its sergeants, for example, reenlisted in 1871; in Troop D, almost no one. Not even one of the troop's five sergeants reenlisted. One, a twenty-eight-year-old Louisianan named George Roberts, transferred to the Twenty-fifth Infantry. Four months later he returned to Dodge's troop and was promptly promoted to first sergeant.[4]

At a time when the other companies had a cadre of veteran noncommissioned officers to train new recruits, D Troop was sadly deficient. As a result, newcomers such as Absalom Ely and Edward Gaston, both twenty-one-year-old mulattoes (one a farmer from Virginia and the other a laborer from West Virginia), found themselves wearing sergeant's chevrons only months after induction. There was no chance they could provide adequate leadership.[5]

One of the major sources of dissatisfaction at Fort Stockton, as was the case with many black units, was health care. Too many doctors seemed to be unwilling to treat black enlisted men. In 1872, for example, the death rate from disease among white soldiers was eleven per thousand; among blacks it was eighteen per thousand. Translated into deaths per hospital admissions, a white soldier admitted to a hospital had twice as good a chance of surviving as a black. While part of the discrepancy may have been a result of the location of most black units in remote areas, racism among doctors also seems to have been a factor.[6]

At Fort Stockton, much of the responsibility for the troubles of 1873 rested squarely upon post surgeon Peter Cleary. Born in Malta, New York, in 1839, he attended Queen's University in Dublin before earning an M.D. degree from the Royal College of Surgeons in London. In 1862 he began a forty-year stint as a military surgeon, during which he rose to the rank of assistant surgeon general. Despite his obvious ability, his four-year tenure at Fort Stockton, Texas, manned exclusively by black troops, indicates that he was one of the most prejudiced officers in the military.[7]

For all Cleary's training and experience, he demonstrated little concern for the ailments of black soldiers. Like Captain Dodge, he believed that "colored troops" were "notorious for having 'miseries' in every part of their bodies," and if these were taken seriously "there would be very few left for duty." Cleary therefore dismissed most complaints by telling patients "to rub themselves with stones or adobes." As a result, there was no shortage of soldiers available for duty. Out of a garrison of 185 enlisted men, exactly 8 were marked as absent sick during a five-month stretch in early 1873. Two men died of illness during the period, indicating that only the severest of symptoms resulted in hosptalization. Obviously. any charge that the surgeon was mistreating or neglecting black patients deserved careful consideration.[8]

On 30 April, Private John Taylor, a Civil War veteran and member of the Twenty-fifth Infantry, reported sick. According to the recollection, thirty years afterwards, of Major Zenas Bliss, acting commander of the Twenty-fifth, Cleary "examined him and gave him some medicine and sent him to duty . . . as he thought there was nothing the matter." During the next two months, Taylor, suffering from "awful pains" in his head, repeatedly sought treatment and was just as repeatedly refused. As his condition worsened, other soldiers "did his guard duty . . . without the Captain's knowledge."[9]

On 5 July, Taylor was admitted to the hospital. Upon making his rounds, Cleary asked him what was wrong. According to a fellow patient, Taylor said that he had "a misery" in his head. The doctor replied, "Oh shit? God damn it: I want you to get up out of that bed and stir around. I don't want to catch you at it any more today."[10]

Allowing Taylor to remain in the hospital overnight, Cleary revisited him the next morning. The hospital steward reported that he had been "out of his head all night," to which the doctor "turned and walked away without uttering another word." The scene was virtually replayed that evening. Cleary questioned Taylor once more on how he felt and was told, "I have an awful pain in my head." Cleary then declared he was "sick of this damn foolishness" and ordered him to be put in the guardhouse.

Confinement at Fort Stockton included daily work in the post garden. The fort, situated in a desert, was blessed with an abundance of water from Comanche Springs. A network of irrigation ditches, constructed and tended by black soldiers, enabled the fort, according to Major Bliss, to have "the best garden I have ever seen at a military post."[11]

On the morning of 8 July, as Taylor's condition worsened, two troopers assisted him to the dispensary to see Dr. Cleary once more. The doctor felt his pulse, remarked cryptically, "You are damn near gone up," and ordered him back to the guardhouse. After the guards had made him as comfortable as possible, the officer of the day, Prussian-born Henry P. Ritzius, discovered his presence. He upbraided the sergeant on guard duty for failing to return Taylor to work. Despite the latter's protest that the prisoner was too ill, Ritzius declared there was "nothing the matter with him, the Doctor says he is playing off," and ordered him to be sent to the field.

With Taylor too weak to walk, the sergeant detailed four men to carry him, presenting a "strange and inhuman spectacle" that caused "considerable excitement and sorrow among the men who witnessed it." The forlorn group progressed about two hundred yards before Ritzius ordered them to return Taylor to the guardhouse. The guard detachment "cheerfully complied," thinking the lieutenant had relented.

Such was not the case. Ritzius ordered Taylor to be deprived of all bedding except one blanket, leaving him nothing to lie on but the "rocky floor," and to have nothing but bread and water. Furthermore, the sergeant was to allow none of the men of the garrison to have any contact with him "whatever." For the rest of the day the guards watched helplessly as, "in a delirious condition," he thrashed around so violently that he was likely to "injure himself against the walls of the cell."[12]

By the next morning he had lapsed into unconsciousness. For the last time he was borne back to the hospital. He remained unconscious throughout that day and night. The following morning, Dr. Cleary arrived at the hospital with another physician, a Dr. Buffington, who was visiting the post. Cleary asked Buffington what he thought might be wrong with the patient. Buffington replied he did not know, but that "the man was dying." Shortly thereafter, Taylor breathed his last.[13]

Taylor's death, after so many weeks of neglect and abuse, traumatized the enlisted men at Fort Stockton. Determined he would not be forgotten, they held a mass meeting on the evening of 11 July and adopted a set of resolutions expressing their "sympathy" for the loss of their "comrade." As it had "pleased Almighty God . . . to take from our midst our friend and comrade," they wished to "record" their appreciation of "his merits and moral worth" and express their "grief and sympathy" to his family. They especially "deplored" his loss because his "upright character, genial disposition, and kind manner were a constant source of happiness to us all." Determined to emphasize his worth, they declared that from the time he first enlisted in the army on 20 September 1863 he had displayed "the true spirit of the soldier" and had set an example "worthy of emulation." After voting to send copies of their resolutions to the *Army and Navy Journal*, they took up a second order of business.[14]

Incensed that none of the officers had shown any concern about Taylor's mistreatment, they mulled over a possible recourse. How could they inform the outside world of Cleary's actions without violating army regulations? Realizing they needed more information, they selected a six-man committee led by infantry sergeants Ellis Russell and Solomon Holloman to question men who "knew of the ill-treatment" of Taylor and others and draw up a statement to be considered the following night. At a meeting on 11 July, forty-five men attached their signatures to a petition addressed to the adjutant general describing the events that preceded the death of John Taylor.

The purpose of their complaint was stated clearly and forcefully: "We believe the deceased came to his death from intentional neglect on the part of the Post Surgeon, P. J. A. Cleary, U.S.A., who from malicious feelings of a personal nature, refused to give or allow him proper treatment." This aside, there was not one pejorative word or phrase in the document; they obviously thought the facts more than adequate to substantiate their case. In signing the document, they affixed their names in a round robin to make it harder to identify the order of signing.

Although a pledge of secrecy had been taken, this was obviously impossible. By the following day, the whites at Fort Stockton were panic-stricken as rumors ran amok. Major Bliss recalled that men were threatening to hang Dr. Cleary and "others in the garrison." They said they "needed no white officers" to run the fort. White panic reached a high point when some women overheard the fatigue parties working in their backyards making threatening remarks. Since Bliss's recollection of the number of men court-martialed and the length of their sentences was greatly exaggerated, it is likely that his memories of the "muttered threats" more accurately reflected white fears than the actual content of the conversations.[15]

There is no doubt that the officers at Fort Stockton were in a panic. After receiving Dodge's summary of the events, General C. C. Augur, commanding the Department of Texas, reported to Sheridan that "there is a great feeling of anxiety" at Fort Stockton, "particularly among the officers who have wives and families." Augur, never an advocate of black military units, informed Sheridan that there was "anxiety" at every post manned exclusively by black troops. They were "so clannish and so excitable, turning every question into one of class," that there was a constant threat that "the whole of the garrison" might turn on their superiors, "not as officers, but as white men."[16]

On the morning of the twelfth, Captain Dodge, undoubtedly already aware of the discontent, was presented with the round robin and asked to forward it through channels to the adjutant general. Instead of complying with the legitimate request, he assembled the signers, read them the rules of war that he deemed applicable, and demanded they withdraw their signatures. Under intense pressure, twenty-four complied. The other twenty-one stubbornly refused.[17]

Dodge's efforts to identify the "ringleaders" of the unrest met with quick success when Sergeant Hollomon, admitting he had helped draft the round robin, turned on his comrades. To save himself, he claimed that First Sergeant Roberts and Private Houston Shelton, both of D Troop, had taken the lead in convincing men to sign the document.[18] Two days after beginning his investigation, Dodge forwarded the round robin together with his own version of the "near mutiny" to departmental headquarters in Austin. General Augur immediately ordered a general court-martial.[19]

Any hopes the accused had of presenting their case to an impartial panel were cruelly disappointed. Augur named Major Bliss to preside over a court made up almost entirely of the same officers at Fort Stockton who were in a great "state of anxiety." One of them, moreover, was Lieutenant Ritzius, who had callously sent the dying Taylor to work and had denied him bedding and comfort throughout his last day on earth. While not specifically charged with wrongdoing by the round robin, he could not have been pleased with its description of his actions. In addition, one of the accused, Sergeant Ellis Russell, objected that Lieutenant Ritzius had said "he would go for me" and did not like him. Although Ritzius admitted that he had once described Russell as "an inefficient non-commissioned officer," he declared that this "would not in any way influence my judgment in this case." He remained on the panel.

From start to finish the court-martial made no pretense of following proper procedures. As Major Bliss recalled, "We tried . . . sixty-two men at one time . . . on the same charges . . . [and] held the court on the back gallery of my old quarters, then vacant, and the prisoners sat around in the back yard near us." Since the backyards of the officers' quarters at Fort Stockton were enclosed by eight-foot-high adobe walls, there was no danger that any of the accused might escape.[20]

Major Bliss greatly overstated the number of the accused. Twenty-one men were tried jointly on 26 and 27 August on charges of "mutinous conduct, to the prejudice of good order and discipline." Ten, including Sergeant Roberts and Private Shelton of the Ninth Cavalry, were alleged to have "originated and organized" an "unlawful and mutinous meeting calculated to . . . create discontent, murmurings and disturbances," and therefore to be responsible for the "mutinous language being used by and among the enlisted men of the garrison." They also had conducted, participated in, or attended a meeting "having as its object the conveying of censure upon their superior officer [Cleary held the rank of captain]." The other eleven were accused only of attending the meeting.

Without benefit of counsel, the accused relied solely on the truth as a defense. They admitted organizing and attending the meeting but denied that it was intended to be mutinous or to incite violence. Uppermost in their minds had been the image of the denial of care to Private Taylor month after month. To a man, they "persisted in their course" and refused to withdraw their signatures, each saying simply: "I prefer to decide the lawfulness of my acts in this case and take the consequences."[21] Heroic as their stand was, the officers were determined that black enlisted men who defied authority would not go unpunished.

After going through the pretense of a trial, the court-martial found all twenty-one guilty, but on reduced charges. The charge that there had been an "unlawful and mutinous meeting" intended to "create discontent, murmurings and disturbances," along with all references to "mutinous language," was quietly put to rest. The ten organizers were found guilty simply of conducting an unauthorized meeting and "demanding . . . an investigation of the official and professional conduct" of Dr. Cleary.

Although Major Bliss apparently realized there had been no intent to mutiny, he deemed it sufficiently criminal that the men had questioned authority and, above all, had refused to recant once given the chance. All ten of the so-called ringleaders received dishonorable discharges and confinement for two years in the prison at Huntsville, Texas. The other eleven, found guilty only of attending the meeting and signing the round robin, received dishonorable discharges and prison sentences of one year.[22]

To justify the sentences, General Augur grossly exaggerated the extent of the threat. "Almost all the enlisted men" at Fort Stockton, not the forty-five indicated by the trial documents, had "banded together" and with few exceptions had refused "to recede from the position they had assumed." He was particularly incensed that so many noncommissioned officers, "whose duty it was to preserve order and sustain constituted authority," had joined the ranks of the discontent. Without citing specific articles of war violated by the meeting, he contended that "such acts of association" were forbidden by "regulations, custom of service, . . . and in themselves [were] wholly subversive of military discipline." Unless curbed, they would speedily "reduce the Army to a mob." To him the sentences were most lenient, especially in light of the fact that only the "ringleaders and those who by their positions as non-commissioned officers were additionally culpable" had been brought to trial.[23]

Though refusing to question Dr. Cleary's treatment of his patients, the army's leaders recognized that his presence at Fort Stockton or, indeed, at any other post manned by black troops might lead to unrest. On 13 August he was reassigned to an installation in New York City. Shortly after the sentences of the convicted troopers had been confirmed, Dodge and Troop D were ordered to trade places with Troop M, stationed at Fort McKavett.[24] New noncoms, new recruits, a new locale, and above all a new physician might allow a new start.

The only officer to reflect upon the ordeal of Private Taylor was Major Bliss. He recalled that, according to Dr. Cleary, there was no way to account for Taylor's death "except that he had been *hoodooed* and that it *so preyed upon him that he died from fright or from a sort of home-sickness.*" In total agreement with the bizarre diagnosis, Bliss innocently aired his own racist feelings: "These men were easily frightened by the idea of being hoodooed, and it made them sick, and perhaps this man died from that cause."[25]

Fort Stockton's "near-mutiny" reveals an incredible solidarity among the black soldiers in defense of their dignity. The incident also reveals how easy it was for the commanders of blacks to overreact instead of dealing with legitimate grievances. The careers of Dodge, Ritzius, and Bliss show that all were capable and conscientious. Eventually they would learn to respect soldiers' hunger for a recognition of their humanity.

6

"Humpy" Jackson, Racist Killer and Folk Hero of the San Saba

In June 1869, Private Boston Henry, F Troop, Ninth Cavalry, was killed near Menard, Texas, by a bullet fired from ambush by John Jackson, a sixtyish farmer possessed of a mind as warped as his back. He had shot the soldier because a black trooper had written a letter to his teenage daughter. Ordinarily such killings evoked little reaction from law enforcement, but in 1869 circumstances were abnormal. Fort McKavett's commander, Ranald Mackenzie, was a strong-willed officer unwilling to tolerate such atrocities. Stationed on the Rio Grande before his transfer to McKavett, he had earned the hatred of racists by his energetic and often arbitrary retaliations for transgressions against his troops.[1] Since military Reconstruction was still in force, he was empowered to dispense justice through military commissions.

In addition, he was pushing his command to the limit in an effort to accomplish the impossible. With but two troops of cavalry and two companies of infantry, he had to escort wagon trains and stagecoaches, maintain law and order, and even select local officials and conduct elections in an area extending from Mason on the east to the Pecos River on the west. At the same time, he was rebuilding Fort McKavett, which had been abandoned during the Civil War. As commander of the Sub-District of the Pecos, he also controlled scouting for Indians along an arc extending from near Laredo on the Rio Grande almost to modern Abilene, Texas.

Too overextended to conduct an extensive manhunt for the killer of Private Henry, Mackenzie still refused to tolerate the crime. The prejudiced-warped memories of his efforts to bring Jackson to justice became one of the lasting myths of the Texas frontier. His failure demonstrates how difficult it was for black soldiers to operate in an area where they were in more danger from civilians than from Indians.

The murder of Private Henry involved a detachment of black infantrymen sent to Menard to operate a sawmill. One of its members, Private William Ecles, became entranced by Narcissus Jackson, a teenager whom he saw daily walking to and from school. With more ardor than judgment, he deposited a letter to her at the local post office. The postal clerk noted the addressee, exclaimed that "no damned nigger had a right to correspond with a white girl," and threatened to kill Ecles. Although this occurred on 1 June, Humpy Jackson brooded over the matter for a week before taking action. On 9 June he was observed carrying a squirrel rifle into the trees across the river from where the soldiers were camped. Minutes later, a bullet fired from the trees killed Private Henry, who had nothing to do with the letter.[2]

Local recollections, which have formed the basis for most accounts of this incident, embellished the matter considerably. The letter was allegedly received by Narcissus, who then showed it to her father. The writer's identity was forgotten. Instead of Private Ecles, he was remembered as being a "yellow skinned" sergeant identified only as "Lanky Jim." Upon reading the letter, "overflowing" with expressions of devotion and a declaration that Narcissus's voice was like "the sweetest music," the mythical Jackson picked up his "trusty old gun," declared it "makes music too," and shot the first soldier he saw, since "a negro was a negro [sic], and all looked alike."[3] No account referred to Private Henry by name or expressed remorse for his murder. One account stated that Jackson later atoned for his error by shooting the guilty trooper.[4]

As soon as the commanders at Forts McKavett and Concho learned of the murder, patrols were sent in search of Jackson. The response from McKavett was limited because Mackenzie was on a campaign with most of the garrison. Captain Henry Carroll dispatched Lieutenant John Bullis with six troopers to investigate. After a sixty-mile scout, Bullis returned empty-handed. A more determined effort from Fort Concho was led by Lieutenant George Albee. With five men, he made a four-hundred-mile scout that took most of the month. Learning that Jackson had sons living in Llano County, he scouted that area extensively without result.[5] Mackenzie, upon returning to McKavett in mid-July, was incensed, but he was too busy organizing another expedition against the Comanches to stage a systematic search.

Incredibly exaggerated recollections, in contrast, claimed that black soldiers "swarmed" from Fort McKavett and searched for months "under the ruthless resolve" of Mackenzie. Easily evading the patrols, Jackson raised "a good corn corp on the side."[6]

The Jackson affair was rekindled in early 1870. On 31 January, Mackenzie responded to an outbreak of cattle rustling near Mason by ordering Captain Carroll to take fifteen men to the town. En route, Carroll chanced upon Jackson driving a herd of horses a few miles east of Menard. During the ensuing pursuit, Jackson was knocked from his horse and captured. Stunned by the fall, hump-backed, deceptively frail looking, and perhaps feigning injury, he convinced Carroll that his condition was too serious for the trip to Fort McKavett. While Carroll was considering his options, Fort Concho's post surgeon, William Notson, arrived.

Acting on Notson's advice, Carroll made a fatal decision. After dispatching a trooper to Fort McKavett to request an ambulance for the prisoner, he left Jackson at his cabin under a guard of three men. With the remainder of his command he rode on to Mason to carry out his orders. Doctor Notson remained in Menard, apparently to check on Jackson's condition. Although Mackenzie would hold Carroll responsible for the decision to leave Jackson with such a small guard, both Jackson's wife and son stated that it was the doctor who allowed him to remain in his home and instructed the guards concerning his treatment.[7]

The troopers assigned to guard Jackson, Corporal Alfred Marshall and Privates Charles Murray and David Brown, were model soldiers. Marshall, a twenty-three-year-old farmer from Kentucky, and Murray, a Virginian one year older, had been among the first to enlist in F Troop. Although Carroll was a harsh disciplinarian, the three were among the few men in the troop with clean records. On the other hand, they had little experience with warfare. Four Indian expeditions departed Fort McKavett in 1869; each time, all three were left behind, with Brown and Murray employed as "carpenters" and Corporal Marshall serving as the post's blacksmith.[8] Although they were probably picked to guard Jackson because Carroll was confident they would follow orders to the letter, their lack of aggressiveness would be a liability in an emergency.

During the afternoon of 2 February the soldiers gradually lost control of the situation. Jackson, lying on a blanket, and his wife and two daughters were inside the cabin, watched by a guard that was rotated every three hours. Notson had instructed the other two to remain outside. No effort was made to prevent visitors. A rancher named Charles Owens was the first to arrive, but he soon left, rifle in hand, riding eastward—perhaps to make sure that Carroll was no longer in the vicinity. He returned an hour later.[9]

Meanwhile, news of Jackson's capture reached Menard. The informer apparently was William Epps, a hired hand of Jackson's, but Dr. Notson, who spent the day in Menard, also discussed the matter freely. The little settlement may have been unusually crowded, because a dance was to be held that night. In the local store a rancher named George Harvey was at the center of a group of at least ten men who were discussing Jackson's plight. A few counseled against a rescue attempt, but to no avail. Eventually it was decided that Harvey, Stephen Cavaness, and Peter Crain would comprise the rescue party.[10]

At Jackson's ranch, Owens had asked Corporal Marshall to remove the guard from Jackson's room. Marshall refused, citing his orders. Harvey, heavily armed and pretending to be looking for a strayed horse, was the first arrival from Menard. In an effort to lure the guards away from their posts, he offered to pay them to help find the horse. Once more, the corporal refused. Shortly after three in the afternoon, Crain and Cavaness rode up, also heavily armed.[11]

The position of the soldiers was hopeless. Some of the gunmen were in the house with Corporal Marshall and the Jacksons; the rest were outside. Gunfire suddenly broke the silence. According to Private Brown, the only soldier to survive, Harvey and Owens opened fire, simultaneously demanding that the soldiers surrender. Brown returned their fire and took cover; Murray dropped his gun in fright and made an effort to flee before being shot down. Corporal Marshall, inside the cabin with the Jacksons, drew his gun as soon as he heard the shots. While he was distracted by the firing, he was allegedly shot by Elizabeth Jackson, who drew a "double barrel pistol" concealed under her skirt. As the Texans entered the cabin where Jackson lay, Brown saw his chance to escape. Plunging over the steep bank of the San Saba River into water so deep he could not touch bottom, he found refuge. Although it was still daylight, the midwinter waters must have been icy, but he eluded a short-lived search. The gunmen, knowing Dr. Notson was scheduled to examine the prisoner soon, wanted to get away before he arrived.[12]

The testimony of Mrs. Jackson and her daughters, the only eyewitnesses other than Brown questioned about the affair, was vague and evasive. They confirmed the presence of Owens, Harvey, Cavaness, and Crain but claimed that the soldiers fired first and denied knowledge of who had fired the fatal shots. Elizabeth, admitting Murray had dropped his gun without resistance, stated, "The other two would not surrender at all." She mused that she did not think "the boys would have hurt them . . . if they would have surrendered." No one asked her to reconcile this with the killing of Murray *after* he had dropped his gun. She closed by stating that she "did not want the soldiers killed" but "did not want them to get Jackson."[13]

Notson arrived soon after the departure of Jackson and his rescuers. While he was surveying the scene, James Jackson, a son of Jackson, appeared and was promptly arrested. Denying any knowledge of the rescue, he stated that he lived about a mile away, had heard shooting, and had ridden up to determine the cause. Notson placed him in custody and set out for Fort McKavett, arriving about ten that evening. Late the following day, Private Brown also reached the fort. He had hidden until dark and then had walked to the ranch of Irish-born Patrick Fields, who lived about nine miles below Fort McKavett. Fields loaned him a horse for the trip to the fort.[14]

Mackenzie was furious. Determined to make an example of the Jacksons, he requested authorization to offer a reward for the killers. After a small detachment led by Bullis determined that the fugitives had fled the country, it burned the Jackson homestead and placed Mrs. Jackson and her daughter Henrietta McTyre under arrest. According to the *San Antonio Daily Herald*, Mackenzie swore that he would "have the man Jackson and the rescuing party, or burn down the country."[15]

Needless to say, recollections of these events form a bizarre tangle of exaggeration, fabrication, and occasional fact. The names of the rescuers were recalled precisely, and such physical descriptions as the scar on the cheek of Peter Crain match those of the contemporary accounts. In contrast, the recollections of the rescue itself were bizarre.

Most puzzling, the timing of the rescue, which occurred about four in the afternoon, became hopelessly confused. John Warren Hunter recalled that the settlers were already at the dance in Menard when news arrived that Jackson was under guard in his home and would be removed the following day to Fort McKavett. The men held their council of war and decided to risk the danger that additional killings might "arouse [the] . . . brutal spirit of revenge" in the black soldiers to the point that they would "throw off all restraints, defy their officers, and wreak a horrible vengeance upon the helpless" settlers. While the rescue party carried out its mission, the others danced out the night to the tune—Hunter must have had a grotesque sense of humor—of "Run Nigger, Run, the Patrol Will Catch You."[16]

The myth makers varied considerably in describing the rescue scene. Hunter placed it in the dead of night, with two soldiers asleep beside a fire just outside the Jacksons' doorway and a third on guard inside. According to another source, the soldier inside was telling Jackson "he wished he was at McKavett so he could write a letter to his girl, 'but she ain't no white girl, boss.'" A third version was equally vivid: Jackson, coughing up blood, lay near the fireplace, his family nearby, while standing over them were *two* soldiers, bayonets poised.[17] Although dramatic license may explain the placing of the rescue at night, it may also have been done to explain Brown's escape.

Contemporary accounts said nothing about Jackson's participating in the gunfight. Brown claimed Mrs. Jackson fired the fatal shot at Marshall; the Jackson women named only George Harvey as shooting at the soldiers. One recollection, in contrast, stated that the soldiers were shot from ambush and had no chance to return the fire. Two others claimed Jackson was the avenger. According to one, Henrietta slipped a pistol to her father; the other, told to J. Evetts Haley, named Elizabeth Jackson as the provider of the deadly firearm.[18]

Private Brown's escape also had several explanations. One account stated that when the initial shot bounced off the stock of his rifle and left him unharmed, he feigned death until he had a chance to escape to the river. Two recollections attributed his survival to the thickness of his skull. The bullet either glanced off, wounding him only slightly, or simply failed to penetrate and lodged just above the eye. According to the last account, Brown, after leaving the military, moved to San Angelo and years later had the bullet removed. Although the details sound authentic, it is pure fiction. There is no chance that Brown, in his deposition, and Mackenzie, in his report on the matter, would have failed to mention a wound.[19]

Exaggerations and falsehoods also characterize the recollections of the renewed manhunt. One account claimed that "seven full companies" combed the countryside. Another tale had Jackson concealing himself on "one of the many peaks" overlooking the road over which the scouts passed and occasionally shooting a soldier from ambush. "It is even asserted that the road from McKavett to Menardville is dotted with negro [sic] graves, victims of his terrible vengeance." As part of the relentless search, "Nearly all the men in the county" were arrested and taken to McKavett to see if Brown could identify them.

In reality, only Jackson's family and two others were held for any length of time. Their fate became a key part of the legend. Elizabeth and her children were held in a "cold, dankish" guardhouse. When she requested blankets and a chicken to make some broth, Mackenzie "cursed her and told her to go to hell." Fortunately, citizens were allowed to provide food and blankets. Jackson meanwhile eluded capture with the aid of food supplied by neighbors.[20]

Since the frontier code of honor demanded retribution for all wrongs, Mackenzie could not be allowed to go unpunished for his misdeeds. After considering an assault on Fort McKavett, Jackson reputedly sent Mackenzie a message threatening retaliation if his wife or daughter "suffered any indignation at his hands."[21] Peter Robertson, briefly held as a possible accomplice, later claimed that he confronted Mackenzie because the colonel had "placed nigger soldiers to watch my home" and had threatened to burn it. Supposedly shaking his finger "within three inches" of Mackenzie's nose, Robertson told the officer that he sympathized with Jackson and thought the killings justified, but that he had nothing to do with them. Mackenzie's hands and knees allegedly trembled, and his "voice betrayed his fright." Completely subdued, he changed his demeanor and assured Robinson that he believed he was innocent. Soon thereafter, Robertson recalled, Mackenzie released the prisoners and "set up the cigars and champagne for the crowd."[22] The account is too preposterous to warrant mention except to illustrate the ability of settlers to fabricate lies about the misbehavior of black troops and their officers.

In reality, the search for Jackson was neither protracted nor massive. Although catching the killers was important to Mackenzie, he had too few resources and too many distractions for an extensive search. Indian raids intensified. One party even struck the ranch of Patrick Fields, who had befriended Private Brown, and absconded with Mrs. Fields. Scouting for Indians took priority over a manhunt for Jackson. Mackenzie also had to maintain detachments at Mason to control the rustling. Even worse, the months of campaigning had taken such a heavy toll on the command's horses that he had to dispatch detachments composed of "infantry because . . . the cavalry horses . . . are nearly worn out by much scouting."

In addition, Mackenzie had a depleted officer corps. E. M. Heyl, commander of one of the two cavalry troops at McKavett, had been wounded in an Indian encounter and was on an indefinite leave. Lieutenant Frederick Smith, exhausted by constant scouting, facing charges that he had mishandled regimental supplies, and depressed because his wife was leaving him, committed suicide. Meanwhile, Mackenzie had turned on his most reliable subordinate, Captain Carroll. Two days after the inquest into the deaths of Marshall and Murray, Carroll was placed under arrest. Soon thereafter, Lieutenant W. W. Tyler was also confined. Although there is no proof that Carroll's arrest was a result of his handling of Jackson's capture, the timing is obviously suggestive. With all these distractions, the Fort McKavett garrison was incapable of any type of manhunt remotely resembling that described by the frontier myths.[23]

Mackenzie did keep Elizabeth Jackson, her daughter Henrietta, Billy Epps, and Tull Smith in a guardhouse for more than a month. After Smith and Epps secured their release by posting bonds, Henrietta was released and Elizabeth Jackson was turned over to a civilian court at Mason. In addition, Mackenzie himself received a leave of absence.[24]

His departure was made easier by a break in the search for Jackson. In early April, a rancher named James F. Allen reported that Jackson, Cavaness, and five or six others were at a ranch about forty-five miles southeast of Fort McKavett.[25] He added that they were rounding up cattle for a drive to New Mexico.

Captain Carroll, recently released from confinement, was scouting in the area for Indians. He dispatched Lieutenant Bullis with nine troopers to check out the report. Although Jackson escaped, the soldiers killed Stephen Cavaness as he tried to elude them.[26]

On 19 April, one day after he had the satisfaction of announcing Cavaness's death, Mackenzie left Fort McKavett, not to return until the end of the year. Soon afterwards, the restoration of civil government ended martial law. In June 1871, Humpy Jackson posted bond of two thousand dollars in Menard and stood trial. Needless to say, he had nothing to fear from a civilian court.[27] Thus ended one of the most infamous causes célèbres of the Texas frontier.

The willingness to forget every positive act of the black troopers in 1869 and 1870 while grossly distorting the saga of Humpy Jackson graphically illustrates the power of racism to dictate memory. In 1870, several residents openly expressed their gratitude to Mackenzie and the buffalo soldiers. Typical of such letters was one from Mason that closed with the observation that what Texas needed was "more Mackenzies to guard her frontier, and a sufficient number of soldiers of the same material [black troops] to guard it with."[28] The appreciative tenor of such observations could not have been in sharper contrast to the mean-spirited diatribes indulged in a half-century later. John Warren Hunter, the most industrious collector of frontier tales, wrote that the "cruelty" of the Indians was "as tender mercies" compared to that of the black cavalrymen, who "would so unblushingly disgrace the uniform of a United States soldier."[29]

Instead of making a folk hero out of a demented killer, historians should place their focus on the cavalrymen who endured the taunts and harassments of the people they were sent to protect. Every trooper knew that he could at any moment join Private Boston Henry, killed without warning by an assassin. Each also might be faced with the same dilemma as Corporal Marshall and Privates Murray and Brown, who refused to abandon their post even when their position had become hopeless. Texas simply was not a nice place for black troopers.

7

Torment and Torture

Captain Ambrose Hooker and the Agony of E Troop

If the men of E Troop assumed that the departure of E. M. Heyl in August 1867 would be the end of their troubles, they were sadly mistaken. They had endured Heyl for a matter of months; their new commander, Captain Ambrose E. Hooker, although not quite as violent, would curse and abuse them for years.

Hooker, like many officers, turned to the military because of the Civil War. Reared in western New York, he studied law until, at the age of twenty, he moved to California in 1852. Employed by a bank, he hobnobbed with the state's elite, dabbled in mining investments, and toyed with politics. At the 1861 Democratic state convention, he declined nomination for state treasurer "when a nomination was equivalent to an election." Instead, he served on the staff of Governor Leland Stanford until war intruded.[1]

Helping to organize the Sixth California Infantry, Hooker became its lieutenant colonel in early 1863. Except for an expedition against an Indian camp on the Sacramento River, he commanded the Beancia Barracks in San Francisco until the war closed. Although he had never been near a battle, he was nominated for a brevet brigadier generalship.[2]

By the war's end, his financial situation had collapsed. When his banking and political friends, always willing to furnish endorsements, did not proffer a suitable job, he applied for a commission, "preferably as a colonel," in the regular army. In June 1866 he was commissioned lieutenant in the Eighth Cavalry.

Desperate for promotion, he secured a captaincy by transferring to the Ninth Cavalry. Before embarking for New Orleans, he tarried in San Francisco long enough to marry Delia A. Bird. When he reached Louisiana, General L. H. Rousseau detained him in New Orleans to serve as his assistant adjutant general. This allowed the newlyweds to enjoy the city's pleasures until Rousseau's sudden death in 1869. Ordered to join his troop at Fort Concho, Texas, he arrived on 30 August.[3]

In the meantime, things had improved for E Troop under the leadership of First Lieutenant David Cortelyou. In 1868, fifty-one men in the Ninth died of disease; only one was from Troop E. Only two members of the troop deserted during the year. Colonel Hatch inspected the troop in October and gave it a solid array of excellents. Even the convicted mutineers had returned from confinement and were quietly serving out their terms. Instead of being applauded for his performance, Cortelyou was dismissed during the army's 1870 reduction, the victim of another of Hatch's unfortunate personnel decisions.[4]

Hooker mistrusted the black troopers from the beginning. Years later, he claimed that a servant had described the mutiny at San Pedro Springs and had quoted "one of the men" as saying he "had better go slow as he has a hard crowd to deal with." He was especially dismayed that the man who had "split open the skull" of Lieutenant Griffin had rejoined the troop. It seemed that a "spirit of insubordination" had been "handed down with the traditions of the Company." Each day, Hooker became more certain that blacks were a "treacherous . . . race utterly devoid of . . . honorable or truthful instincts." To control them, he resolved to be "anything but agreeable."[5]

For a time, all seemed normal. Three weeks after he reported for duty, he participated in Captain John Bacon's expedition against the Comanches. While Bacon was decisively defeating the Indians on 28 October, E Troop was left behind to guard the supply train. In a second attack the next morning, the troop had one casualty. Hooker's horse stumbled and rolled over on him, resulting in a "severe contusion on the head."[6]

In view of his subsequent behavior, the head injury possibly aggravated an existing problem that had subjected him to attacks of neuralgia and migraine headaches for the previous year. It seems possible that the fall contributed to the temper displays that would mar his relations with superiors and subordinates alike.

Racism and head contusions were not the sole causes of his frustration. For years he had mingled with the elite; now he was isolated at remote outposts, his wife unwilling to join him, and surrounded by soldiers he despised. He was also confronted by a vindictive commander, Lieutenant Colonel William Shafter.

Hooker's nemesis was a perfectionist from Michigan. After receiving a Medal of Honor as a major in the Nineteenth Michigan Infantry, he was given command of the Seventeenth U.S. Colored Infantry. In a few months he whipped his recruits into such effective fighters that General George Thomas called him "one of the most successful officers who has ever [served] in the Colored regiments." After the Civil War, Shafter was assigned to the Forty-first Infantry. That regiment was reorganized as part of the Twenty-fourth Infantry in late 1869, and Shafter assumed command of the Twenty-fourth at Fort Concho in January 1870.[7]

Sharp-tongued and vindictive, Shafter was capable of cursing officers who did not measure up to his standards. It was only a question of time before he crossed swords with Hooker. At the end of February, Dr. Notson wryly commented that the "overcrowded condition of the officers' quarters" and some "misunderstandings concerning duties and orders" had resulted in a number of disgraceful charges. Two officers had been placed under arrest, and "more have been threatened with it."[8]

Needless to say, one of the two arrested was Hooker. Shafter was irked because Hooker had allowed Comanches to steal four of his horses. The two also had a brawl concerning the procedures for securing grain rations for Hooker's private horse. Ordered to make a daily requisition, Hooker complained through channels to departmental headquarters. Shafter forwarded the complaint to allow the commanding general to judge "the spirit of insubordination" that marked Hooker's conduct. To Shafter, the issue was simply, "Shall I or Captain Hooker command this post?"[9]

Hooker's arrest ended when illness temporarily confined him to his quarters. Immediately concluding that the captain was "incompetent for active service," Shafter forwarded Dr. Notson's observations on the matter to headquarters. When this produced no result, he ordered Hooker to lead a scout to the upper Colorado. His persecution complex more active than ever, the captain exclaimed that Shafter was "sending me out . . . to get me out of the way, and it is a damned cowardly act." When he demanded an audience, he was cooly told that Shafter had "gone fishing."

Denouncing his superior as a coward and "God damned whelp," he challenged him to fisticuffs before finally leaving on the scout.[10]

Hooker spent three weeks traversing the upper Concho and Colorado Valleys before returning to the fort in early May. He was immediately placed under arrest. When E Troop was transferred to Fort Clark the following month, Notson noted that Hooker had the "unpleasant distinction of leaving Ft. Concho in arrest." At Clark, Hooker was tried for insubordination. When the court-martial convened in July, he admitted he used abusive language and challenged his commander. Although the tribunal characterized Shafter's behavior as undignified, it found Hooker's actions extremely "contumacious" and "insubordinate." Unfortunately, numerous testimonials to his prior good behavior allowed him to escape with only a suspension from rank for three months and a reprimand in orders.[11]

For the men of E Troop, his absence was a relief, since Lieutenant Clarence Stedman shared none of Hooker's racism. One month after Hooker returned to duty in early 1871, five men were in confinement and three others had deserted. Most, however, marked time until their enlistments expired in October. Only six men reenlisted.[12]

Although specifics are lacking, discontent remained high. Since Fort Clark housed several companies, there was less opportunity for blatant mistreatment. In addition, Hooker was often absent. In August 1871 and again the following May, he was sick in quarters for extended periods. Detached service took him away for another six months. In April 1873 he received a medical leave that was extended to June 1874.

Hooker used his leave to make an all-out effort to secure a transfer to the Pay Department. Bankers and politicians from California and Nevada, including Governor Stanford, two U.S. senators, several congressmen, and thirty legislators endorsed his efforts. Although the "leading men of New York" also urged his transfer, it was futile. In June 1874, his mood worse than ever, he returned to Fort Clark.[13]

During the Red River War of 1874–75, E Troop participated in the expedition commanded by Lieutenant Colonel George P. Buell. In a rare moment of glory, Hooker led a successful charge that routed a party of Indians, killing one.[14] The success did nothing to improve his treatment of his troopers. Although they complained to Buell, "nothing was ever done." Hooker later said that Buell considered the complaint to be evidence of a "spirit of insubordination bordering on mutiny." According to him, several noncommissioned officers who had taken "a leading part were summarily reduced to the ranks and rigid discipline was enforced." Neither he nor Buell court-martialed anyone or reported any untoward incidents.[15]

In late 1875, E Troop was transferred to Fort Wingate, the westernmost post in New Mexico. There, Hooker's treatment of his troopers aroused the sympathy of the Fifteenth Infantry's sergeant major. Learning of this, Hooker charged that the sergeant major was continually playing checkers with E Troop's noncommissioned officers and "commenting on" their complaints. When Hooker sought to place him under arrest for "encouraging unrest," Major Nathan Osburne, the post commander, released the sergeant and placed Hooker under arrest. After Osburne had confined Hooker for three months while demanding a court-martial, Hatch abruptly quashed the imbroglio. Faced with an Apache outbreak, he freed Hooker and sent him on a prolonged scout.[16]

For both the troopers and Hooker, the scout was a nightmare. Suffering from migraines, burdened by the cost of supporting an absentee wife, and resentful of being denied the Pay Department position, he vented his frustration on the soldiers.

Private Thornton Jackson was one of many subjected to one of his outbursts. He was packing the captain's tent when Hooker exclaimed that he had never seen a "nigger who could put anything straight." When Jackson looked up in shock, Hooker emitted a spate of curses. A New Englander with only a few months' service, Jackson still had some illusions: "Captain, what do you take me for? I am a soldier and want to be treated as such." He was thereupon "bucked and gagged."

After he was trussed, a guard was preparing a gag when Hooker interceded: "My foot is a good enough gag for the god damned dog." Jackson defiantly replied that he was "no more of a dog" than the captain. Hooker kicked him three times in the neck, saying, "If I uttered another word he would kick every god damned tooth in my head down my throat." Jackson spent the next five days walking, hands bound, handcuffed to a wagon.[17]

The campaign was also hellish for Hooker. He was filled with self-pity at being "alone in the field" with untrustworthy soldiers. Unease grew into fright when he emerged from his tent one morning to see an ominous notice posted on a tree. Scrawled on a grotesquely carved slab of wood was a warning that he had "better go slow" if he wanted to get back to the post.[18]

Until late 1876, the lieutenants in E Troop had demonstrated little of Hooker's bigotry. This changed when F. Beers Taylor, described by his previous commander as so worthless that "his presence with a company is an injury rather than a benefit," discovered he could attain a promotion to first lieutenant by switching places with W. W. Tyler of the Ninth Cavalry.[19] Though often at odds with Hooker, Taylor shared his contempt for blacks.

In 1878, E Troop participated in an expedition into southwestern Colorado. Fortunately for the troopers, Hooker and Taylor spent most of their energy fighting each other. While reprimanding Taylor for failing to pay for a horse taken for his personal use, Hooker resorted to "personal language." Taylor, deeming it a "premeditated insult," sought revenge. The next morning, "publicly . . . and to his face," he called Hooker a "contemptible puppy, liar and coward," slapped him, and challenged him to fight.[20]

Charged with insubordination, he "communicated" his own set of charges against Hooker to officers throughout the regiment. Hatch, confronted with Indian uprisings and civil disorders, was enraged by their antics. Excoriating them for a "disgusting broil . . . unworthy of gentlemen," he ordered Taylor to pay $120 for the horse and each to apologize for his actions. They complied grudgingly, still squabbling over whether the initial outburst was premeditated.[21]

Although Hooker and Taylor reconciled, it was of no benefit to the troopers. Hooker lashed them with whip and tongue to "impress on them the difference between soldiers and 'Cornfield Niggers.'" He constantly berated them for ignorance, but detested most the better educated.

George Nance, an Ohioan with ten years of service, and Hartley Crawford, a South Carolinian in his first term, were his prime villains. Hooker charged that Nance was the "agitator and malcontent of long standing" who had been responsible for his arrest at Fort Wingate in 1876. He also resented the esteem Nance enjoyed among his comrades, who considered him "something of an oracle." Worst of all, Nance acted as if he was the "champion of his race . . . engaged in what he deems to be the amelioration of its present condition." Describing Crawford as a "dead beat malingerer," Hooker complained that he, too, was esteemed by his fellows because he could "read and write well." Worse, the men believed Crawford was "much abused" by the captain.[22]

Nance's statements during an investigation of Hooker's actions suggest intelligence and a philosophical nature. After listing several specific abuses, he stressed Hooker's unfairness and refusal to accord his troopers any respect: "When I have done my best, I have been reprimanded as freely as if the reverse had been the case." Instead of "elevating" the men, Hooker seemingly sought to keep them "in ignorance" and berated them as "brutes."

Specific incidents flowed freely from other soldiers. Corporal Allen Foster recalled an especially vicious slander: A "nigger has as much business to be a soldier as a cur dog to be a saint."[23] He and some comrades, while on patrol, had fired on a squirrel—"as there had been no orders to the contrary." Hooker cursed them and ordered each to carry a forty-pound log while walking a beat.

Their punishment was mild compared to that of Corporal David Peters for a similar incident. While he was leading a cattle-driving detachment, some of the men spotted a flock of turkeys. Without asking his permission, they opened fire. Holding Peters responsible, Hooker called him "a damned idiot," ordered a sergeant to cut off his chevrons, and said, "The damned dog shall carry the turkey until it rots on his back." After Peters was handcuffed, the turkey was tied on his back. He had to walk a beat with it dangling behind him from 2 P.M. until taps that night and again the next morning until 9 A.M.[24]

In 1879, E Troop was stationed at Ojo Caliente, a post located in western New Mexico on the reservation of the Mimbres Apaches. Two years earlier, the Indian Bureau had insisted on moving the Mimbres to the San Carlos Reservation in the Arizona desert. As Hatch had warned, it was impossible to keep them there. After a flight in early 1879, their leader Victorio seemed agreeable to moving to the Mescalero reservation in southeastern New Mexico until he heard he might be tried for the murder of civilians. In August, desperate and confused, he vanished into the mountains with no way to sustain his band except by raiding.

Although news of his flight reached Ojo Caliente, Hooker paid little heed. His command, with fewer than sixty soldiers, simply marked time with routine duties. Ordinarily, a summer monsoon brought relief to the parched mountains, but in 1879 it remained so dry that securing forage for the horses was difficult. Each day they had to be taken to meadows out of sight of the post to graze. Although it should have been obvious that the herd might tempt such adept thieves as the Mimbres, Hooker seemed unconcerned. He normally assigned eight men to guard the horse herd; without explanation, he reduced the number to five. Incredibly, he refused to allow the guards to carry carbines or put saddles and bridles on their mounts. The revolvers, useful only at short range, would be no match for Apache rifles, while the lack of saddles and bridles would make it impossible to escape. Hooker claimed his decision was for the horses' welfare. Saddles might cause sores; bridles would prevent them from grazing. For the guards, his decision was a death sentence.

Although the herd was grazed less than two miles from the fort, a ridge placed it out of sight and would muffle the sound of gunshots. In accordance with orders, one herdsman was placed on "the nearest, highest hill," and another, mounted, moved among the grazing horses. The others picketed their mounts so "they would be handy on the approach of danger" and waited until it was time to drive the herd in.

Hooker changed the guard daily. On 4 September, Sergeant Silas Chapman was in charge. One of more than a dozen South Carolinians who had joined the troop in 1875, he had only recently been promoted. So conscientious that he had saved more than three hundred dollars during his brief service, he probably followed orders to the letter. Of the others, only West Indian–born Abram Percival had more than one tour of duty under his belt. Two, Silas Graddon and William Humphrey, were in their fourth years of enlistment; Lafayette Hooke, a twenty-one-year-old mulatto "waiter" from North Carolina, was the greenest recruit in the company, with only a few weeks' service to his credit.[25]

Whether the herders were as vigilant as possible was probably unimportant. The abundance of arroyos, brush, and boulders made it easy for Apaches to infiltrate "until the herd was completely enveloped." The Indians struck just as the men were preparing to start homeward. The three on foot were killed by rifle fire before they could even mount their horses. The other two tried to escape "towards the main valley but were hemmed in and killed." Although the herd should have been back at the post by 5 P.M., it was dark before Hooker dispatched a search party.[26]

As the magnitude of the loss, five men killed and sixty-eight horses lost, became apparent, Hooker furiously blamed the herders. Showing no remorse for the deaths, he raved that the "God damned cowardly sons of bitches . . . were all asleep." Either that, or they had been gambling instead of keeping watch.

The loss of the horses removed any trace of civility. Lining his troops up, he ranted that he wished "every God damned nigger was in hell and that the Indians would kill every God damned one of them." These tirades reinforced the men's conviction that he was responsible for the deaths. Sending out only five men and denying them carbines, saddles, and bridles seemed too deliberate. Even First Sergeant James Williams, a third-enlistment Louisianan who usually supported Hooker, conceded that "the soldiers needed the saddles and carbines." On the day of the raid, Private John Howard had overheard a guide warn Hooker that Victorio was in the vicinity. "The Captain did nothing but walk up and down on his porch for some time after." Also preying on their minds was resentment that neither Hooker nor any other officer had ever visited a herding detachment to examine its situation.

Hooker's rage did not abate. Although he had only one grave dug for the five bodies, he ordered it to be made extra large because if "any of us spoke he would have another funeral." For weeks after the raid, Ojo Caliente was virtually cut off from the outside world. Every few days Hooker dispatched a squad down the canyon to Cañada Alamosa to pick up dispatches. Every man chosen knew he might be ambushed and killed. Abram Booth, from the same home town as Sergeant Chapman, was one of five chosen for the ride two days after the massacre. Bitterly, he recalled Hooker's remark while he was issuing the orders that they were "the very crowd I want the Indians to get and kill." Booth's language was restrained compared to that of Private Isom Green, also chosen for the mission. He claimed Hooker said they were "the five sons of bitches which he wanted . . . the Indians to kill—god damn the dirty niggers." He continued ranting that he would send out mail parties "until the Indians had killed every god damned one of them."[27]

Hooker almost got his wish. There were several close scrapes with Indians. When Apaches attacked a mail detachment returning to the post on 29 September, only the prompt arrival of Sergeant Williams with a small detachment enabled it to reach the fort. One party in late September reached Cañada Alamosa safely but was unable to return because of an Indian attack.[28]

Fearful for their lives, seventeen men dispatched an anonymous letter to Colonel Hatch describing Hooker's actions. Fifteen were in their first term of enlistment; unlike the old hands, they still believed justice might be possible. Private Booth served as the penman as they charged Hooker with responsibility for the loss of the horses and the deaths of the men. Although such complaints were usually ignored, Hatch and General Pope were so upset over the lost horses that they decided to investigate.

Although a board of inquiry did not specifically condemn Hooker, it questioned his judgment in depriving the herders of carbines, saddles, and bridles. It also criticized his failure to inspect or visit the herders and his inadequate response to the rumors of Victorio's presence. Presented their criticism, Hooker professed he had been exonerated. He and the board simply had "differences of opinion." Hatch, however, was not satisfied.

In December, Hatch dispatched Charles Steelhammer, a tough-minded infantry captain, to Ojo Caliente. Steelhammer spent two days interviewing each enlisted man as well as Taylor, Surgeon A. W. Sewell, and the citizen who had warned of Victorio's presence. After recording each statement, he asked Hooker to respond.

Steelhammer, describing blacks as "excitable, imaginative and disposed to exaggeration," refused to believe what he was hearing until he interviewed Hooker. As the captain denied almost every statement in the men's depositions, and Taylor and the post surgeon supported him, Steelhammer would have accepted their version if Hooker could have concealed his prejudice. Until he joined the Ninth Cavalry, he mused, he had never been "considered profane or coarse." After discovering that blacks could not "appreciate refined English," he had resorted to the use of "strong emphatic language" to "impress on them the difference between soldiers and 'Cornfield Niggers.'" He branded them as "natural born thieves and liars" and admitted that after the loss of the horses he had declared he did not want replacements "until I had something besides Apes and Baboons, Chimpanzees and Monkeys, Kangaroos and Orangatangs [sic] for soldiers." Steelhammer could only conclude that the statement corroborated the "essential part of the troopers' allegations."

The investigator deduced that Hooker's intense prejudice against "the colored race as soldiers" might be related to his "nervous prostration." As a remedy, he suggested stationing Hooker at a post where he would be under a senior officer. "It would make life easier for him and . . . more satisfactory to his men."

After concluding the interviews, Steelhammer surveyed the scene of the attack and absolved the slain herders. With carbines and "from behind shelter," they might have held off the Indians, but this was "extremely doubtful." Given the terrain, "the most vigilant sentry could not have discovered the approach of the Indians." The narrow valley where the horses were grazing was such a natural trap that "only an imbecile would have . . . [sent] a herd into such a place."[29]

Many of the men who spoke to Steelhammer forfeited their careers. Each interview, name attached, was shown to Hooker. To retaliate, he had merely to wait until their enlistments expired. Unfortunately, this occurred for more than twenty during early 1880. Since anyone not in good standing was ineligible to reenlist, the captain killed the careers of Privates Nance, Crawford, Booth, and a dozen others by writing "none" as an evaluation of their character. In addition, this ensured they would be unavailable to testify in subsequent investigations.[30]

With the Apache campaign demanding all his manpower, Hatch gave Hooker a chance to redeem his reputation. After receiving fifty-one mounts in December, the captain was ordered into the field. His performance was miserable. Although his horses were fresh, and his command marched only 250 miles without encountering an Indian during January, he had to shoot six horses that broke down, and only ten mounts remained serviceable at the month's close. In contrast, Captain Carroll, whose troop marched 400 miles, engaged in two battles, lost two men killed, and had to destroy seven horses, reported at month's end that all of his remaining mounts were serviceable.[31]

In March 1880, Hatch organized three battalions to move against the Apaches. Morrow and Carroll commanded two, and Hooker, in compliance with seniority, the third. As Hooker never filed a report on his command's operations, little is known of its movements. A few vignettes suggest his erratic leadership. Although the Indian scouts who accompanied many expeditions were noted for their trustworthiness, the ones assigned to him deserted on 13 March, taking their government-issued guns and gear. Ten days later, a citizen complained to Governor Lew Wallace that Hooker was camped on the Rio Grande, "where there was no danger of seeing Indians." When the citizen reported the theft of 120 horses by Apaches, the captain refused to pursue.[32]

While Morrow and Carroll each engaged the Indians in several hard-fought battles, Hooker never came near an Apache. On 15 April, Hatch placed him in arrest and merged his command with Morrow's. Although released within a few days, his career had ended.[33]

Despite his concentration on the campaign, Hatch had not forgotten Steelhammer's report. He considered a court-martial but concluded that it would be too costly and time-consuming. Instead, he warned Hooker that no amount of "trouble or expense" would prevent a trial if his abuse was repeated.[34]

Hatch was probably influenced by Hooker's poor health. In July a surgeon reported that the captain was suffering from neuralgic attacks during which his eyes were "rendered . . . useless." Unless he received "prompt and vigorous treatment under the most favorable circum-stances," his eyesight would be destroyed.[35] In August he received a leave of absence.

Under the command of Lieutenant Taylor, matters temporarily improved. Transferred to Fort Cummings shortly before the arrival of President Rutherford Hayes, who was making the first presidential visit to New Mexico, Troop E was designated as the honor guard for the occa-sion. What should have been its proudest moment ended in tragedy.

On the eve of the visit, Taylor discovered that Benjamin Hockins, a Kentuckian with fourteen years of unblemished service, was absent without leave. Hockins was located at a "photograph salon" set up for the presidential visit. Although he had earlier been seen drinking, he seemed quite sober. Taken before Taylor, he was ordered to be confined. As a corporal led him from the room, Hockins glanced at Taylor and asked to speak. The officer screamed: "Go on, you G–d d—d black son of a bitch. . . . I could, and will kill you!" Hockins refused to humble himself. He looked at Taylor and said, "I don't think it is right for an officer to call an enlisted man a G–d d—d black son of a bitch. My mother was black . . . but she was a lady and no bitch."

Losing all self-control, Taylor ordered the corporal to disarm the pris-oner and "knock him down." Although he claimed Hockins drew a gun and tried to fire, all other witnesses said the enlisted man surrendered it without resistance. As Taylor and the corporal "flung" Hockins to the ground, he pulled the officer down also. By this time Sergeant Williams began pistol whipping him. Infuriated "with the pain of these blows," Hockins cursed Taylor, calling him a "redheaded Southerner and bastard." He was carried to the guardhouse, still "cursing and crying."

The worst was yet to come. He was "gagged and bucked"—knees forced against his body while his cuffed hands were hooked in front of them with a strong stick "running through . . . to prevent the withdrawal of the arms." The gag, however, was too small to muffle his cries, which were so piercing that they were upsetting the horses stabled nearby.

Any remaining shred of Taylor's patience snapped as he exclaimed, "Will you stampede the herd, G–d d—n you, I'll spoil your countenance for you," and struck him "two or three blows on the head and face with the butt of a carbine, bringing it down vertically." Blood streaming down his face, Hockins ceased his struggles. He was held in double irons until his trial in February 1881.[36]

Although Hockins had nothing but "good" evaluations on his record, Taylor portrayed him as a disreputable soldier. He was helped in this by Hooker, who returned from his medical leave to castigate a buffalo soldier for one last time. During Hockins's first two enlistments, Hooker explained, he had been "relatively a good soldier," but afterwards he developed "vicious and insubordinate qualities, . . . bordering on mutiny." He had defied officers so often that Hooker also had been forced to buck and gag him and put him in irons.

In contrast, Hooker described Taylor, who had once slapped him and called him a "contemptible coward" in front of other officers, as being "very cool and deliberate." For the last time he rehashed his obsession that the "traditions" of the San Pedro Springs mutiny in 1867 still exerted "a great effect" on E Troop.

Unpersuaded by Hooker's rambling testimony, the court could hardly have denounced Taylor's behavior more severely. Hockins had been "docile" until he was provoked by "the most offensive . . . forms of insult of which the English language is capable," including an "insult to his color." In view of "his violent seizure and prostration, the beating with a pistol, his bucking, gagging and shackling; and lastly the blows on his head . . . with the heavy butt of a carbine," it was no wonder that he had "lost his sense of subordination" and retaliated with "insults equal in grossness to those by which he was driven into the outbreak."[37]

Hockins won sympathy, but little else. He had committed a capital offense, resisting and threatening an officer. With the importance of maintaining discipline outweighing any sense of justice, he was sentenced to be discharged and confined for a year at hard labor. After six months at Fort Leavenworth, however, he was pardoned and allowed to reenlist.

Soon after Hockins's conviction, charges were filed against Taylor. A court quickly found him guilty of using "profane and obscene" language on Hockins and striking the man with a carbine butt. After sentencing the lieutenant to be cashiered, the court suggested clemency because of his prior "good record." Accordingly, President Chester Arthur mitigated the sentence to a one-year suspension from rank with forfeiture of one-half his pay.[38]

After testifying against Hockins, Hooker resumed a leave which improved neither his physical nor mental condition. Finding his wife unbearable, he moved in with his brother William, who was operating a ranch in northern Nebraska. While he was sitting at the breakfast table on 20 January 1883, a stroke left him paralyzed, his "rigid face purple and eyes fixed." Five hours later he died.[39]

Not even in death did his tortured body find rest. His widow claimed his brother had poisoned him in order to take valuables he was supposedly carrying. In March, the body was exhumed and taken to O'Neil City, Nebraska, for tests.[40] These, of course, showed no signs of foul play. With his death, sixteen years of torment for Troop E had come to an end.

PART THREE

⚔

Years of Glory

1879–91

8

Major Guy Henry, Champion of the Buffalo Soldiers

The same seniority system that bedeviled Hatch with Nathan Dudley atoned with Major Guy V. Henry in June 1881. Unexcelled as an officer and a publicist, Henry, who had once rejected a commission in a black regiment,[1] would work tirelessly to convince the nation that African Americans made exceptional soldiers. No one, including Colonel Hatch, had a more positive impact on the regiment.

Henry was steered towards the army from the time he was born at Fort Smith, Arkansas, in 1839, son of a frontier officer. Steered by his mother towards a military career after his father died of cholera, he graduated from West Point during the opening weeks of the Civil War. After commanding an artillery battery in South Carolina for two years, he was placed in charge of the Fortieth Massachusetts Infantry. Transferred to Virginia, he participated in Grant's ill-advised assault on Cold Harbor, in which his gallantry was rewarded with a Medal of Honor.

Reverting to the rank of an artillery captain after the war, he found life in the coastal forts tedious. Always industrious and enterprising, he compiled a two-volume *Military Record of Civilian Appointments in the United States Army*, still used by researchers. Plagued by "ague and malaria" in the coastal forts, and anxious for a chance to prove his mettle in combat, he asked for a transfer "to some *white* cavalry unit" in the Southwest.[2] In September 1870 he was assigned to the Third Cavalry, based in Arizona. The following year, he commanded the expedition of Apache scouts that convinced the military hierarchy that they could be relied on in combat with their kinsmen.

Guy V. Henry, major, Ninth Cavalry, 1881–94. Courtesy of the National Archives, Washington, D.C.

Transferred to the Northern Plains in 1873, Henry would endure two harrowing brushes with death. At Camp Robinson, Nebraska, on 26 December 1874 he was ordered to search for prospectors reported to be in the Black Hills. Despite subzero temperatures, he scoured the hills' eastern base to their northern extremity. Finding no sign of intruders, he turned homeward and by 8 January was only a day's march away. One hour after breaking camp, a blizzard struck, cutting off vision and obliterating the trail. Henry ordered his men to dismount, hoping that walking would deter freezing. For hours they plodded on; as the weaker fell, "willing to die rather than make further effort," they were strapped to their horses and the forlorn march resumed. Facing "speedy destruction," he ordered everyone to mount and urge their horses forward at a gallop.

"We all knew," he later wrote, "that this was a race for life; we were helpless; . . . the instinct of our horses could alone save those of us who could hold out." Miraculously, the horses reached the cabin of a squatter and his Sioux wife. The entire command was welcomed into the hovel, where they waited for the storm to abate.[3]

Almost every man required medical care. Henry's wife scarcely recognize him: "His face was black and swollen. His men . . . slit his gloves into strips, each strip bringing a piece of flesh as it was pulled off." One finger had to be amputated, and the left hand remained too stiff for him to close his fingers.[4]

Henry did not return to duty until April 1876, just in time to participate in General Crook's expedition against the Sioux. On 17 June, on Rosebud Creek, a day's march south of the Little Big Horn, Crook collided with one of the most formidable and determined Indian forces ever assembled. Because of the rough terrain, Henry's battalion became dangerously isolated on the extreme left of Crook's lines. His men had driven the Sioux from two successive ridges when an order was received to retire.

The retreating hostiles, who had been luring him into a trap, swarmed to the attack. From "every ridge, rock and sagebrush," Crook's adjutant reported, they "poured a galling fire upon the retiring battalion," inflicting heavy casualties.[5] Striving to keep the retreat orderly, Henry was struck by a bullet that penetrated his cheekbone under the left eye, passed through the bridge of his mouth, and exited under the right eye. Blinded and choking from blood streaming into eyes and mouth, he continued to exhort his men until he slumped unconscious to the ground. As the Sioux pressed onward, men fought hand to hand over his body. After the Indians finally retired, he was brought to the rear and medicated as well as possible.[6]

His stoicism and will to live became enduring legends. Captain Anson Mills found him "covered with clotted blood, his eyes swollen so he could not see and a ghastly wound through both cheeks under the eyes." Mills asked, "Are you badly wounded?" Henry replied, "The doctors have just told me that I must die, but I will not." When correspondent John Finerty offered his own condolences to the stricken officer, he was stunned by the response: "'It is nothing,' Henry said, his voice soft but firm, 'For this are we soldiers!'"[7]

Henry next endured the agony of a two-hundred-mile return trek, lying on a tarpaulin slung between two pack mules, to Fort D. A. Russell. On one occasion the mules shied while rounding a boulder on the trail and pitched him down "among the rocks some twenty feet below." As rescuers gathered around him, Henry was asked inanely, "How did he feel." He responded through clenched teeth, "Bully! Never felt better in my life. Everybody is so kind." Captain A. H. Nickerson, recalling this conversation, stated that "this might possibly from his tone have included the sad-eyed mule which stood . . . nearby."[8]

Once more, Henry endured a lengthy struggle to regain his health. While recuperating, he testified before a congressional committee intent on reducing army expenditures. Although most witnesses sought to protect their own interests, he was most concerned for the welfare of noncommissioned officers. Asserting that the quality of NCOs was of utmost importance to a company, he advocated that their pay should be increased.[9] To improve their efficiency, he also published a booklet, an *Army Catechism for Non-Commissioned Officers and Soldiers*, which he set to work to promote with his usual energy and shrewdness.

After securing testimonials from several officers, including Colonels Hatch and Merritt, he enlisted the support of William C. Church, the editor and publisher of the influential *Army and Navy Journal.* Lauding the work in a review, Church offered to mail a copy to anyone who remitted twenty-five cents. Soon he was inundated with orders that "poured in . . . from all directions."[10] From then on Church would support Henry's many efforts to improve the army.

Shortly after the publication of the *Catechism*, Henry was promoted to major and assigned to the Ninth Cavalry. Assuming command of Fort Stanton in August 1881, he immediately organized a scout to prevent Mescalero warriors from joining Apache raiders in southwestern New Mexico. After three weeks in the field, he was so impressed with his troopers that he wrote the first of many dispatches printed unsigned by the *Army and Navy Journal.*

Displaying neither restraint nor subtleness, he asserted that his men were "cheerful, willing and obedient" soldiers who took such pride in their horses that "I have seen but one man lounging in his saddle." Deliberately challenging the myths propagated about black soldiers, he noted that "there is a class of citizen maligners, belonging to the 'secesh' element, who say 'niggers' can't fight. . . . They say they are hard on horses. . . . Cusack's company [G] at last muster had one sore backed horse, and had marched in September 900 miles." Choosing his words carefully, he stated his troopers were "as honest as others," seldom desert, and "drunken payday sprees are unknown." They were "neat, soldier-like, and very respectful."[11]

Lest readers think him one-sided, Henry included a few negatives. Some officers still had to make out their rolls instead of assigning the task to an enlisted man. The buffalo soldiers did have two weaknesses: gambling, "in which the white brother does not fall far behind," and a "fondness for the fair sex." The latter was a vice, Henry observed dryly, that a white soldier, "from his superior intellect, finds easy to overcome."

His next report described a recent recruit who "appeared to be white." Questioned, the man explained that he had served one term in a white regiment and, "being a sober man," had become "tired of doing guard and other duties for men who got drunk—particularly on pay days—and in the colored regiments there was no trouble in this respect."[12]

Henry knew that his troopers had access to the *Army and Navy Journal* through their post library and would see the "anonymous" dispatches. For men accustomed to being maligned in the media, it must have been exhilarating to see the words of praise. He never had to take them back.

Determined to drive home the virtues of his men, he was often guilty of overkill as he analyzed their characteristics. Today his generalizations would be scorned as patronizing stereotypes, but in the context of his time they were remarkable. His troopers were so happy that from "reveille till late at night, their laughter, cracking jokes, and singing songs is constantly heard." They were "never seen moping, or by themselves, but in crowds; bad and good weather alike they are cheerful." He found their respect for orders to be remarkable. When he first arrived, "it was not an uncommon thing to hear frequent oaths; it was ordered to be stopped, and since then, . . . I have heard not an oath." Concerning hygiene, he noted that after stable duty, "you will see them with their towels going to wash before meals, and in personal cleanliness they are very particular." They were also "the most generous devils I ever saw. I have seen them come into camp with a melon . . . and give away most of it, keeping for the owner the smallest share."[13]

Turning to the relations between the officers and enlisted men, he lauded Lieutenants Eugene Dimmick and Patrick Cusack as "superior" officers who were gathering "complete histories" of their noncommissioned officers by "questioning each man." All had engaged in the Apache war, and several had been "complimented in general orders" or recommended for certificates of merit or Medals of Honor. He closed his assessment by expressing regret that "years ago and not realizing their soldierly capabilities," he had refused "the command of them."[14]

After his command was transferred to Fort Sill, Indian Territory, his letters became less frequent. Always innovative, he soon evoked a "great rivalry" with a decree that the troop with the most men singled out for "cleanliness and soldier-like bearing" each month would be relieved of ten days of fatigue and police duty. In addition, the best marksman in each company was excused for three days and the best overall, for seven.[15]

In February 1882 he noted briefly that the post was lively as the "boys" were amusing themselves "with a series of hops" given in each company's barracks. In April he commended the command's excellent state of health. Out of a garrison of three hundred, not a single person had reported sick in twenty days. He attributed this to the consideration of the officers. In inclement weather, "tattoo roll calls" were conducted in quarters. Men were not "jerked out of hot rooms to stand shivering in the cold and go on sick report the next day."[16]

Always quick to broadcast tributes to his men, he provided the *Army and Navy Journal* with a letter written by "Judge Lewis," a "prominent Southern lawyer" who had visited Fort Sill. After watching the troops "marching . . . and going through the manual of arms," the judge declared that their precision would "convince the most prejudiced that the darkey makes a good soldier." The judge then opined that blacks were not "adapted to anything as [well as] being soldiers in the Regular Army." In relaying the assessment, Henry added a postscript: "What he says of the colored soldiers at Fort Sill . . . is well deserved."[17]

Henry's struggle to eradicate the stigma attached to service with black regiments was not without setbacks. In early 1883 he announced regretfully that Second Lieutenant Frank B. McCoy, a Georgian, had "gone back of the color line" by transferring to the Third Infantry. In addition, Lieutenant Philip Powell, a young Virginian in his second year of service, had "gotten demoralized" and was seeking a transfer to "something that has no color." Expressing regret at their loss, he asserted that "those of us who stick" believe we have "the best soldiers in the service."[18]

Despite his high regard for his men, Henry accepted many racist stereotypes, but never with malice. In answering a letter from S. C. Armstrong, the head of the Hampton Institute for Freedmen in Virginia, he revealed a number of racist assumptions: "If properly led, they will fight well: without such, they have not the staying power of the white man, nor his individuality when thrown upon his own resources. . . . [As] a result of slavery, . . . they are like children. They do not feel the importance of responsibility for property, and in this respect, are neglectful, causing loss to the Government. . . . They are inveterate gamblers, a matter hard to stop, in fact I have never attempted it."[19]

In 1883, Henry determined to improve the marksmanship of his troops, an area in which they had lagged. During March, all hands were employed laying out rifle ranges with "danger flags, wind vanes, etc." The reason, he confided, was that his troopers had been "'sat on' for not shooting, . . . and we propose to shoot or bust, to the satisfaction of the 'powers that be.'"[20]

By September he was convinced that marksmanship could be taught the same as the "manual of arms . . . from constant practice." For one to two hours a day, the troopers practiced aiming their rifles and then, once on the rifle ranges, "put in practice what has been learned in drill." When 274 out of 306 men in the garrison met the standard for designation as marksmen, he "modestly" proclaimed his command to be "the leading garrison" in the country in marksmanship, once more showing that "colored troops . . . [were] soldiers in every sense of the word."[21]

By now, Henry's public relations campaign had met with such success that the buffalo soldiers were at times portrayed as "super soldiers." In January 1885 the Ninth Cavalry was on the verge of conflict with a large party of Boomers in the Oklahoma Territory before the latter surrendered. Referring to the affair, the *Army and Navy Journal* editorialized that had fighting broken out, not a settler "would now be alive." Explaining that each trooper was a "marksman . . . who had no cause to reason why but to do and die," it concluded that "one darkey killed would have infuriated the remainder, and like the blood-hound you could not have held them. When once aroused, they are like the fiercest animals in their attacks."[22]

Taken to task for its outrageous statement, the *Army and Navy Journal* stated that the "bloodhound" characterization had come from "an officer belonging to a colored regiment [quite likely Henry]." It was only speculating what might "be expected if the Ninth was *ordered* into action." There was no intent to suggest they might get out of control or disobey orders.[23]

Unfortunately for the buffalo soldiers, Henry's success in improving their marksmanship led to his transfer. In October 1884 he was placed in charge of all rifle instruction in the Department of the Missouri. When the Ninth was transferred to the Wyoming-Nebraska frontier, he assumed the same responsibility for the Department of the Platte. To help with this, he produced another manual, *Target Practice, or Practical Information for the Rifle Range*, simple enough to be understood by anyone "anxious to learn." Challenging troop commanders, he declared that poor marksmanship was "evidence of either indifference or inefficiency." Once again, the *Army and Navy Journal*, asserting that the booklet "should be in the hands of every man who desires to become efficient in the use of the rifle," made it available for a "nominal price."[24]

In September 1889, Henry returned to regular duty, assuming command of Fort McKinney, Wyoming. Attending the annual departmental exercises at Camp George Crook, Nebraska, in which nine troops from the Ninth participated, he remarked that anyone who doubted the ability of the buffalo soldiers should have seen the "discipline, . . . dash, nerve, and good horsemanship" displayed in the drills.[25]

Avidly watching the exercises was Henry's fifteen-year-old son, Guy, Jr. A future commander of the U.S. Cavalry, he recalled that the exercises were so realistic that there were many hand-to-hand fights. Prisoners were stripped of all their weapons and "left to find their way back to camp." Needless to say, there was "much contention and controversy on the part of the officers."[26]

At Fort McKinney, Henry renewed his efforts to improve the morale and discipline of his troops. One of his pet projects was improving the canteen so that soldiers would have an opportunity after retreat to "get together for amusement." Adding a pool table, tenpin alley, and card tables to the inevitable bar, he requested ideas from "other canteens [that] have any points to give us." Soldiers needed on-post recreational outlets, he argued, because it was unnatural to expect "every man to go to his quarters and sit there . . . with nothing to do." As usual, he followed this up with the inevitable sermon: Officers who "look into every detail of a soldier's life, have few desertions and have men who will follow them into the deadly breach."[27]

In November, Henry revealed that he allowed every man except ten in each troop and those on duty to be free "to go without asking from retreat till taps." Almost all chose to spend their leisure hours having "a good time at the post in their club rooms" instead of frequenting the dives in nearby Buffalo. Then he attached his moral: "The more freedom you give men, consistent with discipline, the better soldiers."[28]

The following January, he pronounced the experiment of giving his troops more freedom a success. Although anyone absent without permission after 11 P.M. was placed in the guardhouse, there were few confinements because of the privileges granted and the canteen. Unauthorized absences had virtually ended.

With the beginning of the Ghost Dance movement in the autumn of 1890, Troops D, F, I, and K of the Ninth, under Henry's command, constituted the first detachment sent to the Pine Ridge Agency. As tensions mounted, Henry drilled his men incessantly to ensure they could handle any task. Soon the precision of his drills captured such admiration that a correspondent, signing himself "Infantry," was left in obvious awe: "At the blowing of a whistle, in a moment's notice a cloud of skirmishers are formed, representing the four sides of a square, bringing a fire in all directions, and being able to move similarly—fighting mounted or dismounted. A second whistle, the original formation is made." They also drilled "moving on a position" by successive rushes by dismounted squadrons, each charge covered by volleys fired by the other squadrons.[29]

Another observer claimed the buffalo soldiers possessed a unique advantage over white troops. The Ghost Dancers feared the black soldiers because the "doctrine of the New Messiah has it that all the whites are to be destroyed but, as the Negro is by virtue of his epidermis, outside the category of the doomed, the red man regards him with a good

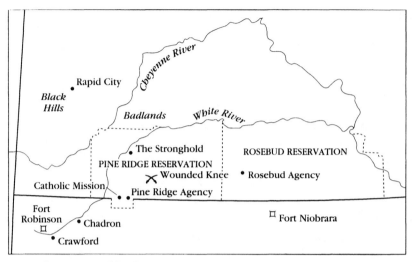

Sioux Campaign, 1890–91

deal of awe when the fight is on."[30] He then suggested that the army should bring in additional black troops.

Henry's opportunity to lead his men into action came on Christmas Eve when General Brooke ordered him to intercept Big Foot's band, which had eluded Lieutenant Colonel E. V. Summer, before it could join the bands of Short Bull and Kicking Bird holed up in a "stronghold" in the Badlands. With his usual energy, Henry covered fifty miles in an all-night march, reaching the vicinity of Short Bull's camp by daybreak. Although Big Foot was not found, Henry's sudden approach induced many of the recalcitrants to return to the agency. Henry's Sioux scouts reported that Short Bull's followers had said, "We give up; we are afraid of those black devils."[31]

Following this success, the buffalo soldiers spent four days combing the rugged countryside, unaware that Big Foot was proceeding forlornly towards the agency. By chance, instead of Henry's well-disciplined troopers the refugees met the Seventh Cavalry under Colonel James Forsyth, a career staff officer whose years of paper shuffling were poor preparation for Indian warfare. When Forsyth botched the delicate chore of disarming them, the bloodbath of Wounded Knee ensued.

About 9 P.M. on 30 December, as Henry's command was bedding down after a forty-mile-trek through the Badlands, a messenger arrived with news of Wounded Knee and orders for them to return to Pine Ridge. Tents "went down like a flash," wagons were hastily packed, and "every man sprang to his horse." Within forty minutes of the messenger's arrival, the troops, "wrapped to the eyes" in shaggy buffalo coats and fur caps, set out "into the inky darkness in the face of a biting wind that sifted the newly fallen snow in the eyes of officers and privates alike." They made the return ride to the agency at a trot so jolting that many were attacked with nausea; Henry deemed that gait the least damaging to horses. When they arrived about 5:30 the next morning, some were "asleep in their saddles from sheer exhaustion."[32] They had barely unsaddled when Corporal William Wilson brought word that Henry's wagon train, trailing the command under the escort of Captain Loud's Troop D, was under attack some four miles away. After two Indian scouts had refused Loud's order to ride for help, Wilson stepped forward. The Sioux gave chase and almost succeeded in cutting him off from the agency. For his bravery he became the last buffalo soldier to earn the Medal of Honor for service in the Indian Wars.[33]

Henry immediately led his exhausted command to the relief of the wagons, dispersing the Sioux with one "irresistible charge." Together, wagons and troopers returned to the agency, where the men, almost constantly in the saddle for thirty hours, "stretched themselves on the ground and went to sleep."[34]

Their work was not over. The hostiles, chagrined at their setback, took out their frustration by setting fire to some out-buildings at the nearby Drexel Mission. Seeing the column of smoke, Brooke ordered Henry to investigate. This was too much. He explained that his men were too tired to "sit in their saddles" and that his horses were so spent they had lain down "as soon as they were tethered." When he requested two hours' rest for his command, Brooke ordered Forsyth's troopers of the Seventh to proceed to the mission.

Through incredible ineptness, Forsyth got his command besieged in a canyon on White Clay Creek, with the Sioux commanding the heights on either side and threatening to cut off his retreat. After some half-hearted efforts at attacking the Indians on the bluffs, the Seventh, thoroughly demoralized, took cover and waited for rescue.

Informed of Forsyth's plight, Henry's troopers prodded the last vestiges of energy out of their exhausted horses. Halting at the mouth of the canyon in which Forsyth was trapped, Henry unlimbered a Hotchkiss gun, divided his dismounted troopers into two battalions, and ordered them to sweep both sides of the canyon. With the Hotchkiss firing away, the buffalo soldiers surged forward, shooting with deadly effect and emitting screams of elation at getting into battle. Confounded by the wave of black soldiers surging towards them, the Sioux took to their heels. Without losing a man, the buffalo soldiers had recorded one of their most celebrated triumphs.

Newspapers across the nation proclaimed that Henry's troops had saved Forsyth from the same fate as Custer's fourteen years earlier. The "untiring Ninth," reported the *Rocky Mountain News*, attacked "furiously the rear of the savage horde, scattering them in every direction . . . [allowing the Seventh] to withdraw slowly and sullenly to Pine Ridge." The *Chicago Inter-Ocean* stated that "half an hour more and the massacre of 1876 would have been repeated. But at the critical moment . . . [the] valiant Buffalo soldiers of the 9th attacked the Indians in the rear, and turned . . . annihilation into safety." Afterwards, "the men of both regiments hugged one another on the field."[35]

With Colonel Forsyth under attack, Henry sprang to his defense. Having worked so long to secure recognition for the Ninth, he now felt constrained to downplay its relief of the Seventh. On 5 January he informed Forsyth that "the service rendered your regiment" at White Bird Canyon was not "entitled to the consideration which seems to be accorded us by the newspapers." Stating that he felt that "no such catastrophe as indicated seemed imminent" for the Seventh, he proclaimed that his command "certainly are not desirous of gaining a little glory at the expense of our comrades."[36]

Forsyth, touched by Henry's support, thanked him "for the spirit of kindness and good feelings" in which his note was written. "There is no doubt, however, that your timely arrival on the 30th aided materially in the withdrawal of my troops, for at that moment it was hard to tell from which direction we were to expect the strongest force."[37]

For the next two weeks, Henry's battalion helped tighten the ring enveloping the holdouts until all finally capitulated. On 21 January, with the campaign over and the assemblage of troops preparing to disperse, General Nelson Miles held a grand review of his forces. A fiercely cold wind swept down a shallow valley where Miles sat astride his "big coal-black horse . . . on the crest of a knoll" to await his troops' passage. Also observing the spectacle from "the summits of the snow-flecked buttes" were blanket-swathed Sioux. Frederick Remington, reporting for *Harper's Weekly*, was most impressed by the "black scowling faces of the Ninth, riding in close ranks with their glittering carbines held at a salute." As they passed, General Miles waved his gloved hand to Henry, "whose gaunt figure was almost lost in the folds of his buffalo overcoat."[38]

The correspondent for the *Omaha Bee*, calling the Ninth "the leading feature of the parade," was more profuse. The buffalo soldiers, sitting "on their horses like centaurs," looked like "Esquimaux rigged out for an active campaign, alike fearless of the elements and storms of shot and shell." Leading them rode Henry, "the fearless man who has led them in their rides over these hills and valleys and both into and out of the mouth of hell."[39]

Miles's review was followed by the return of the units to the comfort of their home posts. The Ninth, however, was ordered to remain on guard at Pine Ridge, with only tents for shelter. Making the best of a bad situation, Henry located their camp in the shelter of a high bluff and settled in to wait out the snowiest winter in years. Soon a thirty-foot-high bank of snow towered over the camp as blizzards with thirty-below-zero temperatures and gale-force winds tormented men and animals alike. Officers took their personal mounts inside their tents during the storms; the enlisted men could only cover their horses "with brush as far as possible."

In unusually philosophical tones, Henry mused that "the darkies don't say much, but they doubtless keep up a devil of a thinking these cold winter nights." To make matters worse, the camp was "overrun with cattle" seeking to share the hay provided the horses. To protect themselves, the troops erected makeshift fences, Henry stated, for "the brutes, anxious for warmth and protection, crowd into our tents and . . . the occupancy of the same by a man and a Texas steer at the same time is not an agreeable thought."[40]

As though cold, snow, and starving animals were not enough, influenza raged. In vain, officers protested the illogic of their continued exposure in the camp when there was shelter at Fort Robinson, "within 24 hours' march." It seemed logical that troopers housed more comfortably would be "prepared for work at any time."[41]

The most moving protest concerning their treatment was penned by Private W. H. Prather of I Troop. In simple verses covering the entire

Ghost Dance episode, he stole credit from no one and applauded the Seventh Cavalry. Simply yet eloquently, he described the Ninth's role:

> As the Second checked the Ninth rode out,
> the Bad Lands to "explo,"
> With Colonel Henry at their head
> they did not fear the foe.
> From Christmas eve they rode
> till dawn of Christmas day.
> The redskins heard the Ninth were near
> and fled in great dismay.
>
> . . .
>
> And now the Campaign's over
> and the soldiers march away.
> All have done their share,
> you see, whether 'twas thick or thin,
> And helped to break the "Ghost dance" up
> and drive the hostiles in.
>
> . . .
>
> All the rest have gone home,
> and to meet the "blizzard's" wintry blast
> The Ninth, the willing Ninth,
> is camped here 'til the last.
> We were the first to come,
> will be the last to leave;
> Why do we stay, why this reward receive?
> In good warm barracks our recent comrades take their ease
> While we "poor devils" and the Sioux are left to freeze
> And "cuss our luck" and wait 'til some one pulls the string
> Which starts "Short Bull" out with another "Ghost dance" in the Spring.[42]

The *Pilot* published the poem because of its "intrinsic worth" and to call attention to "the shabby treatment the gallant regiment is receiving at the hands of the authorities." It concluded that it showed "poor appreciation of the bravery of troops that saved a white regiment from annihilation."[43]

At the crack of dawn on 23 March the buffalo soldiers set out for Fort Robinson, some seventy miles distant. They had originally intended to

Ninth Cavalry trooper, mounted, at the Pine Ridge Agency, 1891. Photo by Moreledge courtesy of the Denver Public Library, Western History Collection.

take several days for the trip, but it soon became obvious that another blizzard was imminent. To avoid a possible disaster, Henry left his wagons behind and hurried his command as fast as possible to Chadron, Nebraska, the closest settlement. Arriving at nightfall, he corralled his horses and rented a skating rink to house his men. By the next morning the blizzard had let up sufficiently for the command to proceed. It was one of the toughest marches in the Ninth's history. Men had to break through deep drifts that concealed the trail so that the route was often lost. Many were ill with the flu, and almost all were suffering from snow blindness. Faces were so blistered and burned from the snow reflection that "officers could hardly be recognized from the privates." In summation, Henry lodged a muffled criticism: "The march was a fitting finale to a hard winter's camp" and "reminded once more" that men should be exposed to winter marches only when absolutely necessary.[44]

Despite being left to confront the blizzards, the buffalo soldiers had not been forgotten. Henry, in the process of being breveted brigadier general, had resolved that they should receive the army's most prestigious assignment—duty at Fort Myer on the outskirts of Washington. Making his initial request to General Schofield, commanding general of the army, on 6 January, he did not let up. On 26 January he asked General O. O. Howard, commanding the Division of the Atlantic, in which Fort Myer was located, to do "a good service" to the "colored troops." His men had earned recognition by their heroic 102-mile march in thirty hours, the relief of their wagon train, and "saving the 7th Cavalry from heavy losses—if not more." Assigning the troops to service at Fort Myer would be "a most gracious way of admitting their deserts." With an uncharacteristic lack of modesty, he requested that all four troops in his battalion be sent to Washington.

Although Howard, a noted champion of blacks, agreed to do "anything proper" to reward Henry's command, he pointed out that the policy of having different regiments represented at Fort Myer would prevent the selection of more than one troop. With Howard's voice added to Henry's, Schofield gave in, "as appreciation for gallant services" in the Sioux campaign.[45]

Rumors of Henry's request spread quickly. By mid-February, the *Cleveland Gazette* was exulting that "forces now at work" might place "these Afro-American cavalrymen where they may be admired by the residents of the national capital and paraded before the thousands which annually visit the city."[46]

Opposition was inevitable. The *New York Herald* reported that many considered it "detrimental to the best interests of the service" to station black troops on the outskirts of Washington, "where the color line is so frequently the cause of discussion." As late as 25 April the *Army and Navy Journal,* which had reported that a troop from the Ninth had definitely been selected, speculated that Secretary of War Redfield Proctor would replace it with one from the Eighth Cavalry.[47]

On 28 February, still enduring the cold at Pine Ridge, Henry had protested the "spirited" efforts to prevent the detail of the Ninth to Fort Myer. While others thought the selection should be based on the social status and record of the officers involved, he thought it should go the "the troops . . . with the best record of good conduct and Indian fighting." He pledged that the troop chosen from the Ninth would include the most experienced soldiers in the regiment who could "associate with their own people and bring credit to them as well as the regiment."[48]

Henry's claims finally prevailed. On 28 April, Secretary of War Proctor ordered him to assume command of Fort Myer and to select a troop from the Ninth for duty with its garrison. The choice of a black unit for "show and parade service" at the nation's capital was not missed by the press. As the *New York Sun* pointed out, bringing a "troop of Buffaloes" to Washington, "with its implication of specially distinguished service and soldierly qualities," is remarkable. For the first time "colored and white troops" would serve together in the capital.[49] The African American weekly *The Cleveland Gazette* eagerly reprinted the Sun's observation. It was a dream come true.

The transfer of the buffalo soldiers was marred by a glaring example of discrimination involving not the men but their officers. When Henry chose K Troop for the assignment, Schofield replaced its officers with his own favorites. Henry Wright, who had succeeded Charles Parker in command of K Troop, had served flawlessly during the recent campaign, while Martin Hughes, his replacement, had been absent on recruiting service in New York City the past two years. Hughes, however, was Schofield's cousin. Although Lieutenant Phillip Bettens of K Troop, in charge of Henry's supply train during the recent campaign, had earned plaudits, he was replaced by Lieutenant A. W. Perry, the son of one of Schofield's closest friends. Asked to justify his action, Schofield responded inanely that his choices were "more polished" and that Captain Wright was "not a man who would shine well in Washington society."[50]

Despite any misgivings about their new officers, the men of K Troop became the rage of Washington. With the perfect platform from which to press his crusade, Henry extolled their virtues to the point of overkill: Blacks made "better soldiers than white men. When a negro [*sic*] enlists and gets on a uniform he is in his glory. It elevates him. He regards enlistment in the Army as something to be proud of."

True enough, perhaps, but Henry also indulged in orgies of genteel Victorian racism:

> The bullying instincts inherent in the colored soldier's character, . . . their natural air of braggadocio and swagger impose on the Indians, and they are afraid of the colored troops, while they have a sort of contempt for the white soldiers. They'll fight like devils, too, these colored cavalrymen. They charge with a yell that is enough to make

ones hair stand, and the Indians are often scared before they are hurt. They don't know what danger is. They are like children in their ignorance of fear. They would go to hell with me, these colored troopers.[51]

Henry closed his litany by noting a unique advantage of stationing buffalo soldiers in the East: If "there should be a Fenian outbreak or a riot of German socialists," white soldiers, made up largely of "Irishmen and Germans," might not fight "with much zeal." A black soldier, on the other hand, "wouldn't want anything better than a chance to kill some of his hereditary enemies, Germans and Irish. He knows they don't like him and he likes them no better." Brutal as these views seem, Henry, after all, had been in the army his entire life.

To ensure that his command received maximum exposure, he conducted daily mounted drills at 6:30 P.M., ostensibly to escape the "early morning heat." Obviously seeking more attention, he delighted "the fashionable world on wheels," who watched the "daring riders" go through the drills "in the Sabre and Carbine manual" and make a series of "dashing charges and counter charges" that were "intensely interesting to the great crowd of Washington fashionables that tarry until the drill is over."[52]

Always the motivator, he had his men up before daylight grooming their horses. Once the horses were in shape, it was the men's turn. The inspection at guard mount turned into an avid competition in which men vied for the duty-release time received by the cleanest. Henry's son, Guy, Jr., who literally grew up in the barracks, recalled that large sums were wagered on who would be selected. Sometimes the inspecting officer "had to undress two men to determine who was the cleanest."[53]

Henry's efforts to demonstrate his men's capabilities could not have more successful. Inspector General R. P. Hughes described his command as "the best instructed cavalry battalion I have yet seen in our army." He commended them for an "exactness in drill [that] I have never seen equaled."[54]

The behavior of the Ninth during its three years at Fort Myer surpassed all expectations. The absence of mishaps in one of the nation's most segregated cities was a result both of Henry's keeping them occupied with drills and official duties and of the availability of social outlets in Washington's black community. It is also likely they were conscious that their actions might enhance the image of African Americans. As the time drew near for them to leave, the *Washington Evening Star* exclaimed that it had never seen "better behaved soldiers." Lauding them for behaving like "gentlemen," it reported that they "speak in highest terms of their treatment by our citizens, not one having been insulted." They had demonstrated that "when they are among gentlemen, they can be gentlemen too. Long live the gallant Ninth."[55]

Effective 30 January 1892, Henry was promoted to the rank of lieutenant colonel, Seventh Cavalry. Although he continued to command Fort Myer and therefore K Troop until early 1894, he bid farewell to the balance of the regiment. Thanking its officers for their "zeal," he lauded the enlisted men one last time for having always "been faithful to do, and prompt to obey, whatever was required of them."[56]

In response, the men of the Ninth used the *Army and Navy Journal* to congratulate Henry and to wish him "happiness and a long life." They closed with a moving assertion that they would never have hesitated "to follow him in any and all dangers . . . because we knew that we had a bold, courageous officer . . . leading us." They also appreciated the fact that any soldier "who might have any well grounded complaint, or who thought himself wronged, could at any and all times have access to him and justice done."[57]

The men of K Troop provided a lasting testimonial. On 23 November 1891 they organized the Guy V. Henry Garrison, affiliated with the Regular Army and Navy Union. The Garrison soon included veterans from the other black regiments as well as from the Civil War and, in time, the Spanish-American War. Henry was made a lifetime honorary member.[58]

His active association with the buffalo soldiers did not end with his departure from the Ninth. In 1897 he assumed command of the Tenth Cavalry. Although he had been with it less than a year when the outbreak of war with Spain led to his promotion to brigadier general, the men of the Tenth became as devoted as those of the Ninth. Trooper John H. Lewis wrote that the regiment had "lost its friend" when Henry was "called to a higher command. He was a man who did not care about your color as long as you was a good soldier. Whatever was done under him, if . . . worthy, would receive proper recognition."[59]

Commanding a division during the conquest of Puerto Rico, Henry served as the island's military governor until poor health forced his return to the States in August 1899. Although tropical service was out of the question, he was anxious to get back to work. After he complained on 13 October that he was tired of his "long play time," he was named to head the Department of the Missouri.

Unfortunately, his frail constitution, its last reserves exhausted, betrayed him. On 23 October he informed the adjutant general that he might be delayed in assuming his new duties because of an attack of pleurisy. The next day, when he learned that the "pleurisy" was actually lobar pneumonia, he asked for a sixty-day leave in which to recover. Three days later, the most revered officer in the history of the buffalo soldiers breathed his last.[60]

As funeral arrangements were being made, the officer in charge received a request from the Guy V. Henry Garrison that its members be allowed a place in the cortege "to pay our last respects to him whose name we esteem." They stressed that many had served under Henry and that he had been an honorary member of the garrison.

Mrs. Julia Henry readily agreed and invited the Garrison to furnish an honor guard to stand watch as her husband lay in state at Saint John's Church. The guard did not wait alone. A steady line of men who had served under Henry were among the hundreds that "trooped through the stillness of the church and passed beside the bier, halting a moment to glance upon the face of the dead." Deeply impressed, a reporter noted that "the tear-dimmed eyes and loyal sorrow" of the veterans, some of whom were literally hobbling, "were testimony to his virtues as a soldier and a man." Just before the services commenced, the members of the Guy V. Henry Garrison filed past.[61]

Julia Henry never forgot the old buffalo soldiers, nor they, her. In an eloquent note she thanked them for the "faithful and loving watch you kept through the long hours of the night, and for the beautiful flowers sent." With an admonition to live so as to "show to the world" that their motto was the same as that of their late leader, "Honor and Duty," she asked them to keep her informed of their organization.

The following Memorial Day, the Garrison assisted in the decoration of graves at Arlington. Soon afterwards, its adjutant wrote Mrs. Henry that they were distressed that the grave of "our namesake" lacked a headstone and desired to "assist in its erection." In due course, an impressive monument commemorated Henry's grave, lying just below and slightly to the left of the Custis-Lee Mansion in full view of the White House and Capitol.[62]

A letter to Julia from John Brown, an aged veteran living in the West Texas hamlet of Denver City, captured the buffalo soldiers' feelings for Henry. What the old veteran's laborious writing lacked in spelling and style was offset by sincerity: "I have long wanted to know wheare you an the gen. wase stacion at but I coud not find out untill I saw his death in the pappers it heurt me so bad I thought I wood write to you an find out if it [is the] truth if it is so the country have lost a good officer an freand to good men[.]"

Brown then asked Julia if she recalled the soldier who had cooked for her family and had taken her son fishing while they were at Fort Sill. He closed with the hope that she would get "this letter an let me heare from you an all of the children."[63]

The reminiscences of Guy V. Henry, Jr., provide the best gauge of Henry's respect for his men. Six years old when his father was assigned to the Ninth, young Henry often accompanied his father "in the perfor-mance of his duties and always when he went into the field." He fondly recalled a young private at Fort Sill (Brown?) who was always willing to play and fish with him. Except for a single term at a boarding school, his early education was entrusted to the black chaplain, Henry Plummer, and two "colored soldiers—deserters who had iron shackles around their ankles." Aged sixteen when his father took command at Fort Myer, he served in effect as aide-de-camp, carrying his father's orders to their recip-ients and deciphering the laborious handwriting. Young Henry fondly recalled his friendship with the troopers, often interceding "to keep them out of trouble." Spending as much time in the barracks as at home, he sensed early that he was never to "tattle" on the men.[64] His father would have had it no other way.

9

Death and Resurrection

Captain Charles Parker and K Troop

Among the thousands of visitors to Arlington National Cemetery on Memorial Day 1892 were five "stalwart" buffalo soldiers "bearing simple wreaths of wild flowers." They walked solemnly up the slopes towards the Custis-Lee Mansion on the ridge's crest, passed it, and strode into a section reserved for the greats and near greats of America's wars. They stopped before a simple slab, paused, and then knelt down and "with the tenderness of women decorated the grave. . . . Tears came to their eyes as they stood with bowed heads and thought of him who had been their commander and friend."[1]

Their pilgrimage would have gone unnoted had not a reporter chanced to observe "one of the most touching scenes" in his life. The soldiers, members of K Troop, Ninth Cavalry, were veterans hardened by years of service on the western frontier. Although their names were not recorded, two most likely were Sergeants George Jordan and Thomas Shaw, both Medal of Honor holders.

Troop K's gallantry during the Ghost Dance episode had resulted in its assignment to serve at Fort Myer, on the outskirts of Washington. The grave before which the men stood contained the remains of Charles Parker, one of the most gentlemanly officers in the history of the Ninth Cavalry. Eighteen years earlier, he had returned from an unjust exile to take command of a demoralized and abused troop. The union, which produced one of the most renowned companies in the army, remained unbroken until Parker's death on 12 December 1890.

Born in western New York in 1843, Parker grew up in Lisbon, Illinois, about fifty miles west of Chicago. Enrolling at the University of Chicago in 1860, he established a reputation as a scholar. Although the outbreak of the Civil War abruptly ended the education of thousands of youths his age, he timed his own participation to minimize the interruption of his studies.[2]

In July 1862 he enrolled for ninety days in the Seventy-first Illinois Infantry, advancing to the rank of captain before returning to school in the fall. In January 1864, after completing most of his degree requirements, he reentered the army as a captain in the Seventeenth Illinois Cavalry. Because he was stationed in Missouri, his only taste of battle occurred during General Sterling Price's ill-fated raid in the fall of 1864. His regiment helped to rout Price's command at Westport on 23 October and pursued its shattered remnants into Arkansas.

Mustered out as a major, Parker resumed his studies and graduated with honors in 1866. His appetite whetted for military service, he applied for a commission in the postwar army. University President J. C. Burroughs endorsed him as "a young gentleman of excellent moral character" whose "executive energy and power of influence over those with whom he comes in contact adapt him eminently to military command."[3] With the additional endorsement of Senator Lyman Trumbull, Parker received a commission in the Ninth Cavalry.

Assigned to Troop L, Parker's career prospered. In July 1867 he was promoted to first lieutenant. As the original captains of the Ninth dropped by the wayside, he moved rapidly up the seniority ladder, earning the praise of every officer he served under. In June 1870 he was promoted to captain and assigned to Troop B, stationed at Fort Davis. There, for the first time, he served directly under Colonel Hatch.

Although Parker carried out his duties with his usual efficiency, he soon incurred Hatch's wrath. Hatch was involved in a bitter feud with "Don Patricio" Murphy, one of two post traders and the dominant merchant in the area.[4] Although it was understood that soldiers were to boycott the Murphy establishment, Parker naïvely concluded that "Col. Hatch's quarrels were not mine" and told his troopers to trade where "they could buy cheapest and best." Worse, he made "occasional visits" to Murphy's house.[5]

It was a bad time to cross a regimental commander because a twenty-regiment reduction of the infantry had thrown almost seven hundred officers out of employment. To ease their plight, cavalry and artillery commanders were instructed to draw upon those officers as replacements for their least competent officers. Colonels could devise their own criteria for purging their rosters. Hatch seems to have had one standard—loyalty.

In December 1870, Parker was ordered to join Major Albert Morrow at Fort Quitman. The two made a lengthy scout along the San Antonio–to–El Paso stage line. Praised by Morrow for his conduct, Parker returned to discover that he had been made "supernumerary," that is, dismissed.

Not one charge or complaint had accompanied Hatch's request. Although Parker for two years had served "creditably" under the direct observation of General J. J. Reynolds, the lackluster commander of the Department of Texas, the latter, "as a matter of courtesy to General Hatch," approved the request. Four years later, Reynolds described Parker's discharge as so "hasty and oppressive" that "plain justice" demanded his restoration.[6]

Stung by Hatch's request for a "competent" officer to replace him and aware it would be assumed he had been dismissed for "inefficiency or something worse,"[7] Parker systematically gathered testimonials. Almost everyone he had served with, including Majors Morrow and Wade, came to his aid. Morrow wrote that Parker was "the last officer in the army" he had expected to see dismissed. Calling him one "of the most efficient officers and honorable gentlemen" he had known, he assured him that "all of your brother officers . . . speak in the highest terms of you officially and socially."[8]

One of Parker's most active backers was Colonel Mackenzie, his commander in 1869. Mackenzie wrote warmly that he knew "no officer of your grade in the Ninth Cavalry that is your superior in all that is required to make a valuable officer." Mackenzie asked Orville Babcock, an aide to President Grant, for help. Obviously concerned, Mackenzie declared that Parker was "one of the best captains in this part of the world. . . . I cannot learn of anything whatever having been done by him."[9]

Although Hatch refused to reconsider, Parker would not give up. He stayed in Texas, supported himself by teaching school, read law in his spare time, and gained admittance to the bar. His case was resurrected year after year.

While he fought to vindicate himself, Hatch was having more than enough trouble with officers whom he had retained. This was especially true of those in K Troop. William T. Frohock, its first commander, had helped organize the Forty-fifth Illinois Infantry during the Civil War. Wounded at both Shiloh and Vicksburg, he was breveted a brigadier general and commissioned colonel of the Sixty-sixth U.S. Colored Infantry.[10] Hatch must have felt fortunate when Frohock was assigned to his regiment.

Frohock's Troop K, stationed at Fort Lancaster, was the first unit of the Ninth to clash with the Comanches in 1867. Several hundred warriors attacked the dilapidated fort and at one point broke "into the post." Frohock led a counterattack that repulsed them. So desperate was the fighting that Frohock's wife and sister-in-law "made themselves useful in serving ammunition." The Comanches lost some twenty warriors; three cavalrymen had been killed.[11] Despite such gallantry, Frohock's tenure with the Ninth ended abruptly in the summer of 1870 because of unprofessional conduct. To avoid a court-martial for gambling with men of his troop, he was forced to resign.[12]

Frohock's successor, J. Lee Humfreville, had spent the Civil War in frontier garrisons in Wyoming. Protecting wagon trails may have been unpleasant, but it was safer than charging Confederate trenches.[13] Assigned to the Ninth Cavalry after the war, he served four years as regimental quartermaster. While he had performed adequately as a staff officer, he was a failure as a troop commander. From the beginning he was both harsh and inconsistent. Periods of neglect alternated with crackdowns.

He also displayed poor judgment in promoting soldiers. Four of his noncommissioned officers had enlisted in Washington, D.C., during the span of a single week in October 1869.[14] Neither they nor First Sergeant Moses Holland, reared only a few miles outside the capital, had reported to the company until after the resignation of Frohock. Humfreville also gave preference to soldiers with light complexions. Two of his sergeants, including Holland, were described as "yellow"; another, as a "quadroon." Such favoritism inevitably led to a situation in which the veterans of the Frohock era were arrayed against the privileged newcomers.[15]

In the summer of 1872, Humfreville was ordered to escort a railway survey party between El Paso and Fort Worth. After the survey was completed in December, the troop returned to its home station at Fort Clark. Upon arriving, Humfreville filed charges against Privates Rufus

Slaughter, Levi Comer, Jerry Williams, and James Imes, accusing them of disorderly conduct, striking noncommissioned officers, and disobedience. Imes, in addition, was accused of pointing a loaded gun at his captain.

The cases were heard by an all–Ninth Cavalry court-martial panel presided over by Major Wade. Humfreville made haphazard presentations and provided little evidence to support his charges. His witnesses, primarily noncommissioned officers who had been involved in the disturbances, contradicted his statements and those of each other. The defendants, on the other hand, presented an abundance of testimony concerning abusive treatment by the captain.

Out of loyalty to a fellow officer, the panel found the defendants guilty and sentenced them to token one- to three-month imprisonments. Reviewers, however, were less accommodating. Technically upholding the verdicts, they remitted the sentences because the prisoners had already been "summarily and illegally punished."[16]

General Augur, commanding the Department of Texas, might have let the matter drop had not Lieutenant Daniel Floyd, a West Pointer on duty with the troop, confirmed the truthfulness of the defendants' complaints. On 23 August 1873, Augur asked his judge advocate to investigate Floyd's allegations. Four months later, Humfreville was confronted by a general court-martial presided over by Lieutenant Colonel Shafter.[17]

Humfreville's first offense, trivial compared to the rest, occurred when he turned his command over to Lieutenant Floyd and spent ten days in Galveston. After returning to duty on 6 December he signed the troop's morning reports to show himself present the entire period. Humfreville paid a high price for his absence, as Floyd, a poor disciplinarian, failed to maintain order and also resented being left alone with the troop.

The tensions within K Troop snapped a week after Humfreville's return to duty. While it was camped near Fort Richardson, preparing for its return march to Fort Clark, conditions got totally out of hand. For days the captain had been frequently absent, either conducting business (his story) or drinking in a bar (Floyd's). Neither he nor Floyd, also often absent from camp, noticed that the men had procured two kegs of liquor and that most, including the noncommissioned officers, were imbibing heavily.

The morning of the fifteenth was bitterly cold as Humfreville departed for one last visit to the fort. As he was leaving, he saw that Private Malachi Pope was intoxicated. Despite the cold, he ordered Pope to be thrown into the creek flowing through the camp. Unable to get out of the icy water without help, Pope began to shiver violently and became "so stiff" that he had to be taken to the post hospital at Fort Richardson. His ordeal left the men more resentful than ever.

Noticing that several soldiers were obviously absent without leave, Humfreville instructed Floyd to arrest each when he returned. After he left, the drinking continued. According to Private William Buchanan, men "were swearing and dancing and carrying on wild."[18]

When Humfreville returned, several men were "carrying logs" while "walking post," a standard punishment. Noticing First Sergeant Holland in an argument with Rufus Slaughter, the senior member of the troop, Humfreville placed Slaughter under arrest.[19] After ordering Jerry Williams, already "walking post," to carry a heavier log, he retired to his tent.

Soon afterwards, Slaughter threw his log down, muttering that "he wasn't going to take it anymore." When he turned to walk away, Holland grabbed him. As the two rolled on the ground, Slaughter pinned the sergeant's arms to his sides. When Humfreville heard the commotion and reappeared, Slaughter was trussed to a tree, his hands tied behind his back. Needless to say, his struggles had drawn a crowd, many urging him on in the fight with Holland.[20]

For a short time matters calmed as men began to take their dinner. When it became obvious the prisoners would not be fed, Williams threw down his log and demanded to eat. Holland refused, and the two were still exchanging words when Humfreville ordered the private to be tied to a tree. With the man helpless, he clubbed him with a carbine, "hard enough to draw blood," and then with a "gambrel stick about the thickness of a man's wrist." Before turning away, he "twisted" the prisoner's nose, "rubbed his fist in his face," and tauntingly asked, "What did you do when you was a slave?"[21]

The uproar, punctuated by Williams's screams, brought men running from all directions. Some got into fracases with sergeants. Others were simply in the wrong place at the wrong time. Humfreville spotted Private James Imes with his gun out of his holster (the private had been cleaning his pistol when he heard the uproar). When the captain accosted him, Imes dropped the gun, but it was too late. While he was "tied by the hands," Humfreville struck him several times with his fist "and once with a revolver or club."

Others, such as Wade, Comer, Robinson, and Tucker—overheard saying that he "had come to see justice done"—were either unlucky enough to attract attention or had been reported by one of the sergeants. Jim Wade, who had played no role whatsoever in the uproar, was guilty only of insubordination when Humfreville called him a son-of-a-bitch. Wade replied, "Captain, you ought not to call me a son-of-a-bitch—my mother is no more of a bitch than yours."

In a fitting finale to the bizarre episode, Humfreville lined up the troop and unleashed a drunken tirade: "Step out any man that wants to fight. I will walk over his dead body or he'll walk over mine—I can whip any man in my troop, let him be old or young, big or little, grizzly or grey."[22]

The ordeal of the prisoners had only begun. Upon beginning the march to Fort Clark, Humfreville ordered them to be "handcuffed in pairs, and fastened in a gang two abreast, by a rope, to the rear of an Army wagon." Day after day, shackled together, they trudged across the Texas prairie. When the troop forded streams, they were dragged through the frigid water with no chance afterwards to change clothes or dry themselves. At the end of the day, each had to carry a twenty-five-pound log and "walk a ring" until midnight. Humfreville "brutally" (the court-martial's description) refused to allow them any fire "for their use in warming themselves or drying their clothes"; likewise, he refused to furnish them a change of clothes. Compounding their torment, he limited each to one blanket at night and denied them coffee and all food save cold bread and meat.

Even worse, the march between Forts Griffin and Concho endured the coldest weather in years. At times the men were pelted with freezing rain and sleet. Lieutenant Floyd testified that one morning a prisoner was "so stiff . . . from the intense cold . . . that he was unable to get up. I had the Sergeant hold him up and drag him around slowly until he got warmed up when he could walk alone."

The prisoner who suffered most was Levi Comer, who collapsed from exhaustion and was dragged for miles shackled to the wagon. His lacerated wrists steadily became more inflamed. One morning, during a layover at Fort McKavett, Floyd saw him "lying on the ground biting a stick making a terrific noise." An examination revealed that his arm was so swollen that he was admitted to the post hospital. Two months later, he was still incapacitated.[23] Farrier Edward Tucker was released from Humfreville's hell on 24 December; Private Wade, six days later. The other four endured their torment until the troop reached Fort Clark on 20 January.

For Captain Humfreville, the court-martial was a nightmare. Even his hand-picked sergeants testified to his atrocities. He was found guilty on four counts involving the "brutal maltreatment" of the prisoners during the forced march, two counts relating to the striking of Williams and Imes while they were tied and helpless, and one for the sadistic ducking of Private Pope. Without a hint of leniency, the court sentenced him to be cashiered. On 3 April 1874 his military career was terminated for conduct "prejudicial to good order and military discipline" and "unbecoming an officer and a gentleman."[24]

Two weeks later, Charles Parker was restored to duty and given command of K Troop. While he received no apology from Hatch, the vendetta was not renewed. As his troubles with such misfits as Ambrose Hooker and Nathan Dudley increased, Hatch surely began to appreciate Parker's efficiency and diligence.

Parker took firm control of his troop. Although Sergeants Holland and Tinner were reduced to the ranks, several of the noncoms were retained, their ranks augmented by some of the men who had provoked Humfreville's wrath. The much abused Jerry Williams was promoted to sergeant; Rufus Slaughter, to trumpeter.[25]

Parker soon noticed the leadership potential of a twenty-four-year-old Tennessean named George Jordan, dark complexioned and only five feet four inches tall. After three years in the infantry, Jordan had transferred to the Ninth in 1870. After his ssignment to K Troop, his record was spotty, at best. During Humfreville's court-martial he was the only trooper to fully support the captain's version of the melee outside Fort Richardson. While carrying a log as punishment for drinking, he claimed he had observed an amazing proportion of the difficulties. He was the only witness to see Private Imes point his gun at Humfreville and to see Williams and Wade throw down their logs and defy the sergeants. In contrast, he never saw Humfreville strike anyone.

Jordan's testimony was so unconvincing that the judge advocate asked him point-blank if he had been bribed: Did you not say that "you were going to do all you could to save Captain Humfreville, and [then] . . . you could get all the money you wanted?" Jordan denied this but acknowledged the captain had given him two and a half dollars for Christmas.

His disastrous testimony induced Colonel Shafter to demand if he "knew the nature of an oath."[26]

Given Parker's trust, Jordan gradually earned his comrades' confidence. Promoted to corporal in September 1874, he waited another five years before receiving a sergeant's stripes.

Typical of the troop's performance under Parker was its assignment to escort surveyors marking the Colorado-Utah boundary in 1879. Upon completing the task, the surveyors' leader wrote Hatch that he was very pleased with the "manner and spirit" in which Parker and his men had performed their duty: "I think highly of the colored troops and I thank you for sending me so excellent a company."[27] Such praise from civilians was rare indeed.

Stationed in Colorado when the Victorio War began, K Troop missed the initial fighting. Such was not the case during the spring of 1880. Under heavy pressure by Hatch's troopers, Victorio retreated into the ranges of western New Mexico. On 11 May, Hatch detached twenty-five men of K Troop, commanded by Sergeant Jordan, to escort a train of provisions to old Fort Tularosa and set up a supply depot for his main force.[28] In addition, Jordan was to offer such protection as he could to the squatters who had settled around the fort.

Entrusted with responsibilities usually assigned an officer, Jordan had a rare opportunity to demonstrate leadership. At the end of an arduous day's march (afoot since its horses had long since worn out), still many miles away from its destination, his detachment learned that Apaches had been seen near Fort Tularosa. Aware that his men were exhausted, Jordan asked if they were able to press on. All said yes. After a respite to eat and "bathe their feet" in a stream to "refresh" themselves, they set out over terrain so rough that a wagon overturned on a steep mountainside.

Arriving at Tularosa early the next morning, Jordan began to strengthen the dilapidated stockade. On the evening of 14 May the Apaches attacked. After repulsing the initial assault, he dispatched ten men to prevent the troops' mules and some cattle from being stampeded. Jordan's description, recalled years afterward, is frustratingly terse: "Keeping under cover of the timber, the men quickly made their way to the herders and drove the Indians away, thus saving the men and stock. . . . After it was all over the townspeople congratulated us for having repulsed . . . more than 100 redskins."[29]

As was typical in the Ninth Cavalry, this encounter received little notice. Hatch's only reference to it was that some "light skirmishing" had occurred. In 1890, Jordan and Captain Parker amassed enough information on the "light skirmish" for the sergeant to be awarded a belated Medal of Honor.[30]

Victorio's death in late 1880 did not end Apache resistance. Nana, who had been his ablest lieutenant, led about forty warriors on a last epic raid. For three months the Apache exiles ranged through their beloved mountains, leaving behind a trail of destruction. Although Hatch committed every available man of the Ninth to their pursuit, almost every battle was initiated by ambushes of small, isolated commands.

Evading a pursuit through the Sacramento and San Andreas Mountains, Nana disappeared into the ranges west of the Rio Grande. Near the mouth of Carrizo Canyon in the San Mateos, about twenty-five miles west of the Rio Grande, his band was discovered by a nineteen-man detachment of K Troop led by Captain Parker. Despite his lack of numbers, Parker rapidly deployed his men to attack before the Apaches escaped. Instead of fleeing, however, Nana counterattacked so fiercely that it was the buffalo soldiers who were in danger of being surrounded and wiped out.

Parker's official account of the battle belies its ferocity. "My command dismounted within 100 yards of the enemy, and was vigorously engaged for more than two hours—without shelter or protection, until their whole force retreated to their rear southwest." Parker especially applauded the leadership of Sergeants Jordan and Thomas Shaw. Jordan, posted in an "extremely exposed position" and with only a few men, was stationed on the right flank. Despite the superior numbers assailing him, he "held his ground" and finally forced the Apaches back, "preventing them from surrounding the command." For this engagement Jordan received a certificate of merit, in the nineteenth century often valued more highly than the Medal of Honor. Unlike the medal, it included a two-dollars-a-month increase in pay.[31]

Shaw, a Kentuckian who had run away from his master to join the Union Army as an eighteen-year-old in 1864, was one of the most experienced soldiers in the regiment. After spending two terms in B Troop, most of the time as a sergeant, he joined the growing number of transfers to Parker's company. In 1881 he was the first sergeant of K Troop. With only a few men at his side, he held the "most advanced position" in

George Jordan, sergeant, Ninth Cavalry, 1879–96, is the soldier wearing a hat, seated in the center of the front row. Jordan was the only buffalo soldier awarded both a Medal of honor and a certificate of merit. The solider also wearing a medal and staingin on the right of the back row is either Sergeant Thomas Shaw or Private Henry Johnson, both Medal of Honor holders who were members of the troop. Courtesy of the Nebraska State Historical Society, Lincoln.

Parker's deployment. Like Jordan, he "refused to yield an inch of ground." One of the best marksmen in the cavalry, skillful and brave, according to one account he "so dismayed the Indians that they gave up the attack and retreated." Parker concluded his recommendation with a statement that indicates the bond between the two men: Shaw "was near me the whole time with the view of rendering his assistance should I fall in the affair."[32]

Parker's command averted disaster, but at a high price. South American–born Charles Perry was a second-term enlistee who had painstakingly saved $335 from his minuscule pay. His dreams for the future ended with a bullet through his head. Guy Temple, the troop's farrier (although only five feet three inches tall), was a twenty-eight-year-old Virginian. Also in his second term of enlistment, he had fought by the side of Sergeant Jordan at Fort Tularosa. He, too, died from a bullet through the head.[33]

The victims of the Apaches' deadly fire included three young Kentuckians who had enlisted within days of one another. They joined up together, trained together, and almost died together. Wash Pennington, shot through the left side, spent more than a year in the hospital before receiving a medical discharge. Jerry Stone, his skull fractured and bleeding internally after his horse fell on him, also remained in the hospital until given a medical discharge in March 1882. John Shidell, also shot through the side, returned to duty several months later; when he reenlisted in 1885, he had risen to the rank of sergeant.[34]

Although Parker secured for Sergeants Jordan and Shaw the medals they well deserved, he received no recognition whatever. When the awarding of brevets for the Indian campaigns was authorized in early 1891, General Pope recommended him for a brevet promotion to major for his "gallant and meritorious conduct" at Carrizo Canyon. There should have been no question concerning his case, but General Schofield curtly quashed the proposal, asserting that there was "hardly enough" in the application to warrant a brevet. There was no appeal, for, as the last sentence in Schofield's note coldly stated, "Captain Parker has since died."[35]

The last decade of Parker's life was marked by a steady decline in his physical condition. Allowed a year's leave in 1882 to "go beyond the sea for . . . his health," he used the respite to observe military exercises. From England he wrote that he had "visited every available military barracks, base, and fortification." Preparing to leave for the continent, he proposed to spend the next six months examining "the discipline and administration of the French and German armies." When he returned, he hoped to be able to "report upon or submit an intelligent opinion upon anything which may come under my observation."[36] He apparently hoped that the trip could remedy his lack of formal military training.

The activities of a company that performs its tasks efficiently leave fewer traces than do those of one that fouls up. K Troop generated no complaints and more than its share of compliments. In the spring of 1887 it was dispatched to Cheyenne, Wyoming, to investigate illegal fencing charges. When it concluded the assignment, the *Cheyenne Leader* expressed regret that the "colored trooper mounted on his . . . spirited charger will no longer be seen upon the streets. . . . The soldiers of the command conducted themselves admirably while camped near the city. . . . Capt. Parker and Lt. [Philip] Bettens were gentlemen of the old school, bearing themselves with dignity but not austerity. They will be missed. . . . Although every resident of this section had solemnly resolved to *hate and detest* the colored troops before their arrival, . . . contempt soon changed to respect."[37]

Despite the troop's excellent record, its members were by no means immune to the temptations of saloons and brothels. One of the most celebrated sprees in its history occurred on the evening of 12 February 1887, at Crawford, Nebraska. During a three-hour stint in a saloon, Private Lee Irving got into an argument with a white prostitute and then turned his anger on the proprietor. After a round of drinks in a nearby establishment, Irving and two comrades returned, fired several shots into the air outside the first saloon, and threatened to return with enough soldiers to incinerate it. As tempers flared, Private Henry Chase, one of Irving's companions, rode his horse into the tavern and demanded to be served. Once obliged by the barkeeper, he took his drink and rode out again.[38]

Irving and two buddies were arrested and brought before a general court-martial presided over by Parker. Even though Parker had brought the charges, the defendants readily agreed to his serving on the panel and also asked him for character references. Their fate was clearly in his hands. He was easiest on George Pumphrey, a Marylander with only two years of service. He stated that the soldier usually did his duty well but that twice he had been observed "acting foolishly" while under the influence of liquor. Parker conjectured that older soldiers selected him as a companion because he had "a good deal of private means and they want him to pay the bill." Although one of Pumphrey's random shots had almost hit a bystander, he received only six months at hard labor and a sixty-dollar fine.

In contrast to Pumphrey, Irving was one of the senior members of the regiment. Accused of chasing the prostitute with a knife in his hand, he denied he had even been in the establishment. In support, a rival saloon keeper stated that Irving had been in his tavern on the evening in question, and Sergeant Jordan testified that Irving had been present for the retreat roll call at the time he was allegedly threatening the prostitute. Parker described Irving as a veteran soldier who generally had "sense enough to keep out of trouble." The vigorous defense resulted in a very light sentence, three months at hard labor and a thirty-dollar fine.

Although Private Chase admitted riding his horse into the saloon, he blamed it on a Texas cowboy identified only as "Clover Bill." Chase was innocently sitting astride his pony in front of the tavern when "Clover Bill" pulled a gun and ordered him to ride inside. Although Pumphrey also testified to the nefarious actions of the cowboy, no one else recalled such an occurrence. As if to atone for the leniency shown Irving, Chase was sentenced to be discharged without honor and imprisoned for one year.[39]

Fortunately for Henry Chase, he served his year at Fort Robinson instead of the military prison at Fort Leavenworth. He conducted himself so contritely that at the conclusion of his term, Colonel Hatch, with the approval of Parker, requested he be allowed to reenlist. Noting that Chase had always been an "excellent duty man," Hatch described his horseback entry into the saloon as a foolish "frolic" for which he had been sufficiently punished.[40]

By their subsequent careers the soldiers showed that the wild night in Crawford was not a valid indicator of their characters. While participating in the Ninth's rescue of the Seventh Cavalry at White Clay Canyon during the Ghost Dance episode, Irving received a minor wound that gave him the distinction of being the regiment's last casualty in combat with Indians. He retired in 1896. Pumphrey had his moment of glory at San Juan Hill. He was one of seven enlisted men from the Ninth to receive a certificate of merit for gallantry during the charge.[41]

Although Parker's troop remained as efficient as ever, nothing could stem the steady decline in his health. Constant "neuralgic" pain forced him to take a six-month leave in November 1887. Visits to hospitals in Hot Springs, Arkansas, and Arrowhead Springs, California, produced little relief. Whenever on duty, he remained as capable as ever. Only a few months before his death, his efficiency report read simply, "an excellent officer in every way."[42]

As the senior captain in the regiment, Parker in August 1890 commanded a battalion, consisting of five troops of the Ninth, in a sham attack on a defensive position held by an infantry detachment under Captain A. W. Corliss. With three companies at his disposal, Corliss was directed to withdraw to the best possible defensive position. After a two-hour wait, Parker was ordered to locate and attack the entrenched infantrymen. Two hours after Parker assumed the offensive, the umpire, Major E. R. Kellogg of the Seventh Infantry, ruled that the positions gained by his troops had made the defense's situation untenable. Corliss, ill-humored as usual, groused that "the officers with me failed to agree to this ruling."[43]

Parker's personal life was far from blissful. His marriage to Mary Brent was childless and of short duration. In October 1880 she complained to the secretary of war that Parker had provided her with "entirely insufficient" support the past two months. Asked to explain, he was terse but bitter. In August, totally exhausted after sixteen straight months in the field, he had been sent to the Las Vegas (New Mexico) Hot Springs to recuperate. His wife refused to leave her mother (living with her at Fort Union, only fifty miles away) to visit him. Although the Parkers never divorced, that was the effective end of their marriage.[44]

Encouraged by Parker and led by Sergeants Jordan and Shaw, the men of K Troop became models of professionalism. Proud of their worth, they were not hesitant in asserting themselves in positive ways. By 1884, stationed at Camp Supply in the Indian Territory, they had organized the elite "Diamond Club," whose gala balls became the envy of the service. On Christmas Eve of that year they "came to the front" with a "grand dress ball" in their barracks. To symbolize their pride in their African ancestry, they grouped the American flag between the colors of the world's only two black republics, Haiti and Liberia. At the entryway, "the Troop letter with crossed sabres, wreathed and surmounted by the word 'Welcome' in gilt lettering," greeted guests.

With the regimental band of the Twenty-fourth Infantry and the Ninth's own string band alternately performing, the ball proceeded with "the utmost decorum." To placate prohibitionists, a coy note appended to the program announced that "gentlemen who desire to 'smile'" would be "assisted" at a bar. Shortly before midnight, a "bountiful repast" was served. It was in the early morning hours before "the last strains of music died away and the guests reluctantly wended their way homeward to dream of 'Ye Merrie Christmas.'"[45] This may not have been the first gala given by K Troop, but it was neither the last nor the most lavish.

After the Ninth moved northward in 1885, the galas became more frequent. On 27 July 1889, Captain Corliss noted that "Troop K, Ninth Cavalry, gave a grand ball in their barracks." Although he did not indicate why the ball was given, it seems likely it was to honor Parker's wife, who had arrived a week earlier for what proved to be an unsuccessful attempt at a reconciliation.[46]

Eight months later, the Diamond Club hosted another extravaganza. In January 1890, Major Henry, writing in the *Army and Navy Journal,* reported, "On Thursday there is to be a grand ball, hall tastefully decorated, with fine supper by Co. K." Participation in the Ghost Dance campaign during the autumn and winter did not dull the Diamond Club's zest for entertaining. On 20 April 1891, K's gala received another rave description in the *Army and Navy Journal.* The correspondent stated that the Diamond Club's "fourth grand reception" celebrated the arrival of the soldiers "from the Bad Lands home again." The "dance orders were neat" and the bill of fare, which "could hardly have been equaled by the celebrated 'Delmonico,'" included "all the delicacies of the season in abundance." To top off the evening, there were "wines, whisky, old cognac brandy, and extra fine cigars." The president and the treasurer of the Diamond Club were Sergeants Jordan and Shaw. The galas, however, most definitely were group endeavors, with committees on finance, decoration, refreshment, invitations, catering, and the bar.[47]

The most compelling evidence for the troop's esprit de corps is found in its record for reenlisting. As early as February 1878, one-half its members had been reenlisted personally by Parker. In 1892, Major Henry, interviewed by a reporter for the *Washington Post,* boasted that its record was "one to be proud of." The twenty senior members averaged twenty-five years of service, and many were nearing the thirty years of service which would entitle them to pensions. "Three of the men [Jordan, Shaw, and Henry Johnson, who had transferred from D Troop] wear medals of honor."[48]

During all his years of commanding K Troop, Parker had followed an odd pattern of evaluation. Most individuals received excellents or very goods when their enlistments expired. In evaluating the troop, however, he invariably found two or more categories on which to mark fair or good. Only when Colonel Hatch or another outsider made the bimonthly inspection did the troop receive excellents across the board. Parker inspected his troops for what turned out to be the last time at the end of June 1890. As though he sensed this might be the case, he issued all excellents.[49]

By October 1890, Parker was too ill to continue with his regular duties. On 20 October he was assigned to duty with the cavalry depot at Jefferson Barracks in Saint Louis. As his condition rapidly deteriorated, he received a leave on 7 November and traveled by train to Washington, D.C. Admitted upon arrival to Garfield Hospital, he died of what was described as cirrhosis of the kidneys on 12 November. His estranged wife, living in Detroit at the time, would console herself with a pension of twenty dollars a month for the balance of her life.[50] The men of K Troop, his only known mourners, were campaigning against the Ghost Dancers and had no way of learning of his death for weeks.

By less than a month he had missed the opportunity to see his troop become one of the most acclaimed in the nation. When they arrived at Fort Myer, Virginia, there was no chance they would forget his years of dedicated service. The grim-faced men who made their Memorial Day pilgrimage to decorate his grave could well be excused for being unable to restrain their tears for the officer who, in the words of the *Star* reporter, had been such "a kind, considerate and conscientious commander."[51]

Not surprisingly, Sergeants Jordan and Shaw received little more consideration from their government than had their captain. Shaw, his body worn out after thirty years of service, retired in 1894 while the troop was still at Fort Myer. He settled in the adjoining hamlet of Rosslyn, where he died the following year. He was buried in Arlington.[52]

Sergeant Jordan completed thirty years of service at Fort Robinson in 1896 and joined Rufus Slaughter and several other troopers in retirement at Crawford. Although he was a substantial property owner with a pension of $37.50 a month, he nevertheless found that America was unwilling to grant equality. In 1900 he asked the adjutant general if it was legal for him to be denied the right to vote. He was informed that although no laws denied a veteran paying taxes the right to vote in Nebraska, the final decision in such cases was left to local officials.[53]

The worst was yet to come. As a result of chronic nephritis, his health worsened during the fall of 1904. Twice his physician, Dr. J. H. Hartwell, requested that he be admitted to the Fort Robinson hospital. Both times he was denied. Advised to apply for entrance to the Soldiers' Home in Washington, D.C., Jordan reluctantly allowed Dr. Hartwell to file a request on 19 October. It was too late. He died five days later.[54]

Convinced that the sergeant had died "for wont of proper attention," Post Chaplain William Anderson, an African American who was also a physician, filed a complaint. As a result, the post commander was informed that "all practicable consideration" should be shown retired soldiers with "records and services . . . as excellent as were those of 1st Sergeant George Jordan."[55] As usual, the military was more generous in death than in life. He was buried with full military honors in a ceremony attended by the great majority of Fort Robinson's personnel. With him died the last survivor of a uniquely successful collaboration between a white officer and his black noncommissioned officers.

PART FOUR

Honor and Dishonor

Episodes from the Barracks and Officers' Row

10

Medals and Courts-Martial

The Enigma of
Sergeant Emanuel Stance

For almost a decade, Emanuel Stance was the only black holder of the Medal of Honor in the military. Despite this honor, his career was punctuated by one crisis after another. Few troopers may have been braver; none had less control over his temper. No one was more likely to be promoted or to be "busted" and reduced to the ranks.

Stance literally grew up in the Ninth. When he enlisted in October 1866 at Lake Providence, Louisiana, he was eighteen and little more than five feet tall.[1] Soon he had added five inches in height and enough muscle to become one of the fiercest brawlers in the regiment. Enlisting the same week as Stance was another East Carroll Parish youth, Moses Williams. Both were assigned to Troop F, Ninth Cavalry; were promoted to sergeant before the end of their first year; and later were awarded Congressional Medals of Honor.[2]

Stance learned the ins and outs of military life under a stern disciplinarian, Captain Henry Carroll. Reared in rural New York near the Canadian border, Carroll had enlisted in the artillery in 1859. Five years later he secured a commission in the Third Cavalry, ensuring him a position in the postwar army. Promoted to first lieutenant in early 1867, he secured a jump to the rank of captain by transferring to the Ninth Cavalry. In May 1867 he was given command of F Troop, a position he held until 1885. Sober, conscientious, and an untiring campaigner, he also possessed a temper that was notoriously short-fused.[3]

As Carroll relentlessly weeded out soldiers who failed to meet his standards, the consequences could be tragic, as in the case of Private Joseph

Dayes. Dayes, from Mobile, Alabama, had briefly served with an infantry regiment in New Mexico before receiving a disability discharge. He remained in the territory, working as a cook and servant for various officers. In April 1877, aged twenty-nine and none too robust, he enlisted in the Ninth Cavalry and was assigned to F Troop. Used primarily as a cook, he fared fine until he was placed on regular duty at the end of the year.

Dayes had not the slightest idea what the various commands and drills meant. Hopelessly out of sync with his comrades, and unable to control his horse, he incurred Carroll's wrath. After receiving no response to a command, the captain stormed up to him, beat him over the head with the flat of his saber, and screamed, "Get, you son-of-a-bitch!" Gashed on both his head and left hand, Dayes retreated in panic to his barracks. He explained to a court that he thought his "safety from further bodily injury depended on my obeying his command to 'get!'" He picketed his horse near the others, took his "saddle and equipment and carbine and placed them together with the other property . . . issued to me as a soldier in my tent. After [this] . . . I eat [sic] my supper and quietly departed."

Unfortunately for Dayes, the items disappeared before his absence was noted. Charged with theft as well as desertion, he was soon apprehended. Found guilty by a court-martial on both accounts, he received a dishonorable discharge and two years of imprisonment.[4] Carroll was censured by the judge advocate general, but the outbreak of war with Victorio made it impractical to pursue the matter. Needless to say, such a role model could not have been beneficial for Sergeant Stance.

Stance began to run afoul of Carroll's regulations in late 1868. In December he was placed under arrest for a few days; the following April, he was fined ten dollars by a garrison court-martial.[5]

Stationed at Fort McKavett in the fall of 1869, he was one of the few men of the Ninth to accompany both of the first two postwar expeditions against the Comanche camps on the upper Brazos. As part of a command led by Carroll, he participated in a pitched battle on 16 September; on that expedition's return, he was attached to a larger scout led by Captain John M. Bacon that worsted the Comanches in two battles on 28 and 29 November.[6]

During the next few months, Stance almost exhausted Carroll's patience before fortune suddenly made him the army's most acclaimed buffalo soldier. Three times during the first two months of 1870, he was convicted by garrison courts-martial on charges of "conduct prejudicial to good order and discipline." Each time, he was given a paltry five-dollar fine.[7] In between trials he participated in several scouts, setting the stage for his moment of glory. On 16 May a band of Indians kidnapped two children from a nearby settlement. In response, Carroll ordered out two detachments to "endeavor to the utmost" to intercept the raiders and recover the children. One, consisting of ten men, was led by Sergeant Stance.[8]

Stance left McKavett on 20 May, marching northward along the trail to Kickapoo Springs. Some fourteen miles out, he spotted a party of Indians driving a herd of horses and gave chase. After a few shots, the Indians abandoned the animals and "took to the mountains" (the timbered escarpment of the Edwards Plateau). With the recovered horses in his possession, Stance halted for the night at Kickapoo Springs and debated his course of action.

He decided to drive the ponies back to Fort McKavett, and fate again smiled on him. About ten miles from the fort, he spotted two government wagons escorted by a small guard. As he surveyed the scene, he observed about twenty Indians "making for" the wagons, obviously intent on plunder. Without hesitation, he ordered his command to charge. The Indians tried to make a stand, but the buffalo soldiers "set the Spencers to talking and whistling about their ears so lively that they broke in confusion and fled to the hills." In this encounter the troopers captured five more horses for their convoy. The Indians made another effort to regain their animals when Stance called a halt at the "eight mile watering hole," but once more a few volleys from the Spencers sent them fleeing. At 2 P.M. the little command arrived back at Fort McKavett and turned over fifteen captured horses.[9]

As scouts went, this one had been comparatively mild. Lasting less than two days, it had covered no more than fifty miles and had resulted in casualties neither to the troopers nor to the Indians. Carroll, however, was so elated by its success that he overlooked the fact that its assigned mission was to search for the kidnapped children. He forwarded Stance's report to departmental headquarters together with a vigorous endorsement. "This marks the fifth engagement in which he has been cited for gallantry and good behavior." Exactly who cited Stance the first four times and for what is not recorded in any known records.

Perhaps because such praise from Carroll was so unusual, the authorities responded with a speed previously used only for white soldiers. On 9 July, scarcely six weeks after the scout's conclusion, Stance was awarded a Medal of Honor. In an eloquent letter of acknowledgment, he promised "by my future conduct" to live up to "the high honor conferred upon me."[10]

The decision to reward Stance while ignoring equal or greater claims is puzzling. A classic example of such an oversight involved another Fort McKavett patrol in August 1871. Lieutenant John Bullis and four men of M Troop were scouting to the west of the fort when they chanced upon some Indians driving a herd of three hundred stolen cattle. The soldiers attacked, and the rustlers fled, leaving the herd behind. Soon afterwards, the Indians, reinforced by the rest of their war party, returned to reclaim the herd and perhaps take a few scalps. Instead of running, Bullis and his buffalo soldiers attacked so furiously that the Indians, an estimated thirty strong, retreated to a wooded hilltop. The troopers not only retained the first herd but also bagged another two hundred head. Lieutenant Bullis was cited for the extraordinary bravery of himself and his four soldiers. No one, however, saw fit even to record their names.[11]

The slight given to the members of Bullis's little band was so much the norm for black soldiers that for years Stance remained the only black Medal of Honor holder. This was anything but the case for white troops of the period. In 1870 alone, forty members of the Eighth Cavalry and seventeen of the First were given Medals of Honor for service against the Apaches in Arizona and New Mexico. Almost all were simply for "gallantry in action." During the Red River War of 1874–75, twenty-five white soldiers from the Fourth and Sixth Cavalry Regiments and Nelson Miles's Fifth Infantry received the medal; not one black regular, cavalry or infantry, received one.[12] Had similar liberality been shown blacks, there would have been dozens of buffalo soldiers carrying the medal by the end of the 1870s.

Although Stance, by the standards of the time, deserved a medal, it was unfortunate he was the only black recipient. It gave him an inflated opinion of himself and likely evoked resentment. The effect on his behavior was the opposite of what Carroll had desired.

In early 1871, Stance was sentenced by a court-martial at Fort McKavett to pay a ten-dollar fine and be reduced to the rank of private.[13] The punishment, most likely inflicted for one or both of his most persistent problems—drunkenness and brawling—may have induced him to leave F Troop. In October 1871 he reenlisted in M Troop. He likely felt his prospects would be better under Lieutenant Byron Dawson, M Troop's acting commander, who was easier going than Carroll and also in need of capable noncommissioned officers.

Nine months earlier, Dawson had taken charge of a troop left in shambles by Captain Heyl of San Pedro Springs infamy. Throughout Heyl's hectic tenure, noncoms were promoted and demoted haphazardly, dozens of fines and imprisonments were handed out, and desertions were frequent. In October 1870, seven men, including First Sergeant John H. Mitchell, deserted en masse. In December, Private George Jacobs, a twenty-one-year-old Washingtonian in his first year in the service, was killed while attempting to escape from the guardhouse. It seems unlikely that anyone could have been displeased when Heyl secured a transfer to the Fourth Cavalry at the close of 1870.[14]

Henry Green, a native of Washington, D.C., completed a three-year tour of duty in the infantry in 1869 before enlisting in the Ninth. Heyl elevated him from private to first sergeant after the mass desertions in October 1870. If Green saw Stance's arrival as a threat to his own status, his apprehension must have grown when Dawson promptly promoted the newcomer to sergeant.

The tensions between the two erupted early on 26 December 1872. Stance had celebrated Christmas so vigorously that he was still inebriated the following day. Told that Green had left the barracks to report his being drunk on duty to Dawson, Stance followed him into the office to plead his case. He was placed under arrest and sent back to the barracks.

Upon Green's return, he was accosted by his subordinate: "If you reported that I was drunk, you reported a God damned lie!" Told to return to his quarters, Stance refused and shoved Green into another soldier: "God-damn you, I can whip you." The two wrestled each other onto a bunk before Stance sank his teeth into his adversary's bottom lip and "*bit it off.*" Revenge exacted, he allowed himself to be escorted to the guardhouse.[15]

A five-officer general court-martial, presided over by Captain Carroll, was convened only eight days after the altercation. In his defense, Stance denied that he had been drunk and claimed that Green had started the fight. On neither point did he receive support. Calling Corporal Lawrence Johnson and Private George Samuels as witnesses, he asked if they "did not see Serg't Green jump on me first." Both replied in the negative. Lieutenant Dawson, who should have been able to judge Stance's state of inebriation, did not testify.

Charged with drunkenness on duty, insubordination, and mayhem, Stance pleaded not guilty to the first two charges but admitted that he had committed mayhem on Green. Convicted on all counts, he was reduced to the ranks, fined ten dollars a month for six months, and confined at hard labor "at the post where his company was stationed" for the same period. Although hard labor sounds rigorous, it often consisted of routine cleanup duty under the eye of a trooper with little incentive to be demanding.[16] In being so lenient, Carroll, who most likely dictated the decision, may have felt that Stance had too much potential to receive the dishonorable discharge his offense merited. In addition, he was reluctant to cashier the regiment's only Medal of Honor holder.

Henry Green had little opportunity to savor Stance's conviction. Before the year was out, he also had been court-martialed, convicted, and reduced to the ranks. When his term expired in October 1874, he did not reenlist.[17] His decision may have been related to Stance's elevation to the rank of sergeant.

Trouble resumed for Stance soon after Green's departure. In March 1875 he was fined five dollars; the next month, a garrison court-martial reduced him to the rank of private and levied another ten-dollar fine. The following winter, he was confined in the post guardhouse for two months. When his second tour of service expired in October, Dawson inexplicably rated his character as good. Thereby allowed to reenlist, Stance promptly chose to remain in Troop M.

After six relatively tranquil months, Stance was promoted to corporal, and in November 1876, to sergeant. Five months later, he was again reduced to the ranks. Once more, incredible as it seems, he climbed back into Dawson's good graces. In April 1878 he was again made corporal; on 14 November, sergeant. It would take one month before liquor and his temper brought him down.[18]

Stationed at Fort Stanton, New Mexico, on 13 December 1876, Stance and fifteen privates were dispatched under the command of Lieutenant J. Hansell French to serve as an escort for Sheriff George Peppin in the nearby town of Lincoln. Lieutenant French and Stance, both reputedly drinking heavily, accompanied Peppin while he attended a session of the county court. That evening, French, more inebriated than ever, had himself "deputized" by the sheriff, had Stance select three enlisted men to accompany him, and commenced a search for "outlaws." Accompanied by the troopers, he disgraced himself by breaking into private residences and frightening the occupants. Before the evening ended, he had insulted Susan McSween, the widow of the slain leader of one faction in the Lincoln County War, and then had stripped to his waist and had challenged her attorney, one-armed Huston Chapman, to fisticuffs. Since French had not been "deputized" until after 9 P.M., it must have been well after midnight before he finally released the three troopers and retired for the evening.[19]

Two of the troopers whom Stance had selected to accompany French were Trumpeter George Washington and Private Louis Horton. Neither could have been in a pleasant mood the following morning when, well before daylight, they turned out with the rest of the detachment to begin the day's duties. Stance designated Horton to cook breakfast while the other men groomed their horses. When Horton asked for help, Washington volunteered, and Stance agreed.

While the troopers' breakfast was baking in the oven, Washington prepared a "private dish" (contents not disclosed) for himself and Horton. As they prepared to dine, Stance appeared and demanded a portion for himself. Perhaps testy from his late hours, Trumpeter Washington refused to share. Stance ordered him to "get it [the food] out of the frying pan then." Declaring that he had no plate in which to put it, Washington replied that he "would do nothing of the kind" and requested permission to report the matter to Lieutenant French. Trivial as this dispute sounds, the rebuff almost resulted in murder.

When Washington commenced eating, Stance declared, "I'll give you a three inch bullet hole" and stormed from the room. In a few moments, he reappeared, loaded gun in hand, and began "abusing" Washington in front of the other men while declaring "you 'sons of bitches' are all trying to take my place." The trumpeter rose, stated that he was going to see French, and started for the door. Stance cocked his carbine and took aim: "I'll blow your damn head off." Before he could fire, Corporal George McCampbell grabbed the gun and, with Horton's help, disarmed him.[20]

Stance's court-martial, presided over by Lieutenant Colonel Dudley, convened on 11 January 1879. This time, Washington was a more formidable opponent than Henry Green. An Alabaman in his third tour of duty, he had consistently received evaluations of "excellent." Although his musical inclinations had kept him from accepting a promotion before the incident, he would afterwards serve as Troop M's first sergeant for almost a decade.[21]

Besides cocking his gun at Washington, Stance was charged with being too intoxicated to perform his duties while in Lincoln. Although acquitting him on the charge of drunkenness, the court found that the following morning, still "under the influence of intoxicating liquor," he loaded his carbine, cocked it, and "threatened to shoot" Washington. Once more, Stance received only token punishment: he was reduced to the ranks and fined sixty dollars. Dudley explained that the leniency was "owing to the excellent character given him by the officers of his company" and to his "having been awarded a medal of honor by Congress for bravery on the battlefield."[22]

Stance's problems in M Troop were not over. In March 1880 he was twice convicted by garrison courts-martial at Fort Bayard and fined a total of fifteen dollars. With this, Dawson's patience snapped. Stance was placed on detached service until October, when he secured a transfer back to F Troop. The move allowed him to resurrect his career.

Through all his difficulties, his main source of pride was his medal. But for a time in early 1881 even this was denied him. He entrusted it "for repairs" to "some parties" and they promptly lost it. Fortunately, his appeal to the adjutant general for a replacement was answered favorably.

Stance's behavior temporarily improved after his transfer, and by October 1881 he again held the rank of sergeant. Even though he was now a fourth-term veteran, he had mellowed little. Impatient, inclined to bully novice soldiers, and at times sadistic, he almost got himself killed in retaliation. Moses Green, a twenty-three-year-old Virginian in his first year of enlistment, was a frequent target of Stance's temper. While the troop was searching for Boomers in Indian Territory in the summer of 1883, young Green provoked a tirade of verbal abuse from the sergeant: "I'll take my carbine and stow you away in the hospital, God damn you, you'd better stop your fooling and go to soldiering."[23]

After the troop returned to Fort Reno in late August, Green was again accosted. The affair began with a scrap between Stance and Private William Davis, during the course of which Stance dropped his pipe. While another sergeant was breaking up the melee, Green brushed past them and left the barracks. Unable to locate his pipe after the trouble with Davis subsided, Stance accused Green of taking it. Making the mistake of talking back, Green was lashed by a torrent of abuse.

Stance snarled that Green "needn't think that when Davis tried to bluff that he could too" and drew his saber. After cutting a small gash on the private's hand, he pinned him against a wall and said that "for two cents he would plunge that saber through him and send him to the hospital." Green asked him to put the saber down and "give him a man's show," but the sergeant refused. Soon afterwards, Stance discontinued his abuse and went outside. When he returned half an hour later, Green was armed with a heavy club and waiting for revenge.

By chance, Green's bunk was located next to the door of the barracks. As Stance strode by, Green struck two savage blows, one full upon the head and the other across an out-thrust arm. The sergeant fell to the floor unconscious, his head bleeding and an arm broken. Satisfied, Green quietly allowed himself to be taken into custody.

At his trial, he admitted the assault but denied he had intended to kill Stance. He had only wished "to lay him up to prevent his injuring me." He knew that if he did not disable the sergeant with the first blow, "he'd get up and injure me, because it is his custom to strike men." As evidence of this, he stated that Private Abe Washington was still in the hospital with his back injured as a result of a blow from Stance. Significantly, no one challenged this accusation.

Once more, the court-martial was lenient. Found guilty of a premeditated deadly assault, Green was confined for nine months at hard labor on the post and required to forfeit ten dollars per month for the same interval. The court attributed its moderation to Stance's "unreasonable . . . conduct towards the prisoner."

When Green returned to F Troop after completing his sentence, Stance made no known effort to retaliate. Getting married in 1886, Green received an evaluation of "very good" at the end of his enlistment.

After being reduced to the ranks for his intemperate actions, Stance once more bounced back. In May 1884, Captain Carroll restored him to the rank of sergeant. This time he held on to his chevrons and was promoted to first sergeant the following spring, shortly before Carroll left the troop to become a major in the First Cavalry.

For the next two years Stance virtually commanded F Troop. Carroll's replacement, Clarence Stedman, was on recruiting service in New York City. By tacking a four-month leave onto the end of this assignment, he delayed reporting until February 1887. After four months on duty, Stedman took another leave to return to the East for a wedding and honeymoon. Not until July was he able to devote his full attention to his troop.[24]

Since Daniel Gibbon, the troop's first lieutenant, had been on sick leave since 1881, the only officer remaining with the company was Second Lieutenant William McAnaney, one of the most enigmatic officers in the army. A native of New York, McAnaney had enlisted in the Eighth Cavalry in 1879 under an assumed name, reputedly to prevent his "low status" from becoming known to his "family and friends." As William Clare, he rapidly rose through the ranks: private, blacksmith—where his ability to treat horses as well as to shoe them caught the attention of his superiors—and then rapidly up the ladder to first sergeant. Recommended for an officer's commission in 1883, he answered every question on the required exam flawlessly. He was commissioned and assigned to the Ninth Cavalry. Six months passed before he felt secure enough to reveal his identity.[25] Although intelligent and personable, his promotion was a reminder to black noncommissioned officers that they, regardless of merit, would never be considered for a commission. McAnaney may also have been a racist.

In early 1887, Private George Pumphrey objected to McAnaney's presence on his court-martial because he believed the lieutenant was "prejudiced against my race." McAnaney customarily made derogatory remarks to black soldiers, telling Pumphrey that he "looked like an end man of a minstrel show" and a comrade that his hands "looked like two hams hanging out in front of a grocery store."[26]

McAnaney was also a frequent consumer of alcohol and a variety of narcotics. He allegedly bragged about his ability to take huge doses of opium without ill effect. Not surprisingly, in light of his "vicious habits," he was on frequent sick leave. Since his substitutes also had to continue with their regular duties, the full responsibility for the troop fell upon Stance.

In 1894, three years after transferring to a white regiment, McAnaney died of a massive drug overdose.[27] Although his service with Troop F had been regarded as satisfactory by his superiors, it is likely that he was at least partly to blame for the disturbances in the troop.

Despite the shortage of officers, Stance's troop at first had few problems. Although Stance was profane and abusive, he was also dedicated. As long as matters ran smoothly, there was no reason for officers to question his leadership. At the conclusion of his fourth tour of duty in September 1886, he was rewarded with a four-month furlough. Significantly, he made one brief visit to Omaha and then returned to duty. As he was unmarried and separated from his boyhood surroundings by twenty years of service, the military apparently was his only home.

During November 1886 the men of Troop F, decked out in full dress uniform, displayed their proficiency at drill before the departmental inspector general. They were elated by his proclamation that they had exceeded his expectations and shown that they were "excellent cavalrymen." On Stance's reenlistment in December, the troop gave a dinner and dance in his honor.[28] It seemed that time and responsibility may have mellowed him.

As 1887 progressed, discipline problems, both major and minor, escalated as recruits became increasingly defiant of the noncoms. Private William Young, the most aggressive offender, had joined the troop at the end of 1884. By November 1886 he had been convicted no less than seven times by garrison courts-martial. Despite a total of five months in the guardhouse, he was more defiant than ever. On 13 April 1887 he picked a quarrel with Private C. E. Woods and with "malice aforethought" injured Woods twice with stones fired from a slingshot.

A general court-martial sentenced Young to be discharged without honor, but the departmental judge advocate disapproved the sentence because it did not include a prison term. His refusal to tolerate leniency meant that Young had to be returned to duty.[29] Stance and his fellow sergeants would have to deal with the incorrigible rebel once more.

Young was not necessarily the most violent of the men in Troop F. While patronizing a "low resort" in nearby Crawford, Private Alex Moody got into a fight with another private, drew his pistol, and inflicted a serious gunshot wound. Moody promptly deserted but was apprehended and given a dishonorable discharge with two years' confinement in prison tacked on.[30]

In June the lack of officers coincided with a flurry of incidents that kept the troop barracks in an uproar. Captain Stedman was absent on his honeymoon, and McAnaney was preoccupied with his imminent departure for a term at the Infantry and Cavalry School at Fort Leavenworth. Sergeant Nathan Fletcher, the longest tenured and most dependable non-commissioned officer in the company, left on 26 May for a four-month furlough. The arrival of ten more recruits to be broken in must have seemed like the last straw to Stance and the other NCOs, some of whom were also in their first term of enlistment. With virtually no supervision from above, Stance apparently pushed the recruits too hard.[31]

One private defied an order to clean the stables, angrily snarling, "Why the devil don't you make some of these other men do something?" Another reacted to an order to tether his horse by accusing the noncoms of "bulldozing" and cursing him ever since he had joined the troop. Compounding his mistake by showing disrespect to McAnaney, he received a thirty-day sentence.[32]

In a dining-hall row on 23 June, David Kendrick broke a bowl over the head of new recruit William Smith. Although Smith had to undergo "surgery" before returning to duty, he was judged to have provoked the incident by drawing a knife on Kendrick. Both men were court-martialed; both were acquitted.[33]

Only one June incident directly involved Stance. He upbraided Private Henry Royster for carelessness while watering the horses and threatened to bring charges unless more care was shown. Royster's insolent response resulted in a ten-day sentence. Although such incidents were inevitable when dealing with new recruits, their frequency suggests a serious rift between the noncommissioned officers and the privates. Despite these squabbles, the troopers enthusiastically greeted Stedman and his bride when they arrived in early July. On the 6 July, Troop F gave a ball in the newlyweds' honor that was attended by Colonel Hatch, Major A. S. Burt, and most of the other officers on the post.[34]

The most serious breakdown in discipline erupted with little warning in the troop barracks during the evening of 17 August. Private Thomas Richardson, who had reported for duty only two months earlier, balked at an order to carry a locker, which he had just cleaned, back to its proper location. Although the locker weighed less than fifty pounds, he asserted, "I can't carry it and will not." Stance ordered him to be taken to the guardhouse. Enraged, Richardson leaped at the sergeant, striking him first with his fists and then with a heavy boot.

As Stance was fending off the attack, he was seized from behind by William Young. Calling to Richardson, "Put it to him, God damn him!" Young ripped off Stance's shirt before he and Richardson were subdued. As he was taken to the guardhouse, he cursed Stance and muttered that "before this thing is over, you will be where I am going tonight." Young received a dishonorable discharge plus six months at hard labor, while Richardson was sentenced to ten months at hard labor and to forfeit eleven dollars a month for one year.[35]

During September, Private Louis Glenn took exception to a relatively innocuous order from Stance. Told to "stop jerking" his horse when watering it, he demanded to see Captain Stedman and uttered a veiled threat, "I am tired of your bulldozing me, Sergeant Stance." He received a five-dollar fine and ten days at hard labor. In November it was the troop blacksmith, George Waterford, who challenged Stance's authority. Ordered to cease making a commotion, Waterford responded that anyone who bothered him was "tired of living." He received a ten-dollar fine.[36]

Such incidents did not mean that the troop consisted solely of disorderly ruffians. One incident, for example, involved Sergeant Ebbert Maden. Maden had enlisted in 1880, had rapidly risen to the rank of sergeant, and had married "one of Omaha's belles" in June 1886. His military career was sidetracked on a November morning in 1887 when he got into a fracas with another sergeant in the company stables. Ruled to have provoked the brawl by calling his adversary a liar, he was reduced to the ranks while his opponent had only to forfeit a month's pay. The harshness of his sentence most likely was because of testimony that he had allowed men on stable duty to play cards by candlelight, exposing the stables to the danger of fire.

Although this incident indicates Maden was a poor noncommissioned officer, this was not the case. In subsequent years he was commended in orders for helping to recapture an escaped prisoner, was acclaimed as one of the best shots in the regiment, and was restored to the rank of sergeant. After participating in the Santiago campaign in Cuba, he was commissioned a lieutenant in a volunteer infantry regiment—a black one, needless to say—and was promoted to captain in November 1899.[37] It was quite an impressive rise for a stable-floor brawler.

The most striking indication that Troop F was not composed solely of malcontents is provided by Sergeant Joseph Moore. Moore spent much of his army career as an educator, organizing post schools for both children and enlisted men under the direction of Chaplain Henry Plummer. He also was credited with establishing a well-attended Sunday School at Fort Robinson. One of the few black cavalrymen at the post deemed worthy of being selected for a stint as acting sergeant major, he became involved in crusades ranging from raising funds for a memorial to abolitionist martyr John Brown to providing aid for the black victims of a Nebraska flood. Like Sergeant Maden, he received a commission as a lieutenant in a black volunteer infantry regiment following the Spanish-American War.[38]

Despite such men as Maden and Moore, the number of discipline problems in Troop F led Colonel Hatch to provide Stedman with additional officers. In November, Lieutenant Joseph Garrard, one of the regiment's most respected officers, replaced the perpetually absent Daniel Gibbon. In addition, Hatch assigned Lieutenant John Alexander, a recent black graduate of West Point, to temporary duty with the troop.[39] The additional officers, however, arrived too late to avert disaster.

Christmas seasons had seldom brought good fortune to Emanuel Stance. Both of his general courts-martial and several of his arrests had occurred during the year-end holidays. On Christmas Eve 1887 he rode into Crawford for a night on the town. Undoubtedly indulging in some combination of drink, sex, and cards, he did not leave for the post until well past midnight. Shortly after sunup, Lieutenant Garrard discovered his body, punctured by four gunshot wounds, midway between Crawford and the fort.[40]

In death he was acclaimed a hero who was unsurpassed "in the esteem of his superiors." A release to the *Army and Navy Journal* emphasized that he wore a "medal awarded by Congress for bravery in *rescuing children from Indians.*" (One wonders if Stance had exaggerated his feat.) Shortly before 10 A.M. on 28 December 1887, all four troops of buffalo soldiers at the fort escorted his body to the post cemetery. Trailing behind were carriages containing the officers and their families. A sixteen-man honor guard fired a farewell salute as the body was lowered into the grave.[41]

Stance left few mourners outside the post limits. Since he apparently had no close relatives, it was speculated that the medal he had cherished over the years and a "manuscript of his life, with drawings," on which he had been working, should be deposited in the "Army Museum."[42] Just what happened to these items is not known.

The identity of his killer or killers was never established. It would be logical to think that someone in Crawford had observed his departure and intercepted him. If this were not the case, his death could have occurred because of a chance encounter with a person harboring the motive and means of killing him.

These possibilities were discarded because of an assumption that the murderer came from his own troop. Within a few hours of the body's discovery, Captain Corliss noted in his diary that the murder "probably" was committed by "men of his own troop." A few days later, a release to the Army and Navy Journal speculated that the "perpetrators of this villainous murder" were soldiers stationed at Fort Robinson. It explained that Stance was very strict because "his troop needed a strong hand, and it took a pretty nervy man to be 1st sergeant."[43]

After a poorly executed investigation, Private Miller Milds, who had had few recorded imbroglios with Stance, was arrested. In January 1887, shortly after Milds had joined the troop, Stance had charged him with being absent without leave. Convicted, Milds had been imprisoned for a month. After that, he steered clear of much of the unrest because he was on stable duty.[44]

Although Milds was confined throughout 1888, he was never brought to trial. Despite Hatch's desire to see justice done, his superiors finally ordered the suspect's release because of the expense that a trial would entail. In lieu of a prison term, Milds, described as a "worthless scamp" suffering from syphilis, was simply discharged from the service.[45]

Since the evidence connecting Milds to Stance's murder was never revealed, there is no way of knowing if he was guilty. In a sense, the swan song concerning the affair was provided by Private Simpson Mann, who joined Troop F more than a year after Stance's death. More than half a century later, Mann remembered being told that two or three members of the troop had killed a sergeant "who had beaten soldiers" and then lied about them to Captain Stedman. As Mann recalled hazily, Stance had been "dirty mean," while Stedman "didn't know as much of the soldiers as he should" and relied too much on what his NCOs told him.[46]

Stance may have been "dirty mean." He certainly was too hot-tempered and too heavy a drinker to be entrusted with a first sergeant's responsibilities. But it is unreasonable to think that he was restored to rank every time he was busted simply because his superiors were indifferent bureaucrats who encouraged sadistic tyrants. He lived in a violent world; his character flaws may have made it more so; nevertheless, he was also a first-class soldier who with different role models and steadier supervision might have lived a more tranquil and longer life.

11

Private Miller's Martyrdom and theTriumph of L Troop

During most of its stay in Texas, L Troop was stationed in the chaparral-covered valley of the lower Rio Grande. In the years since the Texas Revolution, Anglo ranchers had gained title to the land along the river, placed their brands on the longhorns that roamed the chaparral, and employed descendants of the original rancheros, many still loyal to Mexico, to tend the cattle. South of the river, numerous bandits, professedly seeking revenge for past injustices, constantly ran stolen cattle across the river. Their incessant raids at times seemed on the verge of driving the Anglos from the region. Caught in the middle was L Troop.

Typical of the crude border posts was Fort McIntosh, on the outskirts of Laredo. As late as December 1872 it had no troop barracks. An infantry company and some of the officers were quartered in the post hospital, while the black troopers occupied a storehouse. Quarters for sick soldiers and storage facilities were rented at exorbitant rates in Laredo.[1]

Cheap liquor and prostitutes, nonstop gambling, and poor sanitation made border service hazardous to health and morals. Dissipation was so rampant that in 1869, Major T. M. Anderson demanded that the mayor close all saloons at midnight, or "military patrols will do so." The major confined cockfighting, which had been prevalent "in the streets," to the town plaza. To improve sanitation he ordered all garbage to be put in barrels to be picked up by the military. Finally, the "offal from slaughtered cattle" must be taken at least a mile from the public market.[2]

In confronting these hazards, L Troop was fortunate to have excellent noncommissioned officers. Charles Chinn and George Mason, both dark-skinned Kentuckians, served into the 1890s without a blotch on their records. Unfortunately, Chinn departed to become the first sergeant of C Troop in 1877. In 1887 he was one of the first men from the regiment to be promoted to ordnance sergeant. He also penned a tribute to Charles Sumner that was published in the *Army and Navy Journal* in 1874, and, two decades later, he filed suit against a Jim Crow railway law.[3]

Mason, only eighteen when he enlisted in 1867 and still listed as illiterate in the 1870 census (one has to doubt the accuracy of the census taker), served as the troop's first sergeant for more than twenty years.[4] Neither the men serving under him nor the officers over him ever had reason to complain. Other than by a string of "excellent" evaluations, one can deduce his worth only by contrasting the numbers of arrests, courts-martial, and desertions in L Troop with those of other companies.

In early 1869, L Troop was switched to Fort Duncan, near Eagle Pass, part of a subdistrict commanded by Colonel Mackenzie. Detachments led by Lieutenant Charles Parker participated in three expeditions, marching more than two thousand miles and helping destroy three Indian camps. The troop also suffered its first campaign death. While fording the Pecos in June, Private Edward Williams was drowned.[5]

Throughout the months of campaigning there had been few discipline problems. Out of a roster of seventy-eight, the number under arrest averaged slightly over three. Only two men deserted; one was court-martialed. With a return to garrison life in proximity to cantinas and bordellos, discipline deteriorated, in part because of the lack of officers. In February, Parker, the troop's acting commander, was promoted. Since his replacement, E. D. Dimmick, did not arrive for three months and the troop lacked a second lieutenant, the full burden was placed on Captain Jacob DeGress.

A Prussian-born Missourian thrice breveted in the Civil War, DeGress had during the siege of Vicksburg incurred a wound that had ended his wartime service. Although commissioned in the postwar army, he was so prone to epileptic attacks that it was dangerous for him to ride a horse.[6] DeGress alternated between periods of neglect and harshness. In April 1870 he placed eight men under arrest; five received dishonorable discharges. After a quiet summer, fifteen men were confined to the guardhouse in October and another thirteen were fined from twelve to fifteen dollars each. During the final three months of the year, nine troopers received dishonorable discharges with prison terms ranging up to fifteen years. Six others deserted into Mexico.[7]

Some of the offenses were serious indeed. Corporal Denbar Perry, ordered to lead a four-man detachment to a nearby settlement to provide an escort for Lieutenant F. A. Kendall of the Twenty-fifth Infantry, arrived late and inebriated. When Kendall questioned him, he replied in an "unsoldierly and contemptuous manner" that "I've been out with a hundred officers and you are the first one that I ever had trouble with." He refused to relinquish command of the detachment and persuaded the others to abandon the lieutenant and return to Fort Duncan. Despite his mutinous actions, his "previous good conduct" influenced the court to give him "only" fifteen years at hard labor with a steel ball chained to his leg.[8]

Serious though this was, most offenses were trivial. Privates Frank Thomas and Humphrey Williams, for example, stole a pig belonging to Private Henry Fletcher and "did kill, skin, and appropriate a part of the same" to their "own use and benefit." Their appetites whetted, they repeated the act two days later, feasting on one belonging to members of the Twenty-fifth Infantry. Although each animal was valued at only twelve dollars, a court-martial gave them dishonorable discharges plus imprisonment until the expiration of their enlistments.[9]

As a result of the turmoil, few reenlisted when their terms expired. Although the buffalo soldiers were later noted for a high reenlistment rate, this was not true of the original recruits. All companies were decimated, but few as badly as L Troop. In November 1871 its enlisted strength was fifty-nine. In December, twenty-six enlistments expired; two reenlisted. In January, another eighteen expired; one reenlisted. By April its roster had shrunk to fifteen, one of whom was in prison. Not until June did fifty new recruits, more than half from Kentucky, arrive.[10]

Mostly farmers and laborers with a median age of twenty-two, they would fare much better than their predecessors. This was in part because of the reenlistment of Sergeants Chinn, Mason, Bailey Green, and Lawson Smith.

In addition, fate dealt them one of the most gifted officers in the regiment. When DeGress resigned to become the Texas superintendent of education, he was replaced by Francis Moore, regarded by Colonel Hatch as his "best officer . . . in every respect." Reared in Scotland, Moore immigrated to Canada in 1859. Moving to the United States after the outbreak of war, he enlisted in the First Colorado Cavalry in September 1861. During the next two years he helped to turn back a Confederate invasion of New Mexico at Glorieta and scouted for Indians in Colorado. In December 1863 he secured a commission as captain in the Sixty-fifth U.S. Colored Cavalry and had risen to the rank of lieutenant colonel by the end of the war. Temporarily assigned to the Ninth Cavalry in 1866, he so impressed Hatch that he received a regular commission with the regiment.[11] One of his first acts on taking command was to promote George Mason to the post of first sergeant.

One of the troop's least impressive recruits was James Miller. Nineteen, relatively tall for a buffalo soldier at five feet eleven inches, and described as a mulatto, he had been born in Philadelphia, at least one generation removed from slavery. Often sick and seldom selected for scouts, he was hardly a favorite of his superiors. Popular with his comrades, he frequented bars when off duty. These were the cause of most of his troubles in the military.

In early 1872, Company L had returned to Fort McIntosh, to which Laredo's taverns were still accessible. In July, Miller was accused of assaulting a Mexican in a barroom brawl. He was held in the Laredo jail until October, when he was convicted of aggravated assault and returned to confinement. Released in January 1873, he received no additional punishment from the military. He stayed out of further trouble until October 1874, when he was briefly confined for a minor offense and fined eight dollars. Nondescript as his record was, he was destined to become the troop's most tragic figure.[12]

In March 1873, L Troop was transferred downstream to Fort Ringgold, a post with better housing but just as many bars and even thicker chaparral. Responsible for patrolling a seventy-mile stretch along the Rio Grande, the troopers were constantly on the move. A thirty-man picket was maintained at Salinas, about thirty-five miles upstream. Every three days, patrols set out from both Salinas and Ringgold to search for cattle rustlers. The scouts produced impressive mileage figures, 1,348 miles in a two-month span in 1874, but few results until 24 November 1874, when Sergeant James Randolph and three privates surprised a party of rustlers. Opening fire, they captured one and "scattered the rest." Although Randolph was temporarily a hero, his army career ended in disgrace five years later at El Paso when he received a dishonorable discharge for stealing five sacks of corn.[13]

After eight years in the sweltering chaparral, the men of L Troop could not have been displeased in 1875 when they were ordered to move to New Mexico. For them the transfer meant a 1,390-mile trek from Fort Brown, near the mouth of the Rio Grande, via Forts Clark and Davis to El Paso and then northward to their new station. The company arrived at Fort Selden, near Las Cruces, on 27 November, eighty-one days after its departure from Brownsville. Even though Captain Moore was the only officer on the march, no one died, deserted, or was placed under arrest en route, and only three were listed as sick. They had left Fort Brown with fifty serviceable horses and arrived with all fifty still fit. Inspected at Fort Selden by Major James Wade, the troop received across-the-board "excellents" for only the second time in its history.[14]

After stopovers at Forts Selden and Stanton, L Troop was ordered to Fort Union, northeast of Las Vegas. It arrived on 13 January, more than four months after leaving Fort Brown. Although troops at Fort Union no longer had to confront Comanches, they faced a more perplexing situation. In nearby Cimarron, center of the vast Maxwell land grant, all law had broken down. The numerous squatters in the area were threatened with eviction by the Maxwell interests, and gunmen, many of them Texans, were employed by both sides. Among the pawns caught in the maelstrom were the buffalo soldiers.

Three weeks after they arrived at Fort Union, General Pope ordered the stationing of troops in Cimarron to protect local officials. On 16 March, thirty troopers, led by Captain Moore, arrived in the beleaguered town. They met with instant hostility resulting from racism and their being viewed as tools of the Maxwell forces.[15]

Among the most notorious gunfighters in Cimarron were David Crockett, rumored to be a nephew of the hero of the Alamo, and his crony, Gus Heffron. Although Crockett and Heffron have been described by one writer, perhaps with tongue in cheek, as "good citizens," they were known to get drunk, enter stores on horseback, and compel the "clerks to black their boots at the point of a pistol." They did not wait to unleash their racist venom upon the buffalo soldiers.[16]

On the afternoon of 24 March, Crockett encountered two troopers in a saloon, drew his gun, and ordered them to leave. When they reported the incident, Moore forbade anyone to leave camp without permission. Despite this, the two, joined by a comrade, slipped out after taps and, in Moore's words, "threw themselves in the way of trouble."[17]

There was little in their records to indicate they were troublemakers. All were in their fourth year of service. George Small, a twenty-five-year-old Kentuckian who had been selected for numerous scouts and patrols, had incurred a fine of ten dollars in June 1874 and one for three dollars in June 1875. Anthony Harvey, a sailor from Prince Edward Island, Canada, before he enlisted in December 1872, had incurred one three-dollar fine in June 1875. The third soldier, a twenty-seven-year-old Marylander named John Hanson, in April 1874 had been fined five dollars and sentenced to "carry a log" for five days. As a further indication of good character, all had saved modest amounts from their thirteen-dollar-a-month pay checks. Small, for example, had a balance of 167 dollars due in pay, unused clothing allowances, and money on deposit with the paymaster.[18]

Had the troopers intended to challenge Crockett, it seems likely they would have returned to the saloon in which they had been accosted. Instead, they made their way to the bar of the Saint James Hotel. According to Frank Springer, the only recorded eyewitness (and also a partisan of Crockett's), there were about ten men in the bar when the troopers arrived. After a short stay, the soldiers had started to leave when Crockett and his friend arrived. When a soldier "addressed some rough language" towards Crockett and "advanced as if to seize him," the Texan fired—obviously in self-defense.[19]

Springer, however, allegedly told William Pile, an Indian agent in New Mexico, that Crockett shot the soldiers "without provocation on their part, or a word of warning on his."[20] In addition, none of the early newspaper accounts agreed with his first version of events. Even before it learned the identity of the shooters, the *New Mexican* reported that the incident occurred "as three of the colored soldiers . . . were entering the bar" and that "from what we can gather from the bartender there was no provocation whatever." Captain Moore reported that "two or three drunken herders" were already in the bar when the soldiers arrived and had opened fire "immediately" afterwards. Two of the soldiers managed to pull their pistols and perhaps fire a shot or two before they collapsed.[21]

Moore, alerted by the hotel proprietor, began a futile search for the killers. Not a single resident rendered any aid; only one admitted having seen the shooting, and he claimed only to have seen Crockett fire a single shot. As for the buffalo soldiers, Moore reported simply that "although my men are somewhat excited, everything is quiet." His search fruitless, Moore returned to Fort Union in mid-April.

But justice, New Mexico style, was not to be denied. In early August, Crockett and Heffron presented themselves for a hearing. The judge obligingly ruled that "the evidence failed to show any reason for holding them" and ordered their discharge. A few weeks later, Crockett was found guilty of "carrying concealed arms" and fined fifty dollars.[22]

The failure to punish the killers embittered the men of L Troop. With the law uninterested, their only recourse was to "band together and protect themselves."[23] At least one resolved that next time, *he* would be the one to shoot first.

Troop L did not remain long at Fort Union. Following the annihilation of Custer's command in June, the Fifth Cavalry was shifted northward to confront the Sioux, forcing the Ninth to garrison posts in Colorado and Kansas. L Troop was ordered to Fort Lyon on the outskirts of Las Animas, Colorado, a cattle shipping center on the Santa Fe Railroad. Racists were as abundant there as in Cimarron.

With social outlets for buffalo soldiers as limited as ever, the men of L Troop patronized the same bars and brothels as did cowboys and white soldiers. Given the temperament of the cattlemen and the soldiers' memories of Cimarron, another clash may have been inevitable.

An incident on 26 August at a "notorious den of iniquity" whose clientele had been expanded to include buffalo soldiers furnished the prelude for a night of terror. Presided over by a Mrs. McClain, the bordello featured her two teenage daughters. On the day in question, some cowboys called on the McClains and, for causes unknown, one slapped sixteen-year-old "Miss Bell." After they left, mother and daughter went to the vicinity of Fort Lyon, where they poured out their story to some black soldiers, who offered them "their protection." Sometime later, the McClains were observed seated with some of the soldiers under a nearby tree. These occurrences may have had nothing to do with subsequent events, but the editor of the *Las Animas Leader* deduced that the McClains "procured or abetted the murderous scheme" that unfolded that evening.[25]

As the evening wore on, a number of cowmen were drinking at the bar of the Exchange Hotel. About eleven o'clock, Private Miller arrived and made his way to the bar next to two Texans, James Greer and John Sutherland. Greer abruptly ordered Miller to "step aside. . . . I do not drink with a damn nigger!" Drawing a revolver, Greer cursed Miller: "You black son-of-a-bitch, what are you doing here?"[26]

Another version, recalled years later by a Las Animas cowman, stated that Miller had "stepped up to the bar" when Greer challenged him: "Nigger, what are you doing here?" When the soldier replied that he wanted a drink, Greer struck him a blow that caused "a general row."[27]

Humiliation, rage, and memories of his slain comrades in Cimarron combined to cause Miller to vow vengeance as he was ejected from the room. Meeting a group of troopers also out after taps, he received immediate pledges of support. Inside the saloon, Sutherland, soon to be eulogized as "one of the finest and bravest men that ever lived," was chastising Greer for his actions: "You must not say anything to that man, he has done nothing to you." Without warning, Miller and another soldier appeared in the doorway, carbines in hand, and opened fire. Greer was their target, but Sutherland was the one who fell to the floor, mortally wounded. Only one other person, an unnamed "innocent bystander," was hit, even though some of Miller's comrades joined in the shooting. The troopers rushed back to their quarters, but too late. Hearing the gunshots, Sergeant Mason had already checked roll.

After Miller was taken into custody, wild rumors flooded the town. Gangs of enraged cowboys were planning to storm the fort "and kill all the Negroes"; the troopers, afraid Miller would be lynched if confined in the local jail, were going to "burn the town" if this occurred. "From their manner," the intuitive editor of the *Leader* surmised, they "had little fear of their officers or the law." To put his readers on guard, he warned that L Troop was the same detachment that had "caused" the "riotous demonstration" at Cimarron (in which three of their comrades had been gunned down) and that "it is said that Miller was the ring leader in that affair."[28]

Post Commander C. H. Smith made the best of a ticklish situation. After assuring the cowboys that he would "do everything in his power to punish the men that committed the terrible crime," he eased the fears of the buffalo soldiers by insisting that Miller be confined in the post guardhouse. Even though it was obvious that several troopers had been involved, and the names of the men who had missed the roll check were on record, Miller alone had been identified by witnesses. In early

September, five of the absentees were tried before a garrison court-martial, fined, and given thirty-day sentences in the guardhouse.[29]

Murders were as common in Las Animas as in Cimarron, but the shooting of a white man by a black was not to be condoned. The *Leader* piously intoned that all the "armed ruffians [black soldiers] . . . turned loose upon unarmed citizens" must be dealt with severely. Indulging in an orgy of racist hypocrisy, it added that they "must be punished for the sake of their own race." Blacks were "tractable animals" who could be made into "exactly what we give them the opportunity of learning."[30]

With Miller locked away, the town fathers concentrated on the wretched McClains. Believing the women were responsible for the "horrible tragedy," the town "requested" them to leave. One-way tickets to Pueblo were delivered to the conductor of the Santa Fe train "as the family got aboard." Lest anyone think they had been mistreated, the *Leader* described the "ill luck" that befell "those who have had any relations with them." Of Mrs. McClain's three husbands, one had been executed, one shot to death, and the last sent to the penitentiary. Miss Bell, when age thirteen, had married a soldier at Fort Lyon "who has since been sent to military prison." The other daughter had married a man "who was in jail afterwards for stealing."[31] In purging themselves of such founts of vice, the townsmen lost any chance of discovering any connection between them and Miller.

The investigation continued through the fall of 1876. Bent County, in which Las Animas was located, elected a new sheriff, John Spiers, a former school superintendent described as a "kind hearted" man. The town completed a new jail whose cell walls, ceilings, and floors were made of "iron riveted solidly together." A stone wall with half-inch steel doors and heavily barred windows made the structure escape proof and capable of deterring "vigilance committees."[32]

In November, a grand jury indicted Miller and six other troopers for murder. All but two had enlisted in L Troop in early 1872; the majority were Kentuckians. Of the lot, only Nathan Trent, a twenty-five-year-old Virginian, was an obvious troublemaker. In one tour of service he had incurred eight fines for a total of sixty-two dollars and had received two thirty-day stretches in the guardhouse. More typical of the accused were Kentuckians James Payne and William Jones. Neither Payne, the company blacksmith, nor Jones, a plasterer by trade and described as a blue-eyed mulatto, had a transgression on his record.[33]

The trial began on 6 December. Five of the indicted men were released for lack of evidence, leaving Miller and Private Benjamin Smith, a twenty-six-year-old Kentuckian, as defendants. Judge John Henry presided over the trial; Pueblo lawyer M. B. Geary had charge of the defense. Selecting an all-white jury took a day and a half; thereafter, the outcome was certain.

Miller had no chance of acquittal. Smith, in contrast, was identified only by a prostitute, Rachel LeRoy. She had recently recalled looking out a second-story window the night of the shooting and seeing Smith emerge from the saloon. In vain, Smith claimed she had "demanded money" to keep her from making "it hot for him." Sixteen witnesses, most of them buffalo soldiers, testified that Smith and Miller had been in their barracks when they heard the shooting. They had missed Sergeant Mason's roll check because they had left the post after hearing the gunshots "to see what was going on."[34]

Both defendants denied being at the scene of the shooting. One cryptic remark of Miller's, not followed up, indicated that the McClains might have been involved: "The women came to the quarters and said the cowboys were going to whip nigger soldiers. One man asked me to go. I objected." After the testimony had concluded, the counsels made their closing arguments. Shortly after midnight on 17 December the jury received its instructions, deliberated for an hour, and found both Miller and Smith guilty of premeditated murder.

During the trial, distrust of the soldiers spawned wild rumors. In distant Santa Fe, the *New Mexican* reported that stories were "current" that the troopers had rescued the "two negroes confined in the Bent County Jail." It had heard that the prosecution's "principal witness" had been killed "by having his head almost cut off."[35]

The defendants were sentenced to be hanged on 19 January 1877. A thrill seemed to run through Las Animas as its citizens sought to capitalize on the honor of conducting the first legal execution since Colorado had become a state. The only threat to their festivities was Chaplain J. A. M. LaTourette, a reform-minded Episcopalian from New York. To the last hour he endeavored to get the sentences commuted to life imprisonment.

LaTourette's efforts achieved partial success when Governor John Routt, presented with "evidence which tended to throw some doubt" on Smith's guilt, commuted his sentence to life imprisonment. Afraid that Miller might also escape the gallows, the *Leader* vehemently protested that another commutation would "encourage lynch law." If "denied the hanging" after spending thousands of dollars convicting Miller, the citizens "who have waited . . . with so much forbearance" would be discouraged. The *Leader* especially blamed LaTourette. "The Parson . . . probably thinks he is doing God's service," but would he have acted the same way had it been Sutherland who killed the soldier?[36]

While Miller awaited execution, Las Animas witnessed another homicide that dramatized its double standard of justice. Clay Allison, a noted gunfighter and a friend of the men who killed the three troopers in Cimarron, visited the town in company with his younger brother, John. Dropping in on a dance at the Olympic Dance Hall, the Allisons began "trampling" on the toes of other dancers. When the town constable, Charles Faber, attempted to arrest them, Allison pulled a gun and forced him to leave.

Humiliated in much the same fashion as Miller had been, Faber reacted the same way. He found two unnamed "deputies," armed himself with a shotgun, returned to the dance hall, and opened fire without warning. Like Miller, he shot the wrong man; in his case it was Clay's kid brother. It was a fatal mistake. Clay returned the fire, dropping Faber with the first shot, and then fired bullet after bullet into the crumpled body. Faber's unnamed "deputies" took flight.[37]

Just as it had lauded Sutherland, the *Leader* extolled Faber as "an excellent officer, gentlemanly, discreet and brave," whose death would be "a painful blow to the community." After a coroner's jury ruled that Faber had been killed in "the performance of his official duty," Allison was arrested and held for trial. Although Miller and Allison were unlikely cellmates for a few days, justice was much kinder to the gunfighter than to the buffalo soldier.

Taken before the judge who had sentenced Miller, Allison was released on bail with his charge reduced to manslaughter. Governor Routt suggested that "some partiality" might have been shown on "account of color" resulting in Allison's receiving "too much lenity." What he thought when a grand jury refused to indict Allison on the grounds of self-defense was not recorded.[38]

As the day of the execution approached, the town's fascination with its upcoming spectacle heightened. An elaborate gallows, with a sixteen-foot-high cross-beam to support the hangman's rope and a platform, six feet high, with a trap door in its middle, was constructed directly in front of the jail. As if to confirm its handiwork, Miller was asked to inspect the gallows. He "ascended the scaffold, inquired how the drop was operated, and pronounced the structure a success." In the pages of the *Leader* the buffalo soldier had evolved from a barbaric killer into a model inmate, "whiling the time away cheerfully."[39]

To add to the festive spirit, the *Leader* proudly announced that a Negro minstrel, "far superior to anything in the way of amusement ever tendered" the town, would open just two days before the execution. The program, touted as "select, chaste and refined," so as not to "mar the feelings of the most fastidious," consisted of "comic refrains, songs and dances, . . . plantation ditties, . . . selected negro farces, etc." Playing before "a crowded and enthusiastic house," the minstrel show contained "many things to bring the laugh" as cork-faced "darkies" performed their antics.[40]

However amusing the cork-faced "darkies" were, interest in them was less than in the scene that occurred inside the jail the same day. LaTourette had learned that Miller had been courting Bithy Ann Millsed, one of the troop's laundresses. When he suggested it would be proper for them to join in "the holy bonds of wedlock," Miller and Miss Millsed agreed to a ceremony.

Breathlessly, the *Leader* described Miller's union with "the Bride of Death." A deputy acted as the best man, and Sheriff Spiers, "in a good fatherly way," gave away the bride as the chaplain performed the ceremony. Among the seven "privileged spectators" were Sergeant and Mrs. Mason.[41] Whatever the marriage meant to the bride and groom, it was only of momentary interest to the *Leader*. Bithy Ann was never again mentioned in its pages, not even in connection with the execution.

With his spiritual endeavors promising success, LaTourette sent a last-minute plea to the governor for a stay of execution to allow Miller time for "religious preparation for death." Two hours before the hanging, the governor granted a delay to 2 February. By this time Miller had turned fully to the only outlet left him, religion. Professing not to fear death but to feel "as if he was about to start on a long and pleasant journey," he was administered "the rites of confirmation and the holy communion" by the Reverend J. F. Spaulding, the Episcopalian bishop of Colorado. Some, however, questioned his sincerity, for he was heard expressing himself profanely against "being visited as an object of curiosity."[42]

During the hours of counseling, Miller admitted firing the fatal shot but expressed regret that Sutherland had been killed. His intent was to take revenge on Greer. As though "unconscious of having committed a crime," LaTourette observed, he "simply" considered himself "a martyr for his race." He "dwells frequently" on his comrades' murders in Cimarron and "the fact that nothing was done by the civil authorities." When Greer drew the pistol, he "thought his life to be in danger . . . and felt justified in his course."[43] There was no way the residents of Las Animas could appreciate the truths inherent in this statement.

As befitted the occasion, the press gave an almost play-by-play report of Miller's final hours. The condemned man refused a last request to name his accomplices, replying that his mind was "upon God and the salvation of his soul." In addition to three ministers, two unidentified sergeants shared his last hours. After he gave them directions for the disposal of his belongings, one said that he could not stand to stay and see him executed. Miller replied, "Do as you choose. It can't hurt me."

Throughout the agonizing wait, "he spoke with a steady voice and his nerves seemed as steady as iron." Brushing his hair carefully, he donned "a cavalry blouse and pantaloons," a "slouch" hat, and a pair of slippers. Once, he moved to the door and "looked anxiously" out at the crowd that was gathering around the gallows. When the summons came, he ascended the platform with "a full elastic step" and took his place over the trap, "without the quiver of a muscle." An onlooker recalled years later that "the poor negro died what they call game."[44]

The noose was adjusted around Miller's neck, LaTourette recited another prayer, and Sheriff Spiers "read the death warrant in strong and steady voice." After Miller declined a last request to "expiate your crime" by revealing the names of his accomplices, the sheriff prepared to pull the lever.

"Goodbye, Miller, I hope you will go to heaven."

"Goodbye, Spiers, take care of yourself."

"Repeating a prayer, Miller looked out at his comrades in the crowd and said softly, 'Farewell friends, farewell! May God have mercy upon me.'"

The sheriff made two pulls before the trap door sprang open and the prisoner plunged to his death. Unfortunately, the platform was so low that his feet, tightly strapped together, came to rest on a wooden block, keeping his neck from breaking. The block was immediately pushed away and he swung free, muscles contracting violently as he died a "terrible death by strangulation," according to an onlooker. Although the Las Animas reporter was too civic-minded to admit that the town had botched its execution, the *Chieftain* of nearby Pueblo confirmed that something had gone awry. After several minutes elapsed, a doctor "felt the pulse and found Miller still alive." Twenty minutes later he was pronounced dead, cut down, and turned over to his comrades for burial at Fort Lyon.[45]

Although James Miller might have been one of the least distinguished soldiers in the regiment, the dignity with which he conducted himself in the circuslike atmosphere of a racist cattle town provides a rare glimpse into the psyche of a buffalo soldier. The detailed and all-too-revealing comments of the *Leader's* editor reveal graphically the hostility that surrounded the black troopers as they tried to be "all that soldiers should be." In a very real sense, Miller was indeed a "martyr for his race."

Miller's death had a devastating effect on L Troop's morale. By chance, the enlistments of twenty-three men expired during the two months following his death. Two reenlisted.[46] Captain Moore and Sergeant Mason were faced with the task of rebuilding the troop. To their credit they molded it into one of the outstanding units in the cavalry.

During the Victorio War, L Troop participated in at least ten engagements. Two of its members, Privates John Johnson and Major Woodard, both Virginians in their mid-thirties, were killed on 30 September 1879 fighting with Major Morrow at the head of the Cuchillo Negro Canyon. They were buried within feet of where they fell.[47] Having distinguished itself in combat, the company excelled even more with the close of hostilities.

Spared the task of patrolling the Indian Territory against incursions of Boomers, it spent the early 1880s on garrison duty at Fort Elliott in the Texas Panhandle and Fort Lyon. Although inactivity often led to disciplinary breakdowns, it became noted for its excellent conduct and high morale. Just how Mason, with Moore's support, worked his magic is not known, but the statistical evidence is convincing. During the three-year period from 1885 to 1887, ninety-one men deserted from the Ninth Cavalry; three were from L Troop. During the same interval, fifty-one received dishonorable discharges; one was from L Troop.[48] If the observation of General George Crook that "discipline is usually best in companies where trials are fewest" was valid, it may have been the army's best disciplined troop.[49]

In October 1886, the troop was detached from the regiment to serve at Fort Leavenworth, headquarters of the Department of the Missouri and site of the infantry and cavalry schools. It marked the first time a black unit had been stationed at Leavenworth since Grierson had organized the Tenth Cavalry there twenty years earlier. Shortly afterwards, one of the troop's noncommissioned officers sent an ebullient message to the *Cleveland Gazette* indicating their pride. Asserting that the assignment "was like a two-edged sword," he vowed that "regardless of whom it cut, they intend to show the public that the colored soldiers are capable of soldiering wherever there is a military post" and that their discipline would compare "with the best throughout the army."[50]

Never was a prediction better fulfilled. Throughout its tenure the troop performed its duties flawlessly without a hint of disciplinary problems. After it had been at Leavenworth for three years, General Wesley Merritt, commander of the Department of the Missouri, stated it had "the admiration of all who know what a superior organization is." The following year, it was described as the "best troop at Fort Leavenworth."[51]

In the summer of 1890, L Troop was threatened with disbandment as a result of a decision to reduce the number of companies per cavalry regiment from twelve to ten by deactivating Troops L and M and dispersing their members among the remaining companies. Captain Moore asked Merritt for help in keeping his troop together. Arguing that the demise of such an outstanding troop would "work a positive hardship to the service," Merritt suggested that the men of C Troop be dispersed so that L Troop could be redesignated as C Troop. Out of respect for Moore, "one of the very best officers in the service," and for his troop, the army command approved the unprecedented request.[52]

When Moore was promoted to major in early 1892, the new C Troop lucked out again, as fate dealt it Charles Taylor, one of the most charismatic and popular officers in the regiment. Taylor found it easy to work with First Sergeant Mason, as dependable as ever although afflicted by periodic asthma attacks. Completing thirty years of service while stationed at Fort Robinson in April 1895, Mason retired to the regret of superiors and subordinates alike. Captain Taylor lauded him as being "soldierly in demeanor, prompt, attentive to the performance of all duties, and as a disciplinarian strict, impartial and just." Advising soldiers "remaining in service and desiring to succeed" to emulate Mason, Taylor wished him "a pleasant and profitable future.[53]

An occurrence in June 1894 demonstrates the good feelings between officers and rank and file that existed in Taylor's troop and the degree to which the soldiers could emulate the social life of Victorian gentry. In June 1894 the residence of Sergeant and Mrs. Pierre Rock "was the scene of a brilliant gathering" in which the members of the "Jolly Bachelor's Club" gave a "progressive euchre and luncheon in honor of the ladies of the Pleasant Hour club." The pavilion, erected on Sergeant Rock's lawn, in which the luncheon was served was "superbly decorated in pink. Pink china, pink roses; in fact, pink to the right, pink to the left." A repast consisting of "light courses" which "in point of good cooking and taste in arrangement [were] not to be excelled" was served to numerous guests, including the troop's noncommissioned officers, several privates, and Captain Taylor and his staff. Most surprisingly, the account of the occasion appeared not in the pages of an African American newspaper but in the mainstream *Kansas City Times.*[54] At a time when blacks were rarely mentioned in white newspapers except in derogatory terms, this was more remarkable than one might think.

The men most responsible for the troop's success lived out their lives in relative peace. After retiring, Mason remained at Crawford, next door to Fort Robinson. He never left. He died during an asthma attack in April 1916 and was buried in the post cemetery. In a final tribute, the local newspaper described him as "very agreeable and pleasant in all his dealings with his fellow men."[55] Every soldier with whom he had served undoubtedly would have agreed.

As durable as he was capable, Francis Moore rose steadily through the grades of command until in 1903, forty-two years after he first enlisted as a private, he was promoted to brigadier general. Retiring in April 1905, he lived another twenty-three years before dying at the age of eighty-seven. In common with most officers of the Ninth, he left no memoirs or collection of papers. Like Sergeant Mason, he had performed every task assigned much too quietly and efficiently to attract the attention of scholars.

12

A Hero Named Daisy

Lieutenant Matthias Day

No Ninth Cavalry officer was more highly regarded by superiors and subordinates alike than Matt Day. Modest, daring, and an inspiration to his men, he had every quality of the classic hero. After the close of the Indian Wars, however, he adapted to the tedium of routine military life, advanced up the seniority ladder to the rank of colonel, and then retired—to tend his garden. Although a few of his exploits are still marveled at, the man behind them has been lost to history. The story of Day, once known, should make it more obvious than ever that historians need to broaden their scope to include more than the favored individuals who have monopolized the limelight.

The son of a self-styled Ohio "inventor," Matthias Day won his nomination to West Point in 1873 over thirteen rivals. Although he was never a great scholar, his personality would have secured him a commission in the cadet corps had it not been for demerits that piled up at an alarming rate. For "throwing snow in ranks while marching from dinner" one January evening he received three demerits. On more than one occasion "throwing bread in the mess hall" brought similar punishments. He "trifled" in philosophy class, missed roll call at church, and too often was found outside his room after taps. Despite such lapses, he had attained the rank of a cadet sergeant by the beginning of his third year. But all hope of graduating as a cadet officer vanished after taps one evening in October 1875.

While on duty as the barracks inspector, Day abetted the commission of a ridiculously juvenile offense. Well after lights out, Cadet Richard H.

Matthias W. Day, lieutenant and captain, Ninth Cavalry, 1878–1903, awarded the Medal of Honor for action at Las Animas Canyon, August 18, 1879. Courtesy of Special Collections, U.S. Military Academy Library, West Point.

Wilson, brandishing a "dark lantern" and sword borrowed from Day, created a novel disturbance by running through the barracks hall while shouting "raucously." As a result, both cadets were placed on arrest for a month, confined to their rooms, and required to spend their Saturday afternoons marching in dress uniform to and fro in front of the barracks. Needless to say, Day was reduced to the ranks.[1]

Despite his failure to win honors within the corps, he graduated on schedule with the class of 1877, ranked close enough to the bottom to be assigned to a black regiment. Because of the size of his class, he was not assigned to active duty with the Ninth Cavalry until August 1878, when he was ordered to El Paso to assume command of A Troop, whose senior officers were on detached service.

In April 1879, Day led a scout that overtook a Mescalero raiding party about sixty miles northeast of El Paso, routed them, and captured their horses and camp paraphernalia.[2] Transferred to Fort Cummings, located on the southern flank of New Mexico's Black Mountains, his troop totaled 676 miles in scouts during May and June. Switched to Fort Bayard in August, he scouted the rugged headwaters of the Gila River.[3] All this was mere preparation for his real baptism of fire.

In the wake of Victorio's massacre of the Ojo Caliente horse guard (pp. 108–109), Colonel Hatch assigned every available unit to pursue the raiders. The first detachment to come to grips with Victorio consisted of twenty-two men from Troops A and B and three Navajo scouts led by Day and Captain Byron Dawson. While trailing the raiders up the Las Animas Canyon on 18 September, they marched straight into an ambush. Springing the trap about 9 A.M., the Apaches pinned them down with a deadly fire from the canyon rims. By noon the troopers had run so low on ammunition that they were saved from annihilation only by the arrival of a forty-man detachment under Captain Charles Beyer.[4]

Throughout the afternoon, Beyer strove to turn the flank of the Indians and relieve the besieged troopers, but he was repulsed each time. By late afternoon, Dawson's command was so low on ammunition that it had to cease firing, "each man having received a few rounds to repel special attacks." With his ammunition also running short, Beyer ordered a retreat. He "called up" to Dawson to withdraw while his command covered them with rifle volleys.

Although Beyer, never known as an ardent fighter, had ordered an immediate retreat, Day noticed two men unable to travel. One, a recruit named Alfred Freeland, was some four hundred yards "from the rock crested hill, where the troopers were making their stand—all open to fire from the rocky crest of the ridge." Sergeant John Denny, a New Yorker in his third tour of service, volunteered to help him. Freeland tried to hop on one leg as Denny supported him, but he gave out. Another cavalry-man rushed forward to help carry him through a hail of bullets so thick it seemed "no one could pass this open rocky space alive." Denny even-tually received a Medal of Honor; his comrade in the rescue did not even have his name recorded.[5]

Although Day did not mention it in his account of the battle, he also ran the gauntlet of fire to carry Jeremiah Crump, the second wounded soldier, to safety. Captain Beyer was so furious at Day's disobedience of orders that he upbraided him severely. Lieutenant Charles Gatewood, who arrived a few days after the fight, dryly recalled that Day "carried a disabled soldier away under a heavy fire, for which offense the com-manding officer, Beyer, wanted to have him tried by court martial, and for which the Congress of the United States gave him a gold medal." Despite Day's heroism, Crump, a twenty-two-year-old mulatto from New York, died two days later.[6]

Las Animas Canyon was only the beginning of a hectic campaign. In November, in command of A Troop, Day participated in Morrow's dogged pursuit of Victorio deep into Mexico. Trailing the Apaches through a desert left unusually parched by the summer's drought, the thirsty troopers finally reached an anticipated water hole only to find it almost dry. Worse, the Indians "had driven their horses through it and . . . so thoroughly stirred it up, that it was about the consistency of thin mor-tar. Men and animals tried to drink it, but not with much success." As canteens ran dry the following day, "men began to offer a month's pay . . . for just one swallow of water. There was no singing, no joking, no conversation, no smoking . . . , and the banjo . . . that used to enliven the men, on the march and around the camp-fires at night, was silent." Late that afternoon they reached another tank of "clear and cool water" to find that the Apaches had dumped a disemboweled coyote in it and had left it "otherwise disgustingly poisoned." Several who drank of it became violently ill.[7]

John Denny, sergeant, Ninth Cavalry, 1867–97, awarded the Medal of Honor for rescuing a wounded comrade during the Battle of Las Animas Canyon. Courtesy of the Fletcher Christian Collection, Library of Congress.

Despite the shortage of water, Morrow marched on after nightfall and finally overtook the Apaches, who were waiting in ambush. Alerted by his scouts, he drew up his command, only eighty-one strong, many of whom were required to hold the horses, and started up the heights over-looking the trail. Under a full moon, with Lieutenants Day and Gatewood in the van, they made their way up the steep slopes, braving gunfire and dislodged boulders until they reached a sheer wall twenty feet in height. When a flanking attempt ran astray, Morrow reluctantly ordered a with-drawal.

The balance of the night was spent trying to reach water before the command perished. Gatewood recalled that many showed symptoms of "that wild insanity produced by great thirst," but considering "what they had gone through, . . . they were remarkably . . . amenable to discipline." When they finally reached the spring, "White, colored and red men [Apache scouts], horses and mules, all rushed . . . for the water. They drank of it, they rolled in it, they . . . wept and cheered and danced in it, and the mud they made seemed to make no difference in drinking."[8]

During the hellish march, Day was in charge of a rear guard assigned to pick up stragglers unable to keep up. By the time he and his troopers returned to Fort Bayard in early November, they had marched 725 miles since the initial fight on the Las Animas.

While Victorio recuperated in the Sierra Madres for a few weeks, the Ninth Cavalry enjoyed a badly needed respite. No one put the time to better use than Day. On Thanksgiving Day he was married in Mesilla, New Mexico to Miss Emilia Schultz of El Paso. The ceremony, conducted in the parlor of Mesilla's poshest hotel, was performed by New Mexico Supreme Court Justice H. W. Bristol and attended by Governor Lew Wallace and a "large concourse" of friends. The evening was concluded by dancing "until the early hours of morning." With no time for a honey-moon, Day and his bride left the next day for Fort Bayard.[9]

In January 1880 the campaign resumed when Victorio moved back into his homeland. Although Day had relinquished command of A Troop to First Lieutenant John Conline, the illness of Captain Beyer gave him the opportunity to assume leadership of C Troop. On 12 January, near the head of the Rio Perchas, about twenty miles west of Hillsboro, New Mexico, Morrow's troops again encountered the Apaches, who, as always, were lying in ambush. Day led a charge that carried to the foot of their stronghold and then was sent with a small detachment to outflank them. Once again he added to his reputation as a daredevil. With eight men he climbed a steep slope until he reached "the breast high, natural wall of rock which crowned the crest of the gulch." He "sustained the entire fire of the hostile line at this point while climbing into a position which commanded the hostiles on the flank . . . to liberate the soldiers . . . in the bottom of the Gulch."[10]

Day's reputation for gallantry increased with the next engagement. Serving as Morrow's adjutant in a clash in the San Mateo Mountains on 17 January, he carried orders to the various parts of the skirmish line, under fire the entire time. With this task concluded, he demonstrated anew his skill at climbing canyon walls while searching for a spot from which Morrow's mountain howitzer could command the Apache positions. "Assisted by a foothold given by carbines held below by [his] men," he was the "first to climb the cliff." He then relocated the howitzer so that it "speedily dislodged the Indians." During their withdrawal, they managed to kill Lieutenant J. Hansell French, the second Ninth Cavalry officer to die on the battlefield.[11]

Day's service in the Victorio War was less strenuous during the balance of 1880. Through March he remained on Morrow's staff as adjutant and then returned to A Troop. For the next two years he did much campaigning but little fighting. In 1881, while Nana's warriors were ambushing and mauling half a dozen detachments, he led a scout from Fort Stanton on a five-hundred-mile patrol along the Rio Grande without seeing a single Indian.

His riskiest action of the year occurred when Mescalero agent Samuel Russell reported that his charges were drunk on home-brewed *tizwin* and out of control. Although an infantry detachment that tried to intervene had been driven from the Apaches' camp by gunshots, Day "rode alone into [the] camp and quelled the riot."[12]

In the forested foothills of the Sacramentos, with no hostile Indians to fight, life took on an idyllic quality. "The men bring in game, deer and turkey. The . . . colored [soldiers] . . . are apparently happy—from before reveille, till late at night, their laughter, cracking jokes, and singing songs is constantly heard." Even the officers took advantage of the rare opportunity to relax. Day, as exuberant as when a cadet, could not have stood higher in the esteem of his commander, Major Guy Henry. Henry informed the *Army and Navy Journal* that Day was temporarily absent from duty because he had been "worsted" in a "friendly sparring match" and had broken one of the bones in his hand. The victor, Henry explained, was an infantryman who, of course, was more "at home" on foot. Major Henry then noted that Day was the officer who, in a recent Indian fight, "went to the front, under a heavy fire, and carried off a wounded soldier on his back." Any man "capable of such actions is bound to make a good officer."[13]

In the autumn of 1881, Day transferred with the rest of the Ninth Cavalry to the Southern Plains. For him, the next two years were relatively uneventful. In October 1883 he received a six-month leave, his first since reporting for duty. When he returned the following March, he had been promoted to first lieutenant and assigned to I Troop, stationed at Fort Reno, a few miles west of modern-day Oklahoma City. There, his primary duty was not to fight Indians but to protect their land from whites.

By the spring of 1884, relations between the Boomers, as the intruders were called, and the Ninth Cavalry had been following the same pattern for more than two years. Would-be settlers from Kansas entered the unassigned lands in the center of what is now Oklahoma and staked out farms. Troops searched them out, arrested them, and escorted them to the Kansas border. Since convictions before local juries were impossible to attain, the violators were simply released, free to repeat their incursions. Needless to say, too many repetitions of this pattern were stretching the nerves of both sides dangerously thin. Adding fuel to the volatile situation was the intense prejudice held by the settlers against the black soldiers and their white officers.

Excerpts from a poem entitled "Oklahoma and Busted," penned by an anonymous Boomer, summed up the settlers' frustration:

> We had teams and wagons and plenty to eat,
> Were loaded with flour and canned goods and meat,
> And a jolly lot of good fellows together;
> The only drawback—General Pope and the weather.
> We found, when we struck the promised land,
> The soil neither good nor the climate bland;
> But worse than rain or cold or sleet,
> Was the cavalry force we had to meet;

> And as if to add to cold and grief and shame,
> We fellows who went under Captain Payne
> Had to surrender to a troop of niggers
> Without once daring to pull our triggers.[14]

With each confrontation the Boomers became more defiant, the officers less tolerant. Trespassers constantly complained of mistreatment. They detested Day's West Point classmate and friend in the Ninth Cavalry, Lieutenant Charles Taylor, so much that a newspaper described him as "one of a litter of mud turtles born of a Negro woman." Like many West Pointers in the regiment, Taylor had taken an extra year to graduate. A classmate described him as "the image of force and energy and boldness and fortitude . . . [with a] fire and force about him, and superiority to vicissitudes." After being cited for bravery in battle with the Apaches, he volunteered to command Indian scouts and quickly won their trust and the name of "Charley White Hat." On one occasion, when confronted by two gamblers in a Kansas saloon, he "seized them by the neck, one in each hand, and, after knocking their heads together, threw them bodily out into the street." The city fathers had thereupon given him a pearl-handled revolver as a token of their appreciation.[15]

Like many officers assigned to command Indian scouts, Taylor paid little heed to regulations regarding uniform. In Oklahoma his flamboyancy created a storm of criticism from settlers who claimed that just as a religious service was concluding, Taylor came charging into the camp, "dressed in cowboy garb, followed by a company of Negro and Indian soldiers." In a "drunken dialect," he gave them "fifteen minutes to get out of the Territory." Asked what gave him the authority to give such an order, he replied with curses and, acting more like than a "bandit than an officer," threatened to "board our wagons and take our firearms."[16]

Day may not have been as aggressive as "Charley White Hat," but he was equally decisive in handling the Boomers. In April 1884 the Boomer leaders David Payne and W. L. Couch sought to take over Oklahoma Territory by sheer weight of numbers. To keep them out, Captain Carroll had only seven officers and 133 troopers; in April alone, at least six hundred illegal settlers entered Oklahoma, staking out claims, erecting dwellings, and preparing to plow fields. As they had been instructed to submit to nothing except outright force, their leaders may have been trying to goad the black troopers into shooting white civilians, preferably unarmed. If so, they almost realized their goal.

One Boomer recalled the type of defiance that was commonplace: Lieutenant Day "ordered the work stopped, which caused a fight. This fight began with axes, but all weapons were ordered down and then it became a 'fist and choke' fight, which lasted quite a while but no one was seriously hurt."[17]

Another remembered a similar incident between Day's buffalo soldiers and the settlers. On locating a Boomer camp, Day sent a detail to the "main tent" to arrest Payne. The Boomer "met them at the door of the tent with a six-shooter in each hand and . . . said, "No damned nigger can arrest me and if you start to give a command I will start shooting and you (meaning the sergeant) will be the first one I will get. If you want to arrest me, send for a white man." After a slight hesitation, the sergeant sent for Day, who "personally made the arrest."[18]

It was only because of the discipline of the heavily outnumbered buffalo soldiers that they tolerated verbal abuse and on occasion physical pummeling without resorting to the use of their arms. They undoubtedly sensed that shooting whites, under any circumstances, would lead to serious repercussions.

In the absence of atrocities, the Boomers tried to manufacture them, with Day as the prime villain. His most notorious misdeeds, as summarized by C. C. Rister, started on 24 April 1884, when he discovered the father of W. L. Couch plowing a plot of land that would later become part of Oklahoma City. He had Couch trussed "hand and foot" and dumped into a wagon, and then he moved on to arrest Couch's comrades. When one refused to obey quickly enough, the "angry officer" ordered him to be "tied to the wagon," and for more than twelve miles, without a single stop, the man was "led or dragged behind the wagon and when a halt was made for lunch, Day still refused to allow his hands to be unbound."[19]

Rister's account, relying upon Boomer recollections, could not have been more confused. The officer who arrested Couch and tied his comrade to the back of a wagon was not Day but C. J. Stevens, another West Pointer, who had taken those measures for very good reason. Couch, as Corporal Edward Pringle of I Troop explained, had used "indecent, abusive, and insulting language towards me, and towards the other soldiers. He also struck at me with his clinched [sic] fist when I was simply carrying out orders and getting his team unhitched." Stevens added that the elder Couch had lost control of himself and resisted my men. "He called me a son of a b–tch."[20]

Two weeks later, Day did have a confrontation with an equally defiant group of settlers led by W. L. Couch himself. The Boomers' descriptions of Day's actions again made him an arch villain. When he ordered Couch to submit to arrest, the latter refused, declaring that a citizen was not subject to martial authority. Day then ordered part of his men to "seize the Boomers" while the remainder covered them with drawn revolvers. "The effort of the Negroes and Indians [scouts] to carry out the order resulted in as many desperate fistfights as there were pairs of soldiers and Boomers. . . . For several minutes the loud cursing of the contestants, and angry grunts and shouts as they exchanged blow for blow, caused a peaceful camp to become a battleground. Finally the settlers drove their assailants back, much to Day's chagrin and discomfiture." Next, he "ordered his men to stand in line immediately in front of the milling Boomers, with pistols presented." When one of them started for his wagon and refused to halt when told to, Day "twice ordered his men to fire, but they evidently had enough presence of mind to refuse."[21]

It makes a good story: veteran black enlisted men saving a brash young lieutenant from the ignominy of having ordered the slaughter of an unarmed citizen. That Day was also one of the most admired officers in the Ninth makes it all the more appealing.[22] Day's report of the episode, almost equally dramatic, is probably more accurate.

He had only eleven troopers and five Indian scouts; the Boomers, forty-five strong, formed "a line like a rail fence three deep." Day lined up his troopers facing them, while the scouts were ordered to "watch those who had pistols." When Sergeant John Rogers stepped forward to place Couch under arrest, the "whole mob" assaulted him.[23] Rogers's comrades came to his aid but were soon in danger of being overpowered. Day then called out, "This resistance must cease . . . [or] I will resort to arms." At his command to draw arms, "every pistol was drawn [and] leveled" while the "scouts glanced along their carbines and awaited orders." The Boomers apparently interpreted the order to draw pistols as a command to fire.

All the settlers but one submitted to Day's show of force. The one, ignoring an order to halt, continued toward a wagon containing his gun. Ignoring the leveled weapons, he was only a few steps from the wagon when Day gave a last warning, "If you reach that wagon, you are a dead man." He turned back; the crisis had passed.

Placing the squatters under guard, Day immediately turned his attention to another party of settlers that had been observed a few miles away on the north side of the Cimarron. "Tomorrow morn," he informed Captain Carroll, "I shall cross the river, although I am told that there will be a determined resistance. Yet I may as well be hung for a sheep as a lamb so I will notify them at 10 A.M. unless I receive a courier from you."[24]

It seems apparent that Day had come close to perpetrating what would have been considered the murder of an unarmed man. His nerves obviously were frayed, and it was fortunate that soon thereafter he received a leave of absence. Even while taking it, however, he added to his growing reputation.

By the mid-1880s the army was stressing marksmanship as never before. Annual departmental and service-wide contests, open to both officers and enlisted men, attracted national attention. As a rule, the winners were men stationed at permanent posts who had time to devote months to preparation. In addition, cavalrymen, accustomed to carbines, were at an obvious disadvantage to infantrymen in firing the rifles used in the competition. For a cavalryman to come directly from a campaign and do well was next to impossible.

Despite this, the purpose of Day's leave was to enter the competition to determine the best marksmen from the Division of the Missouri. To the amazement of all, he emerged victorious. His feat brought "hearty congratulations" from his rivals and fulsome tribute from the *Kansas City Times*, unofficial sponsor of the event. The newspaper enthused that he was "known throughout his regiment as the 'Daisy' for the many good qualities of which he is possessed." Among the enlisted men who knew him, "he is beloved . . . and many of them were heard to say, 'I'm glad Day won the medal, he's one of the nicest officers in the Service and he can't get too much.'"[25]

With Day as its captain, the team representing the Division of the Missouri (roughly everything between Chicago and the Continental Divide) traveled to Omaha to meet similar squads from the Divisions of the Pacific and of the Atlantic as well as one representing the artillery. Before an audience including General Sheridan and many other high-ranking officers, Day won more laurels. In a competition involving shooting at targets under conditions that were an "approximation to actual service," he was "conceded to be the best skirmisher." In addition, his team easily won the long-distance target shooting.[26] With the rest and relaxation over, he returned immediately to the Indian Territory to confront the most massive intrusion yet.

Throughout the fall of 1884, Boomers led by Couch poured into the Unassigned Lands while General Augur, who had succeeded Pope as commander of the Department of the Missouri, professed to be unsure of his authority to eject them. Not until mid-December did Augur allow Colonel Hatch to proceed against the intruders. Once more, Day, leading the first detachment to confront the intruders, was almost goaded into the use of arms.

Although the temperature was hovering around zero, Day left Camp Russell, a temporary post southwest of present-day Stillwater, with thirty troopers on 21 December. Crossing the ice-covered Cimarron "after a great deal of labor," he located the colonists on Stillwater Creek on Christmas Eve. Four hundred strong, armed with "double barrel shotguns and Winchesters," they rejected an order to surrender their weapons. Day arranged his command in a skirmish line, carbines ready to fire, facing the "massed" settlers. Once more they refused to surrender. Although their defiance obviously angered him, he "hesitated to give orders to fire as the slaughter would have been great." After reporting the incident, he asked for specific permission "to open fire on them" if they refuse to surrender their weapons. "If I cannot use gunfire, I need reinforcements."[27]

Day's report undoubtedly influenced Colonel Hatch's decision to make a show of strength sufficient to convince the settlers that they could not ignore orders. While he was assembling some 375 troopers for a demonstration of power, Day and the Boomers had time to become better acquainted. Day let them know he was waiting for permission to exercise force. Perhaps persuaded by his demeanor that they should change their tactics, they "became exceedingly friendly." By the third day of the standoff, they "stopped carrying their guns" and concentrated on constructing dugouts and rifle pits behind their tents in preparation for a possible siege.

With the weather colder than ever and little to do until Hatch arrived, Day left Sergeant George Wilson and four privates to watch the Boomers while the remainder returned to Camp Russell. Couch even loaned Day a spring wagon to transport rations to Wilson's detachment and promised to inform him if "any other group" tried to move further south. The same superiors who had worried that Day might perpetrate a massacre the previous week were now alarmed that he was "getting too familiar with the intruders" and should be "cautioned not to be embarrassed by an exhibition of sympathy" for them.[28]

Hatch brought the crisis to a decisive close. Unless he demonstrated that he had the power and will "to destroy and confiscate all property of the intruders," he concluded, "serious loss of life will be certain to occur." With six troops of the Ninth Cavalry and one company from the Twenty-fourth Infantry, he moved towards Couch's camp. The chief obstacles to his advance were the icy streams. According to his adjutant, Hatch emerged from swimming his horse across one ford "a complete mass of ice." When he reached the Salt Fork of the Arkansas, its surface was iced over but not yet thick enough to support the weight of supply wagons. Calling upon a trick from his Maine boyhood, he set about constructing an "ice bridge." For twenty-four hours troopers "threw water on the selected roadway until a sufficient thickness of ice was made to bear the command." Fortunately, the bitter cold continued until the command had crossed.[29]

On arriving at the Boomers' camp, Hatch promptly cut off all supplies and reinforcements. As the siege progressed, he decided to make his own reconnaissance to determine the settlers' resolve and size up their fortifications. Believing that "I was unknown to them," he rode over in civilian garb, visited, and casually examined the camp, making special note of the rifle pits and trenches. All the time he kept up a steady conversation until he concluded they had "talked enough" and revealed that he was "one of those fellows they were so down on." Having assured himself that time was on his side, he tightened the siege.

During the next few days, he met with Couch almost daily, urging him to surrender. Their last meeting was on the evening of 26 January. Although Couch, "stubborn to the last minute," blustered, "You will not fight and I know it," Hatch sensed he would yield if allowed to save face. Accordingly, he informed the Boomer that his men would be permitted to retain their arms. Then he delivered an ultimatum: "You must be out of here or moving by 8 o'clock to-morrow morning or we will be obliged to open fire."

The following morning, Hatch deployed his men so that they completely enfiladed the settlers' crude fortifications. Minutes before the deadline, Couch surrendered, proclaiming that he was yielding because of the lack of supplies and not for any fear of Hatch's troops. In victory, Hatch magnanimously released the prisoners upon their promise to return to the Kansas border. Otherwise, he concluded, "I would have been forced to ration and transport them." As for letting them retain their guns, he noted that "we always have to return them anyway."[30]

Although no one could have known it at the time, the winter confrontation was both the climax and culmination of the Ninth's tenure as the policemen of Oklahoma Territory. The following summer, the buffalo troopers resumed their progression northward when they received orders to exchange duties with the Fifth Cavalry, stationed in Nebraska and Wyoming.

"Daisy" Day, however, did not make the move to Nebraska with the regiment. His thirst for adventure unquenched, he learned that the military was in need of officers experienced in desert warfare to serve with the Apache scouts. He promptly volunteered.

Within months he would engage in one of the most epic and ignored sagas in the history of the Apache wars. In charge of the Apache scouts accompanying an expedition led by Captain Wirt Davis, he pushed southward in July 1885 from Fort Huachuca, Arizona, into the Sierra Madres of Mexico. Moving into the mountains, his scouts discovered the trail of Geronimo's band, apparently only a few hours old. Knowing that the regulars, encumbered by the pack train, could never overtake the Apaches, Davis ordered Day to go ahead. Thinking that they would rapidly overhaul the fugitives, he provided them only one day's rations. The lack of food, however, was the least of Day's discomforts during the next few days.

Three days after parting with Davis, the scouts discovered the fugitives "in the mountains a little north and east of Nakari." According to Davis's report, they killed Chief Nana and three others, one the son of Geronimo, and captured fifteen women and children, including "three wives and five children" of Geronimo. The last, although wounded, escaped with the rest of his band.[31] According to Al Sieber, chief of scouts under Captain Emmett Crawford, Day had surprised Geronimo so completely that the hostiles had to leap over a steep bluff to escape capture.[32]

Day, however, paid a high price for his triumph. His ordeal would have gone unreported had not Lieutenant Britton Davis, in command of Crawford's scouts, chanced across his trail the day after the fight with Geronimo. About midmorning, Davis spotted two "dirty, unshaven whites, wearing "undershirts and torn overalls, seated beside a small stream, their feet, swathed in bandages made from their flannel shirts." Nearby were about thirty Apaches. He discovered that the scarecrows were Matt Day, his former classmate at West Point, and the latter's civilian chief of scouts. After devouring Davis's lunch and washing it down with a glass of mescal, Day and his companion described the "nerviest piece of work" Davis had ever known. With rations only for one day, they had replaced their boots with moccasins in order to keep pace with the scouts. Within hours an incessant rain set in and soaked the moccasins until they became useless. For three days they had gone barefoot "over the sharp rocks and through cactus-infested slopes." They had wrapped their bleeding feet in strips torn from their shirts and maintained their pace. When the last of their food was gone, they subsisted on "roots, acorns, [and] horse meat cut from carcasses found lying on the trail."[33] Despite their suffering, they overtook Geronimo and sent him fleeing minus his wives and children. Taking along some horse meat found in his camp, they continued the pursuit. They were taking a break to tend their feet when Davis chanced upon them.

Fortunately, a surgeon was accompanying Lieutenant Davis. When he unwrapped the bandages, he discovered the feet were swollen to twice their normal size, the toes "hardly distinguishable." The doctor pronounced it a "good example of 'elephantitus [sic] of the feet'"[34]

Incredibly, Day refused to give in to his infirmities. After a brief reunion with Captain Davis and the regulars, he and the scouts pushed deeper into the Sierra Madres. On 22 September they again overtook Geronimo. Day "led the charge that dislodged the Apaches" and dealt them yet another reversal. While this was his last action against Geronimo, he had one more delicate task before returning to duty with the Ninth Cavalry.

In March 1886, fifty of the scouts got drunk and began fighting among themselves at Long's Ranch, a supply camp located at the southwestern corner of New Mexico. At what must have considerable risk, Day managed to disarm them before any fatalities occurred.[35]

According to Day, because of a bureaucratic snarl in Washington he was forced to refuse General Miles's request that he remain in command of the Apache scouts. Shortly before the Ninth had left the Indian Territory, he had been designated regimental quartermaster. When his substitutes were unable to account for all the regimental property after the move northward, the adjutant general's office declared Day responsible and withheld his pay. After several months of this, he concluded he had no choice except to return to his regiment and clear up the confusion. Others would have the honor of being involved in the final surrender of Geronimo the following year.[36]

Day was now practically a celebrity. When he returned east in August 1886, the *Kansas City Times* described him as "one of the best and coolest heads among the Indian fighters of the army" and a man with "many years experience as a scout."[37] In November 1887 it reported that "Generals Crook and Hatch and Lieut. Day, with a hunting party, left for the mountains to hunt bear." Significantly, it focused its account not on the generals but on Day, saying that he was "one of the crack shots of the Army and the bear that comes within range of his rifle would do well to follow the example set by Davey Crockett's coon."[38] It seems likely that Crook, under whom Day served in the Geronimo campaign, had requested his presence.

Day's reputation for gallantry was as high as ever as late as 1894. That March he visited his old commander, Lieutenant Colonel Henry, at Fort Meyer. While attending one of Henry's cavalry drills, the still-young officer—long since divorced from his first wife—was introduced to the daughter of the British ambassador, Lord Julian Pauncefote.[39] The following day, Lord and Lady Pauncefote invited him to lunch with them and the young lady. In reporting this tidbit, the *Army and Navy Journal* enthused that Day was a "gallant cavalryman" and that "all are glad to see him thus appreciated."[40]

With the close of the Indian wars, Day quietly accommodated himself to the normal routine of military service. After returning from Arizona, he resumed the position of regimental quartermaster. His role during the Ghost Dance upheaval consisted of expediting the flow of supplies to the troops in the field, a job he may have found tedious but one that he performed flawlessly.

There is no doubt that he remained a favorite of the buffalo soldiers. When the men of I Troop protested the racist actions of Captain Guilfoyle in 1891,[41] they asked that he be replaced by Day. Although the protest achieved little except to lead to harsher treatment by Guilfoyle and some embarrassment for Day, it confirms his continued popularity.[42] Through-out the 1890s his troop and that of Taylor were the most popular ones in the regiment.

The balance of his career was relatively uneventful. Although he missed the Santiago campaign in 1898, he saw considerable action during two tours of duty in the Philippines. After several years with other units, chance allotted him the opportunity to serve a year as the Ninth Cavalry's colonel before he retired in 1912.

Modest to the end, he met with total defeat in 1919 when he was asked to submit an account of his services to the West Point alumni association. The old cavalryman mulled over the matter for a time and then concluded that "writing my record has its terrors . . . even more than the dentist's chair. . . . *I have no record to write*—I presume that is my regret." With that, one of the most storied veterans in the nation clammed up and closed his letter with some patter about his family and garden. For a man with "no history," he had lived a remarkable life.[43]

13

From Asylum to Valhalla

The "Crazy" Lieutenant of G Troop

The most unlikely officer in the history of the Ninth Cavalry was undoubtedly John Conline. Idealistic, sober, and capable, he was also nervous, erratic, and quick to take offense, often over the most trivial slight. Worse, when placed under too much stress he was subject to nervous breakdowns. Three times during his career—once while still at West Point and twice after he was commissioned—he was confined at the Government Hospital for the Insane (Saint Elizabeth's) in Washington, D.C.

Despite his emotional problems, Conline handled himself so coolly in battle with Victorio's Apaches that he won a brevet promotion to major. While superiors feared for the welfare of his men, the buffalo soldiers tolerated his eccentricities, accepted his outbursts, and defended him against criticism.

One of the few historians to mention Conline, after reading a set of charges against him, concluded that he was a discredit "to West Point [and] the army's officer corps."[1] In reality, his career uniquely affirmed that the American dream sometimes came true for even the least likely.

The eldest child of an Irish immigrant couple, John had a tumultuous childhood. His parents moved in the 1840s to Rutland, Vermont, attracted by granite quarries that were worked exclusively by Irish. By the 1850s, discouraged by repeated failures, Thomas Conline resigned himself to a life as the town drunk. Although Mary Conline was as illiterate as her husband, she struggled to provide her children an education. Twelve-year-old John was enrolled in the Rutland High School when her nervous

John Conline, lieutenant and captain, Ninth Cavalry, 1870–89. Courtesy of Special Collections, U.S. Military Academy Library, West Point.

breakdown forced him to fend for himself. Precocious and outgoing, he always found someone willing to provide a job and lodging.[2]

In July 1859, aged thirteen, he was working for an express company in Northampton, Massachusetts, and living with the agent's family when he decided on the military as a career. Methodically, he prepared an application to West Point, proudly stressing that he had concluded a term in High School. He enclosed a statement from a local physician that he had passed a physical exam, was "unusually erect and well-developed for his age," and free of any "deformity, diseases, . . . or disorder of an infectious or immoral character." Eight townsmen endorsed his application, asserting that he had an "active mind much more developed than the average youth his age" and that his "moral character was above reproach." Virtuous he may have been, but he was also sly enough to advance his age to fifteen. He mailed his application to Secretary of War John Floyd and awaited a reply.[3]

When none came, he returned to Rutland, reentered school, and found a job at a railroad depot. In May 1860 he again wrote Floyd, informing him he had grown another two inches and instructing him to retain the application until 1 February 1861—"I will then call for it at Washington." If he could meet the secretary face to face, he had no doubt he would be approved. Before the appointed date arrived, the nation was in dissolution and Floyd had defected to the Confederacy.[4]

Less than a week after the firing on Fort Sumter, Conline enlisted for six months. Upon the expiration of that enlistment he reenlisted in the Fourth Vermont Infantry and took part in more than twenty engagements with the Army of the Potomac. Near the Sunken Road at Antietam, the man next to him was killed by shrapnel; at Little Round Top at Gettysburg, bullets pierced his haversack and canteen; at Fredericksburg, his company formed the rear guard in the right wing's retreat across the Rappahannock. Through it all, he was an "exemplary soldier." But he had not forgotten his dream of West Point. Month after month he carried a revised set of application papers, awaiting a chance to plead his case.[5]

On Christmas Eve 1862, he secured a holiday pass and took a train into Washington in search of Secretary of War Edwin Stanton. When he arrived at the secretary's residence, he was denied entry by the doorman. When he persisted with his request, Stanton's coachman, remembered only as "John," interceded and said: "I will fix it. You shall see Mr. Stanton, wait." What ensued seemed perfectly plausible: "John introduced me to the great and warm hearted Secretary who . . . put his hand on my shoulder and said: 'My son, I have very important business now with the Secretary of State [William Seward]. Please step into my carriage and I will hear what you have to say there.' We both got in the carriage and I was, in short time, chatting familiarly with one who has been called superior to Carnot. He said on the way: 'I will appoint you a cadet at West Point.'"[6]

The following March, Conline reminded Stanton of his promise. "Do not forget" that the appointment is "my greatest hope of serving my country in a capacity which I most ardently desire." He took part in the Gettysburg campaign and helped to subdue the New York City draft rioters before receiving an answer. In August 1863, only days before the start of a new term, he was appointed to West Point.[7]

There could hardly have been a more unlikely plebe. Son of a pauper, so lacking in the social graces that another cadet had to teach him "good manners at the table," Conline, a classmate recalled, "failed altogether to measure up to the exacting standards of the corps." For two years he had scarcely seen a book; now he had to compete with middle-class graduates of prep schools. In addition, he was three months behind most of his classmates, who had reported in June. By a superhuman effort, studying long after taps each night—"blanket over window and transom" to prevent detection—he survived his first year. Out of a class of seventy-eight, he ranked a creditable fifty-eighth.[8]

By the end of his second year, the strain was beginning to tell. He was fifty-sixth out of sixty-three (nineteen had already been dismissed) and would have fared worse had it not been for a tenth-place ranking in drawing. For three terms his conduct had been excellent, but during the spring of 1865 his nerves showed signs of snapping. On 13 February he was placed under arrest "for using highly disrespectful and insubordinate language" to the venerable George Cullom, superintendent of the academy.[9]

The following fall, the strain proved too much. He was found deficient in both chemistry and philosophy. Although he had incurred only thirty-three demerits the entire term, he was judged to have "variable study habits" and to be inattentive to regulations. Faced with possible dismissal after so many months of "overexertion and study," he became, as he termed it, "deranged." For several weeks academy officials failed to recognize the seriousness of his condition, but in late March Cullom informed the secretary of war that Conline had "become a confirmed lunatic" who had been placed under a "proper guard to prevent his committing some act of violence to himself or others." A few days later he arrived at Saint Elizabeth's Hospital for the Insane in Washington.[10]

When the head of the asylum judged him sufficiently improved to be released nine months later, Colonel T. G. Pitcher, who had replaced Cullom as West Point's superintendent, was taken aback. Since Conline was an "utter stranger," he relied upon the director's evaluation of his "fitness to be entrusted with the command of troops" in deciding to readmit him. Dr. E. D. Nichols hesitated and then made the necessary recommendation. Allowed to return to West Point, Conline resumed his third year of study the following September.[11] His original class had already graduated.

He made it through the fall term with deceptive ease. In natural philosophy, one of the courses he had failed, he ranked nineteenth out of forty-one; in drawing, he stood third. But in the spring of 1868 his condition again deteriorated. In January he received a ten-day medical leave, malady not noted. In March he was placed under arrest for "deserting his post while on a punishment tour . . . in contempt of the Superintendent's orders." He was confined for the balance of the spring term to the academic and barracks areas of the campus and required to spend every Saturday afternoon marching across the quadrangle.[12]

The punishment did little for him academically. When he failed chemistry, the academy's academic board recommended his dismissal.[13] Unwilling to admit defeat, "he borrowed enough dollars from an officer then stationed on the post" to go to Washington and lay his case "personally" before President Andrew Johnson. He "asked to be reinstated. And the president did reinstate him."[14]

Exactly what the lame duck president may have done is not known, but on 29 January 1869 the academic board reconsidered Conline's fate. After much deliberation, Albert Church, in his forty-second year as professor of mathematics, moved that Conline be readmitted "in view of the hopes of his permanent recovery as set forth in the letters of Dr. Nichols and the Honorable Gentlemen urging his restoration." It is possible that one of the "honorable gentlemen" was President Johnson. The vote was five to four, as all four military officers, including the commandant of cadets, voted against readmission. When four academicians voted to readmit Conline, they were joined by chemistry professor H. L. Kendrick, whose class Conline had twice failed.[15]

Conline needed no more reprieves. In his last year he finished a respectable thirty-eighth out of fifty-eight in engineering, although his dismal last-place rankings in Spanish and in cavalry tactics brought his overall standing down to fifty-fourth. For the entire semester he received only thirty demerits, three of them for the ludicrous (in light of his academic troubles) sin of "seeking to give information" to a classmate who was reciting in philosophy. On 16 June 1870 he was commissioned. As a classmate remarked, his "length of service as a cadet is unique; none . . . ever served seven years the Laban of academic favor for his Rachel of a diploma."[16]

For Conline, military service seemed a relief. Assigned to D Troop at Fort Stockton, he led scouts, commanded a subpost at old Fort Lancaster, and held such assignments as adjutant and signal officer. He was transferred with his company to Fort Concho at the beginning of 1874, and his status with his superiors was confirmed by his being selected to serve as campaign adjutant for Buell's expedition during the Red River War. Promoted to first lieutenant in November 1875, he took command of G Troop, whose captain, John Bacon, was serving on General Sherman's staff.[17]

Romance had entered Conline's life while he was still at West Point. Guest of honor at an 1870 ball was Mrs. Julia Grant, wife of the president and mother of Cadet Fred Grant. Among her guests were Major and Mrs. W. W. Leland of Saratoga Springs, New York, and their daughter Emma, a student at Vassar. Major Leland, who had served on General Grant's staff during the Shiloh and Vicksburg campaigns, was one of three brothers operating Saratoga's Grand Union Hotel, described by the *New York Times* as "the most sumptuous public house in the world."[18] Introduced to "Miss Emma" during the course of the evening, Conline "became infatuated" with the fragile debutante. Nothing else is known about their romance, but he undoubtedly visited Saratoga Springs while he was waiting to report for duty following his graduation.

In January 1872, Conline secured a leave to visit the Lelands. While he was conversing with the major in the Grand Union, his host suddenly said, "Why don't you get married?" On 22 February, John and Emma were wed in the hotel's ornate ballroom. The outcome would be, Conline reflected, "a verification of the old maxim: 'Marry in haste and repent at leisure.'"[19]

Less than two months later, the Grand Union was sold at a bankruptcy auction.[20] It seems obvious that with financial ruin impending—and with six unmarried daughters—Leland was anxious to transfer Emma's care to Conline. While there is no reason to doubt the bridegroom's sincerity, he was also dazzled by thoughts of what Leland's supposed wealth and political connections might do for his career.

When the newlyweds arrived at Fort Stockton, Major Bliss accommodated them by appointing Conline as post adjutant, relieving him of scouting duties for the balance of the year. Bliss's good offices, however, went for naught. Emma was too fragile, physically and emotionally, for life in a "desert place" without "a tree in one direction for a hundred miles." By mid-June she was pregnant. As her health deteriorated and her fears increased, Conline sent her home in October and four months later secured a leave to be with her during delivery. After a stillbirth, he and Emma returned to Fort Stockton.[21]

By mid-1874, Emma's health was worse than ever and she was again expecting. General C. C. Augur, commanding the Department of Texas, assigned Conline to duty in San Antonio so that Emma would have access to adequate medical care. The baby survived, but when the Ninth Cavalry was ordered to New Mexico, it was obvious Emma could not survive a trip by wagon train. Once more, Conline sent her home, where she arrived, according to her mother, "so changed that I did not know her—mere skin and bones." By July 1876 her health had improved sufficiently that Conline again made the trip east to bring her and his daughter to his station at Fort Garland, Colorado. Since each one-way ticket cost approximately two hundred dollars, he had fallen deeply in debt with no prospects of repaying it.[22]

With tensions rising between the Utes and settlers in western Colorado, Conline was dispatched to head off hostilities. He assured the Southern Utes that the government would protect their reservation from squatters and honor its other treaty obligations. Obviously sympathetic with them, he charged that the settlers' request for soldiers was mainly a result of their desire to sell them fodder at exorbitant prices. Deciding in late November that there was no danger of war, he returned to Fort Garland.

Colonel Hatch commended him for "the manner in which you have conducted the delicate and important duty intrusted to you."[23]

At Fort Garland he found Emma in such a "squabble" with Captain George Shorkley (Fifteenth Infantry) that the post was in an uproar. Shortly after he had left, Emma had begun to experience the nausea of early pregnancy. Convinced she would not survive another childbirth, she asked post surgeon Justus Brown to perform an abortion. When he refused, she "berated him" and procured one at nearby La Veta, "to the great scandal of the military service." By her action she became a pariah in the eyes of the post's officers and their wives.[24]

On returning, Conline was informed that Emma's behavior was so scandalous that she was being "talked about all over the country." Requested to send her away, he refused. In response, Shorkley assembled a list of charges, many of them petty, that was climaxed by a bald assertion that she was insane.[25]

Confronted by the accusations, Hatch suggested that Emma be examined by Post Surgeon Brown. If Brown found her insane, Conline must remove her from the post. Without examining or even visiting Emma, Brown rendered the diagnosis of insanity that had been "his opinion before he began the investigation." Conline still refused to send Emma away and endured arrest for forty days while appealing the order to General Pope. After an investigation by an "impartial" captain of Shorkley's regiment, Pope ordered Emma's immediate removal.[26]

Not one of Conline's superiors considered the financial impact the order would have on the lieutenant or offered him aid. In contrast, the men of his troop rallied to his support. As First Sergeant Joseph Broadus recalled, "I asked him how much did he want. He said seventy-five or eighty dollars if I could spare it. I said . . . he could get a hundred if he needed it and keep it . . . to the expiration of my term of service." Broadus later "deposited" another hundred dollars with Conline. Similarly, Private Samuel Kirkely entrusted eighty-three dollars to him, and others, smaller amounts. None expressed any concern about the safety of their loans.[27]

The return to New York with Emma was not pleasant. Overwrought by the humiliation of being labeled a lunatic and bundled off to her parents, she berated Conline for being too weak to defend her. During a stopover she badgered him into signing "separation papers." Once in New York, the Lelands, embarrassed by the affair, decided to send her to

Europe to study voice. It was a troubled officer who returned to Fort Garland.[28]

As soon as he arrived in April 1877, he was sent back to the Ute country. Dejected though he was, he carried out his orders efficiently, earning plaudits from the Ute agent. One dramatic exploit by Conline and his men was remembered in the Colorado mountains for decades. As he recalled years later, he was visiting at the agency when a courier reported that a wagon carrying a family of eight was wedged in the Uncompahgre River a few miles below the agency. Unless rescued quickly, all would be swept away by waters rapidly rising from the spring thaw. Luckily, the wagon's driver, a saloonkeeper named Bernstein, was carrying a large store of liquor. Its weight plus that of the passengers had kept the waters from dislodging the wagon, but its breakup was inevitable. Conline, "a man of quick decision," Colorado miner Sidney Jocknick later wrote, chose three troopers and galloped down the Uncompahgre Valley, fording its swollen waters twice before reaching the Bernsteins.

Jocknick recalled that Conline attached a lariat to stumps and stretched it across the river. Then "Sergeant Johnson, a stalwart negro," holding to the life line, carried the Bernsteins to safety "one at a time, astride his neck." Conline failed to mention the rope and named a different soldier as the rescuer but told a similar story: Private Hayden, "being the strongest soldier physically who was with us, was stripped naked to avoid friction in the water, and working opposite the tail gate, brought all the family, one at a time, on his naked back to the bank in safety." Conline and the other soldiers "took station mounted" near the front wheels of the wagon to assist "in case the water's force carried him down stream."

Thanking the rescuers profusely, Bernstein offered pay, but Conline refused to accept it. He recalled that Bernstein had two daughters, "beautiful young women about twenty-two and twenty-four years of age." Jockwith referred to them as the "belles of Ouray" and said they "never tired of telling . . . the guests of the Dixon House. . . how they rode out of a dangerous flood to safety on a negro's brawny shoulders, astride his neck."[29]

Any elation Conline felt over the rescue was wiped out by a catastrophic mishap during the return to Fort Garland. In early July, Captain Shorkley reported that on 11 June, Conline had left his troop camped a few miles distant, had ridden into the town of Del Norte, and had engaged in a brawl in a "private gambling room," from which he was "violently ejected." Picking himself up, he allegedly ordered an enlisted man to tell Sergeant Broadus to "bring up the Company and clean out the house or burn it down. I have been struck by a damned Rebel and I will have satisfaction." On 17 June, Denver's *Rocky Mountain News* printed an account of the affair.

The negative newspaper publicity convinced Hatch that he should rid his regiment of Conline. The colonel and Lieutenant Loud, his most trusted adviser, first made a crude effort to secure a confession. Conline stated that on 28 June he and Hatch were "conversing . . . on personal and official topics" when Loud entered and "with much style and flourish" presented Hatch with a sheet of paper. Pasted on it was the clipping from the *Rocky Mountain News*, its margins "'bedeviled' with remarks in red ink with the intention, as expressed by the manner of . . . Loud," to evoke a confession of guilt. As Conline noted grimly, it "did not produce the desired effect."[30]

Sergeants Broadus and Johnson and Trumpeter Charles Johnson supported Conline's denial of the charges. According to them, Conline had instructed the troop to set up camp outside Del Norte while he got a tooth filled and purchased hay. After he returned, he discovered he had left his "pocket books" at the dentist's office and returned for them. It was then that he paid the ill-fated visit to the local saloon.

Broadus and Johnson stated that about 10 P.M., Private George Cook, a white infantryman serving as the expedition's teamster (and Shorkley's spy?), had returned to camp in a drunken condition and claimed that Conline had sent for troops to burn the town. Broadus dispatched Sergeant Johnson to check into the matter. Johnson found his commander "quietly sitting in a bar room and not drinking when I saw him." Conline instructed him that the detachment was to depart at sunrise for Fort Garland. Then the sergeant "walked him to the hotel opposite and he quietly went to bed. I saw no more of him until he rejoined his Company the next day en route to Garland." Johnson added that he had never observed Conline "under the influence of intoxicating liquor in the presence of enlisted men or elsewhere."[31]

Conline's court-martial was scheduled for October 1877. Before it could convene, the months of strain resulted in a nervous breakdown. Hastily ruled insane, he was escorted to Saint Elizabeth's in Washington. When he arrived there, Dr. W. W. Godding, the superintendent, found him "incoherent and irritable." He was so "thin and haggard" that he resembled "a person who had been through some exhausting labor."[32]

The outcome of Conline's commitment was not what Hatch expected. No longer harassed by rumor mongers, the "coherence of his ideas" rapidly improved. The haggard look disappeared, and he made a "quite remarkable" gain in weight. Within a week, Godding was allowing him to go unattended around the grounds. By the first of December the doctor recommended that Conline be released and given a nine-month leave to recuperate. In his opinion, Conline had experienced a "temporary insanity" which had "passed off."[33]

Discharged from the asylum, Conline was immediately brought before a retirement board. Shorkley testified in person, and Hatch and several military surgeons submitted statements. Although Godding vigorously upheld Conline's fitness, the board concluded that he was "liable to a recurrence of insanity and therefore unfit to trust with command." Although General Sherman concurred in a recommendation that Conline be retired without pay, he survived once more. On 1 February 1878, President Rutherford B. Hayes abruptly directed that action on his case be suspended for six months to allow him to recuperate.[34]

Hayes's unusual intervention was apparently a result of an appeal by the Lelands. In October, Emma's mother wrote the president's wife a tearful letter pleading Conline's case: "He has always been a good officer and but for my poor unfortunate child would not now be in trouble. His only fault has been that he took her part without regard to his own interest." She closed by recalling that "I was well acquainted with Mrs. Grant and could have asked her this favor had she been in the position you are now in, but I appeal to you as an Ohio lady like myself . . . to use your influence in [his]. . . behalf."[35]

In June 1878, Dr. Godding examined Conline, pronounced him to be "restored to health," and recommended that he be returned to duty. He assured the lieutenant that if he would "be temperate" in all things, there was "reasonable assurance of mental soundness." On 10 July, Conline formally requested to rejoin his regiment. When Adjutant General Townsend endorsed the request, Sherman reluctantly agreed if Conline would pledge to abstain from liquor and immoderate actions.[36]

Conline's return infuriated Colonel Hatch, who presented him with an ultimatum: "resign your commission or face a General Court Martial."

When Conline refused to resign, Hatch placed him under arrest and asked Pope to order a trial. Asserting that Conline had faked insanity the previous year with "a wonderful piece of acting" to avoid a court-martial, Hatch claimed that the lieutenant's "drunken frolics continue afresh in the minds of citizens." In addition, the colonel charged that Conline had "disgraced the service" by dishonestly "obtaining money from the enlisted men of his Company under any pretext."[37]

Hatch chose to charge Conline with taking money from his men and failing to repay it. As stated, Conline, broke and faced with the expense of transporting Emma back to her parents, had "taken money on deposit" from some of his troopers. In each case he was to hold the funds until the man's term of enlistment expired. After his nervous breakdown, some of the soldiers had inquired about their money. Although he was certain that this charge would ensure Conline's conviction, Hatch could not have been more mistaken, as almost all of his witnesses, in effect, testified for the defendant.

It became obvious that Conline had always intended to repay the loans and had done so at the earliest opportunity. His tardiness in repaying had been the result of a delay in the passage of the military appropriation bill in 1877 which held up pay for several months. By the time his paychecks were delivered, he had been sent to the asylum. On 27 December 1877, the day he was released, he had given Adjutant General Townsend a check for the balances owed men of his troop together with instructions to forward the proper amounts to each one. Because of the expiration of some enlistments and the transfer of soldiers to new posts, it had taken several months to deliver the checks.

Hatch's most serious charge involved twenty-five dollars given Conline by Sergeant Johnson when the latter was facing prosecution for an altercation with another soldier. Promising to secure an attorney with the money, Conline had allegedly retained it for his own purposes, leaving Johnson to fend for himself. Testimony, however, revealed that Conline had contacted an attorney who had advised him that Johnson was in no danger of serious punishment. It was while Conline was waiting to see if the soldier's case came to trial before employing the attorney that he suffered his breakdown. The twenty-five dollars was one of the amounts included in his remittance to the adjutant general. Conline was found "not guilty" on all charges.[38]

Much relieved, Conline proudly wrote Dr. Godding that although "Col. Hatch had me put in arrest and got up a new lot of lying charges against me . . . I wisely concluded to hold my tongue and let him do all that was in his power against me." The result "after having been kept five months in arrest was a unanimous acquittal. . . . I will allow nothing to destroy my peace of mind."[39]

Despite the acquittal, Hatch refused to restore Conline to duty. As late as August 1879, the colonel was arguing that Conline should be retired because the recurrence of his insanity would jeopardize the lives of soldiers under his command. Professing to be acting out of "a feeling of humanity for his misfortune," Hatch argued that it would be a "kindness" to force Conline into retirement. In support, he presented a battery of statements from post surgeons, all advising that Conline was unfit for service.

Adjutant General Townsend was not impressed. Concerning the statements, he noted caustically that it was evident that Conline's "reputation . . . has more to do with it than their knowledge." He also instructed Hatch to revise his summation of Conline's case to show that "these outbreaks came while he was under charges for a trial of which he was acquitted."[40]

After Conline was finally allowed to resume active duty, his career resumed its pattern of acute ups and downs. After a three-day engagement in the Hembrillo Canyon in the San Andreas Mountains on 6–8 April 1880, he and four other officers were "especially commended" for "gallant conduct."[41]

The strain of almost constant campaigning gradually sapped Conline's nerves. According to Lieutenant Day, Conline's actions were becoming more erratic. Day stated that Conline had "a double set" of non-commissioned officers, one for post service and the other for field duty. Charles L. Parker served as first sergeant while the troop was on garrison duty but was replaced by Robert Johnson in the field. A trooper named Green drew the pay of a farrier, while another private did the work. Worst of all, Conline "made and reduced" a Corporal Reid several times in a single day.

Undoubtedly irked by Day's disapproval, Conline turned on him. Day remembered that once "he flew at me like a maniac and like one was quelled by my making faces at him, kicking up, and in other words acting crazy myself." Soon afterwards "he came into my room and formally placed me in arrest and a short time afterward ordered me to be released and to not consider myself to have been in arrest."[42]

In April 1881, Conline secured a thirty-day leave of absence and departed for the East. The journey may have revealed too starkly the emptiness of his life. He had divorced Emma, perhaps unfairly, cutting his ties with the Lelands. His parents were dead, and he had little contact with his siblings. Leading his troopers against the Apaches had given him a sense of purpose; the trip eastward with nowhere to go was too much. The only description of what transpired on the train is his denial that he had brandished a pistol, as had been reported. Some passengers had mistaken his field glasses for a gun. "I walked about the car, looking through the windows with my glasses but I interfered with nobody."[43]

When the train reached Pittsburgh on 30 April, Conline was removed and returned to the all too familiar confines of Saint Elizabeth's. This time, Dr. Godding kept him confined for almost four years. By late 1884 the officer had recovered sufficiently to be allowed to go into the city on his own. On 17 January 1885, Godding concluded that "after a long period of more or less excitement and delusional insanity," Conline had recovered sufficiently to be released. The military complied almost immediately, and on 29 January, Conline was released.[44]

After a six-month leave, he returned to active duty. Colonel Hatch made no protest, leading Conline to conclude that "his hostility" had changed to a "feeling of respect." Although his past would always haunt him, his troubles seemed to be over. Money was no longer a problem. Continuing to draw his salary while an inmate, he had paid off his debts and had accumulated some savings. Untroubled by news of Emma's remarriage, he even enjoyed a brief moment of acclaim.[45]

In 1886, Conline participated in the marksmanship contests of the Department of the Platte. Exhibiting an astonishing steadiness of nerves, he notched his name in the record book. In the championship round he fired ten shots at a target five hundred yards distant, hit dead center on nine, and was only slightly wide on the tenth for a score of forty-eight of a possible fifty. He then captained the departmental team that competed for the championship of the Division of the Missouri.[46]

In 1887 he married twenty-eight-year-old Fannie Strickland, daughter of a Methodist minister in Des Moines, Iowa. A friend later stated that Fannie was an "exceptionally cultivated woman" who by "example, initiative, and influence" gradually uplifted her husband from "the 'back-wardation' of heredity and early association." Two years later they had their only child, a girl named Vivienne. In addition, Conline was promoted to captain.[47]

Ironically, it was Conline's unorthodox methods of dealing with noncommissioned officers that led to his forced retirement. While Major Henry was in temporary command of the regiment, Sergeant Barney McKay complained that he had been unfairly demoted by Conline.[48] Minor as the issue was, Henry used it to invite evaluations from officers who had served with Conline. Thirteen, almost all lieutenants, complied. Typical of the responses was R. T. Emmett's statement that he had never "observed any specific evidence of unsound mind," but, "based on information received from others," he thought Conline "would be at any time liable to a return of his mental trouble if subjected to great excitement." He concluded by describing him as "a man of honor and integrity" whom he held in high respect.[49]

Convinced that both Conline and the service would benefit by his retirement, Major Henry stressed that Conline was "an honorable, hard-working officer, but his condition is such that . . . I should not be doing my duty . . . if I failed to take the action I have." He softened the blow by recommending Conline for a brevet promotion to major and assuring him he would receive a disability pension.

When the retirement board met in April, Conline seemed concerned mainly with refuting diagnoses that his breakdowns were a result of heredity. Maintaining his composure throughout the hearing, he mused that in consideration of the wishes of his "best friends and wife," it might be best if he were "placed on the retired list, for I can see that . . . insanity is, according to the highest authority on such questions, just as liable to recur . . . as . . . any [other] disease."[50]

After his dismissal, Conline in effect lived happily ever after. He moved to Detroit, his wife's girlhood home, and served as its police commissioner during the reform administration of Mayor Hazen Pingree. Early in the new century he moved to Washington, where he could hobnob with other retirees. Visiting in France when World War I broke out, he was so agitated by the German invasion and "his efforts to aid hundreds of Americans to get home, many of them in dire distress" that it produced an "abnormal excitement to his brain and highly organized nervous system." After he returned home, he sent the adjutant general a poignant note that "in case of war with Germany" he would be ready for service "within four hours." As his condition worsened in 1916, he was admitted for a last time to Saint Elizabeth's. In October he died of a heart attack.[51]

William J. Roe described Conline aptly as an "exceptional man who, greatly handicapped, rose superior to all opposition, and by the power of will overcame every inimical force." He declared him to be made of "the same fine clay of strength and valor . . . as those heroes told of in the Iliad . . . or related in the chronicles of chivalry."[52]

Hero or not, Conline received the burial of one. His services were conducted in Saint John's Church, the "Church of the Presidents," across Lafayette Square from the White House. From there a horse-drawn caisson with "caparisoned horse and escort of suitable strength" conveyed his body to Arlington Cemetery. On the slope below and slightly to the left of the Custis-Lee Mansion, amidst the monuments of generals and admirals, he was interred, to be joined in due time by Fannie. Forty-six years later, less than one hundred yards away at the foot of the same slope, there would be buried another descendant of Irish immigrants—John Fitzgerald Kennedy.[53]

14

Sergeant Brent Woods

The Odyssey of a Hero

On 19 August 1881 a detachment of the Ninth Cavalry under Lieutenant George W. Smith rode into the deadliest ambush in the regiment's history. Only the incredible leadership of Sergeant Brent Woods averted a total disaster. While the ambush and Woods's gallantry have been described many times, it was only one event in a thirty-year career that had an inordinate number of ups and downs. Woods's experiences illustrate the importance and difficulty of maintaining good relations between rank and file and officers.

Lieutenant George Smith was probably the last officer in the regiment who would have been expected to stumble into an ambush. He had commanded entire regiments in some of the bloodiest battles of the Civil War and was consigned to the rank of lieutenant only because he had resigned from the army in 1865 and had remained in civilian life for eight years. He had carried out every assignment with an efficiency that would have done credit to a major.

In August 1881, however, Smith was a troubled man. His four-year-old son, "the apple of his eye," had recently died; his wife was the object of malicious gossip concerning an alleged affair with a young infantry officer; and his pay had been withheld because some accounts while he was on quartermaster duty had not balanced.[1] His ensuing actions were so contradictory to everything else in his career that one suspects he was too distracted and depressed to handle an acute crisis.

As Colonel Hatch sought to prevent the escape of Nana's Apaches into Mexico, he ordered Captain Byron Dawson to occupy Gavilan Pass, a gateway to the Chihuahuan Desert. Dawson, lethargic as usual, delayed with the main force while Smith pushed ahead with only seventeen troopers. When Smith reached the mining camp of Lake City on 18 August, he found the miners in an uproar over a raid on a nearby ranch. George Daly, head of the syndicate developing a large silver mine, proposed that Smith combine forces with the miners and pursue the raiders. When Smith replied that he had been instructed to wait for Dawson and the balance of Troops H and B, Daly in effect called him a coward and proposed to pursue himself, with or without the troops.[2] When the miners left the next day, Smith reluctantly joined them.

About 9:30 A.M. Smith and Daly entered Gavilan Canyon. Behind them rode the buffalo soldiers, followed by a motley train of miners and cowboys, many still drinking. As if oblivious to any danger, they rode straight into the ambush. Smith and Daly were killed by the first salvo, and the miners either fled madly down the canyon or collapsed in fright behind boulders. For a moment the panic spread to the soldiers as the senior noncommissioned officer, Sergeant William Baker of H Troop, a man who had won a citation for gallantry from Captain Carroll, broke and ran.[3] The others might well have done the same if it had not been for Woods.

In the eight years since he had left a Kentucky farm at the age of twenty-three, Brent Woods had established himself as "one of the best and bravest soldiers" in the regiment.[4] A mulatto, only five feet six inches tall, he had been assigned to B Troop, where he learned the ins and outs of military life from two future Medal of Honor awardees, Sergeants Thomas Shaw and John Denny. By the time Woods's first enlistment expired, he had advanced to the rank of sergeant and had earned an evaluation of "excellent."[5]

Woods's second five-year term was less tranquil. At Fort Craig in March 1879 he was accused of drawing his pistol on a civilian and was jailed. Although no details are available, his action must have been deemed justified, because the local officials released him almost immediately to the military. Court-martialed, he escaped with a remarkably light sentence, reduced to the ranks and fined one month's pay.[6]

On 7 April, less than a week after his trial, he was granted a ninety-day furlough. After a welcomed stay in his hometown, he was ordered to conduct a detachment of recruits from the Cavalry Depot at Saint Louis

Brent Woods, sergeant, Ninth Cavalry, 1873–1902, awarded the Medal of Honor for the Battle of Gavilan Canyon, 1881. Courtesy of the Fletcher Christian Collection, LIbrary of Congress.

to New Mexico. The Victorio War was in full swing by the time he delivered all of them to their posts.

In a three-week period in early 1880, Woods participated in three hard-fought engagements—in the San Mateo Mountains (12 January), on the head of the Rio Perchas (17 January), and in the Mimbres Canyon in the San Andreas Mountains (3 February). Although the official reports of these engagements are sketchy, the heroics of Woods did not go unnoticed. According to Lieutenant Ballard Humphrey, who had charge of the mountain howitzer at Rio Perchas, Sergeant Daniel Gross, the head gunner, was killed at the height of the battle. Woods immediately offered "his services in working the gun, which I would not have been able to do without his assistance." Humphrey also extolled Woods's bravery at the battle in the San Andreas Mountains. In typical fashion the clash had consisted of assaults upon Apache positions along "the sides of the canyon." As soon as one position was made untenable for the Indians, they reassembled further on and then at nightfall made good their escape. Woods, "at the head" of a detachment, was severely wounded by a bullet in his left thigh. Captains Dawson and Purrington and Lieutenant Humphrey each commended him for "remarkable bravery."[7]

Despite his wound, Woods soon resumed his duties as a noncommissioned officer. Unfortunately, his methods of turning recruits into soldiers were so unorthodox that they resulted in another court-martial. On 23 April Private Allen Dade complained that Woods had with "intent to bully" pointed a loaded gun in his face and had commanded him to "smell of it." No one in the troop save Dade thought the incident serious. Woods explained that he had no intent "to hurt the man or scare him nor anything of the kind." Ever since bringing him from Saint Louis as a recruit, he had endeavored to "instruct him and favor him as a soldier because I did not think he had what belonged to him, in other words good sense."[8]

After Humphrey and Purrington vouched for Woods's character and bravery there was no danger of severe punishment. He was simply sentenced to be reprimanded in orders. Neither a fine nor reduction in rank ensued.[9]

The officers were not always so generous. Woods's fellow sergeant in B Troop, John Denny, acclaimed for rescuing a wounded comrade at the Rio Las Animas in September 1879, had become ravaged by "acute rheumatism." In August 1880 he was reduced to the ranks and assigned to the menial duties of a barracks orderly. In April 1881, still a private, he was given the dangerous task of carrying dispatches by horseback between Deming and Fort Cummings. Woods, in contrast, had been designated provost sergeant. His actions in the midst of the ambush at Gavilan Pass show that he well deserved the honor.[10]

In addition to the deaths of Smith and Daly, several enlisted men were badly hit by the fire of the Apaches. As he deployed the survivors behind the scant shelter available, Woods sized up the situation. Singling out an elevated ridge to their rear from which to make a stand, he ordered a retreat, "firing and retreating in successive lines," until they reached the designated position.

Lieutenant Charles Taylor, who interviewed the survivors shortly after the battle ended, wrote a more graphic account. Woods had "rallied his men, . . . fought his way desperately to a high piece of ground, driving the indians [sic] before him." Despite his small force, he stubbornly "held his ground."[11]

The few civilians who had not fled were stunned. One told Taylor that Woods was "a S.O.B. to fight. I had no idea a darky would fight that way. If it had not been for him, none of us could have come out of that canyon." That, Taylor said, was "the general sentiment" expressed by the survivors.

For almost four hours the troopers held their position. Although Woods had prevented a disaster, three soldiers had been killed, while three others were seriously wounded, leaving only ten able-bodied survivors. The slain men, all from Woods's B Troop, included two veterans and one rookie.

Thomas Golding was a thirty-five-year-old Georgian only three months shy of completing his second tour of duty. A self-described musician when he volunteered in December 1871, he found it so hard to adjust that he deserted six months after reporting for duty. As was the case with many who deserted in their first year, he surrendered himself three weeks afterwards. Allowed to remain in the service, he received a "good" evaluation at the end of his enlistment. He had been the troop's saddler for five years.[12] Monroe Overstreet, a thirty-six-year-old Kentuckian serving as the troop's teamster, was two years into his second enlistment. In contrast, James Brown, a twenty-three-old barber from Virginia, was still in his first year of service.

One of the wounded, Private William Hollins, was also from B Troop. Shot through the lungs, he was kept on the army rolls for the five months remaining in his enlistment and then discharged. His reward was an evaluation of "excellent." The other two wounded men, both seriously hurt, were from H Troop. Private John Williams, in his ninth year of service, had gone before a garrison court-martial three months before the battle. Fined ten dollars a month for a six-month-period, he was returned to active duty. A bullet in his right thigh resulted in an amputation four months later. All fines collected after 30 June, however, were remitted. Wesley Harris, an Ohioan in his third year of service, took a bullet through the right breast.[13]

In midafternoon the Apaches, aware that both Taylor and Lieutenant Eugene Dimmick were converging on their position, broke off the attack. Woods and his command pushed back into the canyon to reclaim Smith's body, the arms and back of which were burned, the nose severed, and the face and "other members" slashed.[14]

Woods and every man in his command should have been recommended for the Medal of Honor on the spot. Instead, they received only the barest of acknowledgments. Colonel Hatch's only reference was a curt note that "Sgt. Woods of B troop . . . , left in command, held his ground until Sgt. [Richard] Anderson [H Troop] came up with the balance of the command." The only military dispatch to pay any tribute to them was an unofficial note, probably written by Major Henry, that the men, "commanded by a sergeant," had "fought in the finest manner" and "deserved great credit."[15] Woods's heroism would go unrewarded for more than twelve years.

With the arrival of the relief forces, all that remained was to bury the dead. A detachment under Sergeant George Turpin of H Troop escorted the bodies to Fort Bayard for burial. Seventeen years later, Turpin, retired and living in Kansas, recalled his breaking "the sad news" to Smith's wife and daughter. He stated that Smith's death had been "greatly regretted by . . . the enlisted men who loved him, as he was always true and brave."[16]

Smith's wife never forgot the bravery and compassion of the buffalo soldiers. Sixteen years afterwards, she was invited to address a reunion of the Society of the Army of the Cumberland concerning her husband. She concluded by commending the troopers who had "continued to fight, and by their bravery without a commander (God bless them) saved the body. . . . A braver set of men never lived."[17]

Despite his actions at Gavilan Canyon, Woods received scant consideration from Captain Dawson. Transferred to Fort Hays, Kansas, his situation disintegrated in April 1882, when he was court-martialed for "conduct prejudicial to good order and military discipline" and reduced to the ranks. The court explained that it had been "lenient" because of his previous record.[18]

Other than a five-dollar fine for being absent without leave in June, Woods's record remained clean for the balance of 1882. Between January and May of 1883, however, he was court-martialed four times for conduct "prejudicial to good order and military discipline," the last of which resulted in the maximum punishment allowable for a garrison court-martial—a month at hard labor and a thirty-dollar fine.[19] Although the specifics of his offenses were not listed, they probably involved insubordination, most likely to First Sergeant David Badie. Although Badie had been commended for gallantry during the Victorio War, his abrasive actions could goad the best of soldiers into defiance.

In August 1884, for example, Sergeant Denny was engaged in "the proper discharge" of orders from "competent authority" when he was challenged by Badie. Despite Denny's explanation, Badie "continued his unauthorized inquiries and remarks" until Denny retaliated with language that was "reprehensible, insubordinate, and a breach of good order and military discipline." Although Denny was convicted, his "long and efficient service as a non-commissioned officer" allowed him to escape with a reduction to the ranks and a fifteen-dollar fine—which was remitted by the post commander.[20] Four years later, Corporal Benjamin Hockens was also court-martialed for intemperate language in response to Badie's badgering.[21]

Although Captain Dawson made no effort to determine why one of his best soldiers had become so incorrigible, he provided Woods some relief by assigning him to the post bakery. When his enlistment expired in October, Dawson evaluated him as "good."[22]

To no one's surprise, Woods transferred to Troop E upon reenlisting and was almost immediately elevated to the rank of sergeant. The promotion of Jerauld Olmsted to the captaincy of E Troop, however, would be disastrous. Olmsted, most of whose experience had been as a quartermaster in the Thirteenth Infantry, would demonstrate how much turmoil an injudicious and headstrong commander could produce. Woods was one of the first of several noncoms reduced to the ranks and replaced by first-termers. In his most bizarre move, Olmsted promoted Melvin Wilkins, a burly, twenty-four-year-old, Canadian-born private, to the rank of first sergeant.

Since Wilkins was just beginning his fourth year of service, barely able to write his name, given to explosive outbursts of temper, and a heavy drinker, his qualifications were obscure to all but Olmsted. Unable to command the respect of veterans, the new sergeant responded with bullying. His special target was Woods. Stationed at Fort McKinney, Wyoming, in early 1886, the hero of the Apache wars was reduced to performing an endless round of fatigue duties such as cleaning the stables.

On 24 March, Wilkins reported that Woods had been absent without leave from a fatigue assignment, had called the first sergeant a "God damn liar," and had struck him in the face.[23] Captain Olmsted quickly filed charges. If he expected to get rid of Woods, he was to be sorely disappointed.

Olmsted's first setback occurred when Woods had him dismissed from the court-martial panel because he was bringing the charges. Worse, the other sergeants testified that Woods had completed his assigned tasks on the day in question and had been relieved of further duties. In addition, they described the first sergeant as the aggressor. William Clay, with fifteen years of service to his credit, stated that Woods, upon being placed under arrest, asked why it had been done. When Wilkins replied that it was for lying, Woods exclaimed: "Any man that says that I lie tells a damn lie."[24]

As Woods turned to stable the two horses he was leading, Wilkins, ten years younger and four inches taller, grabbed him from behind and clamped his teeth onto one of his ears, sending the blood streaming down. After the other sergeants freed Woods and were escorting him to the guardhouse, Wilkins overtook them and screamed, "Don't take him to the guardhouse, give him to me. I'll murder the motherless bastard before I take him." With that, he attacked Woods and "started to beat him again."[25]

Conducting his own defense, Woods skillfully exposed Wilkins's misconduct. Clay stated that he was engaged in a vendetta against the old soldiers in the company and had bragged that "he was going to get the

Captain to 'bob-tail'" all of them. Clay added that Wilkins had been drinking when he ordered Woods's arrest and noted, "He gets up a fuss in the Troop every time when he is drinking."

Benjamin Hockins, another veteran, testified that Wilkins had asked him to swear that Woods was the aggressor. When he hesitated, Wilkins offered to make him a sergeant. When Hockins replied that he was not "hunting Sergeants' stripes in that way," Wilkins responded that he could "go to hell, . . . you are like all the rest of these God damned niggers, you are down on me."[26]

Even though the court-martial panel consisted entirely of Olmsted's fellow officers in the Ninth Cavalry, it acquitted Woods on all counts. Despite this, Wilkins remained first sergeant for another nine months.

In November 1886, after a change of stations to Fort Duchesne, Olmsted took a leave of absence, leaving Lieutenant Eugene Ladd as the troop commander. A few days later, Ladd noticed that Wilkins had been absent for several hours and found him at the post trader's saloon, intoxicated and his face bloody. Irate, Ladd rejected Wilkins's claim that he had been struck while breaking up a fight among some white infantrymen and ordered him to his quarters.

Later that afternoon, Wilkins accused Ladd of prejudice because Major Frederick Benteen, the post commander, was "down on Niggers," and the lieutenant wanted "to keep on the right side of him."[27] Dismissed, Wilkins then dictated a letter to Private Abraham Grayson, the company clerk, and handed it to Ladd. In it, Wilkins requested to be relieved as first sergeant because Ladd, "in the absence of Captain Olmsted," was "doing everything he can to give me a bad name before the Company." Ladd charged him with insubordination, of being absent without leave, and of engaging in a drunken brawl.[28]

Tried on 29 January 1887, Wilkins vainly denied he had dictated the letter or had accused Ladd of prejudice. Olmsted, a member of the court-martial, described him as a "respectful soldier" who "performed his duties faithfully" and was "not addicted to drink." Despite Olmsted's support, Wilkins was convicted and sentenced to be reduced to the ranks and to pay a fine of twenty dollars.[29] When his enlistment expired on 16 February, he returned to civilian life.

As Wilkins's fortunes waned, those of Woods improved. When Colonel Hatch assumed command of Fort Duchesne in January 1887, he selected

Woods as his personal orderly. After Wilkins's court-martial, Olmsted, perhaps hoping to win favor with Hatch, advanced Woods to the first sergeancy. The other noncommissioned officers could not have been pleased by the extraordinary promotion.[30]

Woods's problems with Olmsted were far from over. In October 1887 the captain was charged with insubordination by Major James Randlett, the new commander at Fort Duchesne. After the murder of Sergeant Frank Washington was attributed to a rivalry for the affections of a laundress living with him, Randlett had prohibited all cohabitation on the post. Learning that Sergeant Theophilius White of Olmsted's troop was living with a laundress (and an alleged prostitute) identified only as Edna, he ordered White to return to the barracks and denied him permission to marry Edna. In a blatant act of defiance, Olmsted allowed the pair to wed and attended the ceremony.

Charged with insubordination and brought to trial, Olmsted maintained that Randlett had singled out White because of animosity toward himself, and he described Edna as a virtuous young woman whose only crime was that she worked as a maid for Lieutenant Montgomery Parker, whom Randlett had also charged with insubordination. Always quick with accusations, Olmsted claimed that Randlett had openly condoned promiscuity and prostitution. To Randlett's chagrin, Captain Dawson, a member of the court-martial, testified that he had heard the major say that "plenty of women on laundresses row" would "keep the soldiers satisfied."[31]

Unfortunately for Woods, who had been uninvolved in the affair, he was called to testify. After he confirmed that White and Edna had been living together for nine months, he was asked if Edna was a "known prostitute." He replied tersely that he had "reason and cause to believe she is a woman of that character." Asked if he thought their relationship "was to the scandal and disgrace of the service at this post," he considered a moment and then replied, "*I consider it to be a slander and disgrace to the colored people.*"[32] While that was the extent of his testimony, it had sufficed to add him to Olmsted's list of enemies.

With its captain and first sergeant at odds, discipline within E Troop collapsed as men became openly defiant. When Woods ordered blacksmith Berry Robinson to "stop beating his dog and fall in" for a roll call, Robinson snarled that he would do so when "he got ready."[33] When

Woods admonished Private Hermon Hector for reporting for drill with a watering bridle on his horse, Hector replied in a "threatening, insubordinate, and disrespectful" manner that "I don't want any of your monkeying [or] I will mash your damned head." A garrison court-martial gave Hector a month's confinement.[34]

At the troop dining table on 7 December, Saddler John Steward assaulted another soldier with a poker. When Woods tried to restrain Steward, Corporal Alonzo Scott intervened with "threatening gestures" and "abusive language" that Woods charged was intended to undermine his authority. A garrison court-martial headed by one of Olmsted's friends fined Steward ten dollars for disorderly conduct but acquitted Corporal Scott.[35]

Matters improved somewhat for Woods in 1888, because Captain Olmsted was kept in arrest for most of the first half of the year. When President Grover Cleveland disallowed Olmsted's conviction and dismissal from service in May, Colonel Hatch arranged for Woods to transfer from E Troop. Ironically, he was assigned to B Troop, where he once more came under the command of First Sergeant Badie. When Woods's enlistment expired in November, he showed his disgust with his treatment by transferring to the Tenth Cavalry.

When his enlistment in the Tenth expired in 1893, he asked permission to return to the Ninth and to be assigned to Captain Charles Taylor's C Troop at Fort McKinney, Wyoming. Taylor, who had never forgotten Woods's bravery at Gavilan Pass, supported the request by stating that he had a vacancy and desired Woods's assignment to his troop.

Taylor, who in cooperation with Matt Day was in the process of securing for Sergeant Denny a well-deserved Medal of Honor for the rescue of Albert Freeland in 1879, decided that Woods was also overdue the medal. During early 1894 he secured affidavits from Private Harry Trout, the only man at Gavilan Pass besides Woods still in the regiment, and Sergeant Denny, who had arrived at the site with Taylor.[36] In addition, he prodded a letter of support out of the retired Captain Dawson. Overcoming the skepticism of General Schofield, who found it hard to believe that "services" such as the affidavits described had not been "deemed worthy of official report or notation on rolls and returns," approval was finally gained.

Woods received his medal on 12 July 1894 at a ceremony attended by the entire Fort McKinney garrison. After reciting an account of the Gavilan

Pass ambush, Major E. G. Fechet presented Woods with the medal: "All who know you say that this medal has been worthily bestowed." Reporting the ceremony, the *Kansas City Times* wondered why it "was not awarded long ago."[37]

Promoted to corporal in 1895, Woods was one of three noncommissioned officers chosen to serve as a permanent color guard for all regimental exercises, both mounted and dismounted. Promoted to sergeant and evaluated as "excellent" at the expiration of his enlistment, he signed up for a final tour of duty. Although C Troop was in the fore of the charge up San Juan Hill, in which Taylor was seriously wounded, Woods was not involved. He had been detached to drill the host of recruits enlisted after the outbreak of war. Before this was accomplished, the campaign had ended.[38]

Woods retired from service in 1902 and returned to his native Kentucky. Like most Medal of Honor awardees in the Ninth Cavalry, he had little time to enjoy retirement.[39] He returned to Somerset, Kentucky, his residence when he first enlisted, and settled down on a pension of $29.75 per month. In June 1906, Pearly Woods, either his wife or another relative, informed the adjutant general that he had died the previous March of what the town mayor described as "paralysis." Seventy-eight years later, his remains were moved from a rock-marked county gravesite to the Mill Springs National Cemetery.[40]

15

From Dishonor to Glory

Two Lieutenants of I Troop

Because of the frequent absences of Captain Frank Bennett and First Lieutenant W. W. Tyler, two rookie lieutenants commanded I Troop most of the time between 1875 and 1881. One was a tragic failure whose lapses were all the more glaring because he was the younger brother of Wesley Merritt. The other was one of the most heroic and charismatic figures in the regiment.

If ever a young man was eclipsed by his elder brothers, it was Charles Merritt, the youngest of eleven overachievers in Illinois. While only Wesley gained national acclaim, all except Charles were highly successful. As he neared his twenty-fourth year in 1873, still lacking a vocation, his siblings decided to foist him off on the military. Wesley Merritt, delegated to secure the commission, received little help from the officer to be.

Asked for an autobiographical sketch, Charles Merritt wrote only that he had been reared in Salem, Illinois, and had been "connected" with two brothers in a Springfield publishing enterprise. He closed with a pathetic admission that there had been "no special or important" events in his life.[1] Administered the exam required of applicants, he failed miserably.

Wesley Merritt unwisely refused to accept defeat. Blaming the failure on Charles's "embarrassment and lack of time to refresh his knowledge," he requested that the examining board reevaluate his fitness to be an officer. When the board, dominated by two of Wesley's friends, Major James Forsyth and Captain Michael Sheridan, made a positive recommendation, Charles Merritt was assigned to the Ninth Cavalry.[2] For several months he served as Wesley's aide and even lived with him and his family at Fort Concho.[3]

In 1875, Wesley Merritt assumed command of the Fifth Cavalry, leaving his brother on his own. Soon afterwards, I Troop was relocated at Fort Wingate, the westernmost post in New Mexico, where Merritt for a time displayed a considerable knack for leadership. Placed in charge of a detachment of Navajo scouts in addition to his duties with I Troop, he scouted and campaigned from the Mexican border to southern Colorado. By the end of 1877 he had established a record as creditable as that of any junior lieutenant in the regiment.

Personal problems, however, would be his downfall. At Fort Wingate, on 29 November 1877, Corporal John Rogers, a twenty-nine-year-old Georgian with eight years of service to his credit, audaciously mailed a complaint directly to the secretary of war that Merritt had "made repeated attempts" to break into his quarters, always when he was absent and after his wife had retired. Rogers had complained to Captain Horace Jewitt, the post commander, but Jewett had refused to take action. Three weeks later, Colonel Hatch was ordered to investigate.[4]

After a lengthy investigation, Lieutenant Colonel Swaine of the Fifteenth Infantry recommended that charges be brought against both Merritt and Captain Jewett. On 1 June, Hatch forwarded the papers on the case and awaited instructions. None came.[5] Not only was no court-martial ordered, but in addition the papers were never placed in Merritt's personal file. It seems likely that someone, perhaps General Sheridan, intervened out of respect to Wesley Merritt.

Although Charles Merritt had narrowly avoided the scandal of a trial, he seems not to have learned from his escape. In early 1879 his troop was sent to Ojo Caliente in anticipation of an attempt by Victorio's Mimbres Apaches, recently escaped from the San Carlos Reservation, to return to their homeland. On the evening of 7 February 1879, Merritt was startled by the "hallowing" of Victorio's warriors. When the chief asked for a conference, Merritt agreed to meet him the following morning atop a mountain one-half mile from the post. Showing great bravery, Merritt came unarmed and accompanied only by an interpreter. He agreed to allow the Mimbres to remain as "prisoners" on the Ojo Caliente Reservation and to issue Victorio a pass permitting him to visit the Mescalero reservation to bring in Nana's band. Like his superiors, Hatch and Pope,

Merritt realized that the alternative to subsisting the Mimbres at Ojo Caliente was war.[6]

Although Hatch commended Merritt for bravery and good judgment, the agreement was rejected by the Indian Bureau. In response to Hatch's protest that any attempt to move them back to San Carlos would lead to war, the bureau tentatively agreed to let them settle among the Mescaleros. When Merritt relayed this decision to Victorio in early March, the chief was so upset that yet another promise had been broken that he decided to escape.[7]

Within weeks rumors surfaced that Merritt was too drunk on the night of the Mimbres' escape to "discharge his duty." Captain Ambrose Hooker, recently sent to Ojo Caliente, secured statements from army surgeon C. A. Sewell, forage agent W. J. Hooker,[8] and interpreter Andrew Kelley that Merritt had precipitated the flight by ordering his troops to surround and disarm the warriors. Too inebriated to direct the operation, he entrusted it to First Sergeant Moses Williams. Not surprisingly, in view of the cavalry's lack of numbers and the wiliness of the Apaches, the effort was a fiasco. After a wild exchange of gunfire in which three of the troopers' horses were shot, the Indians made good their escape. Instead of organizing a pursuit, Merritt retired to his tent and remained there until the next day.[9]

Merritt adamantly denied the accusations. He stated that Victorio had refused to go to the Mescalero reservation because he feared reprisals for his having killed two of their warriors. As for the escape, there had simply been too few soldiers to prevent its success. Neither on that night nor at any other time at Ojo Caliente had he been "so much under the influence of liquor as to be unable to properly perform" his duties.[10]

On 9 July, Pope authorized the filing of charges. While awaiting trial in Santa Fe, Merritt destroyed any chance of receiving another reprieve. On the afternoon of 30 July he engaged in a brawl with the Exchange Hotel's bartender and afterwards became so boisterous in a store belonging to the influential Seligman brothers that the police "conveyed him through the public streets" to jail.[11] This most definitely was not "conduct befitting an officer and a gentleman."

When the court-martial convened on 18 August, the witnesses included seven of Merritt's noncoms, headed by First Sergeant Williams and Corporal Rogers. Although it is impossible to ascertain the role their testimony played,[12] the trial's outcome was never in doubt. Merritt was found guilty of being drunk on duty on three occasions at Ojo Caliente, including the night of Victorio's escape and also during the recent incidents in Santa Fe. Sentenced to be dismissed from the service, he waited almost three months before the review proceedings were concluded. When President Hayes finally upheld the dismissal, he was notified that on 26 November his service would be terminated.[13]

After receiving the news at Fort Wingate, Merritt returned to Santa Fe. Once more he checked into the Exchange Hotel. On the evening of 12 December, while engaged in a round of drinks with a friend, he was asked when he planned to leave Santa Fe. He replied, "Never." When he returned to his room, he placed his pistol to his head and pulled the trigger. His burial in Santa Fe's national cemetery was attended by "a great many" citizens and "the entire Military."[14]

George R. Burnett, his successor in I Troop, was an 1880 graduate of West Point whose low academic rank doomed him to a black regiment. He was so handsome that one of his classmates wrote that after "a girl saw Burny it must have been difficult for her to feign admiration for any husband that fate allotted her." He was unusually good natured, his classmate asserted, with "no sullenness nor bitterness nor perfidiousness nor enviousness, nor any of those miserable traits with which preoccupied Nature sometime endows a human being."[15] More important, he was brave to the point of rashness.

Graduating in June 1880, Burnett wasted no time in reporting for duty. Although it was common for graduates to take several months to report, he arrived in Santa Fe on 28 July, less than a month after his appointment. He was immediately ordered to assume command of I Troop at Fort Wingate, since Bennett and Tyler were still on detached service.[16]

Despite Merritt's mishaps, I Troop was one of the better companies in the regiment. Captain Bennett, when on duty, was popular, and Moses Williams was an exceptional top sergeant. As a result, the troop consistently had low desertion and high reenlistment rates. Because few recruits were assigned to the Ninth in the mid-1870s, its roster was split between a core of veterans in their second and third terms and novices thrown into the Victorio campaign as soon as they reported for duty.

The anchor of the troop was Sergeant Williams. A dark-skinned youth reared on a large Louisiana plantation, he nevertheless had secured sufficient education to attract the notice of officers. One of the first men to

George R. Burnett, lieutenant, Ninth Cavalry, 1880–90, awarded the Medal of Honor for action at the Battle of Cuchillo Negro, 1881. Courtesy of Special Collections, U.S. Military Academy Library, West Point.

enlist in 1866, he was promoted to the rank of first sergeant by the end of his first year. Never incurring a demotion or a serious disciplinary action, he served ten years in Carroll's F Troop before switching to Bennett's company. Like George Mason of L Troop, he tended to his duties so smoothly that he left few ripples.

Among the many rookies who joined the Ninth as the Indian troubles escalated was an irrepressible young Marylander named Augustus Walley. Enlisting at Baltimore in November 1878, he reported to I Troop the following April. Like many recruits, he found army discipline so distasteful that he left camp with the intent "in his heart of remaining away." Apprehended and placed under arrest, he was ordered to dig a grave for a deceased comrade. When a band of Apaches suddenly attacked, his guard dropped his carbine and "broke all the southwestern sprinting records." Walley picked up the gun and "from the shelter" of the grave "made things too hot for the invaders." After they retired, he was released from arrest and returned to duty.[17] Since official records do not confirm this account, it may have been much embellished. But based on Walley's subsequent combat record, it is plausible indeed.

Called as a witness at the controversial court-martial of Johnson Whittaker, a black cadet at West Point, Burnett was absent during the first half of 1881. Soon after rejoining his troop in mid-June, he would face the test of his life in the campaign against Nana, the last of the great Mimbres war leaders.

Aware that no single expedition could overtake the Apaches, Hatch assigned their pursuit to a detachment of Indian scouts under Lieutenant Charles Taylor while dispatching other units to occupy likely waterholes and to block the most likely escape routes. With so many different detachments in the field, the Apaches would have little chance of evading all of them. It was a sound plan, but torrential monsoon rains in northern New Mexico washed out the railway line, preventing the rapid transfer of troops to the south. As a result, many of the detachments were so small that they risked annihilation.

As part of the deployment, Burnett and twenty-two men from I Troop scouted the country between Forts Wingate and Bayard without detecting the hostiles. From Bayard they traveled by rail to Fort Craig, arriving on 7 August. Receiving no further orders, Burnett waited impatiently until 13 August. Much to his chagrin, the orders that arrived were delivered by

Lieutenant Gustavus Valois, who was also authorized to replace him as commander. Hatch obviously feared that Burnett was too inexperienced to be trusted on his own. Valois, on the other hand, was a veteran who had just completed a tour as the regimental quartermaster and was awaiting a new assignment.

Although a native of Prussia (his actual name was Heinel), Valois had little combat experience. A quartermaster sergeant during the Civil War, he had served three years as a noncommissioned officer in the Fifth Cavalry after the war before securing a commission in the Ninth. Capable enough in routine assignments, he would display little taste for battle.

Leaving Fort Craig on 13 August, the detachment marched through the San Mateos for two days, arriving at Cañada Alamosa, midway between Ojo Caliente and Fort Craig, early on the morning of the sixteenth. The command had halted to water its horses when a Mexican arrived with the news that Apaches had attacked the Chávez ranch, located a few miles down the Alamosa.[18]

Burnett, growing impatient with the leisurely rate at which Valois was preparing for action, received permission to go ahead with ten men accompanied by a poorly armed party of Mexican civilians. Discovering that all six residents of the ranch, including a woman and her two children, were dead, he spotted an Apache party moving up a ridge to the southwest. Despite his inferior numbers, he took up the pursuit. The Apaches posted a rear guard along the crest of the ridge to deter him while the rest escaped with their plunder and stolen horses.

Aware that a frontal assault would be costly, Burnett posted some of the civilians to the left of the Indians' skirmish line to check any attempt at envelopment. With the balance of the civilians and a few buffalo soldiers, he positioned himself squarely in front of the Apache line and opened fire. While he kept the Indians engaged, Sergeant Williams was dispatched to lead the remaining troopers around the Indians' right flank. When he had worked his command into position to fire on the Apaches, Williams signaled, and Burnett "mounted and charged them until they sought cover behind the next ridge." Burnett then repeated the flanking maneuver.

The Apaches had no intention of making a determined stand until their train of plunder had time to vanish into the Cuchillo Negro Mountains a few miles to the west. Again and again they formed their skirmish line, gave way when things grew too hot, and regrouped at the next high ground. A correspondent for the *New York Herald*, who submitted the most detailed account of a Ninth Cavalry engagement on record, wrote only hours afterwards that "Burnett and his men kept charging, while the Indians kept . . . retreating and motioning him to follow, beckoning with their hands and waving their guns, mostly Winchesters."[19]

The retreat continued until the Apaches reached the mountains. Concealing themselves along the first ridge of the Cuchillo Negroes, they stopped. In addition to having an advantageous position and a superiority in numbers, their Winchesters fired more rapidly than the troopers' single-shot Springfields. Annihilating the buffalo troopers would furnish a modicum of revenge for the wrongs they had suffered.[20]

Undoubtedly annoyed that Valois had not arrived with the balance of the detachment, Burnett approached the Cuchillo Negroes gingerly. As the Apaches opened fire, he ordered his command to take cover. Further advance was impossible; retreat, almost equally dangerous. Undaunted, he sized up the terrain and hit upon a plan that, while risky, furnished the only chance of dislodging the Apaches.

Sure that Valois must be near, he looked around for a volunteer to carry a message instructing Valois to occupy a height to the right of the Indians that would command their position. Instantly, Corporal Rogers, the soldier who had complained about Merritt's advances toward his wife, stepped forward. He started crawling to the rear but then threw caution aside, ran to his picketed horse, and rode through a hail of bullets in search of Valois. Many Medals of Honor were won for less heroic actions.[21]

Instructing his Mexican auxiliaries to continue firing upon the Apache positions, Burnett endeavored to circle their left flank with the cavalrymen. All went well for a time as the squad rode as quietly as possible up a crevice toward a position to the rear and left of the Indians. Suddenly, Sergeant Williams spotted a dark object, perhaps the head of a warrior, silhouetted above a rock and pointed it out to Burnett. The lieutenant dismounted, took careful aim, and fired. Although he thought he "was responsible for . . . one 'good Indian,'" his shot was answered by a volley from the Apaches, who were obviously waiting for the troopers to walk into their trap.

Burnett's horse, frightened by the gunfire, broke away and raced to the rear, sending a feeling of panic through the troopers. "They've got the lieutenant!" someone cried, and most of the troopers started to run. Only Sergeant Williams and Private Walley stood fast. Walley and Burnett, shooting furiously, held the position while Williams overtook the soldiers and led them back into the engagement. The little command yet seemed on the verge of disaster, with bullets ricocheting in from three sides, when the Apache fire abruptly ceased.[22]

Rogers had made good his escape and reached Valois, who was approaching with the rest of the command. After a brief hesitation, Valois started his command toward the suggested prominence. His delay was almost fatal. The Apaches assailing Burnett "broke for the same hill," reached it about "200 yards ahead of Valois," and opened fire, wounding Valois's horse and killing several others.[23]

Caught in the open, Valois's troopers took such cover as they could find in the "long grass and soap weeds." Two, Corporal Monroe Johnson, with a bullet in his right foot, and Private Nathan Gaines, were wounded. Gaines, "shot through the breast," gritted his teeth and stuck to his post. His heroics would have gone unnoted had not the *Herald*'s correspondent heard him exclaim: "Damn my black hide! Who says the colored sojers won't fight?" And "fight he did" until the battle ended.[24]

Now it was Burnett who came to the aid of Valois. Mounting his squad, he rode toward the sound of gunfire. Topping a ridge, he saw that the Indians had Valois trapped. Without hesitation he ordered his men to attack. Charging beyond Valois's line, they dismounted and "held the Indians in check" while Valois hastily retreated, signaling for Burnett to follow.

As Valois retired, he seemed oblivious to the fact that some of his men had gotten pinned down so far in advance of the others that they were unable to join the retreat. Burnett, however, decided they must be rescued. Seeing that Private David G. Martin "was in imminent danger" from three Indians who were sneaking around to his rear, he spurred his horse forward and engaged them at point-blank range while Martin scrambled to safety. Twice, Burnett's horse went down with bullets "through the leather heart on his breast strap"; each time, the animal scrambled to its feet with the officer, clothing stained with the horse's blood, still in the saddle. This was apparently the last scene that Valois saw as he departed the battlefield. As a consequence, the first report sent to Colonel Hatch asserted that Burnett had been "all shot to pieces."[25]

As soon as Martin reached safety, Burnett turned his attention to the plight of three other men. For one, Private James Burton, it seemingly was the end of a hideous year. On 30 January he and Private James Phillips had deserted at Fort Wingate. Arrested a month later, they were awaiting a court-martial that would mean dishonorable discharges and confinements when Nana stormed into New Mexico. Needing all the men possible for his scout, Burnett released them from the guardhouse to join his detachment.

When Valois's command was first fired on, Burton's horse, perhaps struck by an Apache bullet, got out of control and headed straight for the Apache lines. Unable to turn him, the trooper fell to the ground, lying motionless about one hundred yards in front of the Indians. Burnett had assumed he was dead until he heard a cry for help. Before he could call for a volunteer to go to his aid, Private Walley "anticipated me" and galloped up to Burton, "assisted him in the saddle, and mounting behind him rejoined the troop." All the time, the Indians were firing at such a rate, Burnett wrote, that it was "a source of mystery . . . how they escaped unhurt."[26]

With Valois in retreat for Cañada Alamosa and his own ammunition supply depleted, Burnett withdrew from the battlefield. The Apaches, knowing that Lieutenant Taylor and his scouts could not be far away, were more than anxious to resume their trek towards the Mexican border.

Even though only three troopers were wounded, all in Valois's detachment, the fight at Cuchillo Negro is a tribute to the bravery and esprit de corps that characterized the buffalo soldiers. The spontaneous decisions of Corporal Rogers and Private Walley to volunteer for hazardous missions and Private Gaines to continue fighting after being seriously wounded would meet anyone's criteria for gallantry in action.

The unnamed correspondent for the *New York Herald* wrote that the Indians "fought like demons," and except for the "coolness and bravery" of the officers and buffalo soldiers, "we should have suffered great disaster." Stating that Burnett was "as lively as a kitten," he enthused that it was "his first fight, and he deserves great credit."[27]

The letters that Burnett, Williams, and Walley wrote in support of each other's applications for Medals of Honor (made separately between 1890 and 1897) indicate the sense of camaraderie that existed among them. When Burnett applied for his medal in January 1897, Sergeant Williams wrote an account, "six closely written pages in length," describing the battle. Unfortunately, it was not filed, and the only hint of its contents is a statement that "although more in detail, [it] is similar to the statement of Lieut. Valois." Fortunately, an excerpt of Walley's account was preserved. It graphically shows his respect for Lieutenant Burnett.

Declaring that he remembered "all about the fight" in the Cuchillo Negros, Walley, who had received his own medal seven years earlier, included details found in no other account: "You ordered Spencer Martin to Peter Wilson's relief, but he was too slow, so you went yourself— under a heavy fire again—and brought him to the rear. . . . You looked and saw that he [Private Edward Glasby] was surrounded, and . . . and you went with [a detail] . . . and got him out safely."[28]

Burnett was equally unstinting in praising Sergeant Williams for "his skill in conducting the right flank in a running fight of three or four hours, his keen sightedness in discerning the Indians . . . [which] prevented my command from falling into a trap, for . . . rallying my men when I was dismounted . . . and lastly for his coolness, bravery and unflinching devotion to duty in standing by me in an open position under a heavy fire from a large party of Indians at a comparatively short range."[29]

In the years that followed the engagement in the Cuchillo Negroes, the fortunes of those involved differed widely. The clash had its most immediate effect upon Privates Burton and Phillips, the two deserters. A few months later, all charges were dropped because of their "gallant conduct" in the affray.[30]

Burnett recommended Corporal Rogers for a Medal of Honor, but to no avail. Although Rogers remained in the Ninth until the late 1890s, his last few years became increasingly unpleasant. In early 1891 he was accused of circulating a petition among I Troopers to replace Captain Guilfoyle.[31] Although he was allowed to transfer to G Troop after the incident, he had clearly fallen into disfavor. In May, his wife and children were ejected from Fort Robinson "for engaging in a row"; two years later he was ordered to "see that his children attended school and did not loiter around the barracks during school hours." Finally, in October 1895 the post commander denied a request to allow his wife to return to the post.[32]

Moses Williams remained the top sergeant of I Troop until September 1886, when he became the first member of the Ninth to be promoted to ordnance sergeant, a rank previously denied black soldiers. As would be expected, his performance in the new role was exemplary. In 1896 his commanding officer at Fort Buford, North Dakota, described him as "excellent in every respect." Transferred to Fort Stevens, Oregon, he served another two years and then, after thirty-two years of service, retired.

The years away from the Ninth, serving in areas where there were few African Americans, had left him ill prepared for retirement. Although he had listed his status as married, without children, when he reenlisted in 1891 and again in 1896, his wife either had died or had left. With neither family nor community support to rely upon, his health rapidly failed. On 23 August 1899, while living in Vancouver, Washington, he died of natural causes, "alone and without friends." He was fifty-two years old. An inventory of his effects revealed how little he had to show for three decades of dedicated service. The items most suggestive of his personality were nine books, one pair of gold-rim spectacles, a smoking jacket, a gold watch, two bronze army medals, two "society badges," a pack of playing cards, and some fishing line.[33]

For Private Walley, Cuchillo Negro was only the beginning of a long and eventful military career. After the Ninth left New Mexico, he helped remove squatters from the Indian Territory and suppress the Sioux during the Ghost Dance campaign of 1890. Content to remain a private, he was an exceptional soldier. Burnett declared that "I never knew him to receive even as much as a rebuke," and "I venture the assertion that no young soldier is better known in the regiment."[34]

In 1893 he transferred to the Tenth Cavalry and served with it during the Spanish-American War. During the battle of Las Gausimas, fought two days after the Tenth landed in Cuba, he earned (but was unfairly denied) a second Medal of Honor. In the midst of the battle, Major James E. Bell of the First Cavalry had his leg fractured by a Spanish bullet. Captain Charles Ayres, Walley's troop commander, saw that Bell was in great pain from the "shattered bone [that] pierced his flesh." As he looked around for someone to help with the fallen officer, Walley ran to his assistance. Although the Spanish fire was so hot that sixteen men were killed or wounded within thirty feet of them, Walley and three comrades carried the wounded officer to a place of greater safety.

Captain Ayres recommended three of the men for Medals of Honor; inasmuch as Walley already had one, he suggested for him a certificate of merit. The recommendations were originally approved, but a new commander of the Tenth, Colonel S. M. Whiteside, rejected them with the callous observation that it did not appear that the "gallantry under fire" in "carrying a wounded man from the firing line" involved any "extra risk of life." Major Bell was breveted for getting wounded; Captain Ayres was breveted for going to his rescue; but the four privates who carried him to safety were not even mentioned in orders.[35]

A few days after Las Gausimas, Walley participated in the assault on San Juan Hill. Following the Spanish-American War he did two tours of duty in the Philippines and then returned to the States for good. As late as 1905, when he enlisted for the final time, he was still a private. Two years later, two months short of his fifty-second birthday and having accepted a recent promotion to first sergeant, he was granted a well-earned retirement. After brief residences in Montana and Oklahoma, he returned to his native Maryland. The only regimental Medal of Honor winner to reach his ninth decade, he lived until 1938.[36]

Lieutenant Burnett's career was cut short in 1888. Returning from a scout in which he was cited by General Crook for preventing a war between the Utes and cattlemen in western Colorado, he incurred a severe hernia when his horse rolled on him in a fall. While he was recuperating, a malicious fellow officer accused him of having an affair with the wife of a buffalo soldier. Although he was exonerated and his accuser was found guilty of perjury by a court-martial, the scandalous charges compromised his reputation.[37] Given a medical discharge, he taught military science until his death in November 1908 while employed at the Nebraska Military Academy in Lincoln. Like many others in the Ninth Cavalry, his final resting place was at Arlington.

16

"Dear Cecilia"

When a Hero Meets a Maid

Needless to say, men living in areas with few women found it difficult to develop normal contacts with the opposite sex. This was especially true for black soldiers because of the small African American population in the West and the taboos on black-white relationships. With little opportunity to court girls from the civilian community, troopers satisfied their sexual urges by frequenting the "hog ranches," found on the fringes of Western military reservations, which were as available to them as to white soldiers.[1] In addition, an undeterminable proportion of troop laundresses augmented their income by prostitution.

It is likely that the stereotypes concerning black sexuality induced the commanders of African American units to encourage discreet prostitution. In 1878, General E. O. C. Ord recommended that the number of laundresses be doubled for black units because black soldiers "miss the society of women." Fifteen years later, Colonel James Biddle of the Ninth Cavalry spelled it out more plainly: The "colored soldier . . . has a greater . . . desire for women than his white brother. It seems to soothe him to have social relations between the sexes [and]. . . he is more inclined to remain passive and to do his duty better for his indulgence." Biddle's tolerance was not intended to be an invitation to license. Any woman who chose to "indulge the men" must do so in a "very quiet way" or be expelled from the post.[2]

Despite the toleration of prostitution, many sexual taboos were imposed on the buffalo soldiers. Foremost was a prohibition upon liaisons with decent white women. With the possible exception of Corporal Taliaferro at Fort Davis in 1872 (see p. 58), this injunction was rigidly adhered to in regard to officers' wives and other upper-class women. Contacts between black soldiers and lower-class white females, however, were much more likely. Whenever these were detected, post commanders let neither sentiment nor facts impede the defense of the color line. This often resulted in flagrant miscarriages of justice in cases involving soldiers guilty of little more than misinterpreting the remarks of a woman.

In the spring of 1887, Private James Glass of M Troop, stationed at Fort Washakie, Wyoming, was engaged in an unlikely occupation as a part-time "laundress." When Sergeant Edward Hanson went on furlough with his wife, Glass agreed to move into their quarters and accommodate her customers. He not only earned extra income, but he also could exchange pleasantries with the laundresses, many of them white, who lived on suds row.[3]

Mary Snell, a white laundress married to an infantryman, was so forward that Glass mistook her banter for a sexual invitation. When he reacted accordingly, she complained to her husband. In short order Glass was tried by a general court-martial for making an "indecent proposal."

Mary's testimony was none too convincing. After only the briefest of interchanges, Glass had appeared at her door and had stated, "I would like you to do me a favor, to accommodate me." When she retorted sharply, "Do you mean to insult me," he mumbled something and left, obviously discomfited and abashed. She made it plain that his demeanor was in no way threatening and that he did not enter the hut where she was washing clothes. As there were no witnesses to the "insult," it seems doubtful that the judge advocate would have upheld a conviction had not Glass innocently added the details of the matter.

With no counsel to advise him against self-incrimination or honesty, his homely account records a unique slice of garrison life. According to him, Mary Snell had initiated the conversation by

> asking me when Mrs. Hanson would be back. I told her I didn't know. Then I said, "I will be glad when she comes, I didn't have time to do this work." She says, "Why, you are making a great deal of money, ain't you?" I told her yes I was making a little money, but didn't have the time to do it. She asked me if I didn't have a right smart [amount] of money. I said I didn't, I generally deposited my

money about as fast as I got it. She said a great many of you men spend some money with the Indians. I told her I didn't know whether they did or not. She said "isn't there some of them in the hospital"? I told her yes there were some in the hospital, but I didn't know whether or no they were in there from fooling with the Indian squaws. She asked me how much money I had with me. I told her I had none then but that I could always get a hold of a little. . . . I asked her if she wanted some, saying, "if you do, if you come in and stay a little with me, I will give you some." She said she was afraid to fool with "M" Company men, that she would see me directly. I went around to Sergeant Washington's house, and came back to her door and asked her was she coming in. She said, "what?" I said, "are you coming in?" She said, "Coming in for what?" I said, "coming in to do that favor we were talking about a while ago."[4]

To Glass's dismay, Mrs. Snell expressed outrage, refused to accept his explanation that "he didn't mean to insult her," and reported the proposition. No one involved in the court-martial asked a single question. With his guilt admitted, they needed only to demonstrate that decent white women were off limits to black soldiers.

In addition to a dishonorable discharge, Glass received five years in prison.[5] All echelons of the army's review apparatus speedily concurred, and he was ushered off to Fort Leavenworth. Fortunately, that was not the end of his case. Less than a month after he arrived at Leavenworth, Alfred H. Bright, a Milwaukee lawyer, requested a transcript of the court-martial proceedings. Bright emphasized that he intended to seek a pardon for Glass because the soldier had "had no counsel and was himself unable to make a proper defense." When the transcript was not forthcoming, the attorney fired a blistering letter to the secretary of war. "When a man's liberty is at stake," he argued passionately, it was unreasonable to delay providing a transcript. Declaring that Glass had been convicted on insufficient evidence and without benefit of counsel, he labeled the trial a travesty.[6]

This letter produced results. On 16 September a copy of the transcript was mailed. Bright's persistence in pursuit of justice achieved success less than six months later. On 1 March 1888 the secretary of war ordered Glass's release.[7] The ability of a beleaguered private, stationed at a remote outpost, to so quickly secure the aid of an attorney in Milwaukee is likely to remain an unsolved mystery.

Private Glass may have bungled his defense, but this was definitely not the case when one of the regiment's most renowned Indian fighters was tried at Fort Sill for propositioning a maid who worked for his post commander. The ensuing struggle between a sergeant striving to salvage his career and an irate commander, taking place in a society in which normal relationships were hampered by one-sided racial mores, indicates how quickly a soldier could fall from grace if he challenged the color line.

On 5 November 1883, Cecilia Bow, a German-born girl with an outgoing personality, was taking freshly laundered clothing from a basket to be folded and stored. Although this must have been a frequent chore for a maid in a household with six boys stair-stepped from ages two to fourteen, her work was made easier because Captain Charles Beyer, commanding both C Troop and the fort, constantly used men from his company as servants. As she picked up an article of clothing, she spied an envelope addressed to her. It contained a two-page, unsigned letter, lacking a single punctuation mark other than a solitary dash, that combined protestations of devotion with a cold-cash proposition:

> Miss Cecilia Bow dear Lady I am a making a bold and dairing [the writer had a unique system of spelling] adventure . . . as I am so deeply devoted to you . . . I guess whatever it may bee you will gaive me satisfaction when . . . I am known to you—please do not misunderstand me I am not a courting man at all and can not go any further than my money will allow me to and if you think this is any ways intruding please consume it to the flames and let nothing bee ever said about it as I am a True man and can keep a secreat . . . and if you can Trust yourself you can bet on me for I am sertain I will work by your directions and as time is passing by so fast why . . . not take a little advantage . . . if you choose to drop me a few lines . . . please just after it gets dark put a note in the stump at your back gate it is hollow on top and if . . . [you] are favorable I can get a friend that will hand you my notes I sing [sign] no name and would [not] insult you for the hole world but you may accept this and then I would bee contented bee shore and put the note in answer to this in the hollow stump at your back gate and I will get it.[8]

If Cecilia had realized the trouble that would ensue, she would surely have "consumed" the note to the flames. Instead, she presented it to her employer. Beyer was one of the most enigmatic and unimpressive officers in the regiment. Born either in Wurtemburg in the Rhineland or in Brooklyn (both assertions appear in his personal file) in 1842, he had served as a "boy drummer" with the infantry before enlisting in 1858. Primarily interested in "learning music," he became an outstanding trumpeter who served as the regiment's principal musician until the Civil War was safely over.[9]

Six months after Lee's surrender, Beyer was commissioned lieutenant with an infantry regiment stationed in Louisiana. While on detached service with the Ninth Cavalry during its organization, he ingratiated himself with Colonel Hatch and also developed a yen for the cavalry. When the commander of Troop C of the Ninth died in August 1870, Hatch requested Beyer as a replacement.[10]

Beyer's record abounded with contradictions. On one hand his company had an excellent reputation for discipline and conduct and had repeatedly displayed courage under fire. The first two buffalo soldiers to earn the Medal of Honor in action against the Apaches, Corporal Clinton Greaves and Sergeant Thomas Boyne, were from C Troop.[11] But while his men were winning medals, Beyer was being pilloried by the New Mexican press. Although the Las Cruces–based *Thirty-Four* acknowledged that the Ninth's officers, "with two or three exceptions," were the equal of those in any other regiment in the service, it stated that Beyer was "notoriously unfit to command any body of troops in the field."[12] After extolling the bravery of Lieutenants Day, Robert Emmett, and Henry Wright in the encounter on the Las Animas in September 1879, the editor scathingly ridiculed Beyer's behavior.

A civilian scout interviewed following the engagement told the reporter that Beyer had remained "on top of a hill giving orders" during the fight. When asked if Beyer was within "gunshot," the scout scathingly replied that "a gatling gun might have fetched him. . . . The Captain was pretty safe. Thought his hair was too good to be lost." The informant continued that "we retreated to Hillsboro" after the fight, but Beyer "went clear into Fort Bayard."[13] Shortly after the Las Animas engagement, Beyer took the first of two medical leaves that kept him out of action for several months. His men continued to be in every skirmish and battle, but under the leadership of temporary officers such as Lieutenant Day.

Once Cecilia had shown him the letter, Beyer felt honor-bound to defend white womanhood against such effronteries. He also was likely enticed by the ease with which the author could be apprehended. Accordingly, he sealed a blank sheet of paper inside an envelope and instructed Cecilia to deposit it in the hollow of the stump. Shortly after dark, he crept into a place of concealment and awaited the culprit's arrival.

Beyer's zeal cooled as rapidly as the crisp November evening. Becoming "chilled" after an hour's wait, he delegated to Private Alfred Ross, serving as his personal servant, the task of catching the penman. When a shadowy figure walked into the trap and was arrested, Beyer was likely shocked to learn that the culprit was Sergeant George Lyman.[14]

Like many buffalo soldiers, Lyman had grown up in the Blue Grass region of Kentucky. In November 1871, at the age of twenty-one, he had left the farm and enlisted at Lexington. He was five feet nine inches in height and described as a mulatto on the enlistment rolls. He took to the army life, earning an evaluation of "very good" on the completion of his first term. Upon reenlisting, he was promoted to sergeant.[15] He soon had ample opportunity to prove his valor.

On 29 May 1879, after another Mimbres Apache breakout from the Ojo Caliente Reservation, Beyer's troop overtook the refugees and attacked their camp high in the Black Mountains. After a sharp encounter in which Private Frank Dorsey was killed and two other soldiers wounded, the camp was taken and put to the torch. Highly pleased, Beyer cited five troopers for gallantry. Foremost was George Lyman.[16] Adding to his reputation for heroism in battle after battle, Lyman, by the criteria of the period, had more than earned a Medal of Honor.

After the cessation of hostilities, Lyman was one of many who found it difficult to readjust to routine garrison service. In February 1881 he was absent without leave for two days. Reduced to the ranks and placed under arrest, he was convicted by a general court-martial and fined thirty dollars. Departmental headquarters, however, ordered the sentence to be remitted in consideration of "his most excellent character."[17] He soon regained his sergeant's stripes.

Placed on trial for propositioning Cecilia, he received a sterling endorsement of his record from none other than his accuser. Asked to evaluate

Lyman's service, Beyer replied that he had always considered him to be *"as good a soldier as wore the uniform."* He had earned "that reputation," the captain continued, by the "bravery and gallantry" he had displayed in numerous battles in which he had often come under Beyer's "personal observation."[18]

A fine combat record did not weaken Beyer's resolve to make an example of Lyman. Lyman had with *"evil intent"* written a *"vile, scurrilous, and indecent"* letter to an *"honest, upright, well-behaved, hard-working white girl"* that violated "all principles of propriety and decency."[19]

The court-martial panel assembled on 20 November, little more than two weeks after Lyman's apprehension, with Beyer serving as its president. Lyman immediately challenged his participation, arguing that as the chief accuser he could hardly be deemed impartial. After considerable deliberation, the challenge was upheld, and Captain Patrick Cusack assumed the role of presiding officer. Cusack undoubtedly gave the defendant more latitude in presenting his case than would have Beyer.[20]

In retrospect, it is obvious that Beyer blundered in putting so much emphasis on the virtue of Cecilia Bow. This forced Lyman to make her character the dominant focus of his defense. Since he admitted writing the letter, thereby ensuring his conviction, his only hope for leniency was to show that it was not sent with "vile and evil" intent to an "upright and well-behaved" maiden.

Acting as his own attorney, he vigorously cross-examined each of the prosecution's witnesses. Cecilia conceded that she had become well acquainted with him while he was in charge of frequent gardening details at Beyer's house. Although she first asserted that her contact with him had been limited to giving directions, she confirmed that shortly before he had written the fateful letter she had shown him her photos and that he had asked for one. She denied, however, that she had promised one.[21]

Lyman presented numerous witnesses from his troop to explain why he had been led to believe that Miss Bow's favors might be for sale. He concentrated upon her conduct with one Dick Phelps, a rancher employed as a cattle inspector for herds driven north from Texas. Phelps and a cohort named Tom Berk were well known to the soldiers, since they frequently visited the barracks to play poker. Beyer could not have been pleased by the descriptions of the lax conditions in his barracks that were placed in the trial record.

In addition to gambling with soldiers, the cattlemen engaged in liaisons with Cecilia and another maid. The four had been observed drinking beer under the trees that fringed Medicine Bluff Creek, which meandered along the foot of a slope on the north side of the post. On occasion the couples had separately disappeared into the woods and returned some time later. Since fishing in the creek was a common pastime of troopers, Cecilia's outings were a favorite topic of gossip. Confirming their suspicions, Phelps openly boasted of his success, speaking of her, "in a blackguardly" fashion, as "his woman."

Cecilia by no means confined her attentions to Phelps. In her banter with the soldiers with whom she came into contact she exuded a forwardness that, however it was intended, gave them ideas. Several men described suggestive exchanges with her. Private Taylor Bradly recalled bringing a string of fish to Beyer's kitchen and delivering them to Cecilia. After she had joked with him about his success in catching such big fish, he had blurted out, "You are the fish I have been trying to catch." Instead of reacting with shock, she had lightly retorted, "There is nothing like trying" and then made a remark about "the kind of bait" he was using.

Saddler William Mason, later recognized as one of the best marksmen in the regiment, related that Cecilia had often given him the "chance to say things I ought not to have said." On one occasion he was called into the house to help move furniture. As the two were ascending the stairs, the maid "put the handle of a broom under my arm and pushed me upstairs." To him, this gave "all the chance I wanted if I wanted to say anything."

Sergeant Lyman obviously found it more difficult to resist her charms. As he recalled, every time he was working in the captain's yard "she would come out and commence to talk to me in a very familiar and friendly kind of way, more so than any other servant of the garrison." After Phelps had left the post, Lyman had twice noticed her in the company of a Private Young in the post bar room, once "as late as 9:15 P.M."[22] More than anything else, this led him to the unfortunate conclusion that "all [that] was kneeded [*sic*] was to make a proposal to her for what one might require."

He contained his ardor for a few days, but on the fateful day of 5 November he found himself once more alone with Cecilia:

Her and I commenced in conversation I asked her about some pictures that she had got taken down at the post galery—and she said that she would show them to me and went out and was very quick back again and had 2 pictures in her hand and handed them to me I taken them and commense to admire them very highly by calling them daiseys and speaking of her being hansome and after a conversation of about 15 minutes I asked her to gaive me one of the pictures and she said that . . . she had 12 others and . . . that she would give me the choice of the 12—I then asked her what I would do with it and she said why keep it I told her that it would not do me any good and she said take it and wait and see you don't know what good it will do you—at witch she smiled . . . I raise my hat and told her good by and left the kitchen

Upon returning to his quarters, he mulled over Cecilia's remarks while he pondered his next move. After due reflection upon "what others had told me of her" and of what she had just said, he decided it was "saft to wright her a note" with the instruction to "consume it to the flames" if it was not acceptable. In his naïveté he had never dreamed she might disclose it to the captain.

Lyman closed his statement to the court by attempting to explain his motivations. He did not claim "any wright" to associate with any of the officers or their friends and relatives "under any circomestances." As for men such as Phelps and Berk, who "gambled and drank" with the soldiers, however, he considered himself "the equaiels" of them and the "people they associated with." Struggling for words to convey his feelings, he explained that he tried to associate with "my brother soldiers," regardless of color, as long as they responded in a "friendly and familiar" manner. Since he understood Cecilia and her friend "to be the General Company and associates" of Phelps and Berk, he was unaware of a prohibition upon approaching her. With a final explanation that he had been "partly ensnaired by being encouraged from what others had led me to beleave," he respectfully asked "the consideration of your honorable gentlemen."

It is likely that Lyman's claim to equality with lower-class whites hurt his cause. The only interest the court-martial panel showed in the afterwork activities of Cecilia, for example, was to accuse the sergeant's witnesses of "acting as spies upon her actions." The court could hardly have been more Draconian in its verdict. For little more than an honest mistake in judgment, Lyman received a dishonorable discharge and two years' imprisonment.[23]

Fortunately, the judge advocate of the Department of the Missouri took a less impassioned view. While approving the verdict, he recommended that the sentence be mitigated to reduction to the ranks, imprisonment at hard labor for nine months, and a fine of ten dollars a month for the same period.[24] Unfair as even this may have been, it allowed "as good a soldier as wore the uniform" to continue his career.

Upon completing his term of imprisonment, Lyman was transferred to Captain Loud's D Troop, stationed at Fort Riley, Kansas. With his reputation apparently untarnished by his confinement, he regained the rank of sergeant in 1886. Upon reenlisting in 1887, he transferred to A Troop, which remained his home for the balance of his career.

A married man by the early 1890s and with the "dear Cecilia" episode only an embarrassing memory, nothing but honors punctuated the balance of Lyman's career. In July 1895 he was one of three soldiers (including Brent Woods) selected to constitute the regimental color guard. By the outbreak of the Spanish-American War he was the Ninth's color sergeant and was the second best marksman in the Department of the Platte.[25]

His riskiest assignment occurred at San Juan Hill. Carrying the regimental colors, he was an inviting target as the regiment stormed up the slopes. Lieutenant Colonel John M. Hamilton, commanding the regiment, was killed by a Spanish bullet only a few feet away from him. Lyman's "gun barrel was hit," and several bullets "passed through his clothes." One shot creased his head deeply enough that he was stunned and "left for dead." The official record stated simply that he had been slightly wounded.[26]

The war in Cuba ended for him soon after the surrender of Santiago, as an unnamed illness left him hospitalized for several weeks. One more overseas tour of duty awaited him, however, for the Ninth was dispatched to the Philippines in 1900. For months on end, A Troop, with Lyman as its first sergeant, scouted through hostile territory, beat off ambushes, and burned Filipino villages in operations reminiscent of the Apache campaigns twenty years earlier. On 16 October 1901, thirty years after his initial enlistment and eighteen after his disastrous infatuation with Cecilia

Bow, Lyman retired and, like many another old buffalo soldier, returned to his Blue Grass homeland.[27]

The ordeals of Private Glass and Sergeant Lyman only hint at the complexities of interracial relations on the isolated outposts where blacks and whites of necessity worked and lived in close proximity. One can only conjecture that some of the white maids and laundresses who flirted with buffalo soldiers did not reject their overtures. The relatively light punishments ultimately received by the offenders indicate that occasionally a modicum of justice could soften the worst injustices.

17

Sergeant Alexander Jones and the Demise of Captain Beyer

Captain Charles Beyer may not been the bumbling coward described by the New Mexican press, but he had the instincts of a thief where the welfare of his men was concerned. With a wife and six boys to support, he frequently diverted troop rations and supplies to his own household. In addition, he made an excessive use of enlisted men as household servants. In the spring of 1884, after years of enduring his larcenies, his troopers, led by a remarkable noncommissioned officer, rebelled. Although their initial protest occurred shortly after the court-martial of George Lyman, no one, including Beyer, suggested the two episodes were related.

Any elation Beyer felt from Lyman's conviction vanished quickly when he found himself challenged by his hand-picked first sergeant, Alexander Jones. Unlike the other noncommissioned officers in C Troop, Jones, a mulatto from Georgia, had previously served in both the Twenty-fourth Infantry and the Tenth Cavalry. At the end of each tour of enlistment he received a rating of "excellent" and held the rank of first sergeant. Beyer, no doubt pleased that so experienced a soldier had joined his troop in August 1882, rapidly promoted him. On 6 March 1884, Jones became the troop's first sergeant. Beyer would soon learn that it was unwise for a captain as heedless of regulations as he was to entrust his troop to a noncom who was determined, audacious, and the intellectual equal of any officer in the regiment.[1]

Long before Jones joined C Troop there was dissatisfaction with the quality and quantity of food served the company and rumors that its funds were being diverted to Beyer's household. Sergeant John Brown, Jones's predecessor, had surreptitiously gathered evidence of improprieties by retaining vouchers that had been ordered destroyed. Jones carefully studied these and other records, combined them with statements from men who had worked as servants or had seen troop commodities taken to the captain's residence, and pondered his options.

On 18 April, well aware he was laying his neck on the line, he presented Beyer with a letter to be forwarded to the assistant adjutant general of the Department of the Missouri. The captain must have paled as he read the charges. His men were "only half fed" because funds intended for food purchases were diverted, "causing the men's rations to run short and them to go hungry." He had ordered men to work as servants and required them "to perform duties which no man with respect would do or ask another to do." If they refused, he excoriated the entire troop as "a lot of Niggers and of no account whatever." Jones closed by declaring that his statement had been made with "calm deliberation" at the "request of and in behalf of" the troop. Endorsing his complaint were the signatures of twenty-nine enlisted men, including that of George Lyman.[2]

With no alternative, Beyer forwarded the communication together with a letter denying the charges. Departmental headquarters, obviously impressed by the seriousness of the allegations in the letter and by its erudite, error-free composition, dispatched Captain George B. Russell to investigate. Beyer, forewarned, was ready for him.

Three days after Jones presented his letter, Lieutenant Ballard Humphrey met with the troop's noncommissioned officers and accused them of being on the "verge of mutiny" and in "the act of revolt." Asked if "to seek redress through the proper channels" was an act of mutiny, he changed course. Even if Beyer had treated the troop "wrongfully," he argued, it "matters not. . . . I want this matter dropped even if you are right." If not, he threatened to "make it hard for you and . . . make you suffer."[3] When he closed by threatening them with prison if the matter were not dropped, Jones defiantly replied that if the "law would back the Captain in abusing me and every other man of the company, I would go to a military prison."[4] In contrast to his stand, a handful of men, led by Sergeant Jason J. Jackson, recanted their statements. Jackson soon afterwards replaced Jones as first sergeant.

When Captain Russell reached Fort Sill on 9 May 1884, many of the signers of the petition were absent under Lieutenant Humphrey searching for intruders on Indian lands. Humphrey, asked to take their depositions, bullied all into disavowing the complaint. Such was not the case with the ones interviewed at the post by Russell. George Lyman, still serving his term of imprisonment, stated that on several occasions he had been worked "all day without any food" and punished if he complained. Although Jones and Sergeant Brown provided Russell with an abundance of details and documentation to support the complaints, the captain readily accepted the assurances of the post officers that Jones's claims were exaggerated or false. Lieutenant Humphrey, especially vitriolic, charged that the whole affair had been "gotten up" by Jones because his wife had been ordered off the post in a purge of "lewd and abandoned" women.[5]

On 29 May, Russell submitted a report accompanied by the affidavits. He acknowledged that Beyer had been guilty of "poor management" and observed that any company in which the men were so united against their commander was "in a sad state." The cause for this, he speculated, was that the "suspicious and ignorant" black soldiers, feeling "they did not live as well as they might," had been misled by Jones into believing Beyer was at fault. When he advised against further action in the matter and failed to forward the documents presented him by Brown, the case seemed all but closed.

Major Frederick Benteen, who assumed command of Fort Sill in late May, took no action because the matter had been investigated by Russell. Relieved that he had weathered the storm, Beyer confined Jones for several weeks on vague charges of sedition. But the sergeant refused to concede defeat. On 10 August he asked Beyer to forward a second letter inquiring about the results of the investigation. Expressing fear that his original complaint had been "misrepresented," he described the reprisals inflicted on the troop since it was sent. He closed with a hope "that the Dept Commander will cause justice to be done."[6]

Jones's second letter apparently tilted the scales against Beyer. It and Russell's report were immediately forwarded to the departmental judge advocate for consideration. Two weeks later, a court-martial was ordered to try Beyer for conduct unbecoming an officer and gentleman. Headed by Colonel Joseph Potter of the Twenty-fourth Infantry, it contained only one member from the Ninth Cavalry, Major Benteen.[7]

None of the specific charges involved substantial sums of money. Like many other officers, Beyer had established a "slush" fund, which he administered with the advice of a troop committee, to purchase amenities otherwise unavailable. Financed by fines imposed for petty offenses such as being late for roll call and from the sale of surplus produce from the company garden, it provided a modest sum whose expenditure did not go through regular channels.

Beyer, however, allegedly used the fund for his own benefit. In September 1882 he had "sold" the troop his personal shotgun for forty-five dollars; it was to be used for hunting, but he continued to keep it in his quarters. When a request was made for two sets of boxing gloves, he "sold" the troop some "old and worn" ones that had been discarded by his children.

Food irregularities evoked the most heated complaints. The "slush fund" had been charged for two crates of apples, ostensibly to be distributed at Christmas. Instead, Beyer allegedly pocketed the money without buying a single apple. More serious, he "habitually" diverted troop rations such as rice, bacon, bread, coffee, sugar, and beans to his family's use with no semblance of a payment. The only recompense provided soldiers who worked as servants was permission to sell rations drawn from the troop mess.[8]

As the weeks passed while the court-martial was assembling, tensions within C Troop reached a new high. Jones and First Sergeant Jason Jackson, in particular, were at each other's throats. Jones, convinced that Jackson had sold out to Beyer, became even more irate when the first sergeant returned after escorting a convict to the railhead at Henrietta, Texas. Accompanying him was a Miss Bertha Livingston, whom Beyer promptly employed as a maid. According to Jackson, she had been working for one of the town's "first families"; he had met her and they had become engaged after a brief courtship. In contrast, Private George Gibson, who had accompanied Jackson to Henrietta, swore that she was a prostitute with whom he had slept before she had captured the affections of the first sergeant.[9]

Although Jackson and Bertha were regular attendants at post prayer meetings, most members of C Troop accepted Gibson's account of her past. She did not help matters by frequent visits to the barracks, sometimes remaining in Jackson's office until after taps. Throughout August she ate breakfast and supper in the troop kitchen almost daily. Jones, whose own wife had been evicted, wasted no time in informing Beyer of Bertha's past and of her consumption of troop rations.

After a brief investigation, Beyer concluded there was nothing amiss and refused to take action. He claimed that the troop cooks assured him Bertha's alleged dining had consisted only of an occasional sip of coffee. The cooks, however, later testified that they had told him that Bertha was taking meals with the troop almost daily.[10]

Although Beyer may have felt obliged to uphold his chief supporter in the troop, the affair damaged his own shaky reputation. Ironically, it was Sergeant Jackson who dealt him the most telling blow. In defending Bertha's visits, Jackson stated that there had "never bin [*sic*] no objections of laundresses and officers' servants visiting the barracks . . . [and] they have visited this troop . . . ever since I have bin a soldier."[11]

On 2 September, almost on the eve of Beyer's court-martial, the ill will between Sergeants Jackson and Jones erupted into a brawl. While the troop was assembling for breakfast, Jackson noticed his rival talking softly to other soldiers and, convinced that the dialogue was aimed at him, ordered Jones to sit down at the table. Since men had always been free to move around as they waited to be served by the cooks, Jones was so infuriated that he lost his self-control. "I have as much right to walk this dining room as you have to take that God damned whore of yours—you God damned scoundrel and puppy."[12]

When each charged the other with conduct prejudicial to good order and military discipline, General Augur promptly ordered general courts-martial, presided over by Captain Cusack. Each was convicted and let off with a twenty-dollar fine because of the mitigating circumstances of the case.[13] The court obviously considered that the responsibility for the troubles at Fort Sill lay not with the sergeants but with their captain.

When Beyer's court-martial convened in late September, the prosecution's case consisted almost entirely of testimony from the enlisted men. One after another recounted the diversion of foodstuffs and described prolonged tours as household servants with little or no compensation. An inordinate amount of time was devoted to such matters as the quality of the used boxing gloves, the condition and use of the purchased shotgun, and whether any apples purchased with the slush fund had been provided the troop.

Captain Beyer, his wife, and his older children denied each and every allegation. In addition, Sergeants Jackson and Richard Harrison, both of whom had been promoted after Jones's initial petition, supported the captain almost too vigorously. Harrison swore the shotgun had been so available to troopers that he alone had used it to kill 213 turkeys and thirty-nine ducks during a six-week period in late 1882. As proof, he showed a memorandum listing his exploits.[14]

When Russell had investigated Jones's first complaint in May, every officer at Fort Sill rallied to their post commander's defense. At his trial, in sharp contrast, only Lieutenant Humphrey stood by Beyer. The reliability of Humphrey's endorsement of his veracity, moreover, was undermined by another officer who swore he had heard Humphrey call the captain a "damned liar."[15]

Although Beyer and his handful of backers desperately sought to convince the court that the charges were gross distortions concocted by Jones to avenge his wife's eviction for lewdness, they failed. Undeterred, the judge advocate excoriated the captain. Any officer who profited "at the expense of the members of his troop" was guilty of robbery that ranked "lower on the scale than does the pickpocket." The court found Beyer guilty on each charge and, without the slightest suggestion of leniency, sentenced him to be dismissed from the service.[16]

Before taking effect, the verdict had to be reviewed all the way up the line to the President. In many respects, both the sentence and the verdict were unusual. The sums involved were comparatively trifling, and most officers, including those serving on the court-martial, had violated the regulations against using enlisted men as servants. In addition, almost all of the testimony had come from black enlisted men. Judge Advocate General J. N. Lieber, in charge of the final review of the case, stated flatly that the evidence did not "sustain the conviction on the charges as laid." Despite this, President Chester Arthur, acting upon the advice of Secretary of War Robert Lincoln, approved the verdict. On 11 November 1884, the military career of Charles Beyer came to an inglorious end.[17]

Temporarily, the fortunes of Alexander Jones, whose dogged pursuit of justice in the face of incredible odds had led to Beyer's demise, improved dramatically. After the promotion of Gustavus Valois to command of C Troop, Jones replaced Jackson as first sergeant. Valois, however, was frequently absent because of poor health, leaving Lieutenant Humphrey to command the company. As a consequence, Jones became a frequent target of harassment. In November 1886 his protest against excessive guard and fatigue details was ruled "justifiable" by the inspector general for the Department of the Platte.[18]

The worst was yet to come. On 1 July 1887, Valois received a medical discharge and was succeeded by John Conline. When Jones's enlistment expired three weeks afterwards, Conline, almost certainly acting on advice from Lieutenant Humphrey and without the slightest explanation, evaluated his character as "none," thereby denying him the right to reenlist.[19] Even though the records reveal no evidence of any misdeeds by Jones, no one questioned why a man with "no character" had been allowed to hold the rank of first sergeant for almost three years. A lynch mob could not have perpetrated a greater miscarriage of justice.

It is just possible that Jones, as resourceful a soldier as ever wore the uniform, resurrected his career by enlisting in the Twenty-fifth Infantry, the only African American regiment in which he had not yet served. Before long the Twenty-fifth's roster included an Alexander Jones, who eventually won honors in the Philippines. Although in 1897, Jones specifically denied that he had once served in the Ninth Cavalry and had been dismissed without character,[20] one suspects the Ninth's loss had been the Twenty-fifth's gain.

In a sense, Beyer's dismissal, followed closely by the promotion of Captain Carroll, symbolized the transfer of power within the regiment from the Civil War volunteers who had organized and commanded the various troops to West Point graduates. While there would be a definite improvement in efficiency, relations with the rank and file would become more impersonal. The camaraderie and sense of partnership that had characterized the best of earlier times would become increasingly scarce.

18

"Too Indecent for Publication!" The Lonely Passion of Sergeant Dickerson

One of the most speculative topics concerning military life during the nineteenth century concerns the extent of homosexual activity in the army. Other than the celebrated case of Mrs. Nash, a "laundress" who lived with three successive enlisted men in the Seventh Cavalry and whose real gender was revealed only upon *his* untimely death,[1] almost no examples of same-sex activity have been unearthed. None of the published references, however, have made extensive use of court-martial orders and proceedings.

Although Victorian prudery meant that court-martial orders usually avoided specific reference to homosexual activity, such hints as "the specifications will not be published" can serve as giveaways. A survey of orders involving members of the Ninth Cavalry from 1881 to 1889 unearthed three cases dealing with homosexual activity.[2] Although all involved improper advances rather than consensual relations, the details of the cases suggest that at least two offenders had encounters with multiple partners before being exposed. In one of the cases, moreover, there was a distinct possibility that an unpopular first sergeant was falsely accused in order to get rid of him.

Richard Kennedy, a twenty-one-year-old, dark-complexioned youth, five feet eight inches in height, enlisted at Baltimore in May 1880. After preliminary training at Jefferson Barracks in Saint Louis, he reported to A Troop, stationed at Fort Stanton, New Mexico, on 13 October. On 26 February 1881 he was assigned the task of caring for the troop's garden, located at the nearby Mescalero Indian Agency. Also on detached duty at the agency was Corporal Randall Brown, a twenty-eight-year-old, light-complexioned South Carolinian in his second term of enlistment. Corporal Brown was serving as the stable guard for the horses belonging to a detachment of troops stationed at the agency.[3]

On the evening of 3 April, sometime after taps, Brown was preparing to go to bed in the "corral room" adjoining the stables. Kennedy knocked at the door and said he was afraid "to stay in the garden by himself," because he had heard that "Billy the Kid had killed two more men." Brown reluctantly agreed to allow him to sleep on a saddle blanket placed on a work table in his room and then retired for the night. Sometime later he awoke to find Kennedy atop him and in the act of fellatio.[4] Although Kennedy fled when Brown resisted his advances, he was apprehended by a sentry. The following morning, the incident was reported to Captain Michael Cooney, the troop commander.

Like most enlisted men being court-martialed, Kennedy acted as his own counsel. He lodged no objection to Cooney's presiding over the tribunal, even though the captain had ordered his arrest and filed the charges. Declining to cross-examine Brown, he confined his defense to a simple statement that during the night "Corp. Brown woke up and said he was wet, and said I had been sucking him off." Although he neither denied nor confirmed his guilt, no one questioned him.[5] His guilt obviously had been predetermined.

Found guilty, he was given a dishonorable discharge and confined at hard labor for three years. The verdict was quickly approved by reviewing authorities with a mitigation of the imprisonment to one year.[6] The inglorious end of Kennedy's army stint indicates the obvious: some recruits had homosexual urges.

Although Kennedy was apprehended only six months after enlisting and after engaging in a single known incident, such was not always the case. In 1882, Israel Monday was assigned to A Troop. His tour of service seemed uneventful until the night of 21 November 1885, when he was accused of molesting Private Thomas Polk by "feeling over his body to ascertain whether he was asleep and endeavoring to excite Polk's private parts."[7]

According to Polk, the two soldiers' bunks were so close that "the two of us were sleeping together." Upon retiring, he fell asleep but was awakened by Monday's advances. His matter-of-fact description of what followed elicited neither surprise nor skepticism: "From about 10 o'clock P.M. till 1 o'clock A.M. he worked at me and kept me awake." After three hours, Polk "saw what he was trying to do to me and I shoved him away and separated the bunks." The next morning, he reported the incident to the first sergeant, who promptly informed Captain Cooney.[8]

Private Monday confined his questioning to a single query, "Why did you not notify somebody before you struck me?" Since he had pleaded guilty and had neither witnesses to call nor a statement of his own to make, the court was cleared and the panel "maturely considered the evidence." A few minutes later, he was pronounced guilty and sentenced to receive a dishonorable discharge plus two years of confinement.

Although only Polk testified, two recruits, Privates Samuel Carter and Wilson Brown, revealed that they had been the victims of similar molestations. The fact that neither reported the incidents until after Polk's arrest indicates that recruits were especially vulnerable to advances. It also seems doubtful that Monday constrained his urges throughout his thirty months of service before the encounter with Polk.

Most likely, such furtive nocturnal approaches were the most frequent type of homosexual encounters. Until 1875, enlisted men commonly slept two to a bunk; although single beds were the norm thereafter, the crowded conditions of barracks often resulted in their being virtually coupled.

Unlike the other cases, that of First Sergeant Richard T. Dickerson, involving such issues as sexual harassment and entrapment, seems remarkably modern. From the day that he reported to D Troop, Dickerson had stood out among the buffalo soldiers. Unusually old for a new recruit at the age of twenty-four, he was also taller than most, almost six feet in height, and very dark complexioned. His uniqueness, however, lay in his scholarly disposition and academic training. A Virginian by birth, he had been employed as a schoolteacher before enlisting at Cincinnati in mid-1879. Soon after he reported to D Troop, he was detached to work as a clerk in the office of the regimental adjutant, Lieutenant John S. Loud.

Dickerson was almost too good to be true. Neat, precise, and tireless, he was as capable as any assistant Loud had ever had. When the adjutant was promoted to the command of D Troop in early 1880, there was no chance he would forget the clerk's efficiency and diligence.

In early 1881, Dickerson returned to duty with D Troop, at that time one of the most poorly disciplined units in the regiment. With only

Lieutenant Martin Hughes present for duty with the troop, there was constant turmoil. In January, Private Fred Evans had assaulted First Sergeant Israel Murphy verbally and physically. Evans did not desist until another sergeant broke a carbine over his head. Court-martialed, Evans received four months at hard labor and a trivial five-dollars-per-month fine for the same period.[9]

In short order the troop was rocked by two other incidents. On 11 February, Henry Johnson, the hero of the Milk River encounter with the Utes in 1879, got drunk and threatened to shoot a Mexican woman. Arrested, he pleaded guilty and was let off with the token punishment of having thirty dollars deducted from his pay over a three-month period.[10]

Ten days later a fight broke out between Private William Nance, one of the most highly regarded soldiers in the company, and Private John Hatchett, a thirty-year-old Virginian with almost ten years of service. In the midst of the melee, Nance shot his adversary, wounding him so severely that he died three weeks later. Pleading guilty, Nance was sentenced to six months at hard labor and a fine of ten dollars a month for the same period. The court justified its leniency by citing his prior record of good conduct and by concluding that the shooting "in a measure was justifiable."[11]

With eight men also in the guardhouse, Lieutenant Hughes abruptly demoted Sergeant Murphy and elevated Private Dickerson to the position. Although the lieutenant may have thought that Dickerson could handle the troop's paperwork and thereby allow himself time to deal with disciplinary problems, such favoritism shown a soldier who had just reported for duty was bound to create ill will and envy. As Dickerson later stated, "my rapid promotions . . . seem to have been almost a death blow to the older soldiers, and especially to Sergeant [Richard] Miller, who had hoped to get the 1st Sergeancy."[12]

Despite his misgivings, Dickerson took great pride in wearing the "diamond" insignia that designated his rank and worked harder than ever. As he recalled, "Whenever there was anything to be done . . . whether of a clerical or physical nature, I attended to it. . . . I have worked many a night alone until one or two o'clock in the morning." He claimed that he went out of his way to alleviate the distrust of the other noncommissioned officers by assuring them he would "treat them all as men, with no friends to reward and no enemies to punish." Nothing, however, seemed to ease Miller's animosity. "I found it very difficult to get along with Sergeant Miller who has never lost an opportunity to attempt to injure my character."[13]

Dickerson seems to have recognized that it had been a mistake for him to receive the diamond so early in his career and requested several times to be relieved. At the same time, he was snobbish enough to glory in his "reputation among my superior officers . . . as a gentleman among those with whom I have associated." He was also quick to denigrate the low "class of men" that he had to deal with in the troop. The most revealing indication of his psychological frame of reference was a complaint he made after his arrest that he was being treated as if he were "a wild . . . *savage* from the interior of Africa."

In January 1882, D Troop was transferred from New Mexico to Fort Riley, Kansas, the new headquarters for the Ninth Cavalry and the easternmost post of any black unit. Surrounded as they were by nothing more threatening than farms and ranches, there was little for troops to do to break the routine of garrison life. One of the few diversions was the exchange of gossip concerning people's private lives. A favorite topic undoubtedly concerned the relations between Dickerson and the recruits who sometimes visited his quarters.

To Dickerson's relief, Sergeant Miller received a four-month furlough that lasted through most of the summer of 1882.[14] After Miller returned, he allegedly began to plot the downfall of his rival. His opportunity was not long in coming. In October, a new group of recruits reported for duty. One of them was a precocious quadroon still two months shy of his seventeenth birthday. Strikingly handsome and one of the few men in the regiment who was the intellectual equal of Dickerson, Edward L. Baker soon drew the sergeant's attention.[15] Shortly after taps on 27 January 1883, Baker descended the stairs from the troop's second-story barracks room and knocked on the door of Dickerson's quarters, located next to the ordnance storeroom. Sometime later, he left the room.

Waiting for him on the stairway was Sergeant Miller. Miller followed him to the top of the stairs, where Sergeant W. F. Clyde met them. Miller said, "Here he is, shall I take him to the Captain?" Without asking the youth what had occurred in the sergeant's quarters, Clyde nodded in the affirmative and escorted him to Captain's Loud's house.

Undoubtedly irritated by the interruption of his sleep, Loud asked Baker what he had been doing in Dickerson's room. Baker, later explaining that he had "hated to expose the matter," replied, "nothing." Loud then sent him back to the barracks.

At eleven the following morning, Loud and Lieutenant John Guilfoyle questioned Baker again about the incident. His reserve shattered by fears that he might be severely punished, Baker hastily described his encounters with Dickerson. On at least two occasions he had been asked to occupy the first sergeant's quarters during the latter's absence in order to make sure that nothing was taken from the adjoining ordnance room. Both times, he had fallen asleep on the bed and had been awakened by Dickerson's sexual advances. During the first encounter, little more than fondling had occurred, but on the last occasion the sergeant had performed fellatio on him, causing him "to have the same feelings as I would have in intercourse with a woman."[16]

When Baker concluded his account, Loud, without bothering to question Dickerson, ordered him to be reduced to the rank of private and imprisoned. Two months later, a court-martial was convened. All six officers sitting on the court, including both Loud and Guilfoyle, were members of the Ninth Cavalry. In addition, the judge advocate was Lieutenant George Burnett, a recent addition to Loud's troop. Dickerson considered challenging Loud's presence, since he had brought the charges, but concluded that if "I objected to his sitting on my court, I would have deprived myself of the opportunity . . . [to] explain to him the cause of my persecution."[17]

In addition to Baker, two other recruits testified. Private Benjamin Watkins stated that he had been accosted the "third day" after he joined the troop. Watkins related that Dickerson summoned him to his room after taps and told him to "come on and get in bed." "I pulled off my boots and got in bed with him, he says come on let's hurry up, as if I was a girl, . . . feeling me about my privates—pretty close. . . . I got away from him . . . told him no, I didn't play like that . . . and went upstairs and told Sergeant Miller about it."

On Miller's advice, Watkins requested permission the next morning to see the troop commander. Dickerson refused, saying that "if I didn't hush, he would put me in the guardhouse." Since this had allegedly occurred on 24 March 1882, ten months before Dickerson's arrest, and Watkins claimed he had "told it out openly to everyone in the barrack room . . . and several crowded around me to ask about it," it seems odd that no intimations of it reached officers' row. Neither Miller nor anyone else was called to corroborate Watkins's statement.[18]

Private Allen Wells, who had reported for duty in October 1882, testified that he was called to the sergeant's room on 12 November. The two men had drunk "about four bottles" of beer when the sergeant said, "Come on, let's lie down . . . then I took off my trousers and lay down in the bed with him. We lay there for a right smart while . . . and finally he put his hand on my penis and took it out of my drawers, getting it kind of a wet." Wells then "took his hands off, and got up out of bed and left him and went upstairs." He too told of his experience a week or two afterwards and refused subsequent requests to visit the sergeant's room.[19]

After Wells left the stand, Baker repeated the account that led to Dickerson's arrest. Obviously devastated by the charges, Dickerson made only half-hearted efforts at cross-examination. He introduced one defense witness, Private Louis Horton. Horton stated that Baker had told him that Sergeant Miller had detected him leaving Dickerson's room and told him that unless he said Dickerson had fellated him, "he would put general charges against him, so he thought he had better tell it as he didn't want anything like that."[20]

With the conclusion of Horton's testimony, the court adjourned for the day to allow Dickerson time to prepare a statement. Working desperately to stave off disgrace and imprisonment, he filled twelve closely written, incredibly neat pages with an anguished plea that he was the victim of a plot engineered by Sergeant Miller. In style, sentence structure, and grammatical accuracy it was most impressive. At the very least, his denials of guilt and descriptions of the "clique" that had undermined him should have injected a degreee of doubt into the minds of his judges.

He fervently proclaimed his innocence: "God knows that I am not guilty and that I would give the last drop of my heart's blood before I would commit such an unnatural and beastly crime." Two pages later, he interjected anew that he was "being tried not for any offense that I have committed, but for a crime that no human and hardly a beast should be guilty of." In obvious anguish, he continued, "If I was guilty . . . , death would be too easy a punishment for such an unnatural crime."

While he admitted that the recruits had come to his quarters on the dates mentioned, he adamantly denied that "it was for the purpose stated, nor did they ever upon any occasion or under any pretense ever sit or lie upon my bed." Watkins had knocked on his door shortly before tattoo and had asked to borrow some stationery and stamps. He had curtly refused, telling him that "it would require a person whose income was greater than mine to supply a company with stamps and stationery." Wells, he stated, had been employed to straighten the ordnance room in accordance with instructions from Captain Loud.

While Dickerson indicated that Watkins and Wells were willing accomplices in Miller's plot, he obviously believed Baker was acting under duress. He admitted providing him with a few small favors such as some items of clothing left by a private who had deserted. On the last, fateful occasion, Baker had knocked on his door "without being ordered, invited, or enticed to do so by me." Asked what he wanted, Baker replied that he had come to see if he would "let me have a pair of gloves for inspection tomorrow and the trumpet that you promised to get." Dickerson replied that he "would have to wait until Monday for the trumpet but that I would see if I could loan or give him a pair of gloves Sunday morning in time for inspection." Soon afterwards, the private "bade me good night."

When he opened the door to let Baker out, he noticed Sergeant Miller sitting on the steps. His only explanation for Baker's testimony was intimidation. He had been informed that Miller "threatened to put him in the guardhouse unless he said that I inserted his penis in my mouth." He also stated that the private had complained to Private Francis Collins of H Troop that "Miller was the cause of all this trouble." According to Dickerson, Miller had disseminated "disgraceful reports similar to the one for which I am now being tried" about other men in the troop who displeased him, such as Corporal Joseph Brackett.[21]

Although most of his plea could be discounted as the attempts of a man to save himself, he was accurate in claiming that the case was basically a matter of his word against that of his accusers. The most convincing portion of his statement was his analysis of Baker's testimony dealing with his initial confrontation with Sergeants Miller and Clyde: "Why did they . . . march him up to Captain Loud without questioning him concerning the matter? This statement shows that they had prepared their report before hand."

Dickerson's most anguished reflections concerned his relations with Captain Loud, for whom he had worked so tirelessly. "He has never known me to make a wrong report concerning any of the men," nor had he ever had to reprimand Dickerson. Since Dickerson had "served so faithfully," he could not understand why his commander had reduced and confined him without allowing an "opportunity to defend myself." Obviously deeply hurt, he wrote that "I could overlook to a certain degree the conduct of those through whose instrumentality I had been disgraced, but when . . . Capt. Loud 'whom I had served with truth and faith,' had failed to give me a hearing, it was a hard blow."[22]

Although Dickerson's impassioned rhetoric may have raised doubts in the minds of his judges, the charges were too reprehensible to risk his remaining on duty. His plea undoubtedly ameliorated his punishment. Although he could have received several years of imprisonment for the offenses, he was simply sentenced to be dishonorably discharged from the service of the United States. This leniency probably reflected both Loud's ambivalent feelings towards a man who had served him so well and some genuine uncertainty concerning his guilt.

There is no way of knowing whether Dickerson was guilty of the specific charges. The accounts of Privates Watkins and Wells, although none too convincing, were plausible. One wonders, however, why witnesses were not called to support their claims that they had told other troopers about the incidents soon after they occurred. The relationship between Dickerson and Baker was more complex. Whatever the sergeant's sexual proclivities, it seems obvious that he was infatuated, at least in a Platonic sense, by one of the regiment's most personable and talented members.

Of all the people involved, Baker bears the least guilt. No onus could be placed on a youth seduced or molested by such an authority figure as a first sergeant. Even if he testified falsely to save himself from prosecution and dismissal, it is understandable. The proof of his worth lies in what he accomplished after he salvaged his career. After completing his original term of enlistment with the Ninth, he transferred to the Tenth Cavalry. His switch most likely was connected to his wedding plans. Stationed in Wyoming when his term expired, he immediately traveled to Santa Fe, New Mexico, and married the recently widowed Mary Elizabeth Hawley. As the Tenth Cavalry was stationed in New Mexico at the time, it was logical that he would transfer to it. By a quirk of chance, he was assigned to the same troop in which Richard Miller had recently enlisted.

The rest of Baker's career was marked by an unprecedented series of triumphs. In 1890 he was designated as the chief trumpeter for the regiment; the following year, he was promoted to the rank of quartermaster sergeant, a position in which Dickerson would surely have excelled. In 1892, Baker became the regimental sergeant major. Four years later, he was recommended for a leave of absence to attend a cavalry school in Saumur, France, the homeland of his father. Although wounded by shrapnel at San Juan Hill in 1898, he earned a Medal of Honor for saving a wounded comrade from drowning during the fording of the stream at the foot of the hill. It would be the last such medal awarded a black soldier until the Korean War more than half a century later. Although Baker excelled during a two-year stint as a captain in the African American Forty-ninth Volunteer Infantry, he was denied the opportunity to compete for a commission with the regulars. Instead, he was commissioned in the Philippine Scouts, in which he again rose to the rank of captain.[23]

Baker was as adept with the pen as the sword. In 1897, in connection with his position as sergeant major, he compiled and published a pamphlet modestly entitled a *Roster of Non-Commissioned Officers of the Tenth U.S. Cavalry.* The only thing disappointing about it was its title, for it was and is the richest source of information on the troopers of that regiment. In reviewing it, the *Army and Navy Journal* concluded, "If there are any who still question the value of our colored soldiers, they will question no longer after they have read this record of their courage and fidelity, their calm endurance of fatigue and hardship and zealous devotion to the most exacting requirements of military service."[24] In addition, an excerpt from Baker's diary, entitled "A Trip from Montana to Cuba with the Tenth U.S. Cavalry," constitutes one of the most valuable chapters in T. G. Steward's *The Colored Regulars in the United States Army.* It is a tragedy that one of the most unlikely of afflictions for the black soldier, acute alcoholism, forced Baker into early retirement in 1910 and most likely led to his premature death at the age of forty-eight. Impressive as his career was, its most perilous moment was when as a youth he had been caught in a power struggle between two sergeants.[25]

Richard Miller may have used underhanded methods in his vendetta against Dickerson, but his subsequent career indicates that he was a first-rate soldier. Ironically, he received little gain from his rival's demise. Denied the first sergeant's rank he allegedly coveted, he failed to reenlist when his tour of duty expired in 1884. He remained a civilian for eighteen months before enlisting in the Tenth Cavalry.

In August 1886 he was one of two men cited in orders for their courage and determination in a "very daring" effort to capture an Apache outlaw on the San Carlos Reservation. After serving as the trumpeter for his troop from 1890 to 1895, he rejoined the Ninth Cavalry. Promoted to sergeant and stationed at Fort Duchesne in 1897, he earned praise in the *Army and Navy Journal* for helping to organize a nineteen-piece military band, of which he was the drum major. Indicating their love of music, the members received no compensation and bore all the expenses themselves while still being required to "attend to all their duties as soldiers." Nevertheless, they played for a wide variety of post activities and social affairs and were deemed the equal of many regimental bands with "professional musicians paid extra salaries."[26] They also made life considerably more bearable at the isolated post.

As ardent a soldier as a musician, Miller participated in the charge up San Juan Hill the following year and afterwards was sent to the Philippines. On 17 December 1900 he distinguished himself in battle with insurgent Filipinos. Though severely wounded in the thigh by bolo slashes, he continued to fight so fiercely that he received a certificate of merit. The following year, he was selected as the regimental color sergeant.[27]

The court-martial of Dickerson was an embarrassment for all concerned, including Captain Loud. Fourteen years as a regimental adjutant had left him sorely lacking in the art of dealing with soldiers. It took him some time to understand the truth of the dictum that the quality of a first sergeant was more important to a troop than that of its captain. He replaced Dickerson with Sergeant Clyde, who proved to be incompetent and dishonest. This resulted in another year of turmoil before Clyde deserted in early 1885.

By then, Loud finally knew his troop well enough to elevate Madison Ingoman to the position of first sergeant. Ingoman, a thirty-three-year-old Kentuckian, had served one five-year term in the Tenth Cavalry before transferring to the Ninth in 1878. In January 1881, only recently promoted to sergeant, he was assigned to escort a wagon train from Fort Craig to Ojo Caliente. As the train was plodding up the Alamosa Canyon on 21 January, he heard the sound of "sharp firing" ahead of him. Corralling the wagons and leaving them under the guard of the teamsters, he rode ahead with his six-man detachment. Rounding a bend, he discovered seven citizens "defending themselves in a ravine against twenty-five Indians." A furious charge routed the Indians and sent them fleeing. Two days later, still eight miles from Ojo Caliente, Ingoman's train was fired on by some fifteen Apaches positioned atop the canyon walls. Knowing that if he simply took cover the Indians' fire would slaughter his horses, he dismounted his men and led them in an assault on the enemy position. Private William Jones was fatally wounded in the attack, but the Indians retreated in disorder. Although they returned with reinforcements, Ingoman "skillfully covered and conducted the train" to its destination without further loss.[28]

Colonel Hatch, notorious for failing to recognize the gallantry of his men, was so impressed that he commended Ingoman in orders. Although a Medal of Honor would also have been appropriate, none came. Ten years later, Ingoman received a certificate of merit.[29] Although it was considered the equal of the Medal of Honor in the late nineteenth century, its recipients would receive none of the attention focused on recipients of the medal by later generations.

Under Ingoman's guidance, D Troop became one of the most orderly in the regiment. During his first three years as first sergeant, only three men deserted, and only two received dishonorable discharges. In 1889 he switched to the less turbulent life of a quartermaster sergeant, in which position he remained until he contracted yellow fever during the Santiago campaign in Cuba and died on 8 August 1898. In every sense he had been *all that soldiers should be.* John Tracy, another veteran, served as first sergeant until the outbreak of the Spanish-American War.

With such capable first sergeants assisting him, Loud evolved into one the most respected troop commanders in the regiment. When he was promoted to major in 1897, his men presented him with "an extensive officer's equipment." At the presentation they lauded him for his "many acts of forbearance and words of kindness." Often, when they had committed indiscretions, "instead of applying rigid discipline upon us, you have given us gentle counsel and encouragement to perform our duties better." In this way, they asserted, you "made us your sincere soldier friends, and taught us faithfulness in our respective standing."

Taken by surprise, Loud "was visibly affected by this expression of esteem" and the impending separation from his troop.[30]

In view of the success that attended the careers of Baker, Miller, Ingoman, and Loud, it seems almost unfair that Richard Dickerson, as talented as any, in effect vanished into thin air. It is possible that subsequent events, if known, would indicate whether he had been a sex offender, an entrapped victim, or both.

PART FIVE

Racism Resurgent

19

The Ordeal of Chaplain Plummer

The prerequisite for the maintenance of the bond forged between officers and enlisted men in the Ninth Cavalry was the continuation of white supremacy. Although by the 1880s few officers believed that commanding African Americans posed a threat to their status, the presence of black officers was another matter. Even Major Henry, the foremost champion of black enlisted men, feared that more than one or two African American officers would stigmatize the regiment and every officer associated with it.

The first black graduate of West Point was Henry Flipper of the class of 1877. Assigned to the Tenth Cavalry, he had the good fortune to fall under the command of Colonel Benjamin Grierson, one of the most tolerant officers in the army, and to be assigned to the troop led by Captain Nicholas Nolan, an Irishman with twenty-five years of service behind him. Nolan, whose own family had immigrated to America during the famine of the 1840s, empathized with Flipper as a member of a race that had been oppressed as his own had been. Two years later, Nolan learned that a letter from an officer's wife had been published in "some Northern papers" criticizing him and his family "for receiving and entertaining Mr. Flipper."

Nolan charged that the letter was motivated solely by Flipper's color without regard to "his grand attainments." He proclaimed that Flipper's "standing with the officers is of the most friendly nature, and the more he comes in contact with them the better he proves the worthiness of his position."[1]

Nolan was unique in his tolerance. By 1881, Lieutenant Flipper was stationed at Fort Davis among officers whom he later described as "hyenas" and under the command of the acerbic Colonel Shafter. While serving as the post commissary, some of his accounts came up short, a relatively common problem for young officers. Unlike many in similar situations, he was summarily court-martialed. Although acquitted of embezzlement, the primary charge against him, he was convicted of "conduct unbecoming an officer and a gentleman." Following his dismissal in June 1882, the army's officer corps was once more all white.[2]

During the last six years of the 1880s, three more African Americans were commissioned as officers. Each was assigned to the Ninth Cavalry. None were received as warmly as Flipper; instead, they were socially ostracized and subjected to varying degrees of harassment in the conduct of their official duties.

Henry V. Plummer, born in 1844, spent his early years as a slave in Maryland before enlisting in the Navy during the Civil War. Learning to read while in the service, he later worked in a Washington, D.C., post office, pastored a Baptist church, and sporadically attended a seminary until he graduated in 1879. On 1 July 1884, with the support of Frederick Douglass, he was commissioned a chaplain and assigned to the Ninth Cavalry.[3]

Although chaplains held a rank equivalent to captain, they did not exercise command and therefore did not pose the same threat to white supremacy as did black line officers. Plummer, as a result, was initially encouraged as he addressed his duties with a vigor that shamed the lackadaisical efforts of his predecessors. Major Henry, in particular, applauded his ability to attract large numbers of buffalo soldiers to his services.

Henry, so devout that he officiated at burials when on campaigns,[4] had bluntly told a congressional committee that chaplains as a rule were "demoralizing" and "not of much account" because they were "generally old men" so uninterested in their work that soldiers would "not have anything to do with them." In all his years as a regular chapel attender, "I do not think I ever saw over ten soldiers" present at any service.[5] Delighted to discover that Plummer was an exception, he informed the *Army and Navy Journal* that he had heard "one of the best sermons and prayers by the colored Chaplain." He concluded by declaring that he believed Plummer could "discount any of the white Chaplains in the

Service." Eight years later, Lieutenant Colonel George Sanford stated that Plummer inspired the largest church attendance he had ever seen at an army post. He attributed the chaplain's success to the "efficient manner in which . . . [he] carries out his work."[6]

In applauding Plummer, Sanford and Henry were in the minority among the upper echelons of the Ninth's officers. Mary Garrard, wife of Captain James Garrard, was one of the few whites to work closely with the chaplain, serving as his organist for five years. She described him as "energetic, faithful and devoted" and unmatched in his ability to evoke participation in church affairs. She added bitingly: "He has been . . . almost entirely without help or encouragement from the officers and his success with the soldiers is due to his own untiring efforts."[7]

No matter how well Plummer performed his duties, his superiors denied him any semblance of acceptance. After ten years' service, he stated that socially he had been "a stranger to the officers . . . and their families" throughout his tenure.[8]

By the 1890s he was regarded as an overly zealous nuisance. Active in the temperance movement, he opposed post canteens that sold beer and wine. An exposé of the evils of on-post intoxicants at Fort Robinson that he enclosed with his report for March 1892 led to a temporary ban on the canteen's sale of beer, much to the displeasure of his superiors. Although this intervention did nothing to enhance his popularity, it was trivial compared to a more sinister development.

After almost a decade of exemplary service, Plummer was, in the minds of his superiors, metamorphosing into a radical race agitator. In addition to editing a small weekly newsletter, the *Fort Robinson Weekly Bulletin,* that kept soldiers informed on current activities and gossip, he served as a correspondent for the *Omaha Progress,* a black newspaper that many buffalo soldiers read.[9] The remarks concerning post matters that he wrote under the pseudonym "The Owl" were just cryptic enough to awaken latent fears of some sort of "slave uprising."

In April 1893, following the attempted lynching of a former buffalo soldier by a Crawford mob, a circular, reputedly printed on the same press that issued the *Progress,* was distributed at Fort Robinson. It condemned the affair, stated that other soldiers had frequently been abused while in Crawford, and urged a boycott of the worst establishments. Unfortunately, the writer bombastically threatened that if the atrocities continued, "we will . . . reduce your homes and firesides to ashes and send your guilty souls to hell."[10]

Lieutenant Colonel Reuben F. Bernard, a Tennessean with a mediocre military record and an inordinate amount of racism, ordered an investigation to determine the broadside's author. Although he and others believed that Plummer was "at the bottom of it all," they failed to unearth enough evidence to file charges. Sergeant Barney McKay, a veteran with twelve years of impeccable service to his credit, was charged with distributing the manifesto and convicted on the testimony of two soldiers he had recently disciplined. Found guilty by a court-martial presided over by Captain Guilfoyle and consisting entirely of West Pointers who hailed from Southern states, McKay received a dishonorable discharge and two years' imprisonment. Sergeant Thomas Goodloe, who would later serve briefly as the regimental sergeant major, summed up the buffalo soldiers' dismay: "The niggers won't hang together; they are always ready to hang one another."[11] His words would apply equally well to the ordeal facing Plummer.

As Bernard's hostility became more overt, Plummer filed an ill-timed protest concerning housing discrimination. While the other officers were lodged in relatively new duplexes, he had been assigned to older quarters among those occupied by the married noncommissioned officers. When he requested a move into a vacant unit on officers' row as befitted "his rank in the U.S. Army," Bernard reacted brutally. The lieutenant colonel not only denied the request but also stipulated that Plummer's housing assignment was permanent. To add to the chaplain's discomfiture, Bernard had his adjutant read the order to the assembled officers, Plummer in their midst. The adjutant did so, in Plummer's words, with "stentorian accents and rhetorical emphasis."[12]

Perhaps seeking to escape such malevolence, Plummer requested in April 1894 an assignment to lead an expedition of black servicemen into central Africa to introduce "American civilization" and, if possible, "form a nucleus" for a "colony of our people." Although his Quixotic proposal was endorsed by several black leaders and evoked enthusiasm among potential volunteers, it had no chance of acceptance. Six weeks later, the secretary of war ruled that there was no legal authorization for an officer to be detailed for "such a mission."[13]

Less than a month after Plummer's African proposal fell through, a momentary lapse presented his detractors the opportunity to rid themselves of his presence. Essential to their success was Saddler Sergeant Robert Benjamin, a Jamaican immigrant with twenty-one years of service. Intelligent, adept at ingratiating himself with officers, ambitious for promotion, and slow to forgive an offense, he was no inconsiderable opponent.[14]

Plummer seemed unaware that Benjamin harbored deep resentments against him. Years earlier, while stationed at Fort Riley, Kansas, and charged with supervising the post bakery in addition to his pastoral duties, Plummer had reported the Jamaican for failing to attend to his duties properly. The chaplain had continued his offenses at Fort Robinson: failing to attend social gatherings at Benjamin's house, refusing to loan him fifteen dollars, and admonishing his friends for failure to salute properly.[15] In addition to being vengeful, Benjamin also seems to have been an unusually jealous husband. Mrs. Benjamin may have attended too many church socials for his comfort.

Benjamin was also aware of Plummer's disfavor with Bernard, whose support was crucial for him to obtain a coveted promotion to ordnance sergeant, which would raise his monthly pay from twenty-two to thirty-four dollars. He and First Sergeant George Tracy of D Troop had been examined for the position by a board headed by Bernard, but several months had passed without a final decision. There were few soldiers at the post more anxious to curry favor with a superior than Robert Benjamin.[16]

On 2 June 1894, bandsman David Dillon was promoted to sergeant. In celebration, Sergeant Major Jeremiah Jones hosted a small party, including Plummer and Benjamin. One of the topics joshed about over the drinks was Plummer's having recently escorted Mrs. Benjamin to a church ball. By 8:30 P.M. the last of the guests had left. Some, including Benjamin and perhaps Plummer, overindulged, but no one could have foreseen the party's consequences.

Sometime after the gathering had broken up, Plummer began to feel queasy and decided that some milk might soothe his stomach. When he went next door to the Benjamins' to borrow some, Mrs. Benjamin admitted him and told him her husband was absent. After drinking the milk,

Plummer, either tipsy or just lonely because his family was absent, sat down on the floor and began to visit with the Benjamins' eight-year-old daughter.[17] The little girl was a frequent playmate of his sons and was also enrolled in the school he conducted. This was the scene when Benjamin returned.

The sight of the chaplain with his wife and daughter infuriated the Jamaican. He heaped abuse on Plummer and ordered him out of the house. The commotion that followed was as unrestrained as Benjamin's jealous rage. After a hot exchange of words and threats of violence, Plummer departed for home, undoubtedly stunned by the furor evoked by his visit.[18]

The following morning, Benjamin described Plummer's misdeeds to Bernard. He had drunk intoxicating liquor and "caroused" with enlisted men and had even supplied part of the intoxicants. Then, under the influence of liquor, he had behaved in a "disgraceful manner" at Benjamin's house, using crude vulgarities in the presence of Mrs. Benjamin and her daughter. Six days later, Colonel Biddle, having resumed command of the post, endorsed the filing of charges, adding that on 3 June the chaplain was still "odorous with the fumes of liquor." Striving for an appearance of fairness, he said he had "no fault to find with the Chaplain's attention to the post schools or church" and opined that a court-martial was desirable "for his own sake.[19]

Even though a pretrial investigation by Departmental Judge Advocate Enoch Crowder led to the deletion of all charges of intoxication, disgraceful behavior, carousing, and the use of vulgarities, Biddle insisted that he be charged with "conduct unbecoming an officer and a gentleman"—for which conviction required dismissal. Otherwise, Biddle noted grimly, it "would be of no good," because Plummer would be "left with the regiment."[20]

Realizing that he had little chance of receiving unprejudiced treatment, Plummer vainly sought to avoid a trial by asking to be examined by a retirement board for a service-induced infirmity. Although Biddle was more than ready to cooperate, the post surgeon refused to certify the infirmity, and the matter was dropped. In late August the court-martial, presided over by Colonel John C. Bates of the Second Infantry, convened. The defense counsels were Captain Garrard, whose wife was Plummer's most outspoken supporter, and an attorney from nearby Chadron.

During the weeks leading up to the trial, Plummer was the target of a campaign aimed at destroying his reputation and preparing the way for his dismissal. In a series of releases to the *Kansas City Times*, widely read by military men throughout the West, his character was systematically impeached by reports alluding to improprieties so "disgraceful" that they could "not be overlooked" and that would "make his services in the future valueless." The chaplain, who had "made himself obnoxious on other occasions," had defended his actions by pleading that his "relations with the enlisted men had become strained . . . and he was anxious to reinstate himself in their esteem by getting drunk."[21]

Either because of such insinuations or the dwindling interest in civil rights, newspapers that had sympathized with Lieutenant Flipper and Cadet Johnson Whittaker during their courts-martial either ignored Plummer's plight or assumed his guilt. The *Army and Navy Journal*'s only mention of the trial was to print the order terminating Plummer's career. Other papers, such as the *New York Times*, willingly join in the smear campaign. After noting Plummer's proposal concerning an expedition to Africa, the *Times* added that "the scheme was said . . . to have no other object than to distract the attention of the authorities, who had before them the charge of intemperance."[22] In actuality, the colonization proposal had been made several weeks before Sergeant Benjamin initiated the charges of drunkenness.

The testimony of the Benjamins constituted virtually the entire case against Plummer. Although Sergeants Dillon and Jones acknowledged that the chaplain had taken two or three drinks, they contradicted every other aspect of Benjamin's account. Jones, in his ninth year as sergeant major, declared that he had known Benjamin for fourteen years and considered his reputation for veracity so poor that he would not believe him "on oath in any matter where he was personally concerned." Dillon testified similarly and joined Jones in declaring that Benjamin became extremely inebriated during the evening. They confirmed that Benjamin had held a grudge against Plummer for years.[23]

Biddle should have found his key witness an embarrassment. During the middle of the trial, Benjamin dramatically produced a typed letter, signed "We Thirteen," threatening violence against him or anyone else who testified against the chaplain. Unfortunately, an investigation revealed that the threat was typed on a typewriter to which Benjamin had easy access.

Nothing, however, could shake the military's confidence in its star witness. A communication to the *Kansas City Times* stated that "no one," obviously meaning officers, attached "any blame" to Benjamin for reporting Plummer. "It was his duty to do so."[24] Captain Crowder described Benjamin as being "far above the usual standard of intelligence among enlisted men" and concluded that his career had "fully demonstrated" that he merited the "confidence placed in him by his superior officers."

By standing logic on its head, the *Kansas City Times* charged that the "color line" had been "drawn by Plummer's friends," who were exerting "every available influence . . . to prevent the testimony" of witnesses for the prosecution. Piously proclaiming that its only desire was to see a fair trial, the *Times* condemned Plummer's defenders for asserting that "colored people must stand together" and refrain from testifying against one another.[25]

Captain Garrard waged a vigorous defense that evoked constant objections from the judge advocate, Lieutenant Alfred Jackson, whenever Garrard attempted to "show the vindictive nature" of Benjamin. In disgust, Garrard charged that Jackson was "not disposed to let the truth come out" in order to win favor with his superiors. Although no officers testified for Plummer, several white businessmen from Crawford vouched for his character and sobriety. Mary Garrard, his long-time organist, stated that she had observed him frequently both in church and at "his own house on church affairs" and had never once seen him in any way "show any evidence of being under the influence of alcohol."[26] Given the heavy drinking that was endemic among army officers, she undoubtedly had seen many officers under the influence.

Nothing that Plummer or his counsels did was of the least avail in swaying a tribunal predisposed to convict. His attorneys stressed his years of meritorious service, his outstanding record in operating effective post schools, and his unexcelled ability to elicit positive responses to his sermons. To counter these, Biddle produced a copy of Plummer's letter protesting discrimination in the assignment of housing. No one saw any reason to question why an officer with the rank of captain was relegated to quarters among enlisted men. Instead, the court accepted as valid the argument that the tenor of the protest disproved the claim to "meritorious and faithful" service.[27] Such use of a legitimate letter of grievance indicates that Plummer's unforgivable transgression was not so much drinking with enlisted men as challenging the color line and using the wrong tone of voice to his superior officers.

On 3 September the court-martial fulfilled its obligation by finding Plummer guilty of conduct unbecoming an officer and gentleman. As the case passed up the ladder through the judge advocate general and secretary of war to President Grover Cleveland for review, African American leaders throughout the nation petitioned for clemency. They submitted affidavits attesting to Plummer's good character and sobriety and pointing out the ludicrousness of prosecuting a chaplain for having friendly relations with the men who constituted his congregation. It would be November before they received their answer.

While Plummer's fate hung in the balance, Sergeant David Dillon, whose promotion had triggered the events leading to his court-martial, also fell victim to Benjamin's malice. In response to the Jamaican's complaints, Biddle ordered Dillon to stay away from Mrs. Benjamin. Although the court later assumed this was because of harassment and threats, it may have stemmed from Sergeant Benjamin's jealousy. Dillon, a mulatto trumpet player who lived next door and employed Mrs. Benjamin as a laundress, was younger than Benjamin and also unmarried. Testimony indicates that she may have been infatuated with him. Sergeant Houston Lust, a witness to the final imbroglio between Benjamin and Dillon, quoted the latter as saying, "I do not want your God damn wife, as I have returned all recent letters received from her to you, and I have persuaded her to continue with you, and not to leave you for me, as I would not have her for a gracious gift!"[28] The court, obviously uninterested in developing testimony that would reveal any ulterior motives of Benjamin, asked not one clarifying question.

Despite Biddle's injunction, a raucous brawl soon occurred. According to Dillon, he had stopped by Benjamin's house to tell him to "stop lying on me." After a heated exchange, he had turned to walk off when Benjamin called him a "damn dirty Dutch Cur" (apparently a reference to his German birth and light complexion) and threatened to shoot him. As the two tore into each other once more, Sergeant of the Guard Lust placed both under arrest. Dillon's final salvo was a bitter, "Now, God damn you, you report me." This, of course, was exactly what Benjamin intended to do.[29]

Colonel Biddle responded as though Dillon, a former favorite, had betrayed a trust. The sergeant was no run-of-the-mill soldier. Quite possibly the only buffalo soldier born in Germany, he had joined the Tenth Cavalry in January 1877 at the age of twenty-one. Assigned to the regimental band, he soon became the chief trumpeter of the regiment. While he was stationed in Santa Fe shortly before his third enlistment expired, his wife died and he was forced to entrust his children to relatives. As a result of these misfortunes, he did not immediately reenlist.

Dillon's reputation as a musical virtuoso must have been great indeed for the commander of another regiment to recruit him. Upon his reenlistment, Biddle asked the adjutant general to assign him to the Ninth Cavalry because he was such an "excellent musician, something difficult to get." When this failed to evoke quick results, Biddle reiterated his request. As a consequence, Dillon arrived at Fort Robinson on the last day of March 1894. Two months later, he received what was likely a promised reward, a promotion from private to sergeant.[30]

In Biddle's eyes, Dillon's support of Plummer and the altercation with Benjamin demonstrated that he was an ungrateful troublemaker too dangerous to be allowed to remain in the regiment. Charges were immediately brought, a court-martial was hastily assembled, and three weeks after Plummer's conviction, Dillon was found guilty and sentenced to a dishonorable discharge. In callously destroying Dillon's career for so slight an infraction, Biddle was also warning one and all that Sergeant Benjamin was not to be crossed.

Shortly before Plummer's sentence was confirmed, Benjamin received official word that he had been promoted to ordnance sergeant. Of the ten cavalrymen elevated, he was the only African American and the only saddler sergeant. As he packed to leave for his new assignment, Biddle praised him for his "long and faithful service in the regiment."[31]

Grover Cleveland, the first Democratic president since 1860, fulfilled the expectations of his Southern supporters. On 2 November 1894 he approved Plummer's conviction; eight days later, the chaplain's dismissal took effect. In acknowledging receipt of the order, Plummer protested anew that he was being dismissed "upon false testimony and prejudice." He closed with the sad observation that "patriotism and devotion to duty counts for naught against falsehood and prejudice in the regiment under the present regime."[32]

20

The Black Lieutenants

"A Dark Day for the Ninth Horse!"

John Hanks Alexander, the second African American graduate of West Point, reported for duty with the Ninth Cavalry in 1887. Born in 1864 to former slaves in Helena, Arkansas, he graduated from high school at the age of fifteen and taught school in Mississippi a year before enrolling at Oberlin College in Ohio. Intelligent, tactful, handsome, and unassuming, he had all the attributes for success. In addition, his years at Oberlin and summers working as a waiter at a prestigious Cleveland hotel gave him valuable experience in dealing with the Victorian elite.[1] When he arrived at West Point, a *New York Times* reporter described him as a "very clever and intelligent young man, fully equal in appearance and manners to any of the [cadets] . . . and much superior to many of them."[2]

After the dismissal of Johnson C. Whittaker in 1880 ended a decade of unbroken black enrollment at West Point, racists gloatingly predicted there would never be another black graduate from the academy. Even the *Army and Navy Journal* reprinted a diatribe that African Americans were so lacking in the "qualifications to insure success" that no alarm "need be felt" even if another should be admitted. Just as Flipper "had no predecessor at West Point, so will he have no successor on the roll of graduates."[3] Like it or not, any black cadet admitted to West Point would have the eyes of the nation upon him.

Unlike most of the black cadets, who had been appointed by Reconstruction Congressmen in the South, Alexander competed against several whites for a vacancy from Ohio's Fourteenth Congressional District. Although he decisively bested his rivals on the academic tests, he was

John H. Alexander, lieutenant, Ninth Cavalry, 1887–1894. Courtesy of Special
Collections, U.S. Military Academy Library, West Point.

informed that a physical exam had indicated he was "pigeon breasted." With this as an excuse, the congressman relegated him to the status of an alternate and gave the appointment to the son of Morrison Waite, the chief justice of the United States. A caustic West Point observer commented that "it would scarcely do for a Democratic Congressman to give the appointment to a colored boy, so, as a stroke of *finesse*, he was appointed an alternate on account of alleged physical disqualifications."[4]

With the financial help of some Oberlin instructors, Alexander journeyed to West Point and took the required exams alongside the regular appointees. His arrival was greeted with a sardonic prediction that "his successful rival . . . [will] pass the preliminary examination here and relieve the Academy from the duty of carrying another colored boy and his political friends on its shoulders for four years." To everyone's surprise, young Waite was one of only two Ohioans to fail the exam. Not only had Alexander passed, but his "pigeon breast" also had miraculously corrected itself.[5]

His admission was greeted with a blunt warning that "he would receive fair, impartial and courteous treatment from all officers . . . of the Academy, but his social status . . . would be entirely beyond the control of the authorities."[6] In other words, he would be ostracized the same way as his predecessors had been.

Any hopes that he would speedily flunk out were demolished. At the end of his first semester he ranked third in a class of more than one hundred in English and stood ninth overall. Although he never again ranked so high, he consistently remained in the upper half of his class. Despite considerable trouble with engineering, he graduated thirty-second in a class of sixty-four. This was not only higher than the other black graduates during the century but also higher than most of the white officers in the Ninth Cavalry.

Despite his academic success, Alexander amassed so many disciplinary infractions that it is hard to believe his treatment was impartial. More than a dozen times during his first semester, he was issued demerits for "smiling in ranks." He was also guilty of such heinous offenses as "not depressing his toes" while marching to the dining hall, answering mess-hall roll calls either "boisterously" or "inaudibly," wearing an overcoat in the library, and "marching unsteadily." While punishments for minor infractions were frequently levied on plebes by overly zealous (or sadistic) cadet officers, these were most frequently inflicted on lower ranking cadets.

During his first semester at West Point, for example, Alexander accumulated 86 demerits; the combined totals of the eight plebes above him totaled only 52. There was no letup. During his fifth semester at the Academy, he received 90 demerits; this exceeded the combined totals of the twenty-five cadets ranked above him. During his senior year he accumulated 123 demerits during a single semester; only two lowly plebes in the process of flunking out accumulated more. Two weeks before his graduation, he was still being harassed with demerits for such trivialities as "smiling in ranks." As though his nerves were wearing dangerously thin, his final month also saw him receive two citations for "profane expressions."[7]

One of Alexander's more unusual transgressions was for being off limits, ice-skating on the Hudson River late on the afternoon of February 3. His ardor for this pastime resulted in his only known mention in cadet reminiscences of the period. More than forty years later, Major General Mark L. Hersey recalled that one afternoon while he was on duty he encountered "our colored classmate," Alexander, who was off duty:

> The skating was good on the Hudson, and as he passed me I offered him my skates and told him where they hung in my alcove. He went up to get them but Bob Howze, who was in confinement, fired him out and he came down empty-handed. As he passed me, I asked him if he did not find the skates and he said briefly that Howze would not let him have them. When I got off the area, I tackled Bob about it and he, with enthusiastic profanity, let me know that no colored man could enter his room in any social way, in fact, he said that he would never have come to the damned place if he had known he was going to have a nigger for a classmate.[8]

Despite his racism, Robert Lee Howze, a Texan, graduated in the top third of his class and had no difficulty finding success in the regular army. Eighteen years later, he would return to "the damned place" as the commandant of cadets. It was probably just as well that he would have no black cadets to deal with.

Possessed of a keen social conscience whetted by resentment of the injustices inflicted on African Americans, Alexander found it difficult to mask his feelings. In July 1886 several Mississippi blacks from the county where he had once taught were "coldly murdered" for having, in his words, "the courage to stand up and resist . . . insolent, overbearing whites." After pouring out all the dismay concealed from white associates to a friend, he declared that African Americans should defend their "manhood . . . even though the consequences be perdition itself." The failure to resist would simply convince whites more than ever that blacks "had no rights that white men are bound to respect."[9]

Despite such internal fires, he endured the ostracism and harassments at West Point so stoically that black newspapers assured their readers that he was "treated as equal by the boys of his class in their work and play." This was hardly the case. At chapel, for example, he had a pew to himself until another black, Charles Young, was admitted. Writing to one of his closest friends, he compared his situation to that of one who was isolated atop "the highest and most secluded peak of the Himalaya Mountains." He had gone "two years without speaking to anyone." White cadets, in contrast, had friends visiting them and enjoyed "social advantages at hops and with the families of officers which . . . are closed to me."[10] To newspapers, however, he issued such guarded statements as, "I think I got as much fun out of it as the next man."[11]

One small consolation for those few who survived the hell inflicted upon African American cadets was a belated recognition of their worth and grit on graduation day. According to a black newspaper, proud of the youth who had more than held his own in competition with whites, Alexander met with "thunderous hand-clapping" as he stepped forward to receive his diploma.[12]

Unfortunately, it is difficult to assess his reception in the Ninth Cavalry because his personnel file is missing from the National Archives. With Colonel Hatch commanding Fort Robinson, Alexander's initial six-month stint there went smoothly. In March 1888 he was assigned to M Troop, stationed at Fort Washakie in central Wyoming. Transferred with the troop to Fort Duchesne the following June, he remained there until October 1891. In 1890 he served as the acting commander of B Troop, the company to which Lieutenant Charles Young was also assigned. Despite appearances, it was more by chance than design that the only two black line officers in the army were serving with the same troop at such a remote outpost.[13]

Service at Duchesne was relatively pleasant under the command of Major James Randlett, more tolerant and amiable than most of his colleagues. This must have become more apparent to Alexander when in early 1892 he was transferred to Captain Guilfoyle's I Troop at Fort Robinson. After a year with Guilfoyle's troop, he was abruptly replaced by Lieutenant Howard Hickock, a Missourian reporting for his initial tour of duty.

Any satisfaction received from leaving Guilfoyle's command was surely offset by chagrin at being reduced to the status of temporary help. Nominally assigned to the deactivated L Troop, Alexander spent a year filling in for officers on leave or detached service. In a four-month period in early 1893 he served briefly with D Troop, spent ten days as the acting post adjutant, was switched to F Troop for a month, transferred to D Troop for two weeks, and was then placed in charge of the post exchange. The game of musical chairs imposed upon the senior second lieutenant in the regiment ended in the fall of 1893 when he was approved by an examining board for promotion.[14]

More lasting relief offered itself in early 1894 when Wilberforce University, an African American institution at Xenia, Ohio, was added to the list of schools for military training that were staffed by officers on detached service. When Wilberforce's president, an Oberlin graduate, requested Alexander's assignment to his institution, the army was only too pleased to accede. Alexander undoubtedly was delighted to exchange Fort Robinson's ostracism for an academic tour of duty in his adopted state.

He received the orders for his transfer from Colonel Biddle on 26 January 1894, along with a curt expression of appreciation for his "business-like methods" in the conduct of assignments. His tenure at Wilberforce was sadly brief. On 26 March, while sitting in a barber's chair in nearby Springfield, he complained of a severe headache and abruptly collapsed. He died almost immediately, victim of a massive heart attack. A black newspaper conjectured that the attack may have been a result of "excessive cigarette smoking," but it seems likely that stress was also involved.[15]

Alexander's death was recognized as a tragedy both for his family and for all African Americans. The *Kansas City American Citizen* agonized that having such "a young man of unusual brilliancy with a long and useful career before him to be cut down just at the beginning of life . . . is a sad blow to the whole race."[16]

Biddle was more generous to Alexander in death than in life. Groping for platitudes, he commended him for the "zealous performance of every duty" and declared that he had "succeeded in winning the respect and admiration of his brother officers and obtaining from all an acknowledgment of his capacity and worth." He had been "manly, courteous and honorable" and "always a gentleman." Alexander's tragic demise certainly deserved such compliments, but Biddle added a phrase more revealing than he could have wished. One of Alexander's prime virtues was that he had appreciated "the *delicate distinctions of social intercourse* which the *peculiar*, and ofttimes trying, position of his office thrust upon him."[17] According to the leading scholar on Fort Robinson, the "delicate distinctions" were a euphemistic acknowledgment that Alexander "knew his racist colleagues wanted nothing to do with him" and therefore kept to himself.[18]

A more sincere tribute was paid by Fort Robinson's black soldiers. When they organized a chapter of the Army and Navy Union the following year, they named it the John H. Alexander Garrison.[19]

Alexander did manage to develop contacts with civilians, both black and white, in the towns located adjacent to the army posts. In the only journal left by him, he recounted a march from Fort Washakie to Fort Duchesne in the summer of 1888. His entry for the day he left Fort Washakie, a post at which he had been stationed less than five months, is intriguing: "Had quite a pleasant leave taking of the Post. . . . Went up town [Landers, Wyoming] visiting friends this afternoon. Took tea with Miss Roberts. . . . I mess with my captain [Louis Rucker]."[20] There is no reason to think that Landers was the only settlement in which he developed friendships.

After Alexander's death, Lieutenant Charles Young was the army's only black line officer. Born in 1864 in Kentucky to former slaves, he was reared at Ripley, Ohio. After graduating from a "colored high school" at the age of fifteen, he spent three years teaching school and studying at a nearby Jesuit institution before he emulated Alexander and sought admission to West Point. He, too, won out over several white rivals.[21]

Academically, West Point would be very difficult for Young. While he was talented in music and languages, every math and engineering course

Charles Young, lieutenant, captain, and major, Ninth Cavalry, 1889–1913.
Courtesy of the Nebraska State Historical Society, Lincoln.

was an ordeal. At the end of the first term he seemed secure, ranking
midway in a class of seventy. His success combined with Alexander's
lofty rank in the third class evoked a brief note in the *Army and Navy
Journal* that the "Ohio colored lads are doing finely."[22]

His second term was almost his last. Although he ranked in the top
third in both English and French, he failed mathematics. Described as

studious but with "little aptitude" for the subject, he was ordered to repeat the entire year. Redoubling his efforts, he ranked a lofty seventeenth overall and eighth in both English and French at the end of the next year. Despite this achievement, the remainder of his academic tenure was a Herculean struggle against an array of technical and scientific courses. He began his final year ranked next to last, with the most difficult classes yet to come.[23]

His senior year ended in disaster. Failing "Military Engineering and the Science of War," he had to watch his classmates graduate while he waited to learn if he would have another chance. When the academic board granted him three months in which to make good his deficiency, Lieutenant George Goethals, the instructor whose course he had flunked, agreed to remain at the academy and tutor him. During the last week of August, Young passed "with flying colors." On the last day of the month he graduated, ranked last in his class.[24]

Young encountered at least as much hostility as had earlier black cadets. Less polished than the erudite Alexander, he was remembered by a classmate as "a rather awkward, overgrown lad, large-boned and robust in physique, and of a nervous, impulsive temperament" (a description difficult to reconcile with his West Point photo).[25] In contrast to Alexander's years as a popular student at Oberlin, Young had spent most of his life enrolled in or teaching in separate schools. W. A. Hare, an African American who flunked out after a semester at West Point, stated that Alexander was "very popular with the corps" compared to Young, who was "not as much so."[26]

Like Flipper and Alexander before him, Young had to endure prolonged periods during which no white cadets would speak to him. Although Young stoically endured their silence, he was less tolerant of the petty harassments designed to make his life miserable. According to one account, he developed a novel method of responding. A talented song writer, he retaliated for particularly odious acts "calculated to gall him" by composing ballads in either English or French, arranging them to music, and then singing them "to the heavens at a time when its sharp wit would carry home." One unnamed northern cadet replied to such a putdown by "addressing himself" to his comrades within Young's earshot "in language which reflected on the chastity of the negro's [sic] maternal forebears and at the same time consigned him to eternal perdition."

So gross was the insult that a cadet from South Carolina, who had come to appreciate the "suavity" of his black classmate, intervened. Knowing that Young would not dare risk engaging in a fight with a white cadet, he challenged the offender himself. At 4:30 A.M. on a Sunday morning "behind old Fort Clinton," the fistfight took place. The southerner pummeled his adversary unmercifully and then extracted an "apology for his language and broke the ice of silence which had congealed for months about the negro's presence at the Academy."[27] A slightly different version of this encounter placed it "on the famous battleground back of old Fort Putnam" and stated that the victorious southerner was "privately congratulated" by Colonel Hamilton Hawkins, the commander of cadets.[28]

Although Charles Rhodes, Young's classmate, recalled that during his last year "many cadets of character and standing" began to treat him "with the kindness and consideration which had long been his due," matters may not have improved very much. At the beginning of his last semester, cadets were literally fighting to avoid sharing a dining table with him. When Cadet Captain George Langhorne, a Virginian, assigned him a place at the table "to which his scholarship entitled him," so many cadets privately protested that he reluctantly gave in. When he accordingly relegated Young to a lower table, Cadet Lieutenant Morris Barroll of Maryland, to whose table Young had been transferred, objected in such terms that Langhorne, feeling insulted, challenged him to a "bare fist fight." The only disciplinary action taken by the authorities was to issue Barroll a paltry five demerits for "complaining of having to take a certain cadet at his table in the latter's presence." It is no wonder that Young later recalled the "heartaches" he had endured at West Point and stated that "the sole bright things" were the friendship and sympathy of seven cadets, one of whom was George Langhorne; none of those he named was from South Carolina.[29]

Unfortunately for Young, graduation did not mean that whites would no longer fight to avoid his company. When he asked to serve in the cavalry, he was assigned to the Tenth. Since it had no vacancies, he was carried on its roles as an "additional" officer, thereby obliged to be assigned to the first available vacancy, which most likely would occur in a white regiment. To forestall such an event, he was arbitrarily switched to the Twenty-fifth Infantry (black, needless to say), with the proviso that he would be transferred to fill the first vacancy in a "Colored Cavalry Regiment."[30]

Unfortunately for the comfort of the officers in the Ninth Cavalry, Lieutenant Ballard Humphrey died of a heart attack. When Young replaced him, a rebellion erupted. Major Henry, in charge of Fort McKinney, deduced that having all of the black officers in the Ninth would undercut his effort to promote it as an elite regiment. Never reluctant to voice his fears, he petulantly complained that Young's transfer to the "9th Horse is a dark affair. Why should not the 10th have a share, or the 24th or 25th Infantry?"[31]

In temporary command of the regiment, Henry filed a formal complaint that having all three "colored officers" would place the Ninth at a disadvantage in attracting capable white officers and unduly favor the Tenth. To support his protest, he stated that he had been informed that Lieutenant Alexander, stationed at Fort Duchesne, also objected to Young's joining the Ninth because "keeping them together gives no breadth to their efforts to advance their race."[32]

Reporting for duty with B Troop at Fort Robinson, Young met with a reception as hostile as anything at West Point. On 5 April 1890, Colonel Joseph Tilford admonished him for committing four "tactical errors" at guard mount that morning: After opening some boxes, he failed to inspect the contents properly; during the march in review, he gave the command to change directions "before reaching the camp colors," as protocol required; he failed to salute the officer of the day "until after arriving within six yards"; and he gave the command "guide left" before the rear platoon had passed the officer of the day.[33] One doubts that any officer in the regiment's history had been subjected to such nitpicking.

On 24 April, Major Randlett reported that Young had failed to appear for his duty at stables until "about ten minutes before grooming ceased." When questioned about the matter, Young replied that he was on duty elsewhere at the time and promised in the future to comply with the "spirit" of the provision requiring the presence of an officer during stables duty.[34]

Although it was relatively common and often unavoidable for officers to be tardy at stables duty, Tilford informed Young that his response was "entirely" inadequate and that he must correct his behavior or "more severe official action will be taken." During the following week, Lieutenant Eugene Ladd, his superior in B Troop, "frequently complained verbally" of his "habitual lateness" and "carelessness" in his duties. Ordered to explain these actions by Tilford, Young responded that the accusations were "very painful . . . since I hold doing my duty as my sole aim in life." Declaring that he would "scorn to draw pay as an officer" if he neglected his duties, he asked that the negative reports be forwarded to army headquarters together with his explanations.[35]

Before complying, Tilford endorsed his letter with a racist disclaimer that "more consideration [had been] shown him in this regard than any white officer would have received, on account of the misconstruction which others might place [if] . . . severe measures were used against him." He hoped that his warnings would "be a lesson" and that no further measures would be required. The harassments finally let up in late June when Young was informed that his "latest explanation is considered perfectly satisfactory by the post commander."[36]

After both were transferred to Fort Duchesne, Major Randlett and Young were soon on the best of terms. The lieutenant's efficiency reports improved dramatically as he made himself almost indispensable. In March 1892, Randlett placed him in charge of the post exchange; by August, he had added the duties of post adjutant, quartermaster, and recruiting officer. For six months he was also in charge of the post school, and for a time he served as the commissary of subsistence.[37] Seldom had one officer held so many duties. Young handled them flawlessly—a tribute to his work ethic and to his ability to motivate and supervise the troop clerks who helped to handle the record keeping and correspondence.

His service with the Ninth Cavalry was interrupted shortly after Alexander's death in March 1894. With the military science program at Wilberforce still in the planning stage, its president requested Young as a replacement. The military hierarchy, well aware that stationing him at Wilberforce would avert potential "social embarrassments," granted the request with the utmost speed. Informed that Young had not completed the five years of active service required for such an assignment, the high command granted a leave of absence so he could assume the post at once. His official assignment took effect on 31 August, the date on which he completed his fifth year.[38]

Nobody regretted Young's transfer more than Randlett. The major extolled him for "the untiring zeal, fidelity and well directed energy" with which he had performed the duties of adjutant, quartermaster, and exchange officer for the past two years. In the process he had made his post commander's duties "easy and comfortable." Randlett commended him as an officer "eminently worthy" of "confidence and high esteem."[39] Randlett thereupon divided Young's duties among three officers.

At Wilberforce, Young was both tireless and versatile. His efficiency reports abounded with comments that he was "enthusiastic and energetic" and "eminently qualified both from inclination and ability for the position he occupies." In addition to military science, he taught French and mathematics and directed the college band. President Mitchell described him as "thoroughly loyal to the interests of the college" and willing to oblige any request to give service.[40]

Young's closest friend on the Wilberforce faculty was a young sociology professor, W. E. B. DuBois. The latter spent many an evening visiting with Young and his widowed mother, who kept house for Young. According to DuBois's biographer, Young "was the first genuine male friendship" in his life and "one of a handful in which there was genuine affinity." The friendship would endure until DuBois delivered the eulogy at Young's memorial service in 1923.[41]

Young remained at Wilberforce until the outbreak of the Spanish-American War, when he assumed command of the Ninth Ohio Battalion, composed of black national guardsmen. Denied a chance to lead the battalion into combat, he returned to duty with the Ninth Cavalry in 1899 and soon afterwards was promoted to captain. During the next two decades he won accolades for every assignment: as a troop commander in the Philippines, as the superintendent of Sequoia National Park, and as military attaché to Haiti and Liberia. As the lieutenant colonel of the Tenth Cavalry in 1916, he commanded the regiment for several weeks during General John Pershing's Mexican expedition. Commendable as his performance was, his status had become an embarrassing challenge to the color line.

For months during the Mexican campaign, he had "messed" with his subordinate officers in the Tenth, all of whom were white, with "no friction, no quarrel, and no cataclysm." The "heavens above did not fall" and no inspector general reported anything that was not "good and soldierly" of his command.[42] Nevertheless, it seems likely that such a display of "social equality" at a time when lynching was still rampant in many areas and a Southerner resided in the White House was intolerable.

With the outbreak of World War I, Young was prevented from becoming the first black brigadier when "military medical men . . . discovered" in him "a disease no civilian doctor could ever detect." Even though he sought to demonstrate his soundness by riding horseback from Ohio to Washington, where he presented an appearance "astonishingly better than his medical examination indicates," he was forced into retirement. Being denied the opportunity to train and lead a division of black soldiers into battle was undoubtedly the greatest disappointment of his life.[43] He may have had high blood pressure, but the army leaders were also relieved to rid themselves of a man whose every action demonstrated the falseness of their racist beliefs.

One week before the armistice, Young was recalled to active duty and soon afterwards sent back to Liberia as military attaché. It was his final assignment. On 8 January 1922, while on an inspection tour of Nigeria, he died of a kidney infection ("jungle fever," his friends said) and was buried in Lagos. In May 1923, after repeated requests by his widow, the military brought him home for reburial in Arlington.

After a memorial service in New York City in which Franklin D. Roosevelt was among the speakers, the body arrived in Washington on 1 June. Local blacks "made the . . . funeral one of a demonstration in respect to his memory." Every African American school from Howard University down to the elementary level was closed, and "thousands gathered" to pay homage as the funeral procession of regulars, veterans, and cadets marched down Pennsylvania Avenue and across the Potomac to Arlington. The final rites were observed in the Memorial Amphitheater. Fittingly, the last previous service there had been for the Unknown Soldier. Unlike the buffalo soldiers buried in segregated sections on Arlington's fringes, Young's body rested among admirals and generals on the crest of a rolling ridge a short distance to the south of the Monument to the Unknown Soldier.[44] It was a fitting repository for the man who "had smashed to smithereens . . . the absurdity that Negroes can follow only if whites lead."[45]

Young's success may have pleased African Americans all the more because, unlike many successful blacks, there was no hint of any Caucasian ancestry to which racists could attribute his ability. As the *Freeman* of Indianapolis observed approvingly, his "skin" might be "of the darkest hue of the race," but he was "exceedingly clever, a West Point graduate, and a pianist of rare ability."[46]

More important, his tactful, always courteous demeanor could disarm the most unlikely white. After the two returned from the Philippines in 1902, Lieutenant B. R. Tillman, son of the notorious race baiter "Pitchfork" Ben Tillman of South Carolina, invited Young to a banquet. Tillman, obviously not a product of West Point, responded to the objections of some white guests that Young was "a gentleman and a friend of mine."[47]

Young's eulogist, Charles Rhodes, wrote that he "succeeded, through use of tact, self-restraint and what may be called self-effacement, to make steady and permanent headway against race prejudice." One wonders how he navigated the murky morass that passed for racial etiquette. Required by custom to call upon a new officer, for example, he "waited as long as possible, and then having ascertained beyond a doubt that . . . [he] was not at home, called and left his card."[48]

Despite such concessions to convention, he never lost his pride in being an African American nor failed to stand up for his dignity as an officer. When two black volunteer regiments were organized in 1898, he was offered a captaincy. Aware that blacks hoped he would be given command of one of the regiments, he rejected the one-step promotion. He minced no words in explaining that the "consideration of seven millions of my race is not to be ignored by me."[49]

Racial injustice was the topic of a speech he delivered to a student assembly at Stanford University in December 1903. In words that would have done justice to W. E. B. DuBois, he challenged the prevailing philosophy that African Americans should concentrate on vocational training and economic advancement instead of striving for immediate political and social equality. This had not worked in the past and would not in the future. "When the black man has learned the industrial trades and seeks work he runs into the unions, where he is told that no Negroes need apply." He closed his address with a challenge: "All the Negro asks is a white man's chance, will you give it?"[50]

Like so many things in his life, Young's relations with the soldiers he commanded has been misunderstood. Based upon one unfortunate Social Darwinian phrase that black men "by nature" were "more dependent and had less initiative" than Anglos, it has been concluded that he shared "with whites many of the same stereotypical views of blacks."[51] Although the phrase reflected a lifetime of exposure to the teachings of white supremacists, it would still be damning enough if it truly represented his views. Such was not the case.

The quotation was taken from Young's seminal study, *The Military Morale of Nations and Races*, without recognition that the book was written to challenge the racist assumptions of his day. The recent campaigns in Cuba and the Philippines, he asserted, proved that the widespread opinion that African Americans required white officers to be good soldiers was false. Black soldiers took "especial pleasure in the capable [*sic*] of their own race." He summed up his tightly reasoned opus with a declaration that there were "by nature no inferior races." It was only because of the "force of circumstances" that there were "superior placed peoples on the one hand and backward ones on the other."[52]

From his soldiers he demanded and received much. His troop was as well drilled and disciplined as any in the army. An army inspector, after observing it going through its drills at Sequoia National Park, stated that it was "without doubt the best instructed of any of the . . . troops on duty in the parks" and commended Young highly for "keeping it up to proper standard of instruction while attending to his many duties as park superintendent."[53]

Young was more than a severe taskmaster. In the Philippine jungles he was always in the forefront, earning "from his men the nickname 'Follow Me.'"[54] He was also the rare officer who could maintain discipline without distancing himself. Few officers had the sort of rapport that Charles Rhodes detected: "He loved his men and they loved him. . . . It was not an uncommon sight to see him at the piano in his army quarters, surrounded by a happy group of his men, entertaining and being entertained. He possessed their sincere respect as well as their affectionate regard."[55]

As a direct result of his dedication, one of his troopers became the first black enlisted man commissioned in the regular army. As a youth growing up in Washington D.C., Benjamin O. Davis had been thrilled by the sight the elite troop of buffalo soldiers from Fort Myer parading by, "mounted on beautiful, well-groomed horses." After graduating from high school near the head of his class, he applied for admission to West Point. Despite support from a Civil War hero, General John Logan, he found it had become "politically" impossible for an African American to gain admission. In June 1899, after a brief stint in a black volunteer regiment, he enlisted in the Ninth Cavalry and was assigned to Young's troop at Fort Duchesne.[56]

Within months Davis had been promoted to sergeant. When an army expansion in 1901 created a demand for additional officers, Young encouraged him to take the qualifying examination and tutored him relentlessly. Both men knew he must do extremely well to have any chance of being appointed. When he ranked third among the hundreds of noncommissioned officers who took the exam, the military grudgingly offered a commission.[57]

Davis was assigned to the Tenth Cavalry, and his military career mirrored Young's, with frequent tours of duty at Wilberforce and in Liberia. Granted the longevity and good health that fate denied his predecessors, he eventually became the first African American to hold the rank of brigadier general. He also reared a son, Benjamin O. Davis, Jr., who in 1936 became the first black since Young to graduate from West Point and then achieved World War II acclaim as the commander of the Tuskeegee Airmen. The success of the two Davises is all the more remarkable considering that as late as 1940 they were the only black officers on regular duty in the entire army. The younger Davis, ironically, seemed unaware of the debt he owed the officer who had tutored his father at a lonely outpost in the Utah desert.[58]

The careers of the black officers show only too well the limits of the frail entente between blacks and whites in the military. Despite the many instances of racial camaraderie in the Ninth Cavalry, race relations were too dependent on national trends to have any chance of permanent success.

21

The Failure of the Quest

In the spring of 1891, Major Henry's campaign to upgrade the image of the black soldiers achieved its greatest success when K Troop secured the coveted assignment to duty at Fort Myer, Virginia. Soldiers bombarded by negative stereotypes all of their lives must have found it exhilarating to be recognized as members of an efficient, well-disciplined unit worthy of a nation's respect and trust. As a consequence of this, Henry hoped, officers would consider service with the Ninth Cavalry an honor instead of a duty to be avoided.

Even as he packed to accompany his men to Fort Myer, Henry was jolted by a rude reminder of the power of the "sesesh element" among officers to evoke unrest and distrust. As he sat down at his desk on May 1, he discovered a petition from the men of I Troop complaining of abuse by their new captain, John Guilfoyle. Just returned from the Ghost Dance campaign and a frigid winter standing guard at Pine Ridge, they were in no mood to accept Guilfoyle's references to them as a "damned mob." Naïvely trusting that Major Henry could make things right, they requested that he replace Guilfoyle with Matthias Day, who had earned their trust as a lieutenant in I Troop in the 1880s.

Henry must have winced as he studied the stark reminder of the fragility of the bond uniting men and officers. Anxious to avoid a confrontation that would be detrimental to all involved, he called in the troop's noncommissioned officers and advised them to conform to their captain's views, if at all possible. If they still thought they had a "proper complaint," they must file it through the "proper channels"—meaning, of course, Captain

Guilfoyle. Since Henry could not consider petitions that had not gone through the chain of command, he was destroying it. Convinced that they had "acted in ignorance" without any intent to create a breach of discipline, he deliberately "forgot" the names and faces of the men who had signed the protest.[1]

This would have ended the matter had Henry not felt obliged to inform Guilfoyle. If he hoped the latter would learn the importance of according his men respect, he had underestimated the power of racism. Guilfoyle immediately demanded that the signers of the document be court-martialed.[2]

The affair was all the more perturbing because Guilfoyle was both diligent and efficient. Serious and "military" even as a youth, he may have been the lowest ranked student in West Point's history to serve as the cadet adjutant. This anomaly led to a particularly vicious humiliation. As part of his duties as adjutant, he was given the list of cadet officers for the ensuing six months to read aloud while "standing in front of the battalion." To his embarrassment, he learned that he "was no longer the adjutant, or even a cadet officer—he was merely a private!"[3] As a result of his low academic standing, he was forced to accept an assignment to a black regiment.

As a novice lieutenant in 1881, he proved his gallantry during an arduous month-long pursuit of Nana's Apaches that resulted in three bitterly contested battles. Thereafter, it was his good fortune, as well as that of the buffalo soldiers, to serve an extended term as the regimental quartermaster followed by three years as adjutant. He had won Major Henry's respect while serving as his adjutant during the Ghost Dance campaign. His promotion to captain in early 1891, however, revealed him to be hopelessly racist.

Determined to prevent a morale-shattering court-martial, Henry pointed out that his own unfortunate "inability" to recall the names on the petition he had destroyed, or to remember the name of even one of the men who had presented it to him, would make a conviction impossible. When Guilfoyle remained insistent, Henry told him he would forward no more correspondence on the matter.

After Henry departed for Fort Myer, his successor, infantry major Alfred Smith, reopened the investigation but discovered only that Corporal John Rogers and two other men had circulated the petition. Although he ejected Rogers's family from the post, Smith decided against a court-martial because Henry's destruction of the petition and problem with amnesia concerning the names of the signers would make it impossible to sustain the charges.[4]

In a sense, the clash between Guilfoyle and his troop presaged the demise of the "spirit of true comradeship between the white and the black soldiers" that was displayed during the Ghost Dance campaign. As outlined in a pioneering work by L. D. Reddick, the brief "golden day" of acclaim won by Major Henry's troopers would vanish as a result of a resurgence of racism that was undoing the gains of Reconstruction. Simultaneously, Southern officers were "flocking" into the military "in droves," where they became the "counterpart" of the yeomen whites who "did so much to disfranchise and jim crow Negroes in the South."[5]

Efforts to revive the stereotypical image that African American soldiers were too untrustworthy to be relied on in battle achieved major successes with the de facto closing of West Point to blacks and the refusal to recommend black enlisted men for commissions. African Americans, although proud of the accomplishments of black soldiers, recognized that, if denied any chance of promotion, they were in effect cannon fodder allowed "to do the fighting" while the "white man will get the reward . . . [of] honorable promotion."[6]

In a vigorous protest against military racism, the *New York Age* aimed its sharpest barbs at West Point. Blacks could not expect justice from graduates of "the rankest Charity Cesspool of snobbery and colorphobia, outside the University of Virginia, in the Republic." West Point "snobs and colorphobists, educated upon the charity of the tax-payers of the country," would always "stand between the Afro-American private and the first step to a general's epaulets."[7]

Despite the closing of the officer corps to blacks, it took almost two decades to eradicate all positive images of the black soldiers. Racists received a temporary setback when the hoary (and ridiculous) belief that blacks were immune to tropical diseases allowed them to be assigned major roles in the Spanish-American War and the Filipino Insurrection. Once more, African American troops in general and the Ninth Cavalry in particular were allowed to display their valor.

Four troops from the Ninth participated in the climactic assault on the San Juan Heights on July 1, 1898. By chance, they were placed next to

Theodore Roosevelt's celebrated Rough Riders as part of the First Cavalry Brigade, commanded by the officer who had led them in numerous Indian battles—Lieutenant Colonel Henry Carroll. As fate would have it, many of the regular officers, including Carroll and Lieutenant Colonel John Hamilton and Captain Charles Taylor of the Ninth, were killed or seriously wounded in the engagement, leaving Roosevelt to take the lion's share of the credit.

In the charge itself, the men of the Ninth shared equally in the fighting and, as had happened on prior occasions, received their greatest accolades for coming to the aid of white troops. Among the many battlefield accounts that surfaced in the following weeks (most of which glorified the Rough Riders and ignored the deeds of the regulars), one graphically depicts the tendency to cast black troops in supporting roles and indicates the pride that the men of the Ninth Cavalry took in their achievements:

> The Rough Riders were in a bad position on San Juan Hill at one time . . . [and it was] generally admitted they could not have held their position but for the splendid charge of the Ninth Cavalry to their support.
>
> After the worst of the fighting, a rough rider, finding himself near one of the colored troopers, walked up and grasped his hand, "We've got you fellows to thank for getting us out of a bad hole."
>
> "Dat's all right, boss," said the negro, with a broad grin. "Dat's all right. It's all in de family. We call ourselves de colored rough riders."[8]

For the briefest of periods, the national sense of exuberance evoked by the "liberation" of Cuba was strong enough to accord African Americans a share of the glory. It was during the all too brief afterglow, for example, that Sergeants Benjamin Davis and John Green became the only black enlisted men allowed to earn commissions. Once more, fresh waves of racist propaganda would obliterate the recognition earned in battle. Whites, north and south, soon found that the one issue they could unite on was upholding the color line.

For African Americans, the accomplishments of the black regiments in Cuba were not forgotten. According to Rayford W. Logan, an acclaimed historian who grew to manhood during the early part of the twentieth century, blacks had little to help sustain faith in themselves except their pride in the black regiments. "Many Negro homes had prints of the famous charge of the colored troops up San Juan Hill. They were our Ralph Bunche, Marian Anderson, Joe Louis and Jackie Robinson."[9]

This spark of hope would be all that remained of the recognition earned under such leaders as Major Henry and Colonel Hatch. But George Jordan, Moses Williams, Brent Woods, and hundreds of other veterans of the regiment would retain to their dying day a sense of the pride and dignity they had earned. They had more than proven they were "all that soldiers should be."

Notes

CHAPTER 1

1. In addition to Merritt, the only two former regulars seem to have been Captains Henry Carroll (Third Cavalry) and William Bayard (Fourth Cavalry). Although James Brisbin (First Cavalry) was one of the first officers assigned to the Ninth, he remained absent on recruiting service until his promotion to major (Second Cavalry) in 1868.

2. Captains Francis Dodge, John Bacon, and Henry Carroll and Lieutenants Francis Moore and E. O. Dimmick.

3. These figures have been compiled from data contained in Francis B. Heitman, *Historical Register and Dictionary of the United States Army.*

4. Hutcheson, "The Ninth Regiment of Cavalry," in Theodore F. Rodenbough and W. J. Haskin, *The Army of the United States: Historical Sketches of Staff and Line,* 280–82. Hutcheson seemed unaware that he was contradicting himself when he also wrote offhandedly that "many [black soldiers from the volunteer regiments] took advantage of the opportunity to join the regular service and . . . proved of some value as non-commissioned officers." Hutchinson was an 1884 graduate of West Point who had spent much of his early career in the Ninth Cavalry on staff assignments.

5. Ibid., 283.

6. Bigelow, son of the U.S. ambassador to France during the Civil War, was an 1877 graduate of West Point who had learned to appreciate the valor of the buffalo soldiers while winning accolades as a troop commander during the Geronimo campaigns of 1885 and 1886 and later survived no fewer than four wounds during the storming of San Juan Hill. Among the many works on military history that came from his pen was *The Campaign of Chancellorsville,* which still ranks as one of the best studies of that battle (Constance Altshuler, *Cavalry Yellow and Infantry Blue: Army Officers in Arizona between 1851 and 1886,* 32–33).

7. Bigelow, "The Tenth Regiment of Cavalry," in Rodenbough and Haskin, *Army of the United States,* 290.

8. Annual Report of the Adjutant General, in *Annual Report of the Secretary of War,* 1867, 40th Cong., 2d sess., 1867, S. Exec. Doc. 1, serial 1324, 474.

9. Ninth Cavalry, Final Statements, AGO, RG 94, NA. For the three years, 37 percent of recruits were from Kentucky, 24 percent from Louisiana, 19 percent from the Upper South (Tennessee and North Carolina northward), 18 percent from the Lower South, and 5 percent from the prewar free states. I am indebted for the tabulation of the final statements to my wife, Mildred.

10. Testimony of Lewis Johnson, 13 December 1877, *Texas Border Troubles,* 45th Cong., 2d Sess., 1877, H. Misc. Doc. 64, serial 1820, 142.

11. Ninth Cavalry, Final Statements, AGO, RG 94, NA. While it is possible that younger soldiers might have been somewhat more susceptible to disease, it seems unlikely this would have seriously affected the results of the analysis.

12. Register of Enlistments in the U.S. Army, 1798–1914, Microcopy 233, RG 94, NA. The tabulation is based on a compilation of recruits in Troops D, E, F, G, K, and L of the Ninth Cavalry from 1868 to 1877. In glancing over records of other troops, I have detected individuals who gave their birthplaces as Germany, South America, and New Zealand (Maori?), but none are from Africa.

13. Ninth Cavalry, Register of Enlistments, 1871–1877, M 233, NA.

14. Ibid.

15. Rolls, Eleventh U.S. Census, 1870. L Troop, stationed at Fort Duncan, Texas, was enumerated in Kinney County; E Troop, posted at Fort Concho, in Bexar County.

16. William M. Notson, *Fort Concho Medical History, 1869 to 1872,* 14.

17. Earl F. Stover, *Up from Handymen: The United States Army Chaplaincy, 1865–1920,* 88.

18. *Army and Navy Journal,* 9 September 1876, 74. Although the cavalrymen taught by Mullins were from the Tenth Cavalry instead of the Ninth, his observations undoubtedly held as true of one as the other.

19. All three were listed as being illiterate on the 1870 census rolls.

20. *Army and Navy Journal,* 27 January 1877, 395 (emphasis added). Mullins may have been the only observer to report that the buffalo troopers "gamble little." Most other sources claim that gambling was more frequent among them than among whites. His statement may also reflect the truism that the black soldiers, like many others, responded positively to considerate treatment. Because Mullins expected the best and applauded their efforts to improve, he was rewarded with good behavior.

21. *Army and Navy Journal,* 25 April 1874, 580.

22. Ibid., 17 April 1897, 602.

23. Frank N. Schubert, *Buffalo Soldiers, Braves and the Brass: The Story of Fort Robinson, Nebraska,* 117.

24. *Army and Navy Journal,* 8 August 1882, 91.

25. Ibid.

26. Notson, *Fort Concho Medical History,* 14.

27. *Daily New Mexican* (Santa Fe), 30 January 1876, 2; *Army and Navy Journal,* 20 September 1884, 138.

28. Emily Andrews, "Journal of a Trip from Austin to Fort Davis, 1872," 37, manuscript, Center for American History, University of Texas, Austin.

29. Ibid., 8.

30. Guy Henry, "A Sioux Indian Episode," *Harper's Weekly,* 26 December 1896, 1274.

31. "Extracts of Letters from 2nd Lt. Walter Lowrie Finley, 9th U.S. Cavalry, to his Mother, from New Mexico Territory, 1879 to 1881,"11 November 1879, typescript, New Mexico State Archives, Santa Fe.

32. Theophilus G. Steward, *The Colored Regulars in the United States Army,* 147.

33. Grace B. Paulding, "Memoirs," typescript, William S. Paulding Papers, Library of Congress, cited in Marvin E. Fletcher, *The Black Soldier and Officer in the United States Army, 1891–1917,* 99–100. For more specific descriptions of the balls staged by the Diamond Club of K Troop of the Ninth Cavalry, see pp. 152–53.

34. *Cleveland Gazette,* 9 January 1886.

35. Reynolds J. Burt, "Memories," manuscript, Rickey Collection, U.S. Military History Institute, Carlisle, Pa.

36. Ronald Coleman, "The Buffalo Soldiers: Guardians of the Uintah Frontier, 1886–1901," *Utah Historical Quarterly* 47 (December 1979): 436; *Vernal (Utah) Express,* 5 August 1897.

37. *Army and Navy Journal,* 31 May 1890, 757.

38. *Army and Navy Journal,* 17 October 1896, 113; 31 October 1896, 139.

39. Ibid.

40. Beyer to AAG, 23 October 1877, District of New Mexico, Letters Received (hereafter cited as LR), M 1088, NA; Monroe Lee Billington, *New Mexico's Buffalo Soldiers, 1866–1900,* 53–54.

41. *Army and Navy Journal,* 7 October 1882, 228. Technically, "Africus" was guilty of plagiarism, since he did not cite his source.

42. Ibid., 12 August 1882, 29. An excellent description of the murders of Johnson and Grimke is found in W. S. Nye, *Carbine and Lance: The Story of Old Fort Sill,* 245–46.

43. Ellen McGowan Biddle, *Reminiscences of a Soldier's Wife,* 239.

44. *Annual Report of the Secretary of War, 1868,* 40th Cong., 3d sess., 1868, H. Exec. Doc. 1, Serial 1367, 974–75.

45. *Annual Report of the Secretary of War, 1873,* 43d Cong., 1st sess., 1873, H. Exec. Doc. 1, Serial 1597, 212.

46. *Annual Report of the Secretary of War, 1879,* 46th Cong., 2d sess., 1879, H. Exec. Doc. 1, Serial 1903, 404.

47. *Annual Report of the Secretary of War, 1867,* 40th Cong., 2d sess., 1867, H. Exec. Doc. 1, Serial 1324, 474.

48. *Annual Report of the Secretary of War, 1868,* 40th Cong., 3d sess., 1868, H. Exec. Doc. 1, Serial 1367, 768; *Annual Report of the Secretary of War, 1877,* 45th Cong., 2d sess., 1877, H. Exec. Doc. 1, Serial 1794, 49; *Annual Report of the Secretary of War, 1880,* 46th Cong., 3d sess, 1880, H. Exec. Doc. 1, Serial 1952, 33; *Annual*

Report of the Secretary of War, 1888, 50th Cong., 2d sess., 1888, H. Exec. Doc. 1, Serial 2628, 96.

49. General Court-Martial Orders (hereafter cited as GCMO) 85, 9 December 1883, Dept. of the Missouri, Records of the U.S. Army Continental Command (hereafter cited as USACC), RG 393, NA.

50. Ibid., 38, 11 April 1881; and 4, 8 January 1881.

51. Ibid., 68, 16 June 1881.

52. *Army and Navy Journal*, 19 February 1887, 576. Although the style and tone of the communication are similar to the many unsigned communications to the *Army and Navy Journal* from Major Guy Henry of the Ninth Cavalry, the phrase "men of my company" indicates its author was a captain.

53. Guy Henry, testimony, 14 February 1876, "Reorganization of the Army and the Transfer of the Indian Bureau," 44th Cong., 1st sess., H. Rep. 354, 1876, 189–90. Serial 1760.

54. *Army and Navy Journal*, 11 June 1881, 942.

55. General Order (hereafter cited as GO) 88, Fort Robinson, Nebr., Post Records, 1886–94, USACC, RG 393, NA.

56. Cleveland Gazette, 14 July 1894; Schubert, *Buffalo Soldiers*, 133.

57. Salt Lake City Tribune, 28 October 1886.

58. Coleman, "Buffalo Soldiers," 435.

59. Day to AAAG (Acting Assistant Adjutant General), 19 October 1880, District of New Mexico (hereafter cited as DNM), LR, M 1088, NA.

60. *German-American Advocate* (Hays, Kans.), 27 June 1883.

61. Hatch to AAG, Dept. of the Missouri, 10 April 1878, DNM, Letter Sent (hereafter cited as LS), M1072, NA.

62. William H. Leckie, *The Buffalo Soldiers: A Narrative of the Negro Cavalry in the West*, 71–72.

63. Phillips, "The Negro Regulars: Negro Soldiers in the United States Army, 1866–1900," Ph.D. diss., University of Wisconsin, 1970, cited in Fletcher, *Black Soldier and Officer*, 22–23.

64. *San Antonio Daily Herald*, 5 April 1867.

65. Hatch to AAG, Dept. of the Missouri, 3 September 1879, DNM, LS, M 1072, NA.

CHAPTER 2

1. Paul A. Hutton, *Phil Sheridan and His Army*, index.

2. Richard Wormser, *The Yellow Legs: The Story of the United States Cavalry*, 156.

3. Hatch's birth date has commonly been misstated; 22 April 1832 was the date used in an obituary in the *New York Times* (10 April 1889) and subsequently in Heitman, *Historical Register and Dictionary of the United States Army* and in the *Dictionary of American Biography* (8:392). Although most historians understandably have followed suit, Hatch stated that it was 22 April 1831 (File 5556, Appointment,

Commission, and Personal Files [hereafter cited as ACP], 1875, AGO, RG 94, NA.) The same date was also used by the *Army and Navy Journal* (13 April 1889, 655) and by Richard W. Surby, "Biographical Sketch of Brevet Maj.-Gen Hatch," in *Grierson's Raid and Hatch's Sixty-Four Day March*, 191–95. Surby had served as a clerk for Hatch in 1864 and obviously got his information directly from Hatch or from one of the colonel's aides. Surby's account, ignored by most writers, has the most detailed account of Hatch's early life and is the source for most of this paragraph.

4. Surby, *Grierson's Raid*, 191; Hatch to James Harlan, 21 August 1865, 5556 ACP 1875, AGO, RG 94, NA.

5. *Muscatine (Iowa) Weekly Journal*, 31 May 1861.

6. Lyman B. Pierce, *History of the Second Iowa Cavalry*; *Muscatine (Iowa) Weekly Journal*, 2 and 22 September 1861.

7. Surby, *Grierson's Raid*, 145.

8. Hurlburt to President Lincoln, 19 October 1863, Hatch Personal File, 5556 ACP 1875, AGO, RG 94, NA; Wilson to Colonel John Rawlins, 16 September 1863, *War of the Rebellion: A Compilation of the Official Records of the Union and Confederate Armies* (hereafter cited as OR), Series 1, XXX, Pt. 2, 664.

9. Surby, "Biographical Sketch," 193–94.

10. James H. Wilson, *Under the Old Flag: Recollections of Military Operations in the War for the Union, the Spanish War, and the Boxer Rebellion, etc.*, 2:172–73.

11. Surby, *Grierson's Raid*, 193; Pierce, *Second Iowa Cavalry*, 10.

12. Frederick H. Dyer, *A Compendium of the War of the Rebellion*, 3:1160.

13. *Davenport (Iowa) Daily Gazette*, 28 July 1863 (emphasis in the original).

14. Sherman to Major General S. A. Hurlburt, 16 October 1863, *OR*, Series 1, XXX, part 2, 675.

15. Pierce, *Second Iowa Cavalry*, 77.

16. Sherman to Lincoln, 18 October 1863, and Sherman to Lincoln, 13 January 1864, 5556 ACP 1875, AGO, RG 94, NA. Many newspaper correspondents likewise came to admire Hatch: "The Washington Correspondent for the Cincinnati *Commercial* says: 'The best cavalry officer in our Western army is Colonel Hatch, of the 2d Iowa. He has done more raiding, more fighting, and more railroad burning, than any other man'"; *Muscatine (Iowa) Weekly Journal*, 11 March 1864.

17. Col. James B. Chalmers to Hurlburt, 2 July 1863, OR, Series 2, VI, 86.

18. The reports of Hatch, Breckinridge, and Lieutenants Samuel Lewis and E. L. Barden are in OR, Series 1, XXIV, pt. 2, 674–81.

19. Thomas Jordan and J. P. Pryor, *The Campaigns of Lieut.-Gen. N. B. Forrest*, 531; James Dinkins, "The Capture of Memphis by Gen. Nathan B. Forrest," *Southern Historical Society Papers*, 36:191.

20. Jordan and Pryor, *Campaigns of Forrest*, 531. While Dinkins's description is more detailed, it was written more than thirty years afterward and is primarily an embellishment of the account by Jordan and Pryor. The burning of Oxford is not mentioned by the Union officers in the *OR*, but a contemporary account in the *New York Times* (10 September 1864, 2, col. 4) describes both the burning of the town and

of the Thompson mansion. It does not mention Hatch by name. Jacob Thompson had been secretary of the interior in the Buchanan administration. Ironically, at the time his mansion was destroyed, he was in Canada on a mission to outfit raids across the border into the United States. The raid on Saint Albans, Vermont, was one of the results (*Dictionary of American Biography* 18:459–60). Mrs. Thompson was reputed to be one of the most beautiful belles of the South (*Mississippi: A Guide to the Magnolia State*, 256). According to a Union officer, the day that Oxford was burned, some "Southern newspapers fell into our hands glorying over the burning of Chambersburg, Pa" by Confederate forces (Simeon Fox, *The Seventh Kansas*, 52).

21. Reprinted in *New York Times*, 10 September 1864, 2, col. 4.

22. "Report of Capt. Charles T. Biser, 31 August 1864," *OR*, Series 1, XXXIX, pt. 1, 400; Jordan and Pryor, *Campaigns of Forrest*, 550–51. All citations to the OR are to Series 1.

23. Wilson, Report of the Union Cavalry in the Hood Campaign, 29 September–26 December 1864, *OR*, XLV, pt. 1, 551.

24. Stanley, Report on Operations of Fourth Cavalry Corps, 29 September–13 November 1864, *OR*, XXXIX, pt. 1, 907; Schofield, *Forty-Six Years in the Army*, 252.

25. Wilson, *Under the Old Flag*, 2:51.

26. Surby, *Grierson's Raid*, 232; Pierce, *Second Iowa Cavalry*, 142–45; Wilson to A. J. Badeau, 20 November 1865, James H. Wilson Papers, Library of Congress.

27. Pierce, *Second Iowa Cavalry*, 146.

28. Wilson, *Under the Old Flag*, 2:99–121.

29. Wilson to Brig. Gen. R. W. Johnson, 16 December 1864, 7 P.M., *OR*, XLV, Pt. 2, 222; Wilson, *Under the Old Flag*, 2:173 (emphasis added).

30. Thomas to Maj. Gen. H. W. Halleck, 25 December 1864, OR, XLV, pt. 3, 343.

31. John Allan Wyeth, *That Devil Forrest: Life of General Nathan B. Forrest*, 495. Wyeth based his account on "a manuscript of Colonel E. W. Rucker, in possession of the author."

32. Wilson to Thomas, 17 December 1864, 6 P.M., *OR*, XLV, pt. 2, 238; Lee, Report, 30 January 1865, *OR*, XLV, pt. 1, 690.

33. Stephen Z. Starr, *The Union Cavalry in the Civil War*, 3:555; Stanley F. Horn, *The Decisive Battle of Nashville*, 73–154.

34. Wilson, *Under the Old Flag*, 2:174–75.

35. Hatch to Harlan, 21 August 1865, 5556 ACP 1875, AGO, RG 94, NA.

36. Hatch to Grant, 8 September 1866, ibid.; Grant, endorsement to Rep. Hiram Price to Stanton, 10 January 1866; John Simon, ed., *The Papers of U. S. Grant*, 15:619.

37. Grant to Stanton, 2 August 1866, Simon, *The Papers of U. S. Grant*, 16:274–275. The most likely reason that Merritt, a major general during the war, had to accept a lieutenant colonelcy was that the appointment process favored officers in the volunteers (Hatch) over those in the Regular Army (Merritt).

38. Wilson to A. J. Badeau, 20 November 1865, James H. Wilson Papers, Library of Congress; Wilson, *Under the Old Flag*, 2:174. Although none of Hatch's subordinates in the Ninth Cavalry commented on his verbosity, two civilians describe his

talkativeness at great length. See Christian F. Sommer, "Famous Officers I Have Known: Major General Edward Hatch," *Chronicles of Oklahoma* 5 (March 1927): 185–95; *Meriwether's Weekly* (Memphis, Tenn.), 14 April 1883.

39. *Meriwether's Weekly*, 14 April 1883, 309.

40. William Paulding, "Memoirs," manuscript, U.S. Military History Institute, Carlisle, Pa. (hereafter cited as USMHI), 21–22. Like many colonels in the post-war army, Hatch held the brevet rank of major general and was usually referred to by that title.

41. *Daily New Mexican* (Santa Fe), 2 October 1881.

42. A. W. Corliss, Diaries, 1887–89, manuscript, Denver Public Library.

43. Frederick Benteen, Affidavit, 14 January 1888, Olmsted, Court-Martial Proceedings, RR 2868, Records of the Judge Advocate General (hereafter cited as JAG), RG 153, NA.

44. Corliss, Diaries; Frank Schubert, *Buffalo Soldiers, Braves and the Brass: The Story of Fort Robinson, Nebraska*, 96.

45. *Meriwether's Weekly*, 14 April 1883, 309.

46. Circular no. 47, 31 December 1885, Dept. of the Platte, USACC, RG 393, NA.

47. Hatch to AAG, Dept. of the Missouri, 1 October 1877, DNM, LS, M 1072, NA.

48. *Annual Report of the Secretary of War, 1877*, 45th Cong., 2d sess., 1877, H. Exec. Doc. 1, Serial 1794, 43.

49. Hatch to AAG, Dept. of the Missouri, 30 March 1878, DNM, LS, 149, M 1072, NA.

50. Mackenzie to Pope, 24 November 1879, Mackenzie Papers, Gilcrease Museum, Tulsa; for an account of the Ute Commission's negotiations with the Utes, see Robert Emmitt, *The Last War Trail: The Utes and the Settlement of Colorado*, 249–84.

51. *Thirty-Four* (Las Cruces, N.Mex.), 28 April 1880; *Cimarron (New Mexico) News and Press*, 15 April 1880.

52. *The Daily Optic* (Las Vegas, N.Mex.), 19 February 1881; *Thirty-Four*, 6 October 1880. The charge that Hatch was a member of the Santa Fe Ring is almost certainly false. Most likely it was a political ploy by a Democratic newspaper to discredit the Republicans in the upcoming election.

53. Swaine to AAG, Dept. of the Missouri, 5 February 1879, DNM, LS, M 1072, NA.

54. For a detailed account of this episode, see pp. 203–205.

55. *Army and Navy Journal*, 7 February 1885, 543.

56. Reprinted in ibid., 10 January 1885, 461.

57. Copied in ibid., 4 February 1888, 542.

58. *Kansas City Times*, 14 April 1888, 6. There was understandably considerable dissatisfaction concerning the politics that were involved in selecting brigadiers. As one officer pointed out, the system forced officers to become "personal rivals," encouraged them "to be jealous of, and unjust to, each other," and "mortified and injured" the "competency of a large number" to give a "doubtful advantage" to a favored few. *Army and Navy Journal*, 9 October 1886, 217.

59. Corliss, Diaries, entry for 27 November 1888.

60. *Kansas City Times*, 26 November 1887, 6.

61. Corliss, Diaries, entry for 15 March 1889; *Kansas City Times*, 20 March 1889, 6; *Army and Navy Journal*, 30 March 1889, 625.

62. Brisbin to AAG, Dept. of the Platte, 5556 ACP 1875, AGO, RG 94, NA.

63. *Kansas City Times*, 17 April 1889, 6; *Army and Navy Journal*, 20 April 1889, 677.

64. *Army and Navy Journal*, 1 February 1890, 438.

65. Ibid., 7 June 1890, 771.

CHAPTER 3

1. Cusack to Merritt, 15 September 1868, filed with 6663 PRD 1894, AGO, RG 94, NA.

2. *San Antonio Daily Herald*, September 20, 29, 1868.

3. William H. Leckie, *The Buffalo Soldiers: A Narrative of the Negro Cavalry in the West*, 90–91; *San Antonio Daily Express*, 12 December 1869; *Tri-Weekly State Gazette* (Austin), 19 November 1869. The reference to Van Dorn refers to the Wichita expedition of the spring of 1859, which culminated in the Battle of Crooked Creek. William Y. Chalfant, *Without Quarter: The Wichita Expedition and the Fight on Crooked Creek*, 80–91.

4. Carroll to Mackenzie, 13 October 1869, M1647, AGO, 1870, LR, M 619, NA.

5. See Albee personal file, 1318 ACP 1872, AGO, RG 94, NA.

6. Morrow to the AAAG, Sub-District of the Presidio, June 1, 1870, T279, AGO 1870, M 619, NA. Also see Leckie, *Buffalo Soldiers*, 92–93.

7. Macpills to Ed., 10 November 1869, in *San Antonio Daily Herald*, 18 November 1869.

8. Ibid., 11 June 1870; 23 May 1871.

9. Leckie, *Buffalo Soldiers*, 101–102; Clayton W. Williams, *Texas' Last Frontier: Fort Stockton and the Trans-Pecos, 1861–1895*, 156–57; Zenas R. Bliss, "Reminiscences," typescript, Center for American History, Austin, 5:175–83.

10. *San Antonio Daily Herald*, 3 May 1872; *Army and Navy Journal*, 13 May 1872, 646. Marcella Serra, the wife of one of the teamsters killed at Howard's Well and who escaped her Indian captors during the fight, stated that there were two blacks; Serra, Affidavit, 2780 AGO 1872, M 666, NA.

11. For an extreme expression of these fears, see Elizabeth Custer, *Tenting on the Plains, or General Custer in Kansas and Texas*, 321–22.

12. Fifth Military District, General Order No. 10, 20 January 1870, USACC, RG 393, NA.

13. Erwin N. Thompson, "The Negro Soldiers on the Frontier: A Fort Davis Case Study," *Journal of the West* 7 (April 1968): 231. Although Annie Williams was described as white by the post surgeon, there is no mention of her race or color in Pedee's court-martial records (Martin Pedee, Court-Martial Proceedings, PP 2809, JAG, RG 153, NA).

14. Court-Martial Proceedings, PP 2809, JAG, RG 153, NA (emphasis in the original); C. C. Augur to Commanding Officer, Fort Davis, 29 November 1872, Dept. of Texas, LS, M 1114, NA.

15. Mrs. Orsemus Boyd recalled a similar incident when, while her husband was absent, she was awakened by a drunken soldier (white) entering her apartment. She called out and he left quietly. Had she shot and killed him, it would undoubtedly have been considered an attempted rape. Mrs. Orsemus Boyd, *Cavalry Life in Tent and Field*, 168–69. Talliaferro, a native of the District of Columbia, had just completed his third year of duty in the Ninth.

16. Andrews to AAG, 21 November 1872, Dept. of Texas, LR, USACC, RG 393, NA; Thompson, "The Negro Soldiers on the Frontier," 231–32.

17. Augur to C.O., Fort Davis, 29 November 1872, Dept. of Texas, LS, M 1114, NA.

18. Copied in *San Antonio Daily Herald*, 5 December 1872.

19. Charles Kenner, "Guardians in Blue: The United States Cavalry and the Growth of the Texas Cattle Industry," *Journal of the West* 34 (January 1995): 46–54.

20. Merritt to AAG, Dept. of Texas, reprinted in *Army and Navy Journal*, 27 December 1873, 308.

21. *The Nation* 8 (30 October 1873): 201–202. This is the earliest use of the term *buffalo soldier* that I have observed in the press.

22. Leckie, *Buffalo Soldiers*, 128–29.

23. For an extreme example of the degree to which historians have ignored the role of the buffalo soldiers in the Red River War, see James L. Haley's *The Buffalo War: The History of the Red River Indian Uprising of 1874*, 190–91. Haley devotes exactly one paragraph to Buell's expedition and inexplicably states that the destruction of the Indian camps was done by "five companies of the 11th infantry."

24. Leckie, *Buffalo Soldiers*, 108–109; *San Antonio Daily Herald*, 17 February 1875. Technically, Fort Ringgold was designated as Ringgold Barracks until 1878.

25. *San Antonio Daily Herald*, 17 and 20 February 1875.

26. The correspondence in this matter is found in File 1653 AGO 1875, M 666, NA. Also see Leckie, *Buffalo Soldiers*, 108–12.

27. *New York Times*, 20 August 1877, 1, col. 6; *Army and Navy Journal*, 25 August 1877, 41.

28. *Army and Navy Journal*, 25 August 1877, 41.

29. Ord to AAG, 20 May 1875, Dept. of Texas, LS, RG 393, NA; Ord to Shafter, 12 September 1877, Dept. of Texas, LS, M 1114, NA.

30. *New York Times*, 21 January 1876, 1, col. 1.

31. *Army and Navy Journal*, 14 April 1876, 582; 17 June 1876, 728. Also see Ord's testimony before the House Military Affairs Committee in 44th Cong., 1st sess., H. Rep. 354, Serial 1760, 44–46; and in 45th Cong., 2d sess., 1878, H. Misc. Doc. 64, Serial 1820, 103. For evidence of Ord's desire to eliminate the black regiments, see Arlen Fowler, *The Black Infantry in the West, 1869–1891*, 121.

32. Clitz to H. H. Banning, 11 February 1876, 44th Cong., 1st sess., H. Rep. 354, 94, Serial 1820.

33. Anderson to Subcommittee on the Reorganization of the Army, 2 January 1878, 45th Cong., 2d sess., 1878, H. Misc. Doc. 56, 152.

34. Ibid., 115.

35. *San Antonio Herald*, 7 March 1876.

36. Ibid., 15 April 1876, 646.

37. Ibid.

38. *Army and Navy Journal*, 13 May 1876, 646 (emphasis added).

39. Ibid., 17 June 1876, 728.

40. For a description of the confusion of E. K. Davies with E. J. Davis, see Fowler, *Black Infantry in the West*, 119–22.

41. E. K. Davies to B. F. Butler, 7 December 1876, LR, 510 AGO 1877, M 666, NA. Also quoted in Fowler, *Black Infantry in the West*, 19.

42. Cameron to Benjamin Butler, 6 February 1877, LR, 510 AGO 1877, M 666, NA.

43. *Army and Navy Journal*, 7 February 1874, 406; Sherman, testimony, 8 February 1877, 45th Cong., 2d sess., 1878, H. Misc. Doc. 64, Serial 1818, 20.

44. Fowler, *Black Infantry in the West*, 122–25; Walter P. Webb and H. Bailey Carroll, eds., *The Handbook of Texas*, 2:162–63.

45. "Report of the Recruiting Service from October 1, 1875, to October 1, 1876," in *Annual Report of the Secretary of War, 1876*, 72–73.

46. "Recapitulations of the Ninth U.S. Cavalry (Colored) for July and August 1877 (The weakest regiment of cavalry)," "Reorganization of the Army," 45th Cong., 2d sess., 1878, H. Misc. Doc. 56, Serial 1818, 312–18.

47. Hatch, testimony, 8 March 1876, "Reorganization of the Army," 44th Cong., 2d sess., 1876, H. Rep. 354, Serial 1709, 63; Hatch to House Committee on Military Affairs, 8 January 1878, "Reorganization of the Army," 45th Cong., 2d Sess, 1878, H. Misc. Doc. 56, Serial 1818, 90.

48. The classic account of newspaper coverage of the Indian wars is Oliver Knight, *Following the Indian Wars: The Story of the Newspaper Correspondents among the Indian Campaigners*.

49. *Army and Navy Journal*, 4 October 1879, 217.

50. For an excellent summary of the Ute outbreak, see Robert M. Utley, *Frontier Regulars: The United States Army and the Indians, 1866–1891*, 332–42.

51. Dodge filed a detailed report to the assistant adjutant general on 27 October 1879. It is printed in 46th Cong., 2d sess., 1880, S. Exec. Doc. 31, serial 1882, 105–108.

52. Letter filed from Rawlins to *New York Herald*, 19 October 1879, copied in *Army and Navy Journal*, 25 October 1879, 226.

53. Ibid. *Moke*, needless to say, was one of the many Victorian derogatory terms applied to blacks.

54. Ibid.

55. *Army and Navy Journal*, 1 November 1879, 238.

56. Dodge report to AAG, 27 October 1879, 46th Cong., 2d sess., 1880, S. Exec. Doc. 31, serial 1882, 105–108.

57. Leckie, *Buffalo Soldiers*, 208; Walter F. Beyer and Oscar F. Keydel, *Deeds of Valor: How America's Civil War Heroes Won the Congressional Medal of Honor*, 2:258.

58. Johnson to Dodge, 23 March, 1890, in Documents Relating to . . . Blacks Awarded the Congressional Medal of Honor, 1863–98 (hereafter cited as Documents Relating to the Medal of Honor), M 929, NA. Hughes and Parker's comments are in the form of endorsements to Johnson's letter. Dodge, always cold and reserved, simply "concurred in" Hughes's statement.

59. *Army and Navy Journal*, 25 October 1879, 226.

60. *Rocky Mountain News*, 22 October 1879.

CHAPTER 4

1. *Army and Navy Journal*, January 5, 1895, 307; January 12, 1895, 325; "Obituary of Edward Miles Heyl," *Circular No. 5, Series of 1895*, 9 March 1895, Military Order of the Loyal Legion of the United States, Pennsylvania Commandery. None of Heyl's Civil War feats are recorded in the *OR*.

2. Robert G. Carter, *On the Border with Mackenzie, or Winning West Texas from the Comanches*, 169–86. Ironically, Carter's devastating depiction of Heyl's cowardice has even gotten the latter a considerable notoriety in Western novels and popular history. See Terry C. Johnston, *Shadow Riders: The Southern Plains Uprising, 1873*, 80–91, and John Edward Weems, *Death Song: The Last of the Indian Wars*, 149–55.

3. Robert G. Carter, "Diary," manuscript, Panhandle-Plains Historical Museum, Canyon, Texas. A copy of the passages referring to Heyl was provided by Byron Price of the Cowboy Hall of Fame, Oklahoma City; Parker to Wayne Parker, 7 October 1876, Papers of James Parker, U.S. Military Academy Library, West Point.

4. James Parker, *Old Army Memories, 1872–1918*, 18.

5. *Army and Navy Journal*, 8 January 1887, 468; Heyl, Personal Statement, 4143 ACP 1873, AGO, RG 94, NA.

6. Regimental History Committee, *History of the Third Pennsylvania Cavalry in the American Civil War, 1861–1865*, 422.

7. Ibid., 247.

8. Ibid., 174–79.

9. Heyl's application, letters of recommendation, and a copy of the November exam with his answers thereto are found in 4143 ACP 1873, AGO, RG 94, NA.

10. Testimony of Private James Williams, 8 June 1867, Private Irving Charles, Court-Martial Proceedings, PP 2301, JAG, RG 153, NA. For conditions in the Louisiana camps, see William H. Leckie, *The Buffalo Soldiers: A Narrative of the Negro Cavalry in the West*, 9–11.

11. Ibid.

12. *San Antonio Daily Herald*, 5 April 1867.

13. The events of 8 and 9 April are reconstructed from the testimony of many members of E Troop, especially Irving Charles, James Williams, and Lewis Brown. A very good description of the mutiny is in Byron Price, "Mutiny at San Pedro Springs," *By Valor and Arms* 3 (Spring 1975): 31–33.

14. Heyl, testimony, 8 June 1867, Private Irving Charles, Court-Martial Proceedings, PP 2301, JAG, RG 153, NA.

15. Charles, testimony, 9 June 1867, Private Irving Charles, Court-Martial Proceedings, PP 2301, JAG, RG 153, NA.

16. In addition to the testimony of the participants, the mutiny is also discussed fully in Joseph Holt to U. S. Grant, 2 October 1867, John Simon, ed., *Papers of U. S. Grant*, 18:309–14.

17. *San Antonio Daily Herald*, 12 and 26 April, 1 May 1867.

18. Proceedings and reviews of cases of Irving Charles and Charles Woods, Holt to Grant, 2 October 1867, Simon, *Papers of U. S. Grant*, 18:489–94; *Army and Navy Journal*, 14 September 1867, 54; 9 November 1867, 182. Ninth Cavalry, Muster Rolls, Troop E, March–April 1868, AGO, RG 94, NA. Biographical material on Judge Advocate General Holt is from Ezra J. Warner, *Generals in Blue: Lives of the Union Commanders*, 232–33, and Mark Boatner III, *The Civil War Dictionary*, 406.

19. Hatch's list of Specification and Charges against Heyl, undated and minus a file number, is found in Ninth Cavalry, Miscellaneous Regimental Letters, Organizational Records, RG 391, NA; Price, "Mutiny at San Pedro Springs," 33; Ninth Cavalry, Regimental Returns, M 744, NA.

20. Post Adjutant to Lt. Fred Kendall, 29 March 1870, Fort McKavett, Post Records, LS, USACC, RG 393, NA; Personal file of Smith, 2839 ACP 1891, AGO, RG 94, NA.

21. Ninth Cavalry, Regimental Returns, 1867–68, M 744, NA; Ninth Cavalry, Muster Rolls, Troop E, AGO, RG 94, NA, 1867–79. The only three original recruits still in the troop in 1879 were James Williams, William Howard, and Zekiel Sykes. Howard and Sykes retired as thirty-year men in the late 1890s.

22. One officer, J. Lee Humfreville, was cashiered for his barbaric mistreatment of men of his troop. See pp. 000–00.

23. Boatner, *Civil War Dictionary*, 317; Frohock, Autobiographical Sketch, 3229 ACP 1877, AGO, RG 94, NA.

24. Frohock, Court-Martial Proceedings, PP 867, JAG, RG 153, NA.

25. Hatch, testimony, 21 January 1874, J. Lee Humfreville, Court-Martial Proceedings, PP 3768, JAG, RG 153, NA.

26. Summary of the Military Record of Francis S. Davidson, January 1903, filed with 3991 ACP 1875, AGO, RG 94, NA.

27. E. O. C. Ord to JAG, 9 September 1875, Dept. of Texas, LS, M 1114, NA; GCMO 93, 15 November 1875, JAG, RG 153, NA.

28. GCMO 54, 19 November 1873, JAG, RG 153, NA. Radetzki's court-martial also involved charges concerning his "conspiring to defraud the government." The evidence was so flimsy and suspicious that one has to believe his main offense was fraternization. Captain Hooker was on leave at the time of the trial and had nothing to do with it.

CHAPTER 5

1. Francis B. Heitman, *Historical Register and Dictionary of the United States Army*, vol. 1; *New York Times*, 20 February 1908, 7, col. 6; *Army and Navy Journal*, 22 February 1908, 649.

2. Hatch to AAG, 2 February 1870, LR, M493, AGO 1870, M 619, NA; William H. Leckie, *Buffalo Soldiers: A Narrative of the Negro Cavalry in the West*, 90–91.

3. Ninth Cavalry, Regimental Returns, 1872–73, M 744, NA.

4. Ibid.; Register of Enlistments in the U.S. Army, 1798–1914, M 233, NA.

5. Register of Enlistments in the U.S. Army, 1798–1914, M233, NA.

6. "Report of the Surgeon General," in *Annual Report of the Secretary of War, 1872*, House Ex. Doc. 1, 42d Cong., 3 sess., 1872, Serial 1558, 300–301. By the end of the decade the discrepancy in death rates had largely disappeared. In 1879, for example, the death rate from disease among white troops was seven per thousand, and among blacks, eight per thousand ("Report of the Surgeon General," in *Annual Report of the Secretary of War, 1879*, 46th Cong., 2d sess., 1879, H. Exec. Doc. 1, Serial 1903, 404).

7. Heitman, *Historical Register*, vol. 1, s.v. "Peter J. A. Cleary." Heitman incorrectly states that Cleary was born on the island of Malta. See also *Who Was Who in America, 1897–1942*, 229.

8. Dodge to AAG, Dept. of Texas, 14 July 1873, File 3250 AGO 1873, M 666, NA; Fort Stockton, Post Returns, January–June 1873, M 617, NA.

9. Dodge to AAG, Dept. of Texas, 14 July 1873, File 3250 AGO 1873, M 666, NA; George Roberts et al., Court-Martial Proceedings, PP 3542, JAG, RG 153, NA; Bliss, "Reminiscences," typescript, Barker Texas History Center, Austin, 5:163–65. The only previous secondary treatment of this matter is Clayton W. Williams, "A Threatened Mutiny of Soldiers at Fort Stockton in 1873 Resulted in Penitentiary Sentences of Five to Fifteen Years," *West Texas Historical Association Year Book* 57 (October 1976): 78–83.

10. Unless otherwise cited, all information on the affair is from "Petition to the Adjutant General, U.S.A., from the undersigned . . . ," n.d., filed with George Roberts et al., Court-Martial Proceedings, PP 3542, JAG, RG 153, NA.

11. Bliss, "Reminiscences," 5:163.

12. Ibid.; "Petition to the Adjutant General," PP 3542, JAG, RG 153, NA. Despite Ritzius's brutal actions in this instance, he had a long and distinguished career in the military. Under his command Company K, Twenty-fifth Infantry, stationed at Fort Missoula, Montana, in 1890, "stood at the head of the regiment in drill, discipline, and efficiency." In 1885 it had been the first black company to win the prestigious, service-wide Nevada Trophy for marksmanship. In 1890, when I and K Companies of the Twenty-fifth were disbanded as part of a reorganization plan, Ritzius was described as "one of the most popular officers of the regiment, and expressions of regret at leaving the kindly, though firm, rule of their beloved commander, are heard on all sides among the enlisted men" (*Army and Navy Journal*, 6 September 1890, 26).

13. This scenario is based chiefly on the round robin message addressed to Adjutant General, U.S.A., and testimony of various enlisted men given in the court-martial of George Roberts. It also incorporates data from Major Bliss's recollections.

14. *Army and Navy Journal,* 16 August 1873, 15.

15. Bliss, "Reminiscences," 5:153.

16. Augur to Sheridan, 5 August 1873, LR, 3250 AGO 1873, M 666, NA.

17. Ibid.

18. Holloman later enlisted in the Ninth Cavalry, where he served as first sergeant of A Troop until 1898 (Frank N. Schubert, ed., *On the Trail of the Buffalo Soldier: Biographies of African Americans in the U.S. Army, 1866–1917,* 206).

19. Dodge to AAG, 14 July 1873, DT, LR, RG 393, NA; Williams, "Threatened Mutiny," 80.

20. Bliss, "Reminiscences," 5:64; Williams, "Threatened Mutiny," 80–81.

21. Williams, "Threatened Mutiny," 80–81.

22. GCMO 62, in Roberts, Court-Martial Proceedings, PP 3542, JAG, RG153, NA.

23. *Army and Navy Journal,* 3 November 1873, 197.

24. Fort Stockton, Post Returns, August–November, 1873, M 617, NA.

25. Bliss, "Reminiscences," 5:165 (emphasis added).

CHAPTER 6

1. Wayne R. Austerman, "Ranald S. Mackenzie and the Early Years on the Border," *Red River Valley Historical Review* 5 (Summer, 1980): 71–79.

2. Lt. George Albee to Post Adjutant, Fort Concho, 1 July 1869, Fort Concho, Post Records, LR, USACC, RG 393, NA; Capt. George Gamble to AAG, 20 September 1870, Fifth Military District, LR, M 1188, NA.

3. John Warren Hunter, "'Humpy' Jackson Wreaks Vengeance," *Frontier Times* 1 (December, 1923): 1.

4. Margaret Bierschale, *Fort McKavett, Texas: Post on the San Saba,* 63.

5. Albee to AAAG, 1 July 1869, Fort McKavett, Post Records, USACC, RG 393, NA; Special Order 69, ibid.

6. Hunter, "'Humpy' Jackson Wreaks Vengeance," 3.

7. Mackenzie to AAG, 3 February 1870, Fifth Military District, LR, M 1188, NA; William M. Notson, *Fort Concho Medical History, 1869 to 1872,* 24; Proceedings of an Investigation held before Bvt. Brig. Gen. R. S. Mackenzie, 10 February 1870, enclosed with Mackenzie to AAG, 15 February 1870, Fifth Military District, LR, M 1188, NA (hereafter cited as Proceedings).

8. Ninth Cavalry, Final Statements, AGO, RG 94, NA; Ninth Cavalry, Muster Rolls, Troop F, 1866–70, ibid.

9. David Brown, Affidavit, Proceedings.

10. Based on affidavits from several residents of Menard, 9 February 1870, Proceedings.

11. Brown, Affidavit, Proceedings.

12. Ibid. Brown's identification of Mrs. Jackson as the person who shot Marshall is suspect, since it is doubtful that he observed the shooting.

13. Elizabeth Jackson, Affidavit, Fort McKavett, 10 February 1870, Proceedings.

14. Mackenzie to AAG, 15 February 1870, Fifth Military District, LR, M 1188, NA; James Jackson, Affidavit, Fort McKavett, 10 February 1870, ibid.

15. Mackenzie to AAG, ibid.; *San Antonio Daily Herald*, 10 February 1870.

16. Hunter, "'Humpy' Jackson Wreaks Revenge," 2.

17. N. H. Pierce, *The Free State of Menard*, 103, 139.

18. J. Evetts Haley, *Fort Concho and the Texas Frontier*, 268.

19. *San Angelo Standard Times*, Golden Anniversary Edition, 23 July 1936, 11.

20. Pierce, *Free State of Menard*, 103, 139; Hunter, "'Humpy' Jackson Wreaks Revenge," 3–4.

21. Ibid., 3.

22. Ibid., 6–7.

23. Mackenzie to Reynolds, 29 March 1870, Fifth Military District, LR, M 1193, NA.

24. Mackenzie to AAG, 15 March 1870, ibid.

25. Allen, Affidavit, 14 April 1870, in Mackenzie to AAG, 15 April 1870, ibid.

26. Carroll to Mackenzie, 20 April 1870, Fort McKavett, LR, USACC, RG 393, NA.

27. Haley, *Fort Concho and the Texas Frontier*, 270.

28. *San Antonio Daily Herald*, 8 July, 18 November, 29 November 1869.

29. Hunter, "'Humpy' Jackson Wreaks Revenge," 3.

CHAPTER 7

1. Post Surgeon L. A. Edwards to Sherman, 15 April 1874, personal file, Captain Ambrose E. Hooker, 4872 ACP 1873, AGO, RG 94, NA.

2. This sketch of Hooker's pre-1867 career is based on data in his personal file, 4872 ACP 1873, AGO, RG 94, NA. See especially Post Surgeon L. A. Edwards to Sherman, 15 April 1874, and William C. Kibbe to Sherman, 20 January 1874. According to Heitman, Hooker received a Brevet Brigadier Generalship on 13 March 1865. Correspondence in his ACP records, however, show that while he was nominated for the rank of brevet brigadier general of volunteers on 9 May 1868, this honorary rank was disapproved because he had "served throughout the war in California without special distinction."

3. Ninth Cavalry, Regimental Returns, 1867–69, M 744, NA. For Hooker's marriage, see Constance Altshuler, *Cavalry Yellow and Infantry Blue: Army Officers in Arizona between 1851 and 1886*, 169–70.

4. Ninth Cavalry, Regimental Returns, 1868, M 744, NA; Ninth Cavalry, Muster Rolls, Troop E, 1868, AGO, RG 94, NA.

5. Hooker, Statement, 10 December 1879, in Charles Steelhammer to AAG, 11 December 1879, 2434, DNM, LR, M 1088, NA.

6. Company E, Ninth Cavalry, Muster Roll for November–December 1869, AGO, RG 94, NA. Hooker's being "badly wounded" was reported in the first accounts of the battle reaching San Antonio (*San Antonio Daily Herald*, 11 November 1869), but he is not mentioned in any of the official reports of the battle. The Fort Concho post returns and the regimental returns also mention no injury.

7. Paul H. Carlson, *"Pecos Bill": A Military Biography of William R. Shafter*, 22–33.

8. Ibid., 40–41; William Notson, *Fort Concho Medical History, 1869 to 1872*, 24.

9. Shafter to Colonel J. J. Reynolds, 17 February 1870, Dept. of Texas, LR, C 253, RG 393, NA; Shafter to Reynolds, 19 February 1870, Fort Concho, LS, RG 393, NA.

10. GCMO 47, 6 September 1870, Dept. of Texas, in 4872 ACP 1873, AGO, RG 94, NA; Notson, *Fort Concho Medical History*, 24.

11. Notson, *Fort Concho Medical History*, 24.

12. Ninth Cavalry, Regimental Returns, 1871, M 744, NA; Ninth Cavalry, Muster Rolls, Troop E, 1871, AGO, RG 94, NA.

13. The endorsements and petitions are contained in 4872 ACF 1873, AGO, RG 94, NA.

14. William H. Leckie, "Buell's Campaign," *Red River Valley Historical Review* 3 (April 1979): 186–93; Leckie, *The Buffalo Soldiers*, 123–24.

15. Statements of Private Evan Shanklin and Hooker, December 1879, Steelhammer to AAG, 11 December 1879, 2434, DNM, LR, M 1088, NA (hereafter cited as Steelhammer Report).

16. For a summation of Hooker's problems with Osburne in 1876 and his subsequent arrest, see Hatch to AAG, Dept. of the Missouri, 2 June 1876, DNM, LS, M 1072, NA.

17. Steelhammer Report. For another account of Hooker's treatment of his men, see Monroe Lee Billington, *New Mexico's Buffalo Soldiers, 1866–1900*, 192–99.

18. Steelhammer Report.

19. Edward M. Coffman, *The Old Army: A Portrait of the American Army in Peacetime, 1784–1898*, 221; "Charges and Specifications against F. Beers Taylor," 1345, DNM, LR, M 1088, NA.

20. Hooker to AAG, 27 May 1878, LR, DNM, M 1088, NA.

21. Ibid.; Hatch to Taylor, 14 September 1878, DNM, LS, M 1072, NA.

22. Statement of Ambrose Hooker, 10 December 1879, in Steelhammer Report, 11 December 1879, DNM, LR, M 1088, NA.

23. Statement of George Nance, 10 December 1879, and statement of Allen Foster, both in ibid.

24. Peters statement, 10 December 1879; George Nance Statement; and John Howard statement, all in ibid.

25. Ninth Cavalry, Final Statements, AGO, RG 94, NA.

26. Steelhammer Report, 11 December 1879, DNM, LR, M 1088, NA.

27. Statements of Private Arthur Kent, Corporal Richard Williams, and Hartley Crawford, 10 December 1879, in ibid.

28. Ninth Cavalry, Regimental Returns, August–September, 1879, M 744, NA.

29. Steelhammer Report, 11 December 1879, DNM, LR, M 1088, NA.

30. Register of Enlistments, M 233, NA; Ninth Cavalry, Muster Rolls, Troop E, AGO, RG 94, NA.

31. Ninth Cavalry, Regimental Returns, January–April 1880, M 744, NA.

32. E. Montoya to Wallace, 23 March 1880, OIA, N 180, 1880, LR, NMS, M 234; AAG to C.O., Fort Wingate, 13 March 1880, 146, DNM, LS, M 1072, NA.

33. Hatch, Special Field Order, 15 April 1880, published in *Army and Navy Journal*, 15 May 1880, 832.

34. There is a great deal of correspondence concerning Hooker in the files of the District of New Mexico. See especially AAG, Dept. of the Missouri, to Hatch, 2 March 1880, DNM, LR, M 1088, NA; Hatch to AAG, Dept. of the Missouri, 1 September 1880, DNM, LS, M 1072, NA; and AAG, Dept. of the Missouri, to Hatch, 13 September 1880, DNM, LR, M 1088, NA.

35. Surgeon A. W. Sewell to Hatch, 19 July 1880, 4872 ACP 1873, AGO, RG 94, NA.

36. H. P. Cutter, Ass't Judge Advocate General, "Report upon the Record of the Trial of First Lt. F. B. Taylor," 11 September 1881, F. B. Taylor, Court-Martial Proceedings, QQ 2640, JAG, RG 153, NA. Cutter sums up in detail the testimony in the court-martial of Hockins as well as that of Taylor.

37. Ibid.

38. Ibid.; GCMO 60, 4 November 1881, Dept. of the Missouri, USACC, RG 393, NA.

39. Col. P. T. Swaine to AAG, 28 January 1883, 4872 ACP 1873, AGO, RG 94, NA.

40. *Army and Navy Journal*, 31 March, 1883, 514.

CHAPTER 8

1. Marvin E. Fletcher, *The Black Soldier and Officer in the United States Army, 1891–1917*, 20 n. 22.

2. Arrietta Henry to Adj't Gen., 14 September 1869, 1118 CB 1864, AGO, RG 94, NA; Guy V. Henry to Adj't Gen., 30 August 1870, ibid.

3. Richard I. Dodge, *Our Wild Indians: Thirty-Three Years' Personal Experience among the Red Men of the Great West*, 510.

4. *Army and Navy Journal*, 30 January 1875, 383; Cyrus Brady, *Indian Fights and Fighters*, 343–45.

5. Lt. H. R. Lemly, "The Fight on the Rosebud," June 20, 1876, in *The Papers of the Order of Indian Wars*, 14–15. Lemly, Crook's adjutant for the campaign, was stationed with Henry's battalion during the fight, whereas the more oft-cited eyewitness accounts by Anson Mills, John F. Finerty, and John Bourke were all written by men stationed elsewhere on the battlefield.

6. Brady, *Indian Fights and Fighters*, 346–47.

7. Anson Mills, "On the Battle of the Rosebud," in *Papers of the Order of the Indian Wars*, 10; John F. Finerty, *War-Path and Bivouac: The Big Horn and Yellowstone Expedition*, 135.

8. Quoted in Martin E. Schmidt, ed., *General George Crook: His Autobiography*, 196–97; see M. L. Meriwether, "A Week on the Frontier," *Meriwether's Weekly*, 14 April 1883, 308, for Henry's description of the litter on which he was returned to Fort Russell.

9. Henry, testimony, 14 February 1876, "Reorganization of the Army and Transfer of the Indian Bureau," 44th Cong., 2d sess., 1876, H. Rep. 354, 1760, 189–90.

10. *Army and Navy Journal*, 23 July 1881, 1081, and 30 July 1881, 1092.

11. Ibid., 24 September 1881, 163.

12. Ibid., 19 November 1881, 337.

13. Ibid., 5 November 1881, 301.

14. Ibid.

15. Ibid., 7 January 1882, 495.

16. Ibid., 11 February 1882, 612; 22 April 1882, 833.

17. Ibid., 7 October 1882, 219.

18. Ibid., 24 March 1882, 772. Lieutenant Powell apparently recovered from his "demoralization." He remained in the Ninth Cavalry for another twelve years.

19. Henry to Armstrong, 23 November 1883, printed in the *Southern Workman*, date not given, and reprinted in the *Army and Navy Journal*, 26 January 1884, 525.

20. *Army and Navy Journal*, 24 March 1883, 772.

21. Ibid., 22 September 1883, 154. In actuality, with an efficiency rating of 90.55, the Fort Sill garrison ranked number three in the nation (ibid., 29 December 1883, 422).

22. Ibid., 7 February 1885, 544.

23. Ibid., 28 February 1885, 613.

24. Ibid., 1 November 1884, 261.

25. Ibid., 7 September 1889, 20. This statement, like all of Henry's commentaries, was printed anonymously. Its style and content, however, are too similar to all the other commentaries that emanated from wherever he happened to be in the 1880s to leave any doubt concerning his authorship.

26. Guy V. Henry, Jr., "Memoirs," Typescript, 12, USMHI.

27. Ibid.

28. *Army and Navy Journal*, 9 November 1889, 207; 30 November 1889, 271.

29. Ibid., 6 December 1890, 243. The style and content of this is so obviously Henry's that one must conclude he signed it "Infantry" to help obscure his identity.

30. Untitled or dated newspaper clipping, Box 5, Scrap Books, Guy V. Henry, Sr., Papers, USMHI.

31. Unsigned communication from Harney Springs (Henry's camp in the Badlands, 26 December 1890, *Army and Navy Journal*, 3 January 1891, 319. Although Henry quite likely was the author of this dispatch, his other writings on the subject assert no claims of credit for the Sioux abandonment of their positions in the "Stronghold" and return to the agency. Guy Henry, "An Incident of the Sioux Wars," *Harper's Weekly* 40, 26 December 1896, 1273–75.

32. Henry, "Incident of the Sioux Wars," 1273; undated article from the *Washington Star*, Guy V. Henry, Sr., Papers, Scrap Books, Box 5, USMHI; Brady, *Indian Fights and Fighters*, 352–53.

33. John S. Loud, Endorsement to Wilson to Adjt. Gen., 21 August 1891, in Documents Relating to the Medal of Honor, M 929, NA; Frank N. Schubert, *On the Trail of the Buffalo Soldier: Biographies of African Americans in the U.S. Army, 1866–1917*, 480.

34. Uncredited newspaper clipping, "How the Ninth Horse and Its Commander Won Glory," in Box 5, Scrap Books, Guy V. Henry, Sr., Papers, USMHI. In the attack on the wagon train, the Ninth suffered its last fatality in Indian combat. Private Charles Haywood of D Troop was approached by a rider dressed in the uniform of an Indian scout. The two met, shook hands, and had begun conversing when, at such close range as to leave powder burns, the presumed scout shot him in full sight of his comrades (*Chicago Tribune*, 2 January 1891, p. 4).

35. *Rocky Mountain News*, 3 January 1891, 2; *Chicago Inter-Ocean*, undated extract quoted in *Army and Navy Journal*, 17 January 1891, 355; *Harper's Weekly* 35 (7 February 1891): 106.

36. *Army and Navy Journal*, 17 January 1891, 355. In private correspondence Henry was not as deprecating concerning the rescue. A few days after this exchange, he wrote General O. O. Howard that his men had saved the Seventh Cavalry from "heavy losses—if not more" (Henry to Howard, 26 January 1891, O. O. Howard Papers, Bowdoin College, Brunswick, Maine).

37. *Army and Navy Journal*, 17 January 1891, 355.

38. Remington, "The Final Review," *Harper's Weekly* 35 (7 February 1891): 106.

39. *Army and Navy Journal*, 7 February 1891, 409.

40. Ibid., 7 March 1891, 471.

41. Ibid., 14 February 1891, 427; 20 March 1891, 508. The detachment from the Ninth was rotated, two troops at a time, between Pine Ridge and Fort Robinson.

42. Uncredited, undated newspaper clipping, Box 5, Scrap Books, Guy V. Henry, Sr., Papers, USMHI.

43. Ibid.

44. *Army and Navy Journal*, 4 April 1891, 546.

45. Henry to Schofield, 6 January 1891, Schofield Papers, Library of Congress; Henry to Howard, 26 January 1891, and Howard to Henry, 31 January 1891, O. O. Howard Papers, Bowdoin College.

46. *Cleveland Gazette*, 14 February 1891.

47. Ibid., 14 February 1891; Jack Foner, *The American Soldier between Two Wars: Army Life and Reforms, 1865–1898*, 143; *Army and Navy Journal*, 25 April 1891, 602.

48. *Army and Navy Journal*, 7 March 1891, 471 (emphasis added).

49. Ibid., 2 May 1891, 612; *Cleveland Gazette*, 14 February 1891.

50. *New York Times*, 2 May 1891, 1, col. 3; 15 June 1891, 1, col. 6. First Lieutenant P. A. Batteus was also transferred from K Troop to I, most likely as a concession to consistency. His replacement, "White Hat" Charlie Taylor, had gained acclaim as the commander of the Sioux Indian scouts during the recent war. With no inside pull, Taylor's well-earned assignment was the one happy result of Schofield's heavy-handed actions.

51. Undated clipping, *Washington Post*, in Box 5, Scrap Books, Guy V. Henry, Sr., Papers, USMHI.

52. *Philadelphia Inquirer*, 28 June 1891, clipping in ibid.

53. Guy V. Henry, Jr., "Memoirs," 16, Typescript, Guy V. Henry, Jr., Papers, USMHI.

54. Undated clipping, Guy V. Henry, Sr., Papers, USMHI.

55. Undated clipping from the *Washington Evening Star*, ibid.

56. Henry to Officers and Enlisted Men of the Ninth Cavalry, n.d., printed in *Army and Navy Journal*, 5 March 1892, 484.

57. Ibid., 16 April 1892, 591.

58. Undated clipping from the *Washington Evening Star*, Guy V. Henry, Sr., Papers, Box 2, USMHI.

59. Lewis to Editor, *Illinois Record* (Springfield), 25 June 1898, in William B. Gatewood, *"Smoked Yankees" and the Struggle for Empire: Letters from Negro Soldiers, 1898–1902*, 36.

60. The correspondence concerning Henry's fatal illness is contained in his personal file, 1118 CB 1864, M 1064, NA.

61. The correspondence concerning the Guy V. Henry Garrison's part in the funeral is contained in the Guy V. Henry, Sr., Papers, USMHI; extensive coverage of the funeral is contained in the *Washington Post*, 28 October 1899, 4; 30 October 1899, 3; and 31 October 1899, 1, and in the *Washington Evening Star*, 30 October 1899, 3, and 31 October, 1899, 1.

62. Mrs. Guy V. Henry Correspondence Folder, Box 2, Guy V. Henry, Sr., Papers, USMHI.

63. Brown to Mrs. Henry, 14 November 1899, ibid.

64. Guy V. Henry, Jr., "Memoirs," 6–16, Typescript, USMHI.

CHAPTER 9

1. *Army and Navy Journal*, 11 June 1892, 729.

2. Charles Parker, Autobiographical Sketch, n.d., 1590 ACP 1871, AGO, RG 94, NA.

3. Burroughs to AAG, 20 December 1866, and Parker to Trumbull, 25 January 1871, both in ibid.

4. For a description of Murphy's establishment, see Clayton W. Williams, *Texas' Last Frontier: Fort Stockton and the Trans-Pecos, 1861–1895*, 106: "Murphy had three large buildings at an excellent location. The buildings, each 130 feet long, formed three sides of a square, and on the fourth side there was a wall about 12 feet high."

5. Parker to E. J. Davis, 3 January 1872, 1590 ACP 1871, AGO, RG 94, NA. Parker wrote that Lieutenant G. W. Bosworth had reported he had heard Hatch threaten "to ruin every officer who visited the house of Mr. Murphy socially."

6. Parker to Davis, 3 January 1872, and Reynolds to Hames Cobum, Chairman, House Military Affairs Committee, 20 March 1874, ibid.

7. Only ten captains of cavalry were declared "supernumerary." The only other one from the Ninth was William Bayard of C Troop, who had been court-martialed twice during his four years of service.

8. Morrow to "My dear Parker," 3 February 1871, 1590 ACP 1871, AGO, RG 94, NA.

9. Mackenzie to Parker, 19 February 1871, and Mackenzie to Babcock, 19 February 1871, ibid.

10. For Frohock's Civil War record, see Mark M. Boatner III, *The Civil War Dictionary*, 317; Frohock, Biographical Sketch, 3229 ACP 1877, AGO, RG 94, NA.

11. William H. Leckie (*The Buffalo Soldiers: A Narrative of the Negro Cavalry in the West*, 85) states that the attacking force consisted of "Kickapoos, Lipans, Mexicans, and white renegades." A more detailed account provided the *Santa Fe Weekly New Mexican* (29 November 1879) by regimental adjutant John S. Loud describes them as Comanches.

12. See p. 80.

13. Humfreville's record is found in 1838 ACP 1874, AGO, RG 94, NA.

14. This is not as freakish as it might seem. Well over 90 percent of all recruits for the Ninth Cavalry in 1869 were enlisted in the last ten days of September and the month of October. The majority of these were enrolled in Washington, D.C. Two of the new sergeants, William Jenifer and George Washington, had prior enlistments in the infantry.

15. This is based on a study of K Troop's muster rolls, 1870–74 (AGO, RG 94, NA). None of Frohock's appointees remained in the military long enough to be included in Frank N. Schubert's encyclopedic *On The Trail of the Buffalo Soldier: Biographies of African Americans in the U.S. Army, 1816–1917.*

16. The court-martial proceedings and sentences of Slaughter, Williams, Imes, and Comer are in PP 3034, JAG, RG 153, NA.

17. An excellent summation of the testimony is found in Judge Advocate General Joseph Holt to the secretary of war, 21 March 1874, in PP 3768, JAG, RG 153, NA.

18. Buchanan, testimony, 30 January 1873, Rufus Slaughter, Court-Martial Proceedings, PP 3034, JAG, RG 153, NA.

19. It is extremely difficult to juxtapose Slaughter's troubles with those of Williams. Much of Humfreville's testimony is in sharp conflict with that of all of the enlisted men, including his hand-picked sergeants.

20. Rufus Slaughter, Court-Martial Proceedings, PP 3037, JAG, RG 153, NA.

21. Testimony of Private George Duval, 365, Humfreville, Court-Martial Proceedings, PP 3678, JAG, RG 153, NA. There was some discrepancy among witnesses concerning whether the Slaughter affair or the Williams affair occurred first.

22. Ibid.

23. Floyd, testimony, ibid.; Comer, Statement, Court-Martial Proceedings, PP 3087, JAG, RG 153, NA.

24. GCMO 23, 3 April 1874, AGO, filed with PP 3768, JAG, RG 153, NA. Only two officers in the Ninth testified in defense of Humfreville. One was Lieutenant Ballard

Humphrey, who had been assigned to K after the infamous march to Fort Clark; the other was Colonel Hatch. Hatch was also the only member of the regiment to sign a petition to the secretary of war recommending clemency. In 1881, Humfreville mustered enough political support to get his dismissal revoked—upon the condition that he not apply to reassume his commission (GCMO 29, 4 February 1881, AGO, ibid.).

25. Ninth Cavalry, Muster Rolls, Troop K, AGO, RG 94, NA. Most of the men involved in the disturbances of 15 December 1872 fared much worse than did Williams and Slaughter. Edward Tucker and Levi Comer, two of the prisoners chained to the wagons, deserted in separate incidents during the last half of 1875. Imes took a disability discharge in early 1875. Wade completed his term but did not reenlist.

26. Jordan, testimony, Humfreville, Court-Martial Proceedings, PP 3768, JAG, RG 153, NA.

27. R. J. Reeves to Hatch, 26 July 1879, DNM, LR, M 1088, NA.

28. This place is not to be confused with the Tularosa southwest of Fort Stanton at the foot of the Sacramento Mountains. Although most writers spell it Tularosa, the military documents and maps of the nineteenth century use Tulerosa for it. It is located a few miles east of the Arizona line and roughly eighty miles north of Silver City.

29. Walter F. Beyer and Oscar F. Keydel, *Deeds of Valor: How America's Civil War Heroes Won the Congressional Medal of Honor*, 2:274–75.

30. Hatch to AAG, Dept. of the Missouri, 21 May 1880, 6058 AGO 1879, M 666, NA; Beyer and Keydel, *Deeds of Valor*, 2:274–75; Preston Amos, *Above and Beyond in the West: Black Medal of Honor Winners, 1870–1890*, 17–18.

31. George Jordan, "Soldier's Record, etc.," Documents Relating to the Medal of Honor, M 929, NA.

32. Beyer and Keydel, *Deeds of Valor*, 2:276–77; Amos, *Above and Beyond*, 20–22; Parker to Adjt. Gen., 14 March 1890, 11891 PRD 1893, AGO, RG 94, NA. Hatch's official report on this engagement is exceedingly vague: "I had, on the first [of August], ordered 'K' Troop of the cavalry to Rio Quemado to head him [Nana] off, which resulted in a sharp fight with loss to us of two killed and four wounded in the company." Although he later stated almost incidentally that Parker was one of several officers who "displayed energy and courage and are entitled to honorable mention," his negligence cost Parker a brevet years later. It is also likely that Lieutenant Loud, his regimental adjutant, wrote the report and forwarded it without Hatch's seeing it. The day on which it was sent from Santa Fe, Hatch was at Ojo Caliente coordinating operations against Nana. That was also the day on which he would have learned by courier of the death of his wife in Washington, D.C. (Loud to AAG, DM, 3 October 1881, DNM, LS, M 1072, NA; *Daily New Mexican*, 2 October 1881).

33. Ninth Cavalry, Final Statements, AGO, RG 94, NA.

34. Ninth Cavalry, Muster Rolls, Troop K, 1881–82, AGO, RG 94, NA.

35. "The Case of Charles Parker," 1590 ACP 1871, AGO, RG 94, NA. Probably the main reason for Schofield's denial was the lack of a description of the battle at Carrizo

Canyon. In reporting battles, both Hatch and Major Morrow were exceedingly sketchy. Rarely were officers, and almost never enlisted men, singled out by name for their actions. Parker's brief description of the battle in support of Medals of Honor for Jordan and Shaw is practically the only account of the fight.

36. Parker to Adjt. Gen., 31 August 1882, 1590 ACP 1871, AGO, RG 94, NA.

37. *Cheyenne Leader*, 20 October 1887 (emphasis added).

38. The description is based on transcripts of the courts-martial of Privates Henry Chase, Lee Irving, and George Pumphrey. All are filed under RR 2389, JAG, RG 153, NA.

39. Ibid.

40. Hatch to AGO, 20 April 1888, Fort Robinson, LS, USACC, RG 393, NA.

41. Schubert, *On the Trail of the Buffalo Soldiers*, 86, 217, 342; Theophilus G. Steward, *The Colored Regulars in the United States Army*, 280.

42. Ninth Cavalry, Regimental Returns, 1887, M 744, NA; Parker, Efficiency Report, 1 May 1890, 1590 ACP 1871, AGO, RG 94, NA.

43. Tilford to AAG, Dept. of the Platte, 11 September 1890, Fort Robinson, LS, USACC, RG 393, NA; A. W. Corliss, Diaries, 1884–90, entry for 28 August 1890, manuscript, Denver Public Library, Denver, Colorado.

44. Veterans' Administration File 296,801, NA; Mary Brent Parker to Hatch, 27 October 1880, with endorsements; Parker to Adjt. Gen. R. C. Drum, 12 December 1880, both with 1590 ACP 1871, AGO, RG 94, NA. The Parkers made a brief, unsuccessful try at a reconciliation at Fort Robinson, Nebraska, in 1889. She was living in New York City at the time of his death. The men in Troop K, apparently thinking he had divorced her and unaware of any close relatives, were unsuccessful "claimants to his estate" (Captain Henry Wright, endorsement on Mary Parker to Adjt. Gen., 7 December 1891, ibid.).

45. *Army and Navy Journal*, 10 January 1885, 471; *Kansas City Times*, 19 December 1884, 5.

46. Corliss, Diaries, entries of July 18 and July 27, 1889, manuscript, Denver Public Library..

47. *Army and Navy Journal*, 25 January 1890, 463.

48. Undated clipping from *Washington Post*, 1891, Scrapbooks, Box 5, Guy Henry Collection, USMHI.

49. Ninth Cavalry, Muster Rolls, Troop K, 1890, AGO, RG 94, NA.

50. Parker's death certificate and medical history are contained in Veterans' Administration Pension File 296,801, NA.

51. *Army and Navy Journal*, 11 June 1892, 729.

52. Amos, *Above and Beyond*, 22.

53. Jordan to AGO, 1 October 1900, 34516 AGO 1900, General Records Office, AGO, RG 94, NA. The adjutant general's response is indicated on the endorsement page.

54. Jordan to Adjt. Gen., 19 October 1904, 934489, Document File, AGO, RG 94, NA.

55. William Anderson, Monthly Chaplain's Report, November 1, 1904, quoted in Schubert, *On The Trail of the Buffalo Soldier,* 249. Also see 946848, Documents File, AGO, RG 94, NA.

CHAPTER 10

1. Stance gave his age as nineteen when he enlisted in 1866. The age he gave for all subsequent enlistments, however, indicates he was only eighteen at the time.

2. Unless otherwise indicated, personal data come from Registers of Enlistments in the United States Army, 1798–1914, M 233, NA, and from Ninth Cavalry, Muster Rolls, Troop F, AGO, RG 94, NA.

3. Biographical data on Carroll come from his personal file in the AGO, 3754 ACP 1874, RG 94, NA.

4. James Dayes, Court-Martial Proceedings, QQ 1568, JAG, RG 153, NA; Hatch to AAG, Dept. of the Missouri, 2 January 1880, DNM, LS, M 1072, NA.

5. Ninth Cavalry, Muster Rolls, F Troop, 1867–68, AGO, RG 94, NA.

6. Ninth Cavalry, Muster Rolls, F Troop, 1869, AGO, RG 94, NA; Ninth Cavalry, Regimental Returns, M 744, NA.

7. GO 2 and 9, 20 January and 5 March 1870, Fort McKavett, Post Records, USACC, RG 393, NA.

8. SO 73, 19 May 1870, Fort McKavett, Post Records, USACC, RG 393, NA.

9. Stance to Post Adjutant, 26 May 1870, Documents Relating to the Medal of Honor, M 929, NA. The repeating Spencer carbines, so effective in the Civil War, were soon afterwards replaced by single-shot, breech-loading Springfields.

10. Stance to Adjt. Gen., 24 July 1870, ibid.

11. *Army and Navy Journal,* 2 December 1871, 247.

12. These tabulations are derived from data in *The Medal of Honor of the United States Army,* 210–34. An exception was the awarding of medals to three black Seminole scouts attached to Mackenzie's Fourth Cavalry.

13. Ninth Cavalry, Muster Rolls, Troop F, March/April 1871, AGO, RG 94, NA.

14. Ninth Cavalry, Muster Rolls, Troop M, 1869–71, ibid. In Heyl's defense it should be noted that he and his command had performed admirably in the Indian campaigns of 1869 and consistently received better than average evaluations when inspected by superiors.

15. The description of the imbroglio between Stance and Green is based upon the court-martial record. Green's version of the encounter was seconded by Sergeants Monroe Houston and Horace Johnson and by Private William Smith (Emanuel Stance, Court-Martial Proceedings, 3 January 1873, PP 2295, JAG, RG 153, NA).

16. Ibid.

17. GCMO 55, 15 December 1873, Dept. of Texas, General Orders, RG 393, NA; Ninth Cavalry, Muster Rolls, Troop M, 1873, AGO, RG 94, NA.

18. Ninth Cavalry, Muster Rolls, Troop M, 1874–78, AGO, RG 94, NA; Ninth Cavalry, Regimental Returns, 1874–78, M 744, NA; Register of Enlistments, M 233, NA.

19. This account is based on the testimony given in a court of inquiry hastily convened by Lieutenant Colonel N. A. M. Dudley to investigate Lieutenant French's bizarre behavior. Although several townspeople, including Houston Chapman, testified, the court cleared French of all charges. Reading between the lines, one might conclude that while French was prone to alcoholism and exceedingly hot-tempered, he was also a young second lieutenant trying to ingratiate himself with Dudley. The most significant parts of the court of inquiry are quoted in Frederick Nolan, *The Lincoln County War: A Documentary History*, 362–69. A more detailed description of Lieutenant French's alcoholism is found in Frederick Nolan, "The Men at Fort Stanton," *Quarterly of the National Association for Outlaw and Lawman History* 18 (October 1994): 37–38.

20. This account is based primarily on testimony by Washington, Horton, and McCampbell in Emanuel Stance, Court-Martial Proceedings, 11 January 1879, QQ 1019, JAG, RG 153, NA. See also GCMO 17, 24 February 1879, Dept. of the Missouri, USACC, RG 393, NA.

21. Ninth Cavalry, Muster Rolls, Troop M, 1879–87, AGO, RG 94, NA. Before leaving the career of Sergeant Washington, I should note that he was the victim of inexcusable carelessness by Colonel Hatch's staff, most likely Assistant Adjutant General John Guilfoyle. On 7 October 1887, Sergeant Frank Washington, B Troop, was shot and killed by one of his men, Private Thomas Collins (Ninth Cavalry, Muster Rolls, Troop B, AGO, RG 94, NA; Fort Duchesne, Medical History, October 1887). On 10 December 1887 the *Army and Navy Journal* identified the slain sergeant as George Washington of M Troop. No correction was made. The *Army and Navy Journal* error led to an error in relation to Washington's death in Frank N. Schubert, ed., *On the Trail of the Buffalo Soldier: Biographies of African Americans in the U.S. Army, 1866–1917*, 451.

22. GCMO 17, 24 February 1873, Dept. of the Missouri, USACC, RG 393, NA (emphasis added).

23. Moses Green, Court-Martial Proceedings, 14 September 1883, QQ 4302, RG 153, JAG, NA.

24. Ninth Cavalry, Regimental Returns, 1885–87, M 744, NA; Corliss, Diaries, Entry for 1 June 1887; Stedman's life and career are described in detail by his old West Point classmate and friend Captain Robert G. Carter in *Fifty-second Annual Report of the Association of Graduates of the U.S. Military Academy*, 110–15.

25. Unless otherwise indicated, all information on McAnaney comes from file 3651 ACP 1886, AGO, RG 94, NA.

26. Private George Pumphrey, Court-Martial Proceedings, 16 March 1887, RR 2389, JAG, RG 153, NA.

27. Ninth Cavalry, Regimental Returns, 1886, M 744, NA; Surgeon E. L. Swift to the Surgeon General, U.S.A., 3 April 1894, 3651 ACP 1886, AGO, RG 94, NA. Although he

died on 2 April 1894, of a massive overdose of opiates and sulphonal, the *Army and Navy Journal* charitably attributed it to "blood poisoning."

28. Schubert, *On the Trail of the Buffalo Soldier*, 400; Ninth Cavalry, Regimental Returns, September–December 1887, M 744, NA; *Cleveland Gazette*, 27 November 1886.

29. GCMO 43, 21 May 1887, Dept. of the Platte, USACC, RG 393, NA.

30. GCMO 44, 24 May 1887, ibid.

31. Ninth Cavalry, Regimental Returns, 1887, M 744, NA.

32. Frank N. Schubert, *Buffalo Soldiers, Braves and the Brass: The Story of Fort Robinson, Nebraska*, 84–85. Also see Frank Schubert, "The Violent World of Emanuel Stance, Fort Robinson, 1887," *Nebraska History* 55 (Summer 1974): 203–19.

33. GCMO 140 and 156, Fort Robinson, Post Records, 1887, USACC, RG 393, NA; Schubert, *On the Trail of the Buffalo Soldier*, 252.

34. Although a brief item in the *Army and Navy Journal* stated that Stedman "gave his troop a ball" (30 July 1887, 6), it seems more likely that the reverse was the case. Captain A. W. Corliss noted in his diary on July 7 that "the colored soldiers" gave a ball the previous night (Corliss, Diaries, manuscript, Denver Public Library).

35. Thomas Richardson, Court-Martial Proceedings, September 5, 1887, RR 2626, and William Young, September 28, 1887, Court-Martial Proceedings, RR 2670, JAG, RG 153, NA. Richardson was returned to duty in early 1888 and immediately defied authority again, saying, "This post is not a fit place for a man to serve. . . . I don't like soldiering and I would rather be in prison . . . than to be here." He was accommodated with a dishonorable discharge plus four years in prison (Thomas Richardson, Court-Martial Proceedings, 16 February 1888, RR 2862, JAG, RG 153, NA). It would have been better for all concerned if men such as Young and Richardson had been permitted to sever their military ties before committing serious breaches of discipline.

36. Schubert, *Buffalo Soldiers, Braves and the Brass*, 85; Schubert, *On the Trail of the Buffalo Soldier*, 453.

37. Schubert, *Buffalo Soldiers, Braves, and the Brass*, 84; *Cleveland Gazette*, 24 July 1886; Schubert, *On the Trail of the Buffalo Soldier*, 284–85.

38. Schubert, *On the Trail of the Buffalo Soldier*, 284–85; Fort Robinson, Post Order no. 143, 22 August 1886, USACC, RG 393, NA.

39. Garrard to Adjt. Gen., Ninth Cavalry, 10 October 1887, 4384 ACP 1887, AGO, RG 94, NA. Unlike most of the West Point graduates in the Ninth Cavalry, Garrard had graduated near the top of his class in 1874. After serving twelve years in the artillery, he transferred to the Ninth in 1886. Alexander, previously unassigned to any troop, was temporarily assigned to Troop F on October 7 (Ninth Cavalry, Regimental Returns, M 744, NA).

40. The most complete account of Stance's death is in Schubert's "The Violent World of Emanuel Stance"; the basic source materials for the events surrounding his death are found in Schubert's *On the Trail of the Buffalo Soldier*, 400. In addition to being very limited, the records concerning his death contain bizarre conflicts. According to Schubert, an entry in the Post Medical History states that he was found

dead by the side of the road; a letter written by the same post surgeon stated that he died in the post hospital.

41. *Army and Navy Journal*, 31 December 1887, 442; Schubert, *On the Trail of the Buffalo Soldier*, 400.

42. *Army and Navy Journal*, 14 January 1888, 482.

43. Corliss, Diaries, entry for 25 December 1887; *Army and Navy Journal*, 14 January 1888, 482. A detailed account of the investigation of his death is contained in Schubert, "The Violent World of Emanuel Stance."

44. GCMO 16, 16 February 1887, Dept. of the Platte, USACC, RG 393, NA; Ninth Cavalry, Regimental Returns, July 1887, M 744, NA.

45. For a description of the arrest and confinement of Milds, see Schubert, *Buffalo Soldiers, Braves and the Brass*, 86–87.

46. Mann, Interview by Don Rickey, Jr., February 1965, manuscript, Nebraska State Historical Society, Lincoln.

CHAPTER 11

1. "Colonel Edmond Shriber's Inspector-General's Report on the Military Posts in Texas, November 1872–January 1873," *Southwestern Historical Quarterly* 67 (April 1967): 571.

2. Anderson to AAG, 14 November 1869, M60, DT, 1869, M 1193, NA.

3. See above, p. 15.

4. Ninth Cavalry, Muster Rolls, Troop L, 1867–89, AGO, RG 94, NA.

5. Ninth Cavalry, Regimental Returns, 1869–70, M 744, NA; Ninth Cavalry, Muster Rolls, Troop L, 1869–71, AGO, RG 94, NA.

6. 1729 ACP 1871, AGO, RG 94, NA; Walter P. Webb, ed., *The Handbook of Texas*, 1:482.

7. Ninth Cavalry, Regimental Returns, 1870–71, M 744, NA; Ninth Cavalry, Muster Rolls, Troop L, 1870–71, AGO, RG 94, NA.

8. GCMO 81, 17 December 1870, Dept. of Texas, USACC, RG 393, NA.

9. Ibid. It was not unusual for a single court-martial order to cover several cases.

10. Ninth Cavalry, Regimental Returns, 1871–72, M 744, NA; Ninth Cavalry, Muster Rolls, Troop L, 1871–72, AGO, RG 94, NA.

11. Moore's personal file, M1382 CB 1866, M 1064, NA.

12. Ninth Cavalry, Muster Rolls, Troop L, 1872–74, AGO, RG 94, NA.

13. Ibid.; GCMO 23, 7 March 1879, Dept. of the Missouri, USACC, RG 393, NA.

14. Ninth Cavalry, Muster Rolls, Troop L, September–December 1875, AGO, RG 94, NA.

15. Monroe Lee Billington, *New Mexico's Buffalo Soldiers, 1866–1900*, 63–67; Chris Emmett, *Fort Union and the Winning of the Southwest*, 370–73; Frank Springer, Deposition, 9 August 1878, in Frank Angel, Report of Investigation of Governor S. T. Axtel, 3 October 1878, Interior Department, Appointment Division, LR, Territorial

Governors of New Mexico, 1845–78, RG 98, NA; *The Weekly New Mexican*, 21 September 1878.

16. William A. Keleher, *The Maxwell Land Grant: A New Mexico Item*, 69; *Daily New Mexican*, 10 October 1876.

17. Moore to C.O., Fort Union, 25 March 1876, DNM, LR, M 1088, NA.

18. Ninth Cavalry, Muster Rolls, Troop L, 1876, AGO, RG 94, NA.

19. Springer, Deposition, 9 August 1878.

20. *Daily New Mexican*, 21 September 1878.

21. Springer, Deposition, 9 August 1878; *Daily New Mexican*, 25 March 1876, 21 September 1878; *Rocky Mountain News*, 26 March 1876; *Leader* (Las Animas, Colo.), 31 March 1876; Moore to C.O., Fort Union, 25 March 1876, DNM, LR, M 1088, NA. An extremely garbled account of the shooting is found in Keleher, *Maxwell Land Grant*, 69.

22. *News and Press* (Cimarron, N.Mex.), 11 August 1876, copied in *Daily New Mexican*, 16 August 1876; *Daily New Mexican*, 13 September 1876.

23. *Leader* (Las Animas, Colo.), 19 January 1877.

24. Ibid., 1 and 8 September 1876.

25. Ibid., 1 September, 15 December 1876; *Colorado Chieftan* (Pueblo), 3 February 1877.

26. Articles in the DeBusk Memorial, 2:145–49, CWA Manuscripts, Colorado Historical Society, Denver (hereafter cited as Articles in the DeBusk Memorial).

27. *Leader*, 1 September 1876; Articles in the DeBusk Memorial, 147.

28. *Leader*, 1 September 1876; Ninth Cavalry, Muster Rolls, Troop L, August–October 1876, AGO, RG 94, NA.

29. *Leader*, 1 September 1876.

30. Ibid., 8 September 1876.

31. Ibid., 6 and 27 October 1876.

32. Ninth Cavalry, Muster Rolls, Troop L, 1872–77, AGO, RG 94, NA. During Major Albert Morrow's campaign against Victorio, Jones was one of six enlisted men to be cited for bravery in a battle on September 29, 1879 (Morrow to AAAG, 5 November 1879, DNM, LR, M 1088, NA).

33. *Leader*, 8 and 15 December 1876, 2 February 1877.

34. *Daily New Mexican*, 30 December 1876.

35. *Leader*, 2 January 1877.

36. Ibid., 26 December 1876.

37. Ibid., 22 December 1876; 5, 12, and 26 January 1877; *Colorado Chieftain*, 3 February 1877; Chuck Parsons, *Clay Allison: Portrait of a Shootist*, 30–31.

38. *Leader*, 19 and 26 January 1877.

39. Ibid., 12 and 19 January 1876.

40. Ibid., 19 January 1877.

41. Ibid.

42. Ibid., 26 January 1877.

43. Ibid.

44. *Leader,* 1 September 1877; Articles in the DeBusk Memorial, 149.

45. *Leader,* 2 February 1877; *Colorado Chieftain,* 3 February 1877; Articles in the DeBusk Memorial, 149.

46. Ninth Cavalry, Muster Rolls, Troop L, January –February 1877, AGO, RG 94, NA.

47. Ninth Cavalry, Final Statements, and Muster Rolls, Troop L, ibid.

48. The figures have been tabulated by an analysis of data in the regimental returns for the period indicated.

49. *Army and Navy Journal,* 7 May 1887, 816.

50. *Cleveland Gazette,* 6 November 1886. Although the correspondent signed himself, J. J. J., he almost certainly was Sergeant James J. Jackson.

51. Merritt, endorsement on Moore to Adjt. Gen., 2 August 1890; and Moore, Efficiency Report, 15 December 1891, both in 1382 CB 1866, M 1064, NA.

52. Moore to Adjt. Gen., 2 August 1890, ibid.

53. *Army and Navy Journal,* 11 May 1895, 608.

54. *Kansas City Times,* 15 June 1894, 3.

55. *Crawford Tribune,* 15 April 1916, quoted in Frank N. Schubert, ed., *On the Trail of the Buffalo Soldier: Biographies of African Americans in the U.S. Army, 1866–1917,* 289.

CHAPTER 12

1. Register of Delinquencies and Special Order 183, 22 October 1875, USMA Archives, West Point.

2. Major General Charles P. Summerall, "Report of Engagements and Part Taken by 1st Lieut. M. W. Day, 9th Cavalry," Typescript, Personal files, 2710, Matthias W. Day, Cullom Library, USMA, West Point. (Summerall compiled the report for Day's widow, who forwarded it to West Point.)

3. "The Ninth Cavalry," no author, n.d., typescript, U.S. Cavalry Association Library, Fort Riley, Kansas.

4. Both William H. Leckie (*The Buffalo Soldiers: A Narrative of the Negro Cavalry in the West,* 210–11) and Monroe Lee Billington (*New Mexico's Buffalo Soldiers, 1866–1900,* 90–91) mistakenly place Lieutenant Colonel N. A. M. Dudley in command of Dawson's force. Leckie relied upon an erroneous preliminary report (Loud to AAG, Dept. of the Missouri, 23 September 1879, 6058 AGO 1879, M 666, NA). Dan L. Thrapp (*Victorio and the Mimbres Apaches,* 240–41) bases his accurate but sketchy account on Major Morrow to AAAG, DNM, 5 November 1879, 6058 AGO 1879, M 666, NA. Morrow enclosed the reports of Dawson and Beyer, but they are missing from the files. Day's account is in Day to Captain C. W. Taylor, 22 August 1894, 7598 AGO 1894, General Correspondence (Document) File, 1890–1914, AGO, RG 94, NA.

5. Day to Taylor, 22 August 1894; Preston E. Amos, *Above and Beyond in the West: Black Medal of Honor Winners, 1870–1890,* 13. Freeland remained in the

hospital until he received a medical discharge 2 June 1882; *Grant County Herald* (Silver City, N.Mex.), 29 September 1879; Ninth Cavalry, Regimental Returns, 1879–82, M 744, NA.

6. Charles Gatewood, "Campaigning against Victorio in 1879," *The Great Divide*, April 1894, 102; *Grant County Herald*, 29 September 1879; Ninth Cavalry, Final Statements, AGO, RG 94, NA.

7. Gatewood, "Campaigning against Victorio," 103.

8. Ibid.

9. *Thirty-Four* (Las Cruces, N.Mex.), 3 December 1879.

10. Summerall, "Report of Engagements and Part Taken by 1st Lieut. M. W. Day."

11. Ibid. Colonel Hatch confirmed the value of the mountain howitzers in fighting Apaches: "The Indians select mountains for their fighting ground, and positions almost impregnable, usually throwing up stone rifle pits where nature has not furnished them and skillfully devising loopholes. The Mountain Howitzer is simply invaluable. It knocks the stone fortifications down readily and, served by an old artillery man, Lieut. [Ballard S.] Humphrey . . . the accuracy of its fire is something wonderful" (Hatch to AAG, Dept. of the Missouri, 25 February 1880, 6058 AGO 1879, M 666, NA). Lieutenant French, afflicted by frequent bouts of alcoholism and facing a possible court-martial, may have in a sense committed suicide. Lieutenant Walter Finley, also present at the fight in the San Mateos, wrote that French "did not come into camp with the rest of the troops, but staid [sic] out on the mountain. After . . . about half an hour we heard three shots fired. . . . In the morning they found his body, he had evidently been shot from behind as he was climbing a hill" (Finley, "Extracts of Letters . . . to his Mother," January 20, 1880, typescript, New Mexico Archives).

12. Summerall, "Report of Engagements of . . . 1st Lieut. M. W. Day," manuscript, file 2780, Cullom Library, USMA, West Point.

13. Correspondent to editor, 20 October 1881, *Army and Navy Journal*, 5 November 1881, 301.

14. *Wichita (Kansas) Eagle*, 12 April 1883.

15. Leckie, *Buffalo Soldiers*, 250; C. C. Rister, *Land Hunger: David L. Payne and the Oklahoma Boomers*, 40; Fish, "Memories of West Point," 1:349; "Charles William Taylor," *Seventieth Annual Report of the Association of Graduates of the United States Military Academy* (1939), 134–38; Undated newspaper clipping from the "*Register*," no place of publication given, Cullom File 2819, USMA Library, West Point.

16. James B. Cooper to Robert Lincoln, 17 November 1883, filed with 2653 AGO 1879, M 666, NA.

17. W. A. McCurry, Interview, n.d., Pioneer Papers, Oklahoma Historical Society, Oklahoma City.

18. Grant Harris, "With Capt. David L. Payne at Rock Falls," manuscript, Mrs. Howard Searcy, Compiler, "Unpublished Narratives of Oklahoma Pioneers," Oklahoma Historical Society.

19. Rister, *Land Hunger*, 146–47.

20. Pringle's statement is enclosed with Stevens to AAAG, Fort Reno, 28 May 1884, 2653 AGO 1879, M 666, NA.

21. Rister, *Land Hunger*, 148.

22. See, for example, the account in Leckie, *Buffalo Soldiers*, 250.

23. He is the same "Corporal" Rogers who performed so gallantly in Lieutenant George Burnett's clash with Nana's Apaches at Cuchillo Negro in August 1881. pp. 244–45.

24. Day to Carroll, 8 May 1884, 2653 AGO 1879, M 666, NA.

25. *Kansas City Times*, 10 September 1884, 2.

26. Ibid., 11 October 1884.

27. Day to Post Adjt., 25 December 1884, 2653 AGO 1879, M 666, NA. A letter by an unidentified Boomer stated that "Day said he would give us five minutes to surrender; if we did not he would fire on our city, which he failed to do. . . . I counted nineteen rifles leveled at the head of Lieutenant Day. . . . The soldiers then withdrew with the promise that they would not molest our mail or anyone coming into our town" (*Kansas City Times*, 4 January 1885, 4).

28. Day to Post Adjt., 1 January 1885, 2653 AGO 1879, M 666, NA.

29. *Kansas City Times*, 31 January 1885, 4.

30. Hatch to AAG, Dept. of the Missouri, 30 January 1885, 2653 AGO 1879, M 666, NA; *Kansas City Times*, 31 January 1885, 4.

31. Crook to the AAG, Div. of the Pacific, 17 August 1885, as quoted in Dan Thrapp, *Al Seiber: Chief of Scouts*, 303. Nana was not killed in the skirmish, and any wound to Geronimo was very slight.

32. H. W. Daly, "The Geronimo Campaign," *Arizona Historical Review* 3 (1930): 72.

33. Britton Davis, *The Truth about Geronimo*, 175. Apaches on the move (and cavalry units as well) commonly killed horses that broke down.

34. Ibid.

35. Summerall, "Report of Engagements and Part Taken by 1st Lieut. M. W. Day."

36. Day to Charles Gatewood, Jr., 26 June 1926, Charles Gatewood Papers, Arizona Historical Society, Tucson.

37. Quoted in *Army and Navy Journal*, 28 August 1886, 86.

38. Copied in *Army and Navy Journal*, 3 December 1887, 363.

39. On 1 May 1885, while Day was serving with the Apache scouts in Arizona, Emilie Day secured an uncontested divorce in El Paso. She remarried shortly afterwards, but Day remained unwed until 1916, four years after he retired from the military (Veteran's Administration Pension File 1,593,162, NA).

40. *Army and Navy Journal*, 24 March 1894, 513.

41. See pp. 310–12.

42. Frank N. Schubert, *Buffalo Soldiers, Braves and the Brass: The Story of Fort Robinson, Nebraska*, 88–91.

43. Day to Robinson, 8 May 1919, USMA Archives, File 2710 (emphasis added).

CHAPTER 13

1. Monroe Lee Billington, *New Mexico's Buffalo Soldiers, 1866–1900*, 121–22.

2. Unless otherwise stated, biographical data on Conline come from the statements he made to an army retirement board in 1890 (File 1055 ACP 1873, AGO, RG 94, NA [hereafter cited as Conline, Retirement Statement]. Also see William J. Roe, "John Conline," *Forty-Eighth Annual Report of the Association of Graduates of the United States Military Academy*, 78–83).

3. Application of John Conline, File 308/1859, USMA, Cadet Application Papers, 1805–66, M 588, NA.

4. Conline to Floyd, 20 May 1860, ibid.

5. Conline, Retirement Statement.

6. Ibid. The "Carnot" referred to, of course, was Lazare Carnot (1753–1823), the great war minister of Revolutionary France.

7. Application of John Conline, File 308/1859, USMA, Cadet Application Papers, 1805–66, M 588, NA

8. Conline, Academic Rank, USMA Archives, West Point; Conline, Retirement Statement; Roe, "John Conline."

9. Conline, Academic Rank; Register of Delinquencies; and SO 23, 1865, Post Orders, all in USMA Archives.

10. Cullom to George P. Delafield, 29 March 1866, Letters Sent by the Supt. of the USMA, 1845–1902, M 1089, NA.

11. Pitcher to E. Nichols, 20 December 1867, ibid.; SO 18, 1868, Post Orders, USMA Archives.

12. Conline, Academic Rank, and SO 27, 1868, Post Orders, USMA Archives.

13. Conline, Academic Rank, USMA Archives.

14. Roe, "John Conline," 81.

15. Academic Board Minutes, 29 January 1869, USMA Archives, West Point.

16. Conline, Academic Record, USMA Archives; Roe, "John Conline," 83.

17. Fort Stockton, Post Returns, M 617, NA; Ninth Cavalry, Regimental Returns, M 744, NA.

18. Conline, Retirement Statement; *New York Times*, 16 June 1870, p. 5, col. 1; 1 July 1870, p. 2, col. 2.

19. Conline, Retirement Statement; Fort Stockton, Post Returns, 1872, M 617, NA; *Army and Navy Journal*, 2 March 1872, 470.

20. *New York Times*, 11 April 1872, p. 6, col. 1.

21. Fort Stockton, Post Returns, M 617, NA; Conline to the Secretary of War, 21 March 1873, 1055 ACP 1873, AGO, RG 94, NA.

22. Ninth Cavalry, Regimental Returns, M 744, NA; Mrs. A. M. Leland to Mrs. Rutherford B. Hayes, 29 September 1877, 1055 ACP 1873, AGO, RG 94, NA.

23. Loud to Conline, 1 October and 9 November 1876, DNM, LS, M 1072, NA.

24. Emma's differences with Captain Shorkley are summed up in Shorkley to AAG, 1 January 1877, and Shorkley to AAG, 29 January 1877, DNM, LR, M 1088, NA.

25. Shorkley to AAG, 29 January 1877; Shorkley to AAG, 16 March 1877, DNM, LR, M 1088, NA; Shorkley to AAG, 23 December 1876, DNM, Register of LR, M 1097, NA.

26. Shorkley to AAG, 29 January 1877; Shorkley to AAG 16 March 1877; Conline, Charges . . . against Asst. Surgeon J. M. Brown, U.S.A., 6 April 1877; and Capt. E. R. Pratt to Cmdg. Off., DNM, 10 March 1877, all in DNM, LR, M 1088, NA.

27. Broadus, testimony, 23 December 1878, John Conline, Court-Martial Proceedings, QQ 933, JAG, RG 153, NA. Also see the testimony of Conline, Kirkely, and Charles Johnson, ibid.

28. Emma Leland to Adjt. Gen., 28 June 1879, 1055 ACP 1873, AGO, RG 94, NA.

29. Conline to Secretary of War, 7 March 1910, ibid.; Sidney Jocknick, *Early Days on the Western Slope of Colorado, 1870–1883*, 172–75. Conline stated that Sergeant Robert T. Johnson was one of the three troopers present at the rescue.

30. Conline, Charges . . . against 1st Lieut. John S. Loud, 7 August 1877, DNM, LR, M 1088, NA.

31. Depositions, 17–19 August 1877, enclosed with Conline to AAG, Dept. of the Missouri, 19 August 1877, DNM, LR, M 1088, NA.

32. Godding, Statement, Army Retirement Board Hearing, January 1878, 1055 ACP 1873, AGO, RG 94, NA.

33. Ibid.

34. The proceedings against Conline are summed up in "Case of John Conline, 31 July 1878," 333 ACP 1878, filed with 1055 ACP 1873, AGO, RG 94, NA.

35. Mrs A. M. Leland to Mrs. Rutherford B. Hayes, 29 September 1877, 1055 ACP 1873, AGO, RG 94, NA.

36. "Case of John Conline, Summary, 31 July 1878," ibid.

37. Hatch to Conline, 23 August 1878, and Hatch to AAG, Dept. of the Missouri, 27 September 1878, DNM, LS, M 1072, NA.

38. Testimony of Charles Johnson, Sgt. Broadus, Sergeant Robert Johnson, Attorney W. W. Pierson, and Conline and GCMO 7, 22 January 1879, all in Conline, Court-Martial Proceedings, QQ 933, JAG, RG 153, NA.

39. Conline to Godding, 27 February 1879, Records of Saint Elizabeth's Hospital for the Insane, RG 407, NA.

40. Hatch to Townsend, 5 August 1879, filed with 1055 ACP 1055, AGO, RG 94, NA. Townsend's comments are contained in his endorsement of the letter.

41. GO 5, 4 August 1880, DNM, General Orders, RG 393, NA.

42. Day to Post Adjt., Fort Robinson, 20 February 1890, 1055 ACP 1873, AGO, RG 94, NA.

43. *Army and Navy Journal*, 16 April 1881, 775; Conline, Retirement Statement.

44. Godding to the Adjutant General, 17 January 1887, 1055 ACP 1873, AGO, RG 94, NA.

45. Conline, Retirement Statement; Godding to AGO, 3 March 1884, and Charles Leland to Godding, 6 February 1885, 1055 ACP 1873, AGO, RG 94, NA.

46. *Army and Navy Journal*, 28 August 1886, 86.

47. Roe, "John Conline," 82.

48. This is the same Barney McKay who was discharged after one of the most controversial courts-martial in the Ninth's history. See pp. 285–86.

49. Henry to AAG, Dept. of the Platte, 2 March 1890, and Emmett to Henry, 17 February 1890, 1055 ACP 1873, AGO, RG 94, NA.

50. Henry to AAG, 4 March 1890, ibid.; Conline, Retirement Statement.

51. Roe, "John Conline," 82; Conline to Adjutant General, 11 November 1914, 1055 ACP 1873, AGO, RG 94, NA.

52. Roe, "John Conline," 83.

53. Adjt. Gen. to C.O., Fort Myer, Virginia, 17 October 1916, 1055 ACP 1873, AGO, RG 94, NA.

CHAPTER 14

1. Stephen Lekson, *Nana's Raid: Apache Warfare in Southern New Mexico, 1881*; Smith, Personal File, 2838 ACP 1873, AGO, RG 94, NA.

2. Lekson, *Nana's Raid*, 28–29; George A. McKenna, *Black Range Tales Chronicling Sixty Years of Life and Adventure in the Southwest*, 184–85; *Army and Navy Journal*, 3 September 1881, 119; *Grant County Herald*, 27 August 1881.

3. Affidavit of Private Henry Trout, 24 June 1894, 5931 PRD 1894, AGO, RG 94, NA. Sergeant Baker is inaccurately identified as Edward L. Baker, one of the most noted black soldiers in the army, in Irvin H. Lee, *Negro Medal of Honor Men*, 76.

4. See the testimony of Lieutenant B. S. Humphrey and of Captain George Purrington, 9 December 1880, Brent Woods, Court-Martial Proceedings, QQ2224, JAG, RG 153, NA.

5. Data on Woods are gleaned from the Enlistment Registers and from Muster Rolls, Troop B, 1873–78, AGO, RG 94, NA.

6. Ibid.

7. Ninth Cavalry, Muster Rolls, Troop B, 1880, ibid. These battles are described from the viewpoint of Lieutenant Matthias Day on pp. 196–97. Also see Hatch to AAG, Dept. of the Missouri, 5 February 1880, filed with 6058 AGO 1879, M 666, NA; *Arizona Star* (Tucson), 12 February 1880; Dan L. Thrapp, *Victorio and the Mimbres Apaches*, 262–63. For Woods's role in the fights, see testimony of Ballard Humphrey, Brent Woods, Court-Martial Proceedings, QQ 2224, JAG, RG 153, NA.

8. Woods, Court-Martial Proceedings, QQ 2224, JAG, RG 153, NA.

9. GCMO 10, Dept. of the Missouri, RG 393, USCC, NA.

10. Ninth Cavalry, Muster Rolls, Troop B, 1881, AGO, RG 94, NA; Ninth Cavalry, Regimental Returns, 1881, M 744, NA.

11. Taylor to Adjt. Gen., 10 April 1892, 5931 PRD 1894, AGO, RG 94, NA, filed with Woods, Medal of Honor documents, M 929, NA.

12. Ninth Cavalry, Final Statements, Organizational Records, RG 391, NA; Ninth Cavalry, Muster Rolls, Troop B, AGO, RG 94, NA.

13. Ibid.; Ninth Cavalry, Muster Rolls, Troop H, 1881, AGO, RG 94, NA.

14. *Grant County Herald,* 27 August 1881; Hatch to AAG, 3 October 1881, 6058 AGO 1878, M 666, NA; McKenna, *Black Range Tales,* 184–85; *Army and Navy Journal,* 27 August 1881, 81; Private Henry Trout, Deposition, 24 June 1894, Captain Byron Dawson to AAG, 6 April 1894, with endorsement by Charles Taylor, 5 June 1894, all in Documents Relating to the Medal of Honor, Roll 2, M 929, NA.

15. *Annual Report of the Secretary of War, 1881,* House Ex. Doc. 1, 47th Cong. 1st sess., 1881, Serial 2010, 127; *Army and Navy Journal,* 3 September 1881, 99.

16. Turpin to editor, *Topeka State Journal,* 10 February 1898, in "Scrap-Books," Kansas State Historical Museum, 10:257, Kansas State Historical Society, Topeka.

17. "Captain Geo. W. Smith," in *Proceedings of the Army of the Cumberland, 14th Corps* [1894–97], 125, cited in Don Rickey, Jr., *Forty Miles a Day on Beans and Hay: The Enlisted Soldier Fighting the Indian Wars,* 306.

18. GO 60, 6 April 1882, Fort Hays, Post Records, USACC, RG 393, NA.

19. GO 16, 30 February 1883; 25, 25 February 1883; 48, 5 April 1883; and 82, 22 May 1883, ibid.

20. GO 83, 4 September 1884, ibid.

21. GO 162, 22 August 1888, Fort Robinson, Post Records, USACC, RG 393, NA.

22. Ninth Cavalry, Muster Rolls, Troop B, 1883, AGO, RG 94, NA.

23. GCMO 39, 7 May 1886, Dept. of the Platte, USACC, RG 393, NA.

24. Brent Woods, Court-Martial Proceedings, RR 1910, JAG, RG 153, NA.

25. Ibid.

26. Hockins, testimony, ibid.

27. Ladd was courting and eventually married Benteen's niece and adopted daughter, Violet Norman.

28. GCMO 14, 10 February 1887, Dept. of the Platte, USACC, RG 393, NA; Melvin Wilkins, Court-Martial Proceedings, RR 2348, JAG, RG 153, NA.

29. Ibid.

30. Ninth Cavalry Muster Rolls, Troop E, 1883–88, AGO, RG 94, NA; *Army and Navy Journal,* 9 April 1887, 734.

31. Dawson, testimony, Jarauld Olmsted, Court-Martial Proceedings, RR 2868, JAG, RG 153, NA.

32. Ibid.

33. Post Order 152, Fort Duchesne, Post Order Book, 1886–88, USACC, RG 393, NA.

34. Post Order 159, 3 November 1887, ibid.

35. Post Order 175, 13 December 1887, ibid.

36. Documents Relating to the Medal of Honor, Brent Woods, M 929, NA.

37. Ibid.; *Army and Navy Journal,* 11 August 1894, 874–75; *Kansas City Times,* 5 August 1894.

38. *Army and Navy Journal,* 28 March 1896, 540; Ninth Cavalry, Regimental Returns, 1898, M 744, NA.

39. Of the eleven Medal of Honor winners from the Ninth, one (Stance) was killed and one (William Williams) deserted. Of the others, two (Moses Williams and Thomas

Shaw) died the year following retirement; two (Woods and Denny), four years afterwards; one (Henry Johnson), six years later; and two (George Jordan and Thomas Boyne), seven years later. Of the other two, Clinton Greaves survived for twelve years, while Augustus Walley lived until 1938.

40. *Army and Navy Journal*, 28 March 1896, 540; Preston E. Amos, *Above and Beyond in the West: Black Medal of Honor Winners, 1870–1890*, 29–30; Documents Relating to the Medal of Honor, Brent Woods, M 929, Roll 2, NA; Frank N. Schubert, *Black Valor: Buffalo Soldiers and the Medal of Honor, 1870–1898*, 170.

CHAPTER 15

1. Charles Merritt to Adjutant General, 29 August 1873, 3502 ACP 1873, AGO, RG 94, NA.

2. Wesley Merritt to Townsend, 21 September 1873, ibid.; Don E. Alberts, *Brandy Station to Manila Bay: A Biography of Wesley Merritt*, 214–16.

3. Alberts, *Brandy Station to Manila Bay*, 216.

4. Polk to Hatch, 20 December 1877, M 571, DNM, Register of LR, M 1097, NA.

5. Ibid.; Hatch to Polk, 1 June 1878, 1313/1878, ibid.

6. Dan L. Thrapp, *Victorio and the Mimbres Apaches*, 213–14.

7. Ibid., 215.

8. W. J. Hooker was the brother of Captain Hooker and had just incurred a severe financial loss when a fire supposedly suppressed by Merritt reignited and destroyed thirty-five tons of hay belonging to Hooker. See Monroe Lee Billington, *New Mexico's Buffalo Soldiers, 1866–1900*, 111, and Hatch to Merritt, 22 April 1879, DNM, LS, M 1072, NA.

9. Hooker to Adjt. Gen., 18 May 1879, 1339, DNM, Register of LR, M 1097, NA.

10. Merritt to AAG, 18 May 1879, ibid.

11. "Charges and Specifications against Lt. Charles Merritt," 2 August 1879, 1960, DNM, LR, M 1088, NA.

12. The proceedings of Merritt's court-martial were filed under QQ 1351, JAG, RG 153, NA. After repeated searches, the staff of the National Archives have been unable to locate the file.

13. GCMO 59, 8 November 1879, filed with 3502 ACP 1873, AGO, RG 94, NA.

14. *Army and Navy Journal*, 20 December 1879, 320; *Weekly New Mexican*, 20 December 1879.

15. Wellington Fish, "Memories of West Point, 1877–1881," 363–65, typescript, USMA Library, West Point.

16. Francis B. Heitman, comp., *Historical Register and Dictionary of the United States Army*, vol. 1; Ninth Cavalry, Regimental Returns, 1880, M744, NA.

17. *Cleveland Gazette*, 14 February 1891. The account was datelined Pine Ridge, S.Dak., where Walley was stationed.

18. All previous accounts, based almost exclusively upon the undocumented information in Walter F. Beyer and Oscar F. Keydel's *Deed's of Valor: How America's Civil War Heroes Won the Congressional Medal of Honor*, state that it was about 9:30 or 10:00 A.M. when the Mexican rode into the camp. Burnett recalled that it was "almost noon" (Burnett to Moses Williams, 20 June 1896, in Williams to President Grover Cleveland, 29 July 1896, 1970 PRD 1890, AGO, RG 94, NA). A correspondent, writing the day of the clash, stated it was about 2:00 P.M. (*New York Herald*, 18 August 1879, 2).

19. *New York Herald*, 18 August 1881, 2.

20. Beyer and Keydel, *Deeds of Valor*, 1:278–79; Burnett to Williams 20 June 1896; *New York Herald*, 18 August 1881, 7; Preston E. Amos, *Above and Beyond in the West: Black Medal of Honor Winners, 1870–1890*, 23–24.

21. In 1891, Lieutenant Burnett recommended Rogers for a Certificate of Merit. For reasons not specified, the recommendation was not approved (13292 PRD 1891, AGO, RG 94, NA).

22. Burnett to Williams, 20 June 1896; *New York Herald*, 18 August 1881, 7.

23. *New York Herald*, 18 August 1881, 7. Since the *Herald's* correspondent was apparently with Valois, his account is followed when it seems obvious that he was an eye witness.

24. Ibid.

25. Valois to Adjt. Gen., 10 September 1889, filed with 5723 ACP 1884, AGO, RG 94, NA; Undated extract from a note from Burnett to the Adjt. Gen., filed with ibid. Since the correspondent for the *New York Herald* departed the scene of the battle with Valois's force, all remaining details of the fight were supplied by Williams, Walley, and Burnett in their subsequent applications for the Medal of Honor.

26. Burnett to Adjt. Gen., 21 August 1890, 12608 PRD 1890, AGO, RG 94, NA. Once more, Burnett's eyewitness account, written only nine years after the fight, is in sharp conflict with the description in Beyer and Keydel, *Deeds of Valor*, 2:279–81, on which previous accounts of these events have been based. It is unfortunate that they did not cite their sources.

27. *New York Herald*, 18 August 1881. The style of the dispatch indicates that Major Guy Henry, who arrived at Fort Craig with Colonel Hatch on August 17, the date and place referred to in the report's dateline, wrote it. Since Henry apparently was not at Cañada Alamosa on August 16, another officer, most likely Valois, was the source of the eyewitness observations.

28. Excerpt, Walley to Burnett, 5 January 1897, Brief, Burnett's Application for the award of a Medal of Honor, 5723 ACP 1884, AGO, RG 94, NA. The reference to the letter written by Moses Williams is also from this brief.

29. Burnett to Williams, 20 June 1896.

30. *Army and Navy Journal*, 1 April 1882, 782.

31. See pp. 311–12.

32. Frank N. Schubert, ed., *On the Trail of the Buffalo Soldier: Biographies of African Americans in the U.S. Army, 1866–1917*, 360–61.

33. Capt. A. C. Markley to Adjt. Gen., 16 November 1899, Case of Moses Williams, 297257 AGO 1899, Documents Relating to the Medal of Honor, M 929, NA; Amos, *Above and Beyond*, 27.

34. Burnett to Adjt. Gen., 21 August 1890.

35. Captain Charles G. Ayres to Adjt. Gen., 23 October 1899, 197231 AGO 1899, "Case of Private Augustus Wally," Documents Relating to the Medal of Honor, M 929, NA. Walley described his Cuban service in a statement reprinted in Herschel V. Cashin et al., *Under Fire with the Tenth U.S. Cavalry*, 264–65.

36. Frank N. Schubert, *Black Valor: Buffalo Soldiers and the Medal of Honor, 1870–1898*, 87.

37. Jarauld Olmsted, Court-Martial Proceedings, RR 2868, JAG, RG 153, NA.

CHAPTER 16

1. Excellent summaries of prostitution are found in Anne M. Butler, *Daughters of Joy, Sisters of Misery: Prostitutes in the American West, 1865–1890*, 122–50 and Darlis A. Miller, "Foragers, Army Women, and Prostitutes," in Jensen and Miller, *New Mexico Women: Intercultural Perspectives*.

2. Ord, testimony before the Banning Committee, 10 February 1876, 44th Cong., 1st sess., 1876, H. Rep. 354, 106; Biddle to AAG, Dept. of the Platte, 10 August 1893, Fort Robinson, LS, RG 393, USACC, NA.

3. Ninth Cavalry, Regimental Returns, 1887, M 744, NA; James Glass, Court-Martial Proceedings, RR 2553, JAG, RG 153, NA.

4. Ibid. "Sergeant Washington" was the same soldier whom Emanuel Stance threatened to kill at Fort Stanton in 1878 (see pp. 165–66).

5. GCMO 67, 26 July 1887, Dept. of the Platte, USACC, RG 393, NA.

6. Bright to the Judge Advocate General, 22 August and 5 September 1887; Bright to the Secretary of War, 12 September 1887. Both are filed with RR 2253, JAG, RG 153, NA.

7. SO 49, 1 March 1888, Records of the Secretary of War, RG 107, NA.

8. The letter to Cecilia was filed with George Lyman, Court-Martial Proceedings, QQ 4415, JAG, RG 153, NA.

9. Beyer's personal file, M316 CB 1870, M 1064, NA.

10. Ibid.

11. Preston E. Amos, *Above and Beyond in the West: Black Medal of Honor Winners, 1870–1890*, 8–13. Amos mistakenly states that the troop's ranks included Sergeant John Denny, the third medal winner in the Apache wars. He was a member of B Troop.

12. *Thirty-Four*, 2 June and 7 April 1880.

13. Ibid., 29 September 1879.

14. Testimony of Beyer and Ross, George Lyman, Court-Martial Proceedings, QQ 4415, JAG, RG 153, NA.

15. Register of Enlistments, M 233, NA.

16. Beyer to Post Adjutant, Fort Bayard, 16 June 1879, DNM, LR, M 1088, NA.

17. GCMO 42, 18 April 1881, Dept. of the Missouri, USACC, RG 393, NA.

18. Beyer, testimony, George Lyman, Court-Martial Proceedings, QQ 4415, JAG, RG 153, NA (emphasis added).

19. GCMO 2, 4 January 1884, Dept. of the Missouri, USACC, RG 393, NA.

20. Unless otherwise indicated, all information concerning the case comes from the proceedings filed under QQ 4415, JAG, RG 153, NA.

21. Ibid.

22. Private Young, who did not testify, was most likely Charles H. Young of C Troop. There were no white troops stationed at Fort Sill at the time.

23. GCMO 2, 4 January 1884, Dept. Of the Missouri, USACC, RG 393, NA.

24. Ibid.

25. Frank N. Schubert, ed., *On the Trail of the Buffalo Soldier: Biographies of African Americans in the U.S. Army, 1866–1917*, 272.

26. Herschel V. Cashin et al., *Under Fire with the Tenth U.S. Cavalry*, 117. Lyman was one of four members of the Ninth Cavalry who was interviewed by Cashin (Ninth Cavalry, Regimental Returns, July 1898, M 744, NA).

27. Ninth Cavalry, Regimental Returns, M 744, NA.

CHAPTER 17

1. Register of Enlistments, M 233, NA; Ninth Cavalry, Muster Rolls, AGO, RG 94, NA; Frank N. Schubert, ed., *On the Trail of the Buffalo Soldier: Biographies of African Americans in the U.S. Army, 1866–1917*, 241–42.

2. Jones to AAG, Dept. of the Missouri, 18 April 1884, filed with Charles Beyer, Court-Martial Proceedings, RR 580, JAG, RG 153, NA.

3. Jones to AAG, Dept. of the Missouri, 10 August 1884, ibid.

4. Jones, testimony, 2 October 1884, ibid.

5. Humphrey to Russell, 20 May 1884, enclosed with ibid. Beyer made a similar accusation during his court-martial.

6. Jones to AAG, DM, 10 August 1884, ibid.

7. Endorsements to ibid.; GCMO 50, 11 November 1884, AGO, RG 94, NA.

8. GCMO 50, 11 November 1884, AGO, RG 94, NA.

9. The testimony of First Sergeant Jackson and Private Gibson is found in Jackson, Court-Martial Proceedings, RR 737, JAG, RG 153, NA.

10. This is based on testimony in ibid.

11. Ibid.

12. The testimony of Sergeants Jackson and Jones on this matter is in Jones, Court-Martial Proceedings, RR 737, JAG, RG 153, NA.

13. Both sentences are contained in GCMO 59, 30 October 1884, Dept. of the Missouri, filed with ibid.

14. Harrison's and all other testimony is found in Charles Beyer, Court-Martial Proceedings, RR 580, JAG, RG 153, NA.

15. Post Surgeon J. W. Keane, 9 Oct. 1884, ibid.

16. GCMO 50, 11 November 1884, AGO, RG 94, NA.

17. Ibid.; Lieber to Lincoln, 30 October 1884, filed with Beyer, Court-Martial Proceedings, RR 580, JAG, RG 153, NA.

18. Schubert, *On the Trail of the Buffalo Soldier,* 241–42.

19. Ninth Cavalry, Muster Rolls, Troop C, 1887, AGO, RG 94, NA.

20. General Document File, 1030444, AGO, RG 94, NA.

CHAPTER 18

1. Don Rickey, Jr., *Forty Miles a Day on Beans and Hay: The Enlisted Soldier Fighting the Indian Wars,* 170–71.

2. I surveyed the General Court-Martial Orders for the Department of the Missouri, 1881–84, and for the Department of the Platte, 1885–89. Since nineteenth-century officers used a variety of euphemisms in referring to deviant behavior, it was likely that some cases were missed. Often it was necessary to consult the court-martial transcripts to determine what the real offense was.

3. Register of Enlistments, M 233, NA; Ninth Cavalry, Regimental Returns, 1880–81, M 744, NA.

4. Brown, testimony, Richard Kennedy, Court-Martial Proceedings, QQ 2650, JAG, RG 153, NA.

5. Kennedy, statement, ibid. Both the wording of the charge and the testimony indicates that the terms fellatio and oral sex were missing from the vocabularies of both the enlisted men and the officers. The necessity to use Anglo-Saxon four-letter vulgarities to express their meaning produced language so shocking to Victorian sensitivities that the court-martial order simply charged Kennedy with "conduct prejudicial to good order and military discipline" and primly noted that the "specification will not be published."

6. GCMO 79, 23 July 1881, Dept. of the Missouri, USACC, RG 393, NA.

7. GCMO 88, 15 December 1885, Dept. of the Platte, USACC, RG 393, NA.

8. Israel Monday, Court-Martial Proceedings, RR 1709, JAG, RG 153, NA. Polk, in his fourth year of service, was one of the most highly regarded soldiers in the troop and soon afterwards was promoted to the rank of sergeant. During his second tour of duty he married, and later he served in both the Spanish-American War and the Filipino Insurrection (Schubert, *On the Trail of the Buffalo Soldier,* 332).

9. GCMO 79, 23 July 1881, Dept. of the Missouri, USACC, RG 393, NA.

10. GCMO 68, 16 June 1881, ibid.

11. GCMO 54, 2 May 1881, ibid.

12. "Sworn" statement of Dickerson, 26 March 1883, Richard Dickerson, Court-Martial Proceedings, QQ 3830, JAG, RG 153, NA. Although Miller, a twenty-six-year-

old Kentuckian, had no more tenure in the regiment than did Dickerson, he had been on duty with D Troop ever since enlisting in 1879.

13. Ibid.

14. Ninth Cavalry, Regimental Returns, 1882, M 744, NA.

15. Baker's photo is included in Herschel V. Cashin et al., *Under Fire with the Tenth U.S. Cavalry*, 318. Biographical data are from Schubert, *On the Trail of the Buffalo Soldier*, 23–24; and Rayford Logan and Michael Winston, eds. *Dictionary of American Negro Biography*, 45–46. The most thorough description of his life is found in Schubert, *Black Valor: Buffalo Soldiers and the Medal of Honor*, 145–63.

16. Baker, testimony, QQ 3630, JAG, RG 153, NA.

17. Dickerson, "Statement," ibid.

18. Watkins, testimony, ibid.

19. Wells, testimony, ibid.

20. Horton, testimony, ibid.

21. Joseph Brackett was a thirty-one-year-old Virginian who completed ten years of service in the Ninth Cavalry in December 1882. Although he received a character evaluation of "good" upon the expiration of his tour of duty, he did not reenlist (Register of Enlistments, M 233, NA; Ninth Cavalry, Regimental Returns, M 744, NA).

22. Dickerson, "Statement," QQ 3830, JAG, RG 153, NA.

23. Schubert, *On the Trail of the Buffalo Soldier*, 23–24; Oscar G. Villard, "The Negro in the Regular Army," *Atlantic Monthly* 91 (June 1903): 726. Above all, see the outstanding essay on Baker in Schubert, *Black Valor*, 145–63.

24. The full title of Baker's booklet is *Roster of Non-commissioned Officers of the 10th U.S. Cavalry, with Some Regimental Reminiscences, Appendixes, etc., Connected with the Early History of the Regiment; Army and Navy Journal* 18 September 1897, 35.

25. Theophilus G. Steward, *The Colored Regulars in the United States Army*, 255–79. Schubert, *Black Valor*, 160–61.

26. Baker, *Roster*, 49; *Army and Navy Journal*, 29 May 1897, 733; Schubert, *On the Trail of the Buffalo Soldier*, 295.

27. Schubert, *On the Trail of the Buffalo Soldier*, 295; *Army and Navy Journal*, 2 February 1901, 555.

28. Enlistment Rolls, February 1873; Ninth Cavalry, Muster Rolls, Troop D, 1878–81, AGO, RG 94, NA; Monroe Lee Billington, *New Mexico's Buffalo Soldiers, 1866–1900*, 101; *Army and Navy Journal*, 26 February 1881, 608.

29. Ninth Cavalry, Muster Rolls, Troop D, AGO, RG 94, NA; 6647 PRD 1891, AGO, LR, RG 94, NA.

30. *Army and Navy Journal*, 21 August 1897, 5.

CHAPTER 19

1. Nolan to Robert Newton Price, 4 and 18 September 1879. Excerpts printed in *Army and Navy Journal*, 11 October 1879, 176.

2. For the particulars of Flipper's court-martial, see Bruce Dinges, "The Court-Martial of Lieutenant Henry O. Flipper," *American West* 9 (January 1972): 12–16; Charles M. Robinson, *The Court-Martial of Lieutenant Henry O. Flipper.*

3. Earl Stover, "Chaplain Henry V. Plummer, His Ministry and His Court-Martial," *Nebraska History* 56 (Spring 1975): 21–22.

4. John F. Finerty described such a burial shortly before General Crook's fight with the Sioux at the Rosebud in 1876: "The burial service was impressively read by Col. Guy V. Henry over the grave" (*War-Path and Bivouac, or the Conquest of the Sioux*, 56).

5. Henry, testimony, 14 February 1876, House Report 354, 44th Cong., 1st sess., 1876, serial 1760, 188.

6. *Army and Navy Journal*, 29 November 1884, 343; Sanford to AAG, Dept. of the Platte, 3 May 1892, Fort Robinson, LS, RG 393, USAC, NA.

7. Quoted in Stover, "Chaplain Henry V. Plummer," 25.

8. *Army and Navy Journal*, 29 November 1884, 343; Edward M. Coffman, *The Old Army: A Portrait of the American Army in Peacetime, 1784–1898*, 226.

9. Stover, "Chaplain Henry V. Plummer," 29.

10. Stover, "Chaplain Henry V. Plummer," 30.

11. Quoted in Frank N. Schubert, *Buffalo Soldiers, Braves and the Brass: The Story of Fort Robinson, Nebraska*, 91. Goodloe may or may not have made the statement. Private Matthew Wyatt, one of the soldiers testifying against McKay, quoted him as saying so (McKay, Court-Martial Proceedings, File 447, JAG, RG 153, NA).

12. Stover, "Chaplain Henry V. Plummer," 30–33; Post Order 37, 11 May 1893, Fort Robinson, Post Records, USACC, RG 393, NA.

13. Stover, "Chaplain Henry V. Plummer," 33; Schubert, *Buffalo Soldiers, Braves and the Brass*, 130–31.

14. Frank N. Schubert, ed., *On the Trail of the Buffalo Soldier: Biographies of African Americans in the U.S. Army, 1866–1917*, 34.

15. Stover, "Chaplain Henry V. Plummer," 38.

16. Ibid., 39; Schubert, *On the Trail of the Buffalo Soldier*, 34; *Army and Navy Journal*, 1 July 1893, 745.

17. I am assuming Mrs. Plummer was absent, because she was not called to testify concerning the evening's events nor was she mentioned in any of the testimony.

18. My interpretation of the events that led to the difficulties between Plummer and Benjamin is based on a careful reading of the testimony in Plummer, Court-Martial Proceedings, File 748, 1894, JAG, RG 153, NA.

19. Biddle to AAG, Dept. of the Platte, 9 June 1894, Fort Robinson, LS, USACC, RG 393, NA.

20. Stover, "Chaplain Henry V. Plummer," 36–39.

21. *Kansas City Times*, 24 June 1894, 6; 16 August 1894, 5; 17 August 1894, 7.

22. *Army and Navy Journal*, 10 November 1894; *New York Times*, 3 November, 1894, 4.

23. Stover, "Chaplain Henry V. Plummer," 42–43.

24. Copied in *Army and Navy Journal*, 30 June 1894, 769.

25. *Kansas City Times*, 30 August 1894, 7.

26. Stover, "Chaplain Henry V. Plummer," 40; Schubert, *Buffalo Soldiers, Braves and the Brass*, 133.

27. Stover, "Chaplain Henry V. Plummer," 41.

28. Testimony of Sergeants Lust and Dillon, Dillon, Court-Martial Proceedings, JAG, RG 153, NA.

29. Ibid., 45.

30. Register of Enlistments, 1871–77; Schubert, *On the Trail of the Buffalo Soldier*, 122.

31. *Army and Navy Journal*, 27 October 1894, 141; 3 November 1894, 154.

32. Stover, "Chaplain Henry V. Plummer," 44.

CHAPTER 20

1. Willard B. Gatewood, "John Hanks Alexander of Arkansas: Second Black Graduate of West Point," *Arkansas Historical Quarterly* 41 (Summer 1982): 114–16.

2. *New York Times*, 13 June 1883, 1.

3. Sidney Herbert to Editor, *Savannah (Georgia) News*, reprinted in *Army and Navy Journal*, 26 August 1882, 71.

4. *Army and Navy Journal*, 23 June 1883, 1055; 30 June 1883, 1082.

5. John Marzalek, "John H. Alexander," in Logan and Winston, eds., *Dictionary of American Negro Biography*, 9; *Cleveland Gazette*, 2 July 1887.

6. *Army and Navy Journal*, 23 June 1883, 1055.

7. Register of Delinquencies, 1883–1887, Alexander, Archives, USMA; Semiannual Conduct and Merit Roles, ibid.

8. Maj. Gen. Mark L. Hersey to Maj. Gen. William J. Smith, 21 March 1929, Cullom File 3232, Special Collections, USMA.

9. Alexander to John P. Green, March 27, 1886, quoted in Gatewood, "John Hanks Alexander of Arkansas," 122.

10. Ibid., 119–21.

11. *Cleveland Gazette*, 2 July 1887.

12. Ibid.

13. Ninth Cavalry, Regimental Returns, 1887–94, M 744, NA.

14. Ibid., 1893.

15. Post Order 7, 26 January 1894, Fort Robinson, USACC, RG 383, NA; Gatewood, "John Hanks Alexander of Arkansas," 125–27; *Cleveland Gazette*, 31 March 1894.

16. *Kansas City American Citizen*, 30 March 1894, quoted in Gatewood, "John Hanks Alexander of Arkansas," 128.

17. *Army and Navy Journal*, 14 April 1894, 570.

18. Ibid., 54.

19. Frank N. Schubert, *Buffalo Soldiers, Braves and the Brass: The Story of Fort Robinson, Nebraska*, 156.

20. Alexander, "Trip of M Troop, 9th Cavalry, from Fort Washakie, Wy. to Ft. Du Chesne, Utah," manuscript, Huntington Institute, Burbank, Calif.

21. Nancy Gordon Heinl, "Charles Young," in Logan and Winston, eds., *Dictionary of American Negro Biography*, 677; Charles D. Rhodes, "Charles Young," *Fifty-third Annual Report of the Association of Graduates of the United States Military Academy*, 152.

22. *Army and Navy Journal*, 17 January 1885, 493.

23. Merit and Conduct rolls, USMA Archives, West Point.

24. *New York Times*, 1 September, 1889, 6; Rhodes, "Charles Young," 153; Logan and Winston, eds., *Dictionary of American Negro Biography*, s.v. "Charles Young," 677. Lieutenant Goethals later won fame as the builder of the Panama Canal.

25. Rhodes, "Charles Young," 154.

26. Hare to Green, 28 June 1885, quoted in Gatewood, "John Hanks Alexander of Arkansas," 120.

27. E. H. Lawson, "One of Twelve Million; Unrevealed Facts in the Life Story of Col. Charles Young, West Pointer," *The Washington Post*, 26 May 1929, 11.

28. *Army and Navy Journal*, 28 August 1909, 1487.

29. Rhodes, "Charles Young," 156; *Army and Navy Journal*, 26 January 1889, 432; Register of Delinquencies, Barroll, 13 January 1889, Archives, USMA; Young to Col. Delamere Skerett, 26 July 1916, Cullom File 3030, Special Collections, USMA.

30. The correspondence concerning the ludicrous handling of Young's assignment is summed up in the various endorsements to Major Guy Henry to the Adjutant General, 3 January 1890, filed with 5345 ACP 1889, AGO, RG 94, NA.

31. *Army and Navy Journal*, 16 November 1889, 229.

32. Henry to Adjt. Gen., 3 January 1890, filed with 5345 ACP 1889, AGO, RG 94, NA. Just when and to whom Alexander expressed these sentiments is not known. He was absent on leave from 6 November 1889 to 9 February 1890. Henry released essentially the same protest to the *Army and Navy Journal*, which published it under a bold heading: "The Ninth Horse Objects." *Army and Navy Journal*, 18 January 1890, 402.

33. Post Adjt. to Young, 5 April 1890, filed with 5345 ACP 1889, AGO, RG 94, NA.

34. Randlett to Post Adjutant, 24 April 1890, ibid. Fort Robinson's post records indicate that tardiness or absence at stable duty by officers was not at all unusual.

35. Young to AAG, Ninth Cavalry, 7 May 7 1890, filed with 5345 ACP 1889, AGO, RG 94, NA.

36. Tilford to Young, 25 June 1890, Fort Robinson, LS, RG 393, USACC, NA.

37. Ninth Cavalry, Regimental Returns, 1892–94, M 744, NA.

38. The correspondence concerning his assignment to Wilberforce is found in his personal file. See especially, Mitchell to Senator John Sherman, 14 April 1894, together with its many endorsements, 5345 ACP 1889, AGO, RG 94, NA.

39. Fort Duchesne, Post Order 20, 18 May 1894, filed with ibid.

40. Efficiency reports, ibid.; Logan and Winston, eds., *Dictionary of American Negro Biography*, s.v. "Charles Young," 677; *Cleveland Gazette*, 3 November 1894.

41. David L. Lewis, *W. E. B. DuBois: The Biography of a Race, 1868–1919*, 176.

42. "Charles Young," *The Nation* 144 (8 February 1922): 141.

43. Ibid.; Logan and Winston, eds., *A Dictionary of American Negro Biography*, s.v. "Charles Young," 677; Young to DuBois, 20 June 1917, in Herbert Aptheker, ed., *Correspondence of W. E. B. DuBois, 1877–1934*, 1:222.

44. "Charles Young," *The Nation* 144 (8 February 1922): 142; *Washington Post*, 1 June 1923, 3; *New York Times*, 2 June 1923, 11.

45. "Charles Young," *The Nation* 144 (8 February 1922): 141.

46. *Freeman* (Indianapolis), 27 December 1902, quoted in Schubert, *On the Trail of the Buffalo Soldier*, 490.

47. Ibid., 31 January 1903.

48. Rhodes, "Charles Young," 153; Schubert, *On the Trail of the Buffalo Soldiers*, 490.

49. Marvin E. Fletcher, *The Black Soldier and Officer in the United States Army, 1891–1917*, 64.

50. Ibid., 116.

51. Edward M. Coffman, *The Old Army: A Portrait of the American Army in Peacetime, 1784–1898*, 229. The phrase is from Charles Young's *Military Morale of Nations and Races*, 214.

52. Young, *Military Morale*, 217, 273.

53. Logan and Winston, eds., *Dictionary of American Negro Biography*, s.v. "Charles Young," 679.

54. Ibid.

55. Rhodes, "Charles Young," 154.

56. Benjamin O. Davis, Jr., *Benjamin O. Davis, Jr., American; An Autobiography*, 1–3.

57. Fletcher, *Black Soldier and Officer*, 74.

58. Davis wrote that his father never informed him how it was that "an enlisted man in the black 9th U.S. Cavalry Regiment, at the turn of the century," was able to "go before a regional U.S. Army board at Fort Leavenworth, Kansas, and obtain from it a solid recommendation that he be given a Regular Army commission" (Davis, *Autobiography*, 3).

CHAPTER 21

1. Henry to AAG, Dept. of the Platte, 1 May 1891, Fort Robinson, LS, RG 393, NA.

2. Frank N. Schubert, *Buffalo Soldiers, Braves and the Brass: The Story of Fort Robinson, Nebraska*, 88–89.

3. "John F. Guilfoyle," *Fifty-third Annual Report of the Association of Graduates of the United States Military Academy*, 1922, 80–84; Parker, "My Experiences as a Cadet at West Point, 1872–1876," 8, manuscript, USMA Library, West Point.

4. Henry to AAG, Dept. of the Platte, 20 May 1891; Smith to AAG, Dept. of the Platte, 26 June 1891, Fort Robinson, LS, RG 393, NA.

5. L. D. Reddick, "The Negro Policy in the United States Army, 1775–1945," *Journal of Negro History* 34 (January 1949): 18–21.

6. *New York Age*, 13 February 1892.

7. Ibid.

8. *Army and Navy Journal*, 2 September 1898, 17.

9. Rayford W. Logan, *The Betrayal of the Negro: From Rutherford B. Hayes to Woodrow Wilson*, 335.

Bibliography

MANUSCRIPTS

Arizona Historical Society, Tucson. Charles B. Gatewood Papers.

Center for American History, University of Texas, Austin.

  Emily Andrews. "Journal of a Trip from Austin to Fort Davis, 1872."

  Colonel Zenas R. Bliss. "Reminiscences." 5 vols.

Bowdoin College Library, Brunswick, Maine. General Oliver O. Howard Papers.

Colorado Historical Society, Denver. "Articles in the DeBusk Memorial."

Denver (Colorado) Public Library. Western History Collection. Captain A. W. Corliss. "Diaries, 1884–1894."

Gilcrease Museum, Tulsa, Okla. General Ranald S. Mackenzie Papers.

Huntington Institute, Burbank, Calif. Lieutenant John Hanks Alexander. "Trip of M Troop, 9th Cavalry, from Fort Washakie, Wyoming, to Fort Du Chesne, Utah, 1887."

Kansas State Historical Society, Topeka. Kansas State Historical Collections. "Scrapbooks" (Colonel Henry Carroll and Lieutenant George Washington Smith).

Library of Congress, Washington, D.C.

  William C. Church. Papers.

  General James H. Wilson. Papers.

Nebraska State Historical Society, Lincoln. Don Rickey. Interview Files.

New Mexico Archives, Santa Fe. Lieutenant Walter L. Finley. "Extracts of Letters to His Mother, 1879–1872."

Oklahoma State Historical Society, Oklahoma City. Mrs. Howard Searcy, comp. "Unpublished Narratives of Oklahoma Pioneers."

Oklahoma State Historical Society, Oklahoma City. Pioneer Papers.

Panhandle-Plains Historical Museum, Canyon, Texas. Lieutenant Robert G. Carter. "Diary."

U.S. Military Academy Archives, West Point.
Post Orders.
Registers of Delinquencies and Academic Ranking.
U.S. Military Academy Library, West Point. Special Collections.
Wellington Fish. "Memories of West Point, 1877–1881." Typescript.
Lieutenant James Parker. "My Experiences as a Cadet at West Point, 1872–1876."
———. "Papers."
Personal (Cullom) Files of Graduates of the United States Military Academy.
John H. Alexander. 3205
George R. Burnett. 2876
John Conline. 2365
Matthias W. Day. 2710
Mark L. Hersey. 3232
Clarence Stedman. 2363
Charles W. Taylor. 2819
Charles Young. 3330
U.S. Military History Institute, Carlisle, Pa.
Reynolds J. Burt. "Memories." Rickey Collection.
General Guy V. Henry, Jr. "Memoirs."
Colonel Guy V. Henry, Sr. "Scrapbooks and Papers."
Colonel William S. Paulding. Papers.
U.S. National Archives and Records Service
Records of the Adjutant General's Office, Record Group 94.
Appointment, Commission, and Personal Files (ACP)
Albee, Lt. George E. 1318 ACP 1872.
Burnett, Lt. George R. 5723 ACP 1884.
Carroll, Capt. Henry. 3754 ACP 1874.
Conline, Lt. John. 1055 ACP 1873.
Davidson, Lt. Francis S. 3991 ACP 1875.
Day, Lt. Matthias W. 2859 ACP 1885.
DeGress, Capt. Jacob. 1729 ACP 1871.
Frohock, Capt. William T. 3229 ACP 1877.
Garrard, Capt. Joseph. 4384 ACP 1887.
Hatch, Col. Edward. 5556 ACP 1875.
Heyl, Capt. Edward M. 4143 ACP 1873.
Hooker, Capt. Ambrose E. 4872 ACP 1873.
Humfreville, Capt. J. Lee. 1838 ACP 1894.
McAnaney, Lt. William C. 3651 ACP 1886.
Merritt, Lt. Charles. 3502 ACP 1873.
Olmsted, Capt. Jarauld A. 3831 ACP 1873.
Parker, Capt. Charles. 1590 ACP 1871.
Parker, Lt. Montgomery D. 5235 ACP 1879.

Plummer, Chaplain Henry V. 6474 ACP 1881.
Radetzki, Lt. Gustav M. 6072 ACP 1872.
Smith, Lt. Frederick. 2839 ACP 1891.
Smith, Lt. George Washington. 2838 ACP 1873.
Taylor, Lt. F. Beers. 797 ACP 1878.
Young, Lt. Charles. 5345 ACP 1889.
Other manuscript files.
Principal Records Division, Letters Received (LR), 1890–94.
General Documents File, 1890–1917.
Ninth Cavalry, Muster Rolls, 1866–1900.
Ninth Cavalry, Final Statements, 1866–91.
Records of the Judge Advocate General's Office, Record Group 153.
Court-Martial Proceedings, 1866–94.
Byer, Capt. Charles (1884). RR 580.
Charles, Pvt. Irving (1867). PP 230
Chase, Pvt. Harry; Pvt. Lee Irving; and Pvt. George Pumphrey (1887). RR 2389.
Comer, Pvt. Lee (1874). PP 3087.
Dayes, Pvt. James (1880). QQ 2868.
Dickerson, Sgt. Richard (1883). QQ 3830.
Dillon, Sgt. David (1894). No. 590.
Frohock, Capt. William T. (1870). PP 867.
Glass, Pvt. James (1887). RR 2553.
Green, Pvt. Moses (1883). QQ 4302.
Humfreville, Capt. J. Lee (1874). PP 3768.
Kennedy, Pvt. Richard (1879). PP 2650.
Jackson, Sgt. Jason (1884). RR 737
Jones, Sgt. Alexander (1884). RR 737.
Lyman, Sgt. George (1884). QQ 4415.
McKay, Sgt. Barney (1893). No. 359.
Merritt, Lt. Charles (1878). QQ 1351.
Munday, Pvt. Israel Munday (1885). RR 1709.
Olmsted, Capt. Jarauld A. (1887). RR 2837.
Olmsted, Capt. Jarauld A. (1888). RR 2868.
Pedee, Pvt. Martin (1872). PP 2809.
Plummer, Chaplain Henry V. (1894). No. 748.
Richardson, Pvt. Thomas (1887). RR 2626.
Richardson, Pvt. Thomas, and Pvt. William Young (1888). RR 2862.
Roberts, Sgt. George (1873). PP 3542.
Slaughter, Pvt. Rufus (1874). PP 3034.
Stance, Sgt. Emanuel (1872). PP 2295.
Stance, Sgt. Emanuel (1879). QQ 1019.

Taylor, Lt. F. Beers (1881). QQ 2640.

Wilkins, Sgt. Melvin (1887). RR 2348.

Woods, Sgt. Brent (1879). QQ 2224.

Woods, Sgt. Brent (1886). RR 1910.

Young, Pvt. William (1887). RR 2670.

Records of the United States Army Continental Commands, Record Group 393.

Department of the Missouri, 1875–85.

General Court-Martial Orders.

Letters Received.

Letters Sent.

Department of the Platte, 1885–94.

General Court-Martial Orders.

Letters Received.

Letters Sent.

Division of Texas, 1871–75.

Letters Received.

Post Records (Medical Histories, Letters Received, and Sent, and General Orders).

Fort Concho, Texas, 1867–75.

Fort Davis, Texas, 1867–75.

Fort Duchesne, Utah, 1886–96.

Fort Garland, Colorado, 1875–78.

Fort Hays, Kansas, 1882–84.

Fort Lyon, Colorado, 1876–77.

Fort McIntosh, Texas, 1867–75.

Fort McKavett, Texas, 1867–75.

Fort Riley, Kansas, 1883–84.

Fort Robinson, Nebraska, 1886–94.

Fort Sill, Indian Territory, 1881–84.

Fort Stanton, New Mexico, 1878–81.

Fort Stockton, Texas, 1867–75.

Fort Union, New Mexico, 1876–79.

Fort Wingate, New Mexico, 1876–81.

Records of Saint Elizabeth's Hospital for the Insane, Record Group 407.

Patient Files.

National Archives Files on Microfilm

Records of the Adjutant General's Office, Record Group 94.

Index to General Correspondence, 1890–1917. M 698.

Letters Received by the Adjutant Gen, 1861–70. M 619.

Letters Received by the Adjt. Gen., 1871–80. M 666. (Only large, consolidated files listed.)

2815 AGO 1874. Papers Relating to the . . . Red River War. Rolls 159–64.

1653 AGO 1875. Papers Relating to . . . Mexican Border Troubles. Rolls
195–211.

1405 AGO 1878. Papers Relating to . . . Lincoln County War. Rolls
397–98.

2653 AGO 1879. Papers Relating to . . . Intrusions into Indian Territory,
1879–93. Rolls 471–88.

6058 AGO 1879. Papers Relating to the Victorio Outbreak, 1879–81. Rolls
526–28.

Letters Received by the Adjutant General, 1881–90. M 689.

Register of Enlistments in the U.S. Army, 1798–1914. M 233.

Returns from U.S. Military Posts, 1800–1916. M 517.

Records Relating to the U.S. Military Academy, 1812–67. M 91.

U.S. Military Academy Cadet Application Papers, 1805–66. M 688.

Letters Sent by the Superintendents of West Point. M 1089.

The Negro in the Military Service of the United States, 1639–86.
M 858.

Letters Received by the Commission Branch of the Adjutant General's
Office, 1863–70. M 1064.

Beyer, Capt. Charles. B316 CB 1870.

Henry, Major Guy V. H1118 CB 1864.

Moore, Capt. Francis. M1382 CB 1866.

Records of the Judge Advocate General's Office, Record Group 153.

Registers of the Records of the Proceedings of the U.S. Army General
Courts-Martial, 1809–90. M 1105.

Records of the United States Army Continental Commands, 1821–1920.
RG 393.

Department of Texas, 1865–70.

Letters Sent. M 1165.

Letters Received. M 1193.

District of New Mexico, 1865–90.

Register of Letters Received. M 1097.

Letters Received. M 1088.

Letters Sent. M 1072.

Records from more than one record group.

Descriptive Commentaries from the Medical Histories of Posts. M 903.

Returns from Regular Army Cavalry Regiments, 1833–1916 (Regimental
Returns). M 744.

Documents Relating to . . . Blacks Awarded the Congressional Medal of
Honor, 1863–98. M 929.

Documents relating to . . . Blacks Nominated for Appointment to the U.S.
Military Academy during the Nineteenth Century. M 1002.

Records of the Veterans Administration, Record Group 15.

General Index to Pension Files, 1861–1934. T 288.

PUBLISHED DOCUMENTS

A*nnual Reports of the Secretaries of War,* 1866–98. These were published as part of House of Representatives Executive Document 1 by each regular session of Congress. Congressional serial set numbers for the most significant years are:

1866, 1285.
1867, 1324.
1868, 1367.
1869, 1412.
1870, 1446.
1871, 1503.
1872, 1558.
1873, 1597.
1874, 1635.
1875, 1674.
1876, 1742.
1877, 1794.
1878, 1843.
1879, 1903.
1880, 1952.
1881, 2010.
1883, 2182.
1885, 2369.
1888, 2628.
1891, 2921.

U.S. Congress. House. *Reorganization of the Army.* 45th Cong., 1st sess., 1876. H. Misc. Doc. 56. Serial 1773.

———. *Reorganization of the Army etc.* 44th Cong., 1st sess., 1876. H. Rep. 354. Serial 1760.

———. *Texas Border Troubles.* 45th Cong., 2d sess., 1878. H. Misc. Doc. 64. Serial 1820.

U.S. Congress. Senate. *Burnside Report on Reorganization of the Army.* 45th Cong., 3d sess., 1879. S. Rep. 555. Serial 1837.

———. *Relief of Lt. George W. Smith.* 45th Cong., 2d sess., 1876. S. Rep. 213. Serial 1808.

———. *The Ute Outbreak.* 46th Cong., 2d sess., 1880. S. Exec. Doc. 31. Serial 1882.

NEWSPAPERS AND PERIODICALS

Arizona Star (Tucson), 1879–80.
Army and Navy Journal, 1866–1916.
Cheyenne (Wyoming) Leader, 1885–90.
Chicago Defender, 1922–23.

Chicago Inter-Ocean, 1889–91.
Chicago Tribune, 1862–90.
Cimarron (New Mexico) News and Press, 1880.
Cleveland (Ohio) Gazette, 1885–98.
Colorado Chieftain (Pueblo), 1873–77.
The Crisis (New York), 1916–23.
Daily Optic (Las Vegas, N.Mex.), 1879–80.
Daily New Mexican (Santa Fe), 1875–81.
Davenport (Iowa) Daily Gazette, 1862–63.
German-American Advocate (Hays, Kans.), 1883–85.
Grant County Herald (Silver City, N.Mex.), 1879–81.
Kansas City (Missouri) Times, 1884–94.
Las Animas (Colorado) Leader, 1875–77.
Lawrence (Kansas) Daily Journal, 1881.
Meriwether's Weekly (Memphis, Tenn.), 1883.
Muscatine (Iowa) Weekly Journal, 1861–65.
The Nation (New York), 1873.
New York Age, 1890–98.
New York Herald, 1881.
New York Times, 1862–99.
Rocky Mountain News (Denver, Colo.), 1876–80.
Salt Lake City Tribune, 1886–96.
San Angelo (Texas) Standard Times, 1936.
San Antonio Daily Herald, 1867–75.
Thirty-Four (Las Cruces, N.Mex.), 1879–81.
Topeka State Journal, 1898.
Tri-Weekly Gazette (Austin, Texas), 1869–73.
Vernal (Utah) Express, 1891–96.
Washington Post, 1889–1929.
Weekly New Mexican (Santa Fe), 1875–79.
Wichita (Kansas) Eagle, 1883–84.

ARTICLES

Austerman, Wayne R. "Ranald S. Mackenzie and the Early Years on the Border." Red *River Historical Review* 5 (Summer 1980): 71–79.
"Charles Young, Colonel." *The Nation* 114 (8 February 1922): 141.
Coleman, Ronald. "The Buffalo Soldiers: Guardians of the Uintah Frontier, 1886–1901." *Utah Historical Quarterly* 47 (December 1979): 421–39.
Conway, Walter C., ed. "Colonel Edmond Shriver's Inspector General's Report on the Military Posts in Texas, November 1872–January 1873." *Southwestern Historical Quarterly* 67 (April 1967): 559–83.

Daly, H. W. "The Geronimo Campaign." *Journal of the U.S. Cavalry Association* 19 (1908): 247–62.

Dinges, Bruce. "The Court-Martial of Lt. Henry O. Flipper." *American West* 9 (January 1972): 12–16.

Dinkins, Captain James. "The Capture of Memphis by Gen. Nathan B. Forrest." *Southern Historical Society Papers* 36:180–96.

Gatewood, Charles. "Campaigning against Victorio in 1879." *The Great Divide*, April 1894, 102–104.

Gatewood, William B. "John Hanks Alexander of Arkansas: Second Black Graduate of West Point." *Arkansas Historical Quarterly* 46 (Summer 1982): 114–32.

Henry, Guy V. "A Sioux Indian Episode." *Harper's Weekly* 42 (26 December 1896): 1088–96.

Hunter, John Warren. "'Humpy' Jackson Wreaks Vengeance." *Frontier Times* 1 (December 1923): 1–8.

Kenner, Charles. "Guardians in Blue: The United States Cavalry and the Growth of the Texas Cattle Industry." *Journal of the West* 34 (January 1995): 46–54.

Leckie, William. "Buell's Campaign." *Red River Valley Historical Review* 3 (April 1979): 186–93.

Lemly, Lieutenant H. R. "The Fight on the Rosebud, 1876." in *Papers of the Order of Indian Wars*, 13-21. Intro. by John Carroll. Fort Collins, Colo.: Old Army Press, 1975.

Nolan, Frederick. "The Men of Fort Stanton." *Quarterly of the National Association for Outlaw and Lawman History* 18 (October 1994): 37–45.

Price, Byron. "Mutiny at San Pedro Springs." *By Valor and Arms* 1 (Spring 1975): 31–34.

Reddick, S. D. "The Negro Policy in the United States Army, 1775–1945." *Journal of Negro History* 34 (January 1949): 18–21.

Remington, Frederick. "The Final Review." *Harper's Weekly* 35 (7 February 1891): 106–107.

Rhodes, Charles. "Charles Young." In *Fifty-third Annual Report of the Association of Graduates of the United State Military Academy*, 151–54. Saginaw, Mich.: Seeman & Peters Press, 1922.

Roe, William. "John Conline." In *Forty-eighth Annual Report of the Association of Graduates of the United States Military Academy*, 78–83. Saginaw, Mich.: Seeman & Peters Press, 1917.

Schubert, Frank. "The Violent World of Emanuel Stance." *Nebraska History* 55 (Summer 1974): 203–19.

Somers, Christian F. "Famous Officers I Have Known; Major General Edward Hatch." *Chronicles of Oklahoma* 5 (March 1927): 187–95.

Stover, Earl. "Chaplain Henry V. Plummer: His Ministry and His Court-Martial." *Nebraska History* 56 (Spring 1976): 21–30.

Thompson, Edwin N. "The Negro Soldiers on the Frontier: A Fort Davis Case Study." *Journal of the West* 7 (April 1968): 217–35.

Villard, Oscar G. "The Negro in the Regular Army." *Atlantic Monthly* 91 (June 1903): 725–30.

Williams, Clayton. "A Threatened Mutiny of Black Soldiers at Fort Stockton in 1873."
West Texas Historical Association Year Book 57 (October 1976): 78–83.

BOOKS

Alberts, Don E. *Brandy Station to Manila Bay: A Biography of Wesley Merritt.* Austin,
Texas: Presidial Press, 1981.

Altshuler, Constance. *Cavalry Yellow and Infantry Blue: Army Officers in Arizona
between 1851 and 1886.* Tucson: University of Arizona Press, 1991.

Amos, Preston E. *Above and Beyond in the West: Black Medal of Honor Winners,
1870–1890.* Washington, D.C.: Potomac Corral of the Westerners, 1974.

Aptheker, Herbert, ed. *The Correspondence of W. E. B. DuBois, 1877–1934.* 3 vols.
Boston: University of Massachusetts Press, 1973.

[Baker, Edward]. *Roster of Non-commissioned Officers of the 10th U.S. Cavalry with
some Regimental Reminiscences, Appendices, etc., Connected with the Early History
of the Regiment.* Saint Paul, Minn.: Wm. Kennedy Printing Co., 1897.

Beyer, Walter F., and Oscar F. Keydel. *Acts of Bravery: Deeds of Extraordinary
American Heroism.* (Reprint of vol. 2 of Deeds of Valor, 1903.) Stamford, Conn.,
Longmeadow Press, 1994.

———, eds. *Deeds of Valor: How America's Civil War Heroes Won the Congressional
Medal of Honor.* Stamford, Conn.: Longmeadow Press, 1994.

Biddle, Ellen McGowan. *Reminiscences of a Soldier's Wife.* Philadelphia, J. B. Lippen-
cott, 1907.

Bierschale, Margaret. *Fort McKavett, Texas: Post on the San Saba.* Salado, Texas:
Anson Jones Press, 1966.

Bigelow, John. *The Campaign for Chancellorsville.* New Haven: Yale University Press,
1910.

Billington, Monroe Lee. *New Mexico's Buffalo Soldiers, 1866–1900.* Niwot, Colo.:
University Press of Colorado, 1991.

Boatner, Mark M., III. *The Civil War Dictionary.* New York: David McKay Co.,
1959.

Boyd, Mrs. Orsemus. *Cavalry Life in Tent and Field.* Intro. by Darlis Miller. Lincoln:
University of Nebraska Press, 1982.

Brady, Cyrus. *Indian Fights and Fighters.* Intro. by James T. King. Lincoln: University
of Nebraska Press, 1971.

Brown, D. Alexander. *Grierson's Raid.* Urbana: University of Illinois Press, 1954.

Butler, Anne M. *Daughters of Joy, Sisters of Misery: Prostitutes in the American West,
1865–1890.* Urbana: University of Illinois Press, 1985.

Carlson, Paul H. *"Pecos Bill": A Military Biography of William R. Shafter.* College
Station: Texas A&M University Press, 1989.

Carter, Robert R. *On the Border with Mackenzie, or Winning the West from the
Comanches.* New York: Antiquarian Press, 1961.

Cashin, Herschel V., et al. *Under Fire with the Tenth U.S. Cavalry.* New York: Arno Press, 1969.

Chalfant, William. *Without Quarter: The Wichita Expedition and the Fight on Crook Creek.* Norman: University of Oklahoma Press, 1991.

Coffman, Edward M. *The Old Army: A Portrait of the American Army in Peacetime, 1784–1898.* New York: Oxford University Press, 1986.

Custer, Elizabeth. *Tenting on the Plains, or General Custer in Kansas and Texas.* Norman: University of Oklahoma Press, 1971.

Davenport, Edward A. *History of the Ninth Regiment Illinois Cavalry.* Chicago, Donohue & Henneberry, 1888.

Davis, Benjamin O., Jr. *Benjamin O. Davis, Jr., American: An Autobiography.* New York: Penguin Books, 1992.

Davis, Britton. *The Truth About Geronimo.* Lincoln: University of Nebraska Press, 1976.

Dodge, Richard. *Our Wild Indians: Thirty-Three Years' Personal Experience among Our Red Men of the Great West.* New York: Anchor House, 1959.

Dyer, Frederick H. *A Compendium of the War of the Rebellion.* 3 vols. Des Moines, Iowa: Dyer Publishing Co., 1908.

Emmett, Chris. *Fort Union and the Winning of the Southwest.* Norman: University of Oklahoma Press, 1965.

Emmitt, Robert. *The Last War Trail: The Utes and the Settlement of Colorado.* Norman: University of Oklahoma Press, 1954.

Finerty, John F. *Warpath and Bivouac, or the Conquest of the Sioux.* Intro. by Oliver Knight. Norman: University of Oklahoma Press, 1961.

Fletcher, Marvin E. *The Black Soldier and Officer in the United States Army, 1891–1917.* Columbia: University of Missouri Press, 1974.

Foner, Jack. *The American Soldier between Two Wars: Army Life and Reforms, 1865–1898.* New York: Humanities Press, 1970.

Fowler, Arlen. *The Black Infantry in the West, 1869–1891.* Westport, Conn.: Greenwood Press, 1971.

Gatewood, William B. *Smoked Yankees" and the Struggle for Empire: Letters from Negro Soldiers, 1898–1902.* Urbana: University of Illinois Press, 1971.

Hagan, Thomas. *United States–Comanche Relations: The Reservation Years.* New Haven: Yale University Press, 1976.

Haley, J. Evetts. *Fort Concho and the Texas Frontier.* San Angelo, Texas: San Angelo Standard-Times, 1952.

Haley, James L. *The Buffalo War: The History of the Red River Indian Uprising of 1874.* Garden City, N.Y.: Doubleday & Co., 1974.

Heitman, Francis B., comp. *Historical Register and Dictionary of the United States Army.* 2 vols. Washington, D.C.: Government Printing Office, 1903.

Horn, Stanley F. *The Decisive Battle of Nashville.* Baton Rouge: Louisiana State University Press, 1956.

Hutton, Paul A. *Phil Sheridan and His Army*. Lincoln: University of Nebraska Press, 1985.

Jensen, Joan, and Darlis A. Miller. *New Mexico Women: Intercultural Perspectives*. Albuquerque: University of New Mexico Press, 1986.

Jockwick, Sidney. *Early Days on the Western Slope of Colorado, 1870–1883*. Glorietta, N.Mex.: Rio Grande Press, 1968.

Johnson, Terry C. *Shadow Riders: The Southern Plains Uprising, 1873*. New York: St. Martin's Paperbacks, 1991.

Jordan, General Thomas, and J. P. Pryor. *The Campaigns of General Nathan Bedford Forrest and of Forrest's Cavalry*. Intro. by Albert Castel. New York: Da Capo Press, 1996.

Kelleher, William A. *The Maxwell Land Grant: A New Mexico Item*. New York, Argosy-Antiquarian Press, 1964.

Leckie, William H. *The Buffalo Soldiers: A Narrative of the Negro Cavalry in the West*. Norman: University of Oklahoma Press, 1967.

Lee, Irvin H. *Negro Medal of Honor Men*. New York: Dodd Mead, 1967.

Lekson, Stephen H. *Nana's Raid: Apache Warfare in Southern New Mexico, 1881*. El Paso: Texas Western Press, 1987.

Lewis, David L. *W. E. B. DuBois: The Biography of a Race, 1868–1919*. New York, Henry Holt Co., 1993.

Logan, Rayford W. *The Betrayal of the Negro: From Rutherford B. Hayes to Woodrow Wilson*. New York: Collier Books, 1965.

———, and Michael R. Winston, eds. *Dictionary of American Negro Biography*. New York: W. W. Norton, 1982.

Lynk, Miles. *The Black Troopers, or the Daring Heroism of the Negro Soldiers in the Spanish-American War*. New York: AMS Press, 1971.

McKenna, James A. *Black Range Tales Chronicling Sixty Years of Life and Adventure in the Southwest*. Chicago: Rio Grande Press, 1963.

The Medal of Honor Winners of the United States Army. Washington, D.C.: Government Printing Office, 1948.

Mississippi: A Guide to the Magnolia State. New York: Hastings House, 1938.

Mills, Anson. *My Story*. Washington D.C.: Press of Byron S. Adams, 1918.

Mills, Charles K. *Harvest of Bitter Regrets: The Army Career of Frederick W. Benteen, 1834–1898*. Glendale, Calif.: The Arthur H. Clark Co., 1985.

Moore, William H. *Chiefs, Agents & Soldiers: Conflict on the Navajo Frontier, 1868–1882*. Albuquerque: University of New Mexico Press, 1994.

Nye, Wilbur S. *Carbine and Lance: The Story of Old Fort Sill*. Norman, University of Oklahoma Press, 1937.

Nolan, Frederick. *The Lincoln County War: A Documentary History*. Norman: University of Oklahoma Press, 1992.

Notson, William M. *Fort Concho Medical History, 1869 to 1872*. Intro. by Stephen Schmidt. San Angelo, Texas: Fort Concho Museum, 1974.

Parsons, Chuck. *Clay Allison: A Portrait of a Shootist.* Seagraves, Texas: Pioneer Books Publishers, 1983.

Pierce, Lyman. *History of the Second Iowa Cavalry.* Burlington, Iowa: Hawk-eye Steam Book Co., 1865.

Pierce, N. H. *The Free State of Menard.* Menard, Texas: Menard News Press, 1952.

Regimental History Committee. *History of the Third Pennsylvania Cavalry in the American Civil War, 1861–1865.* Philadelphia, Pa.: Franklin Printing Co., 1905.

Rickey, Don, Jr. *Forty Miles a Day on Beans and Hay: The Enlisted Soldier Fighting the Indian Wars.* Norman: University of Oklahoma Press, 1963.

Rister, Carl Coke. *Land Hunger: David L. Payne and the Oklahoma Boomers.* Norman: University of Oklahoma Press, 1956.

Robinson, Charles M. *The Court-Martial of Lt. Henry O. Flipper.* El Paso: Texas Western Press, 1994.

Robinson, James B., ed. *Southern Historical Society Papers.* 40 vols. Richmond, Va.: Broadfoot Publishing Co., 1991.

Rodenbough, Theodore, and W. J. Haskins. *The Army of the United States: Historical Sketches of Staff and Line.* New York: Argonaut Press, 1897.

Schofield, John M. *Forty-Six Years in the Army.* New York: Century Co., 1897.

Schubert, Frank N. *Black Valor: Buffalo Soldiers and the Medal of Honor, 1870–1898.* Wilmington, Del.: Scholarly Resources, 1997.

———. *Buffalo Soldiers, Braves and the Brass: The Story of Fort Robinson, Nebraska.* Shippensburg, Pa.: White Mane Publishing Co., 1993.

———, ed. *On the Trail of the Buffalo Soldier: Biographies of African Americans in the U.S. Army, 1866–1917.* Wilmington, Del.: Scholarly Resources, 1995.

Simon, John, ed. *The Papers of U. S. Grant.* Carbondale: Southern Illinois University Press, 1975.

Starr, Stephen Z. *The Union Cavalry in the Civil War.* 3 vols. Baton Rouge: Louisiana State University Press, 1979–85.

Steward, Theophilus G. *The Colored Regulars in the United States Army.* New York: Arno Press, 1964.

Stover, Earl F. *Up From Handymen: The United States Army Chaplaincy, 1865–1920.* Washington D.C.: Department of the Army, 1977.

Surby, Richard. *Grierson's Raid and Hatch's Sixty-Four Day March.* Chicago: Round and James, 1865.

Thrapp, Dan L. *Al Sieber: Chief of Scouts.* Norman: University of Oklahoma Press, 1964.

———. *Victorio and the Mimbres Apaches.* Norman: University of Oklahoma Press, 1974.

Utley, Robert M. *Frontier Regulars: The United States Army and the Indians, 1866–1891.* New York: MacMillan Publishing Co., 1973.

War of the Rebellion: A Compilation of the Official Records of the Union and Confederate Armies. 128 vols. Washington, D.C.: Government Printing Office, 1865–1928.

Warner, Ezra. *Generals in Blue: Lives of the Union Commanders.* Baton Rouge: Louisiana State University Press, 1964.

Weaver, John D. *The Brownsville Raid.* New York: W. W. Norton, 1970. Reprinted, with a new foreword by Lewis L. Gould. College Station: Texas A&M Press, 1992.

Webb, Walter P., and H. Bailey Carroll, eds. *The Handbook of Texas.* 3 vols. Austin: Texas State Historical Association, 1952.

Weems, John Edward. *Death Song: The Last of the Indian Wars.* New York: Doubleday, 1976.

Williams, Clayton W. *Texas' Last Frontier: Fort Stockton and the Trans-Pecos, 1861–1895.* Ed. Ernest Wallace. College Station: Texas A&M University Press, 1982.

Wilson, James H. *Under the Old Flag: Recollections of Military Operations in the War for the Union, the Spanish War, and the Boxer Rebellion, etc.* 2 vols. New York: D. Appleton and Co., 1912.

Wormser, Richard. *The Yellowlegs: The Story of the United States Cavalry.* Garden City, N.Y.: Doubleday and Co., 1966.

Wyeth, John Allan. *That Devil Forrest: Life of General Nathan B. Forrest.* Baton Rouge: Louisiana State University Press, 1989.

Young, Charles. *Military Morale of Nations and Races.* Kansas City, Mo., 1912.

Index

CPSIA informa
at www.ICGtes
Printed in the U
FFOW01n1054
3820FF

6 144665